Vol. 5

Story and Art by
Tokihiko Matsuura

Tuxedo Gin
vol. 5
Action Edition

Story and Art by Tokihiko Matsuura

Translator/Kenichiro Yagi
Touch-up & Lettering/Adam Symons
Cover & Graphic Design/Carolina Ugalde
Editor/Andy Nakatani

Managing Editor/Annette Roman
Production Manager/Noboru Watanabe
Editor in Chief/William Flanagan
Sr. Dir. of Licensing & Acquisitions/Rika Inouye
VP of Marketing/Liza Coppola
Sr. VP of Editorial/Hyoe Narita
Publisher/Seiji Horibuchi

Published by VIZ, LLC
P.O. Box 77010
San Francisco, CA 94107

Action Edition
10 9 8 7 6 5 4 3 2 1
First printing, March 2004

For advertising rates or media kit,
e-mail advertising@viz.com

www.viz.com

www.animerica-mag.com
store.viz.com

CONTENTS

Chapter 1
IT'S ALL OVER... • 5

Chapter 2
ANYTHING FOR LOVE • • • • • • • • • • • • • • • • • • •29

Chapter 3
KOTONE •51

Chapter 4
WHICH ME IS BEST...? • • • • • • • • • • • • • • • • •71

Chapter 5
HEAVEN, HEAR MY CALL... • • • • • • • • • • • •91

Chapter 6
SPLASH •111

Chapter 7
BEWARE OF PENGUINS!! • • • • • • • • • • • • •133

Chapter 8
NANA-CHAN •153

Chapter 9
I'VE FALLEN FOR YOU • • • • • • • • • • • • • • •173

Ginji Kusanagi is 17 years old and on top of the world. He just made his debut as a pro boxer and he's about to go on a first date with the girl of his dreams, Minako Sasebo. On the eve of his big date, Ginji gets into an "accident" and dies. An odd guardian angel (or perhaps it's more of a Buddhist spirit) tells Ginji about a loophole in the cycle of life, death, and reincarnation – all he has to do is live out the life of a penguin, and then he can come back to life in his former body. For now, Ginji's settling into life as Gin-chan the penguin. But will love be able to bloom between a boxing penguin and a beautiful girl...?

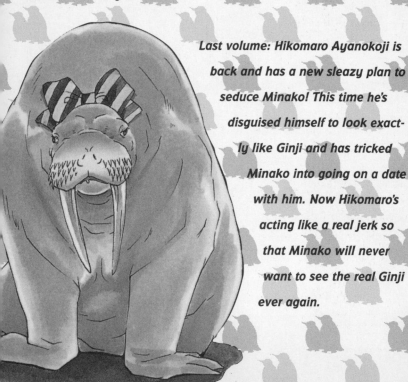

Last volume: Hikomaro Ayanokoji is back and has a new sleazy plan to seduce Minako! This time he's disguised himself to look exactly like Ginji and has tricked Minako into going on a date with him. Now Hikomaro's acting like a real jerk so that Minako will never want to see the real Ginji ever again.

CHAPTER 1
IT'S ALL OVER...

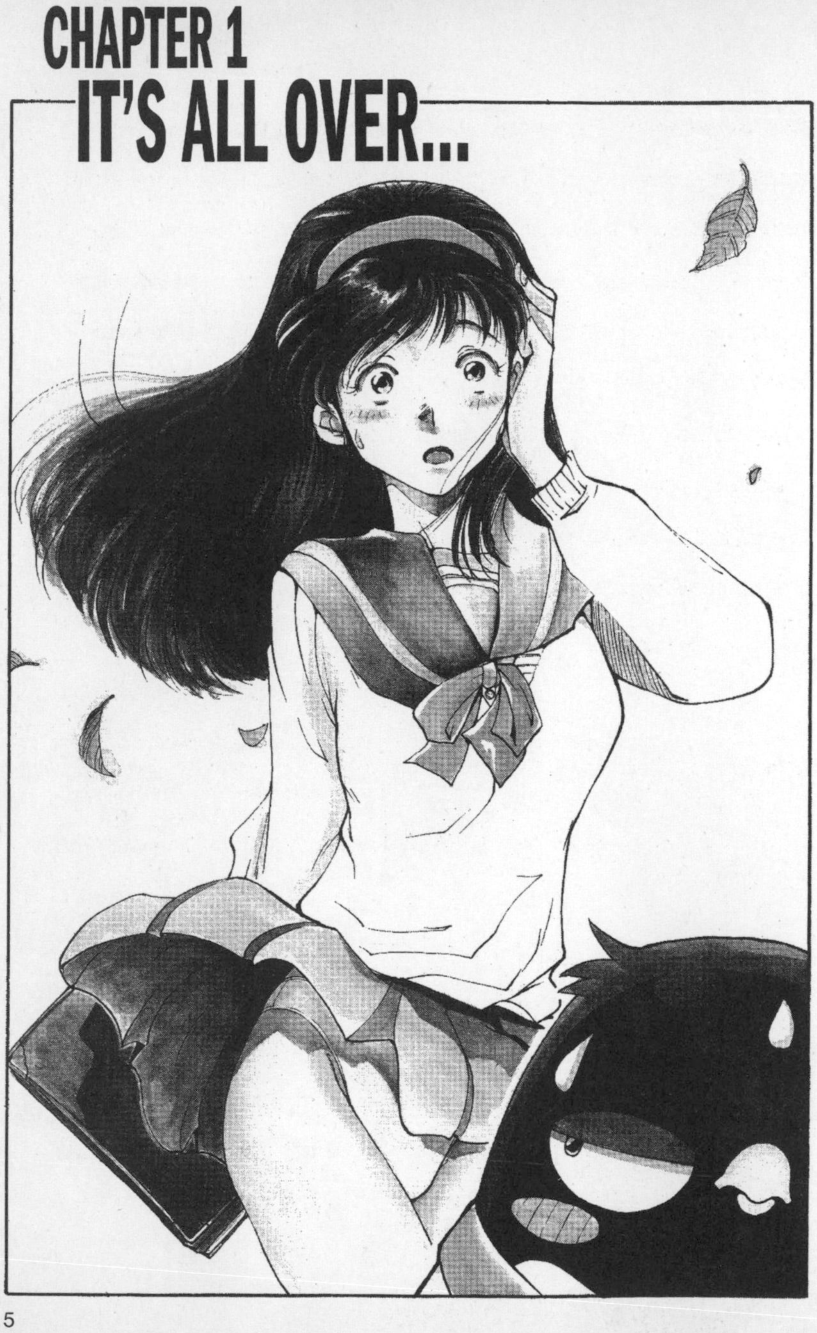

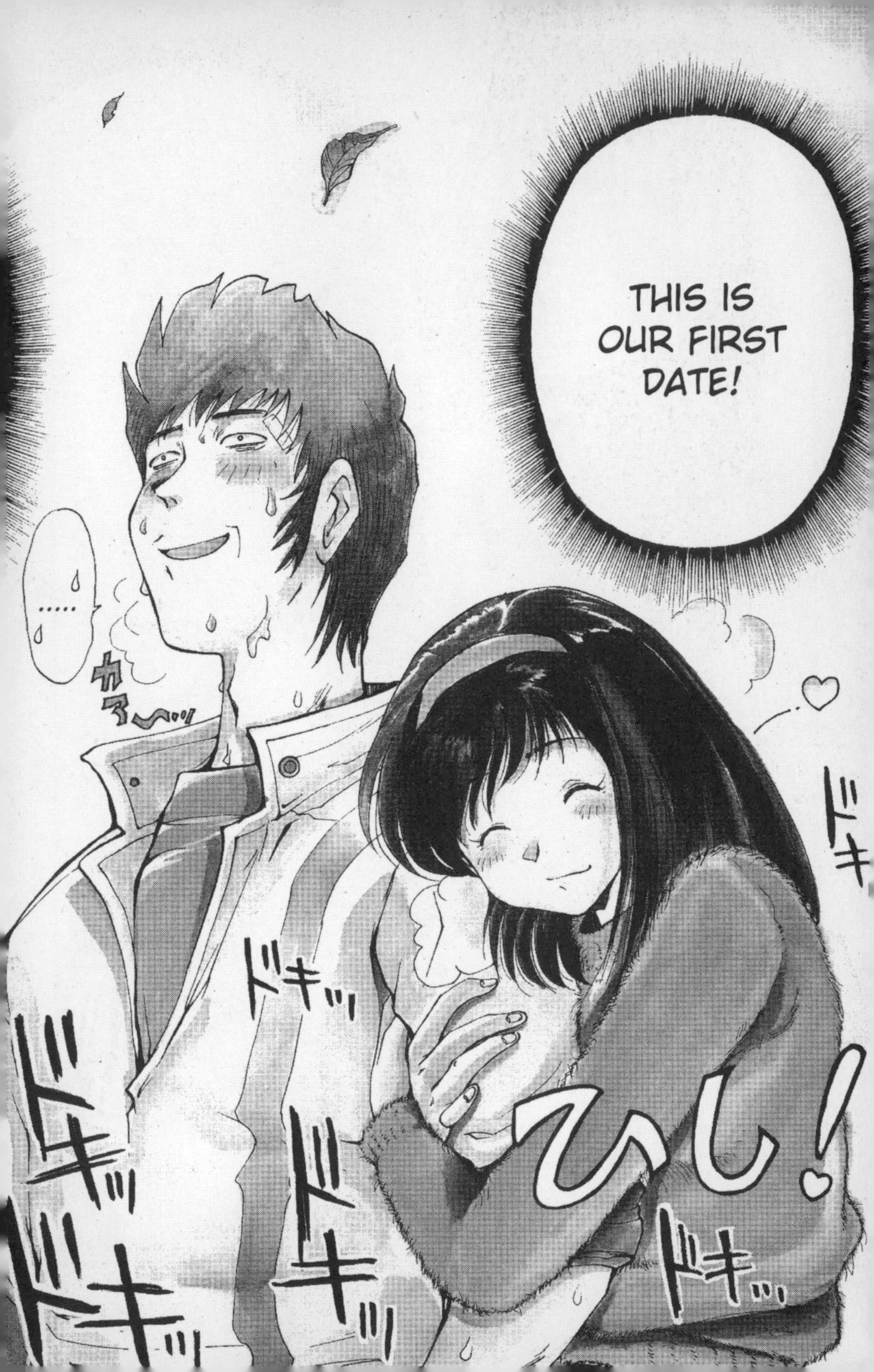
THIS IS OUR FIRST DATE!
ドキ
ひし!
ドキッ
ドキッ
ドキッ
......
カァ〜ッ
ドキッ
ドキッ

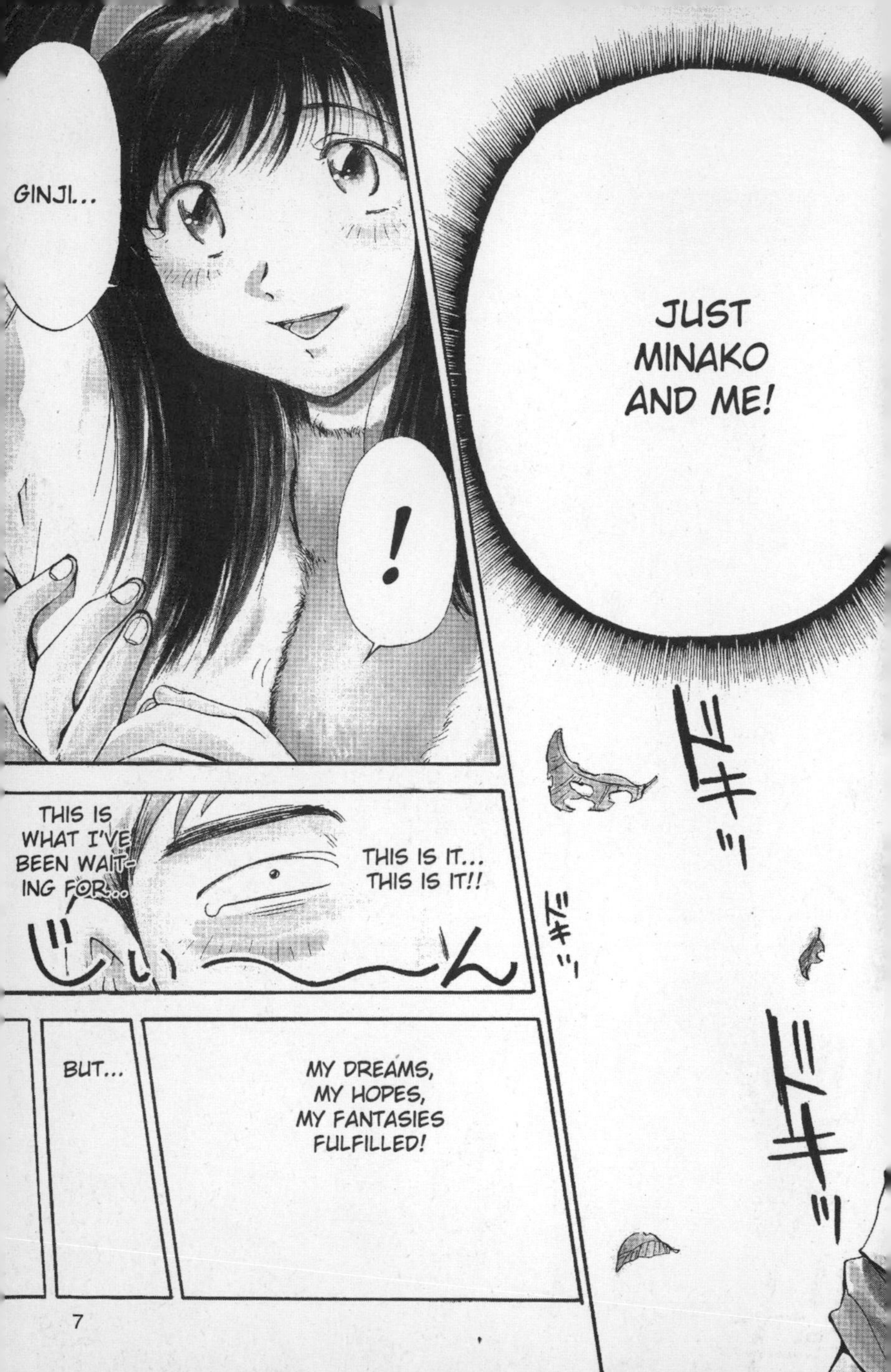
JUST MINAKO AND ME!
ドキッ
ドキッ
ドキッ
GINJI...
!
THIS IS IT... THIS IS IT!!
THIS IS WHAT I'VE BEEN WAIT-ING FOR..
じい～～ん
MY DREAMS, MY HOPES, MY FANTASIES FULFILLED!
BUT...

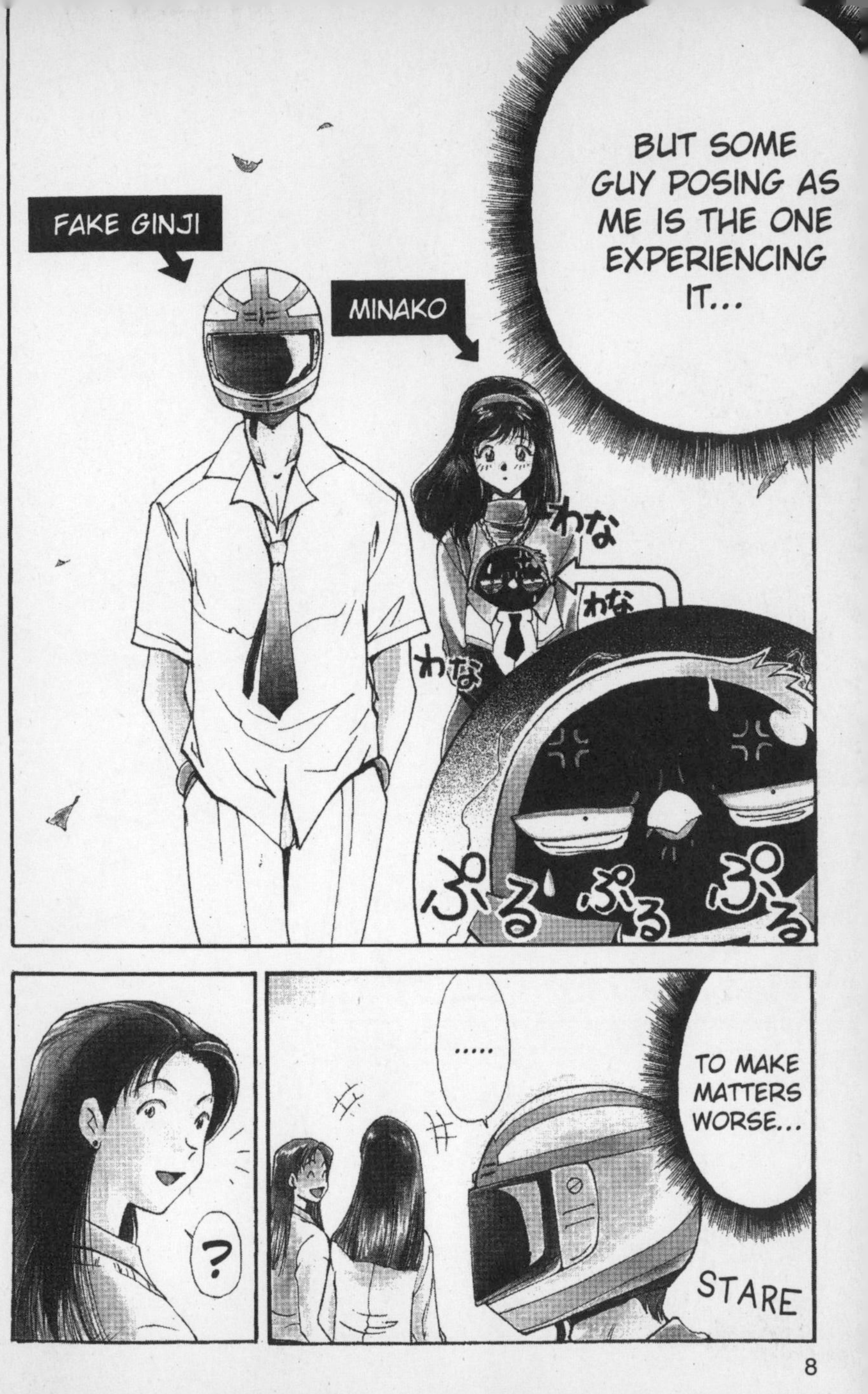
BUT SOME GUY POSING AS ME IS THE ONE EXPERIENCING IT...
MINAKO
FAKE GINJI
わな
わな
わな
ぷる ぷる ぷる
TO MAKE MATTERS WORSE...
......
STARE
?

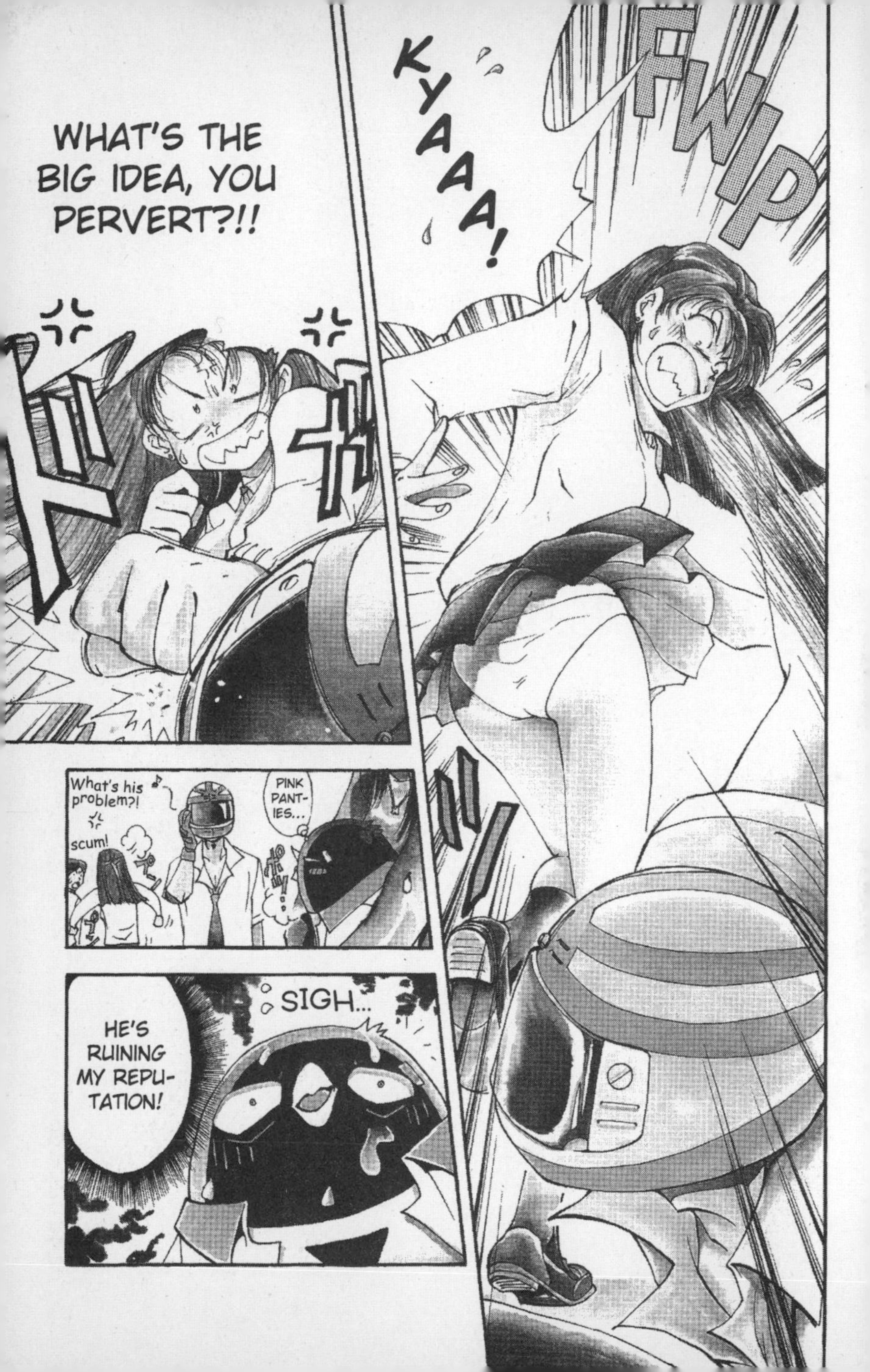
FWIP
KYAAAA!
WHAT'S THE BIG IDEA, YOU PERVERT?!!
PINK PANTIES...
What's his problem?!
scum!
SIGH...
HE'S RUINING MY REPUTATION!

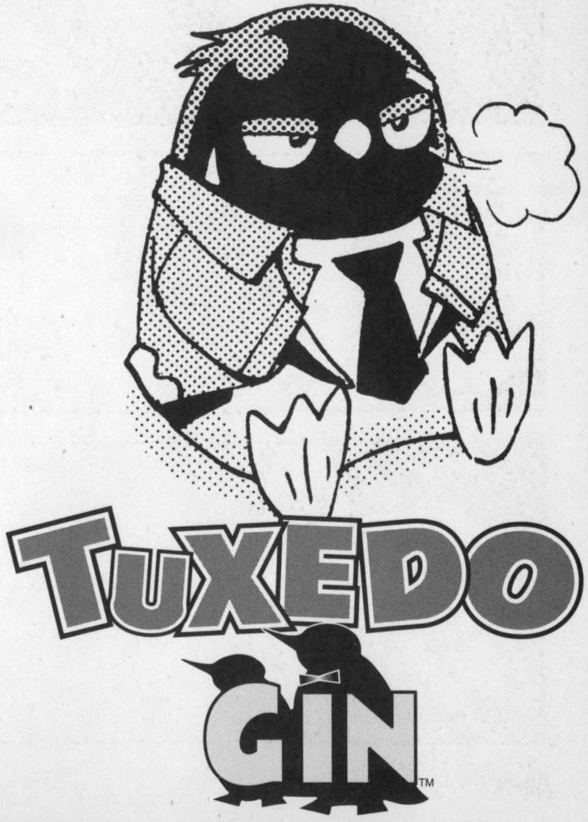

TUXEDO GIN™

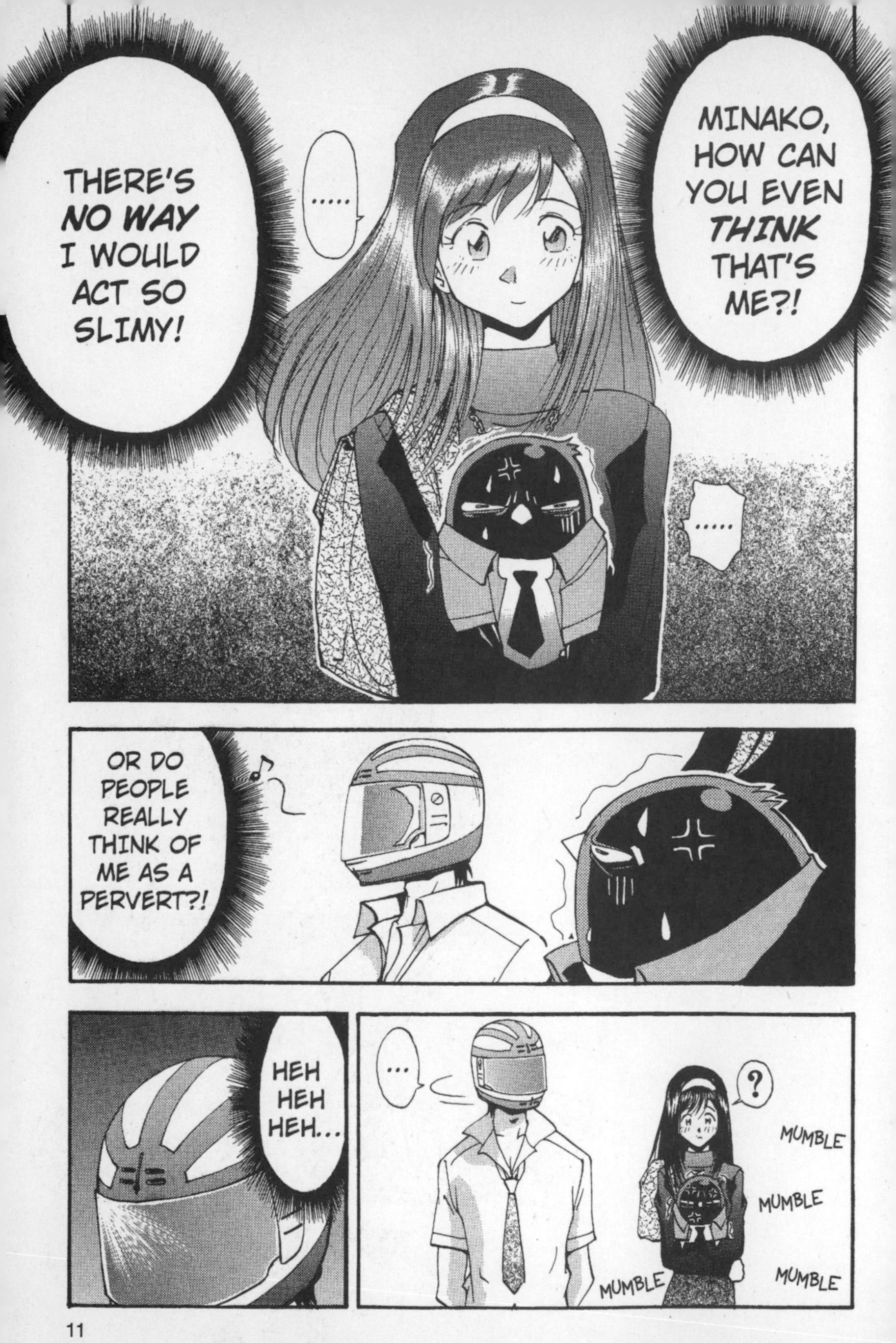
MINAKO, HOW CAN YOU EVEN *THINK* THAT'S ME?!
THERE'S *NO WAY* I WOULD ACT SO SLIMY!
......
.....
OR DO PEOPLE REALLY THINK OF ME AS A PERVERT?!
...
?
MUMBLE
MUMBLE
MUMBLE
MUMBLE
HEH HEH HEH...

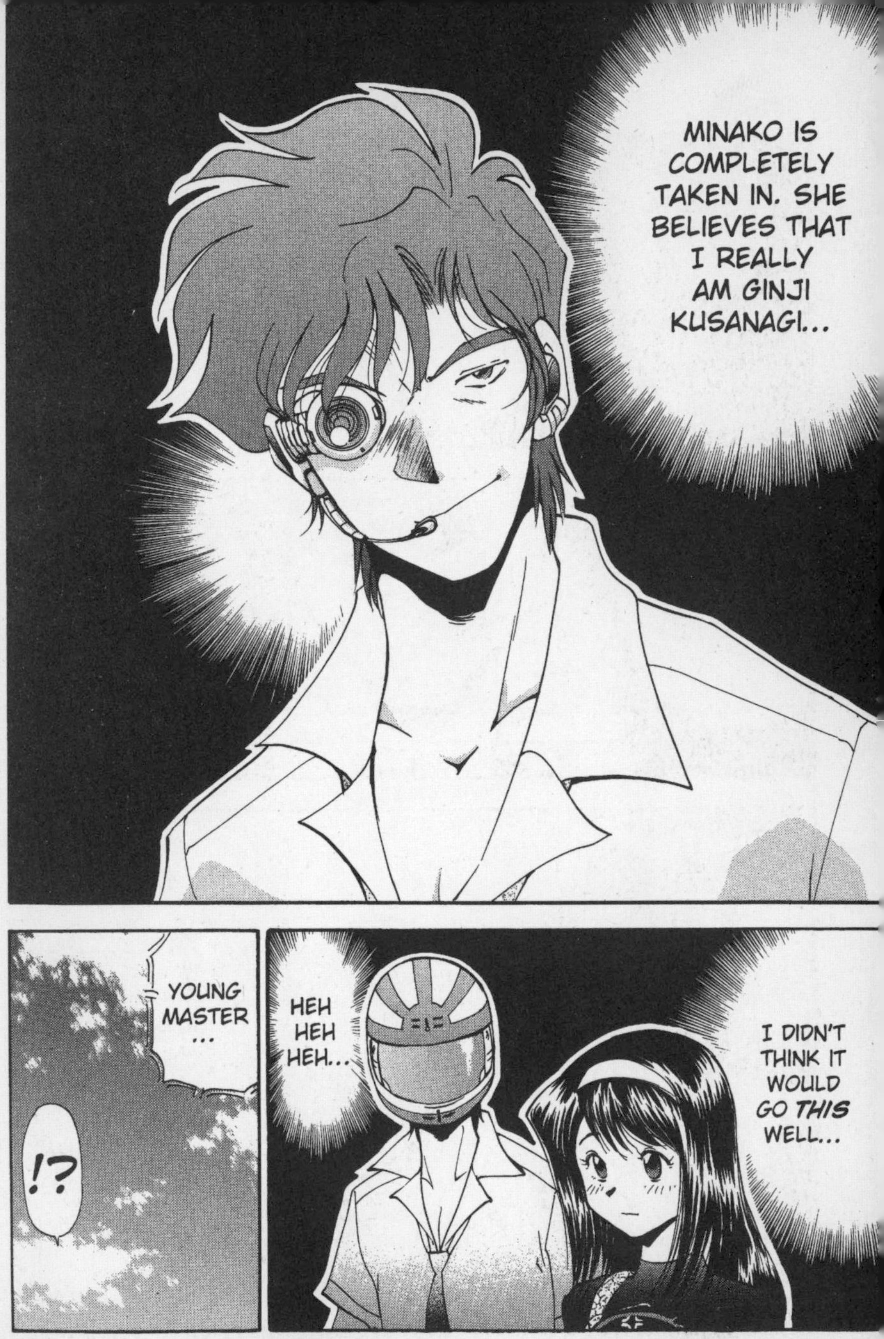
MINAKO IS COMPLETELY TAKEN IN. SHE BELIEVES THAT I REALLY AM GINJI KUSANAGI...
I DIDN'T THINK IT WOULD GO *THIS* WELL...
HEH HEH HEH...
YOUNG MASTER ...
!?

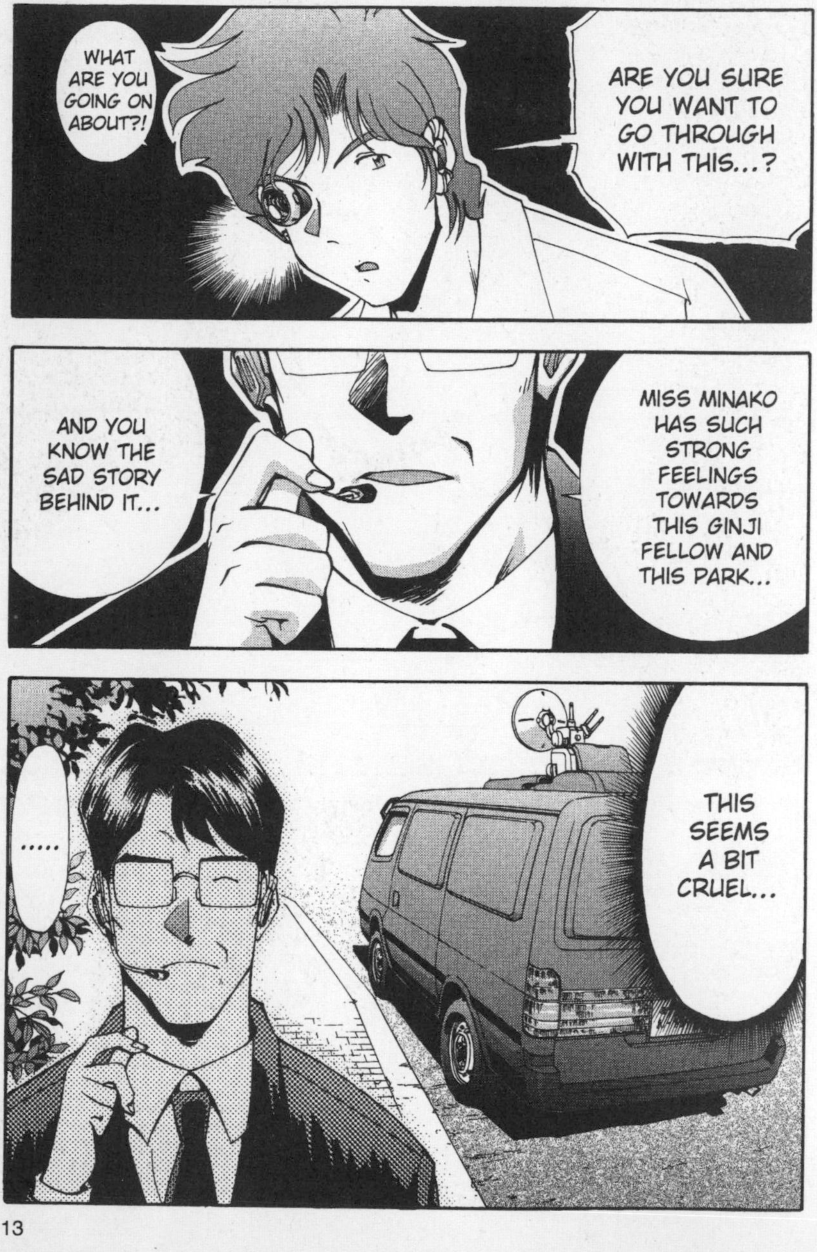
ARE YOU SURE YOU WANT TO GO THROUGH WITH THIS...?
WHAT ARE YOU GOING ON ABOUT?!
MISS MINAKO HAS SUCH STRONG FEELINGS TOWARDS THIS GINJI FELLOW AND THIS PARK...
AND YOU KNOW THE SAD STORY BEHIND IT...
THIS SEEMS A BIT CRUEL...
.....

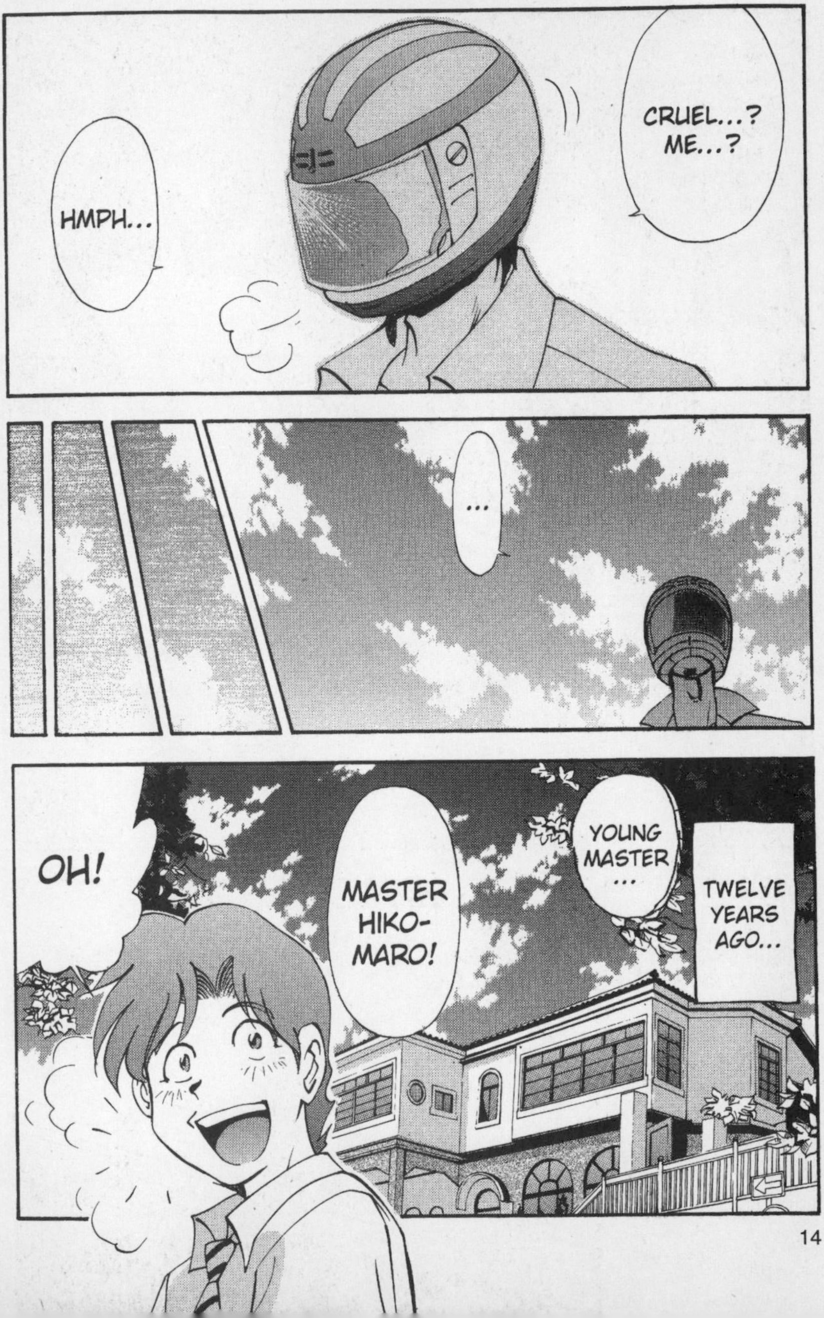
CRUEL...? ME...?
HMPH...
...
TWELVE YEARS AGO...
YOUNG MASTER ...
MASTER HIKO-MARO!
OH!

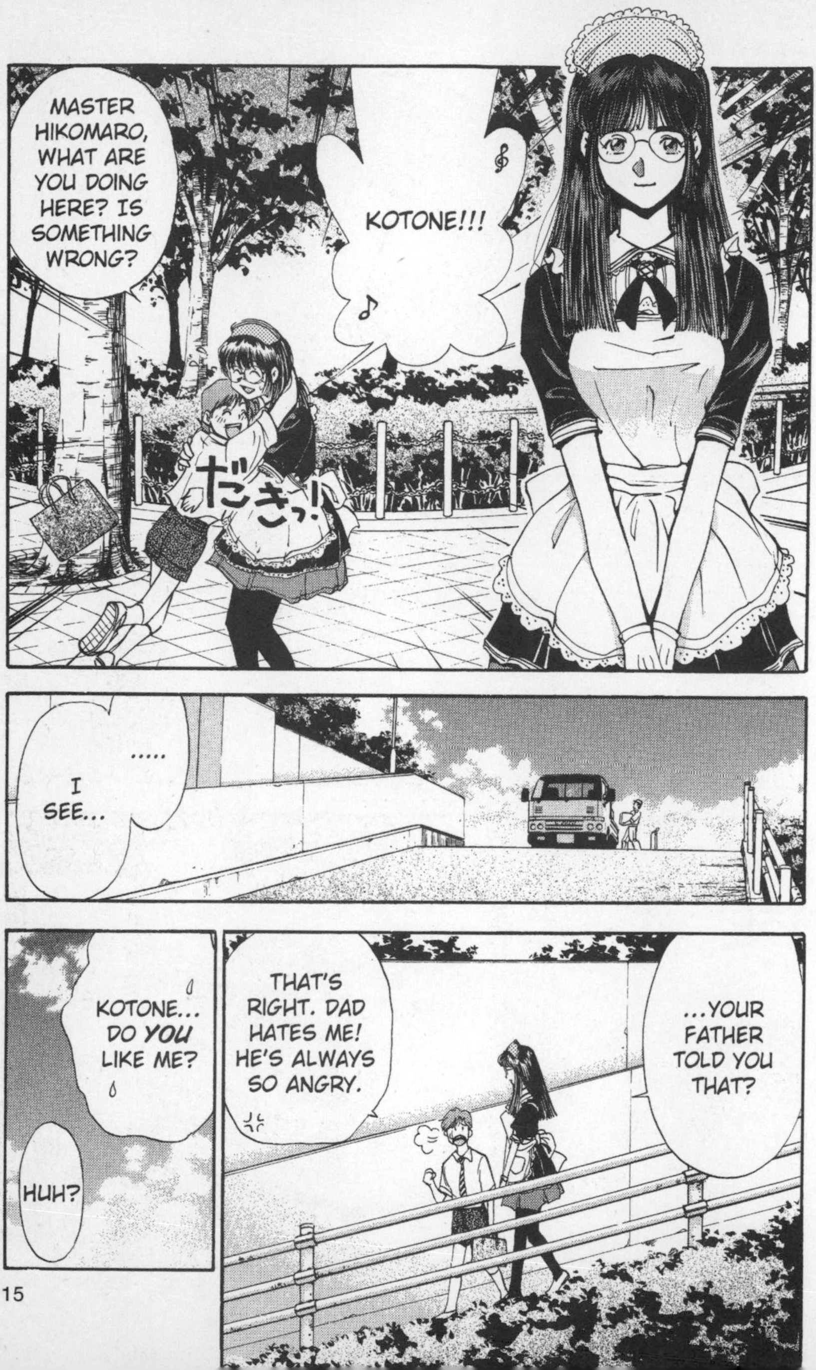
KOTONE!!!
MASTER HIKOMARO, WHAT ARE YOU DOING HERE? IS SOMETHING WRONG?
だきっ!!
..... I SEE...
...YOUR FATHER TOLD YOU THAT?
THAT'S RIGHT. DAD HATES ME! HE'S ALWAYS SO ANGRY.
KOTONE... DO *YOU* LIKE ME?
HUH?

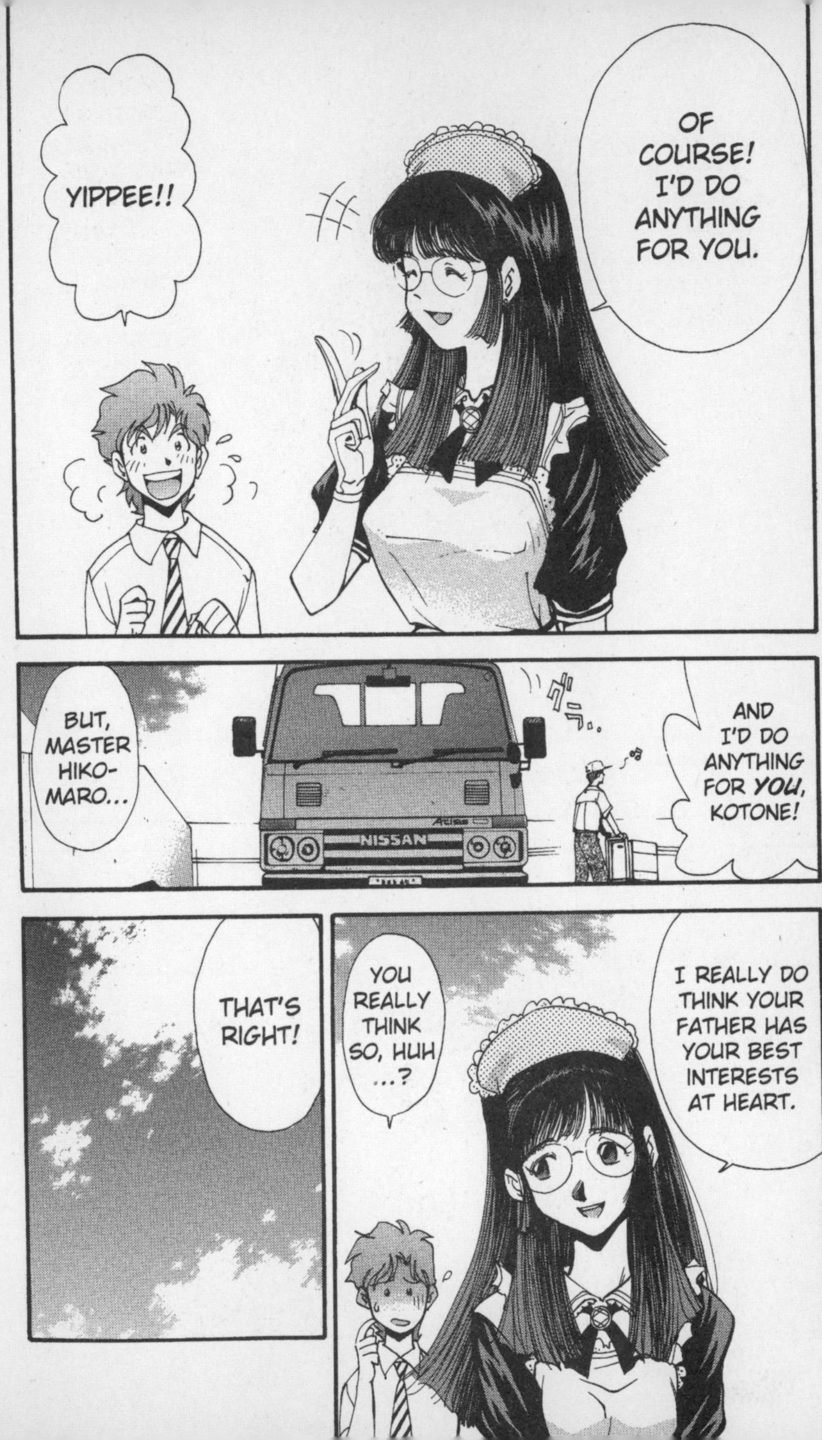
OF COURSE! I'D DO ANYTHING FOR YOU.
YIPPEE!!
AND I'D DO ANYTHING FOR *YOU*, KOTONE!
BUT, MASTER HIKO-MARO...
I REALLY DO THINK YOUR FATHER HAS YOUR BEST INTERESTS AT HEART.
YOU REALLY THINK SO, HUH ...?
THAT'S RIGHT!

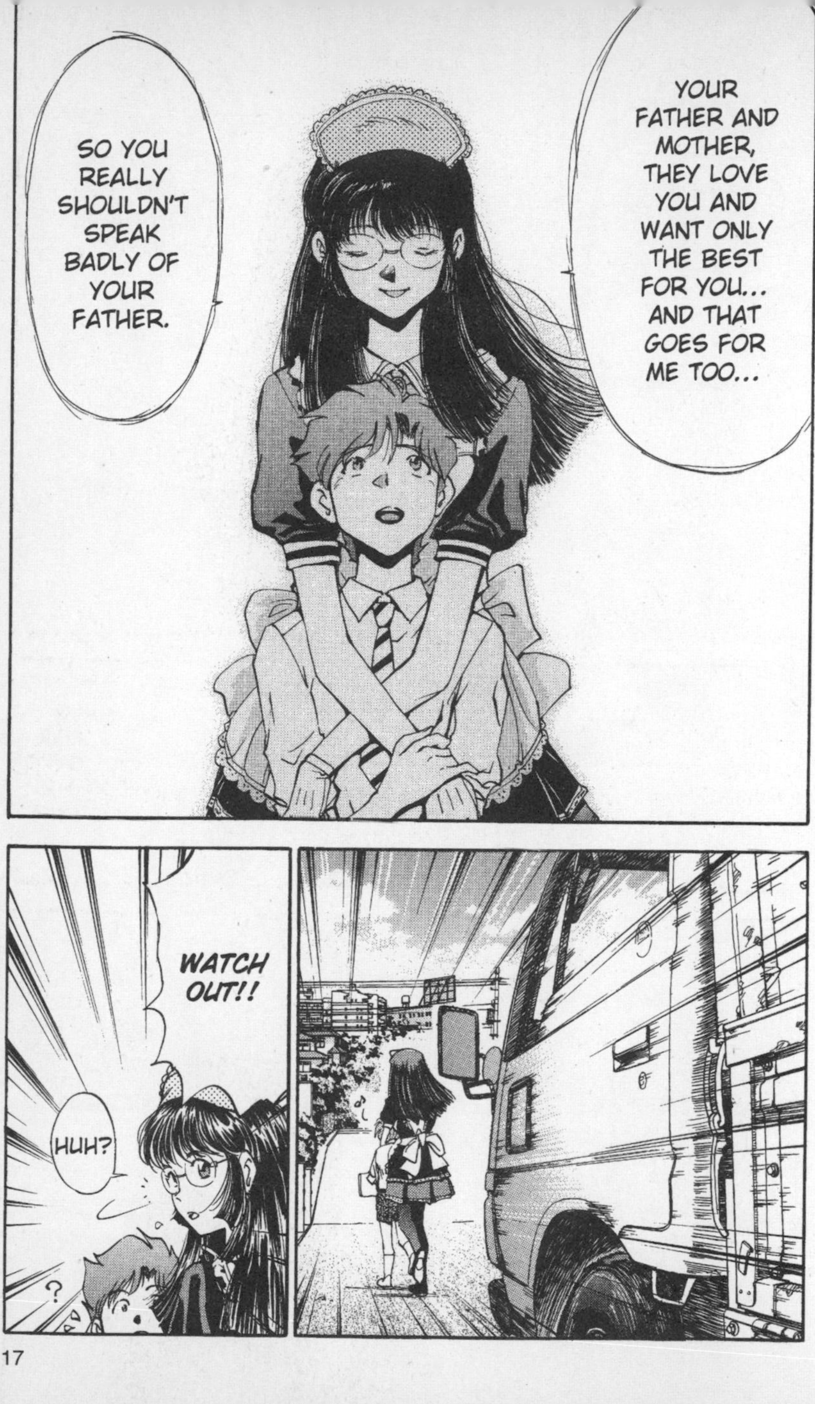
YOUR FATHER AND MOTHER, THEY LOVE YOU AND WANT ONLY THE BEST FOR YOU... AND THAT GOES FOR ME TOO...
SO YOU REALLY SHOULDN'T SPEAK BADLY OF YOUR FATHER.
WATCH OUT!!
HUH?
?

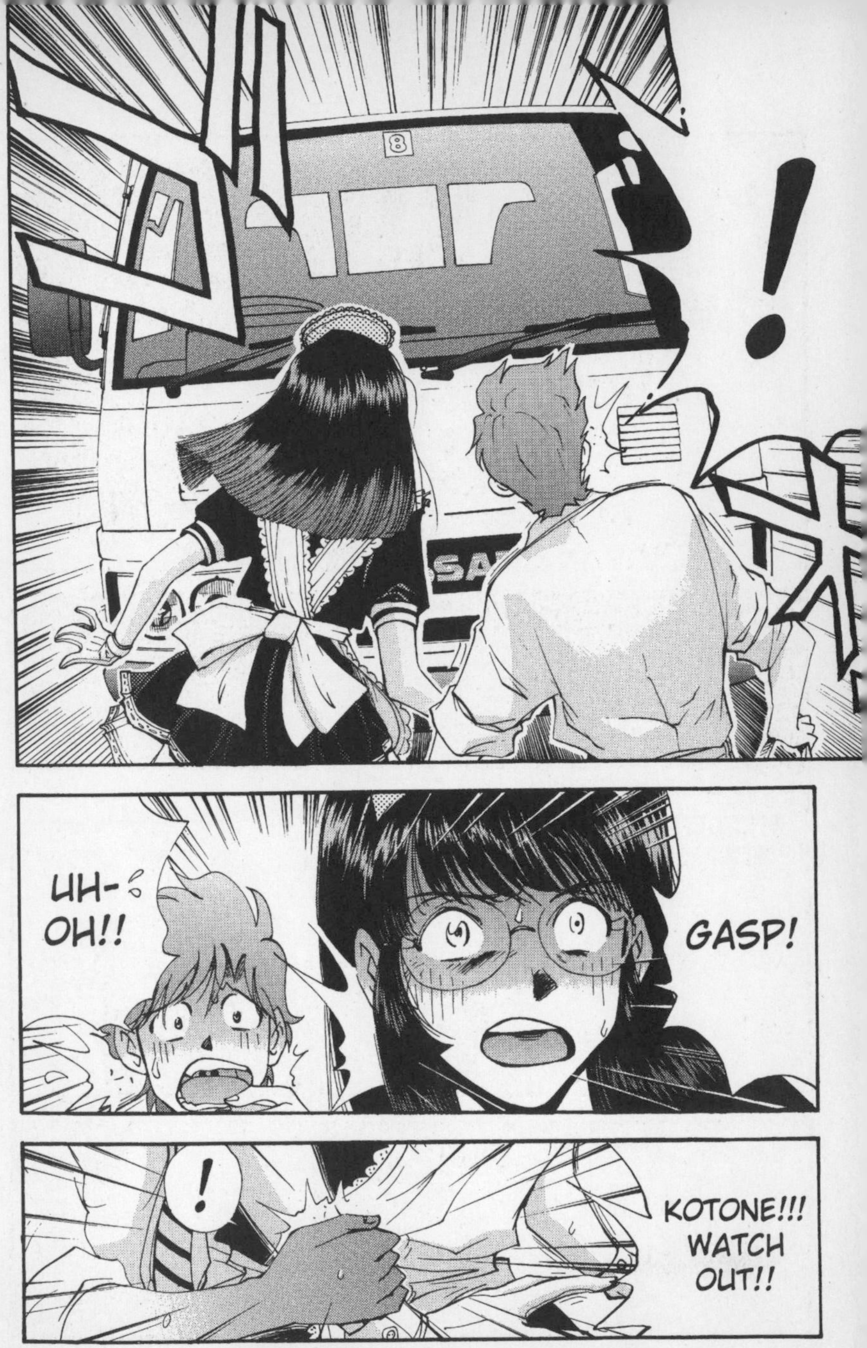
!
GASP!
UH-OH!!
KOTONE!!! WATCH OUT!!
!

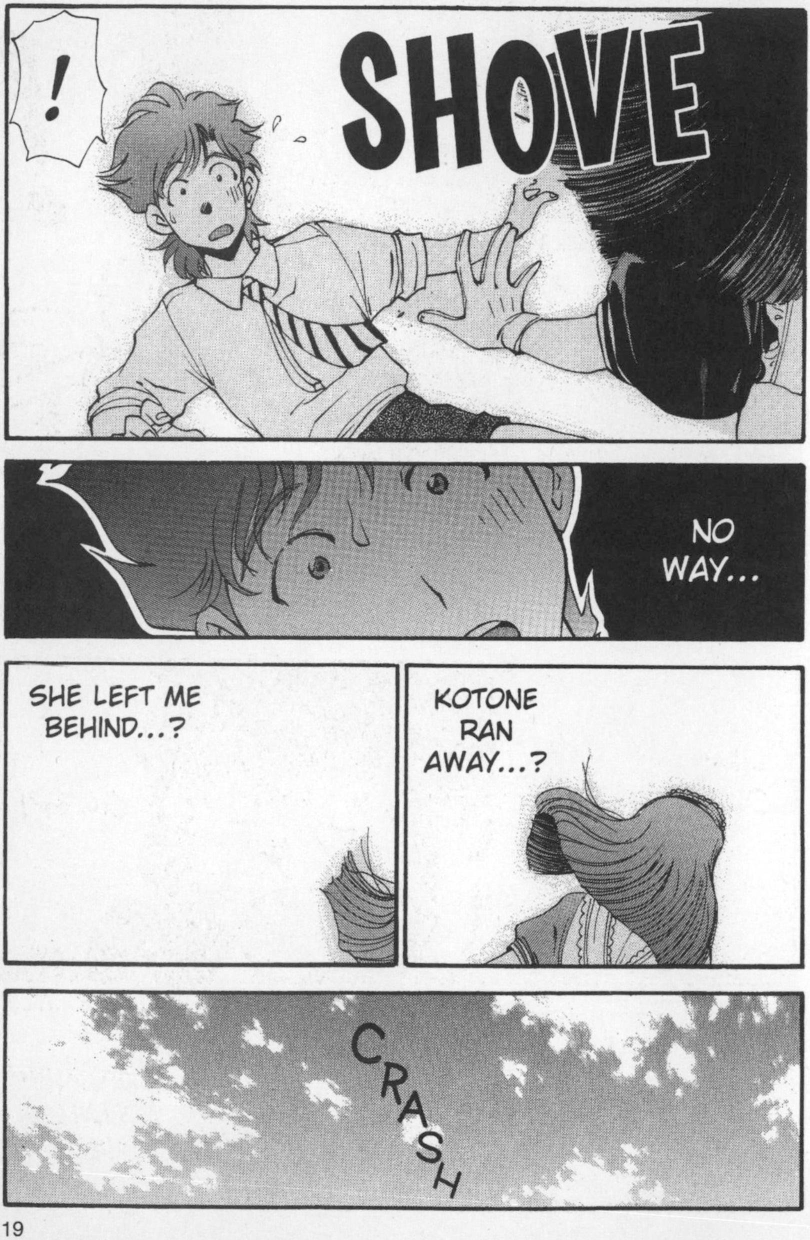
SHOVE
!
NO WAY...
KOTONE RAN AWAY...?
SHE LEFT ME BEHIND...?
CRASH

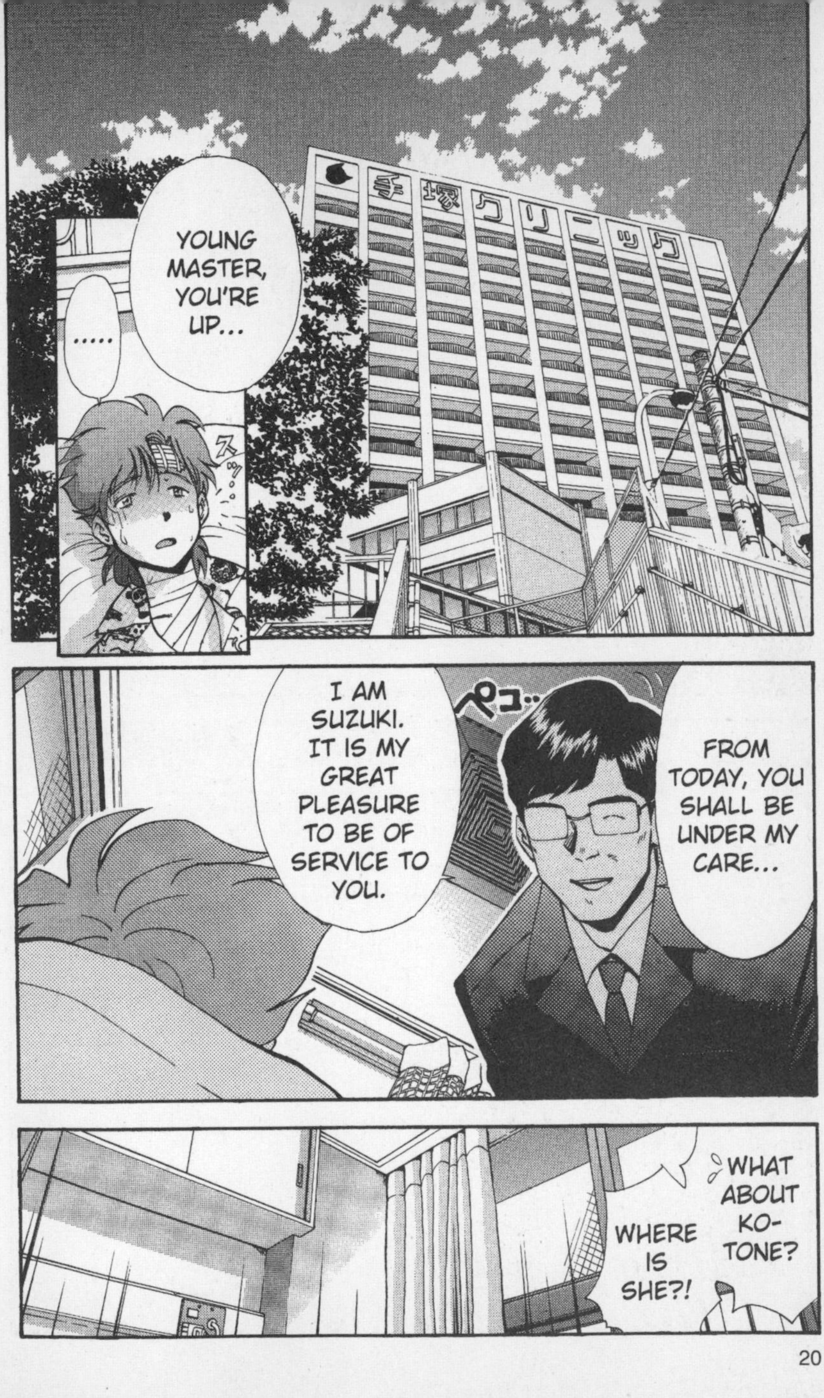

手塚クリニック
YOUNG MASTER, YOU'RE UP...
.....
ス
FROM TODAY, YOU SHALL BE UNDER MY CARE...
ペコ
I AM SUZUKI. IT IS MY GREAT PLEASURE TO BE OF SERVICE TO YOU.
WHAT ABOUT KO-TONE?
WHERE IS SHE?!

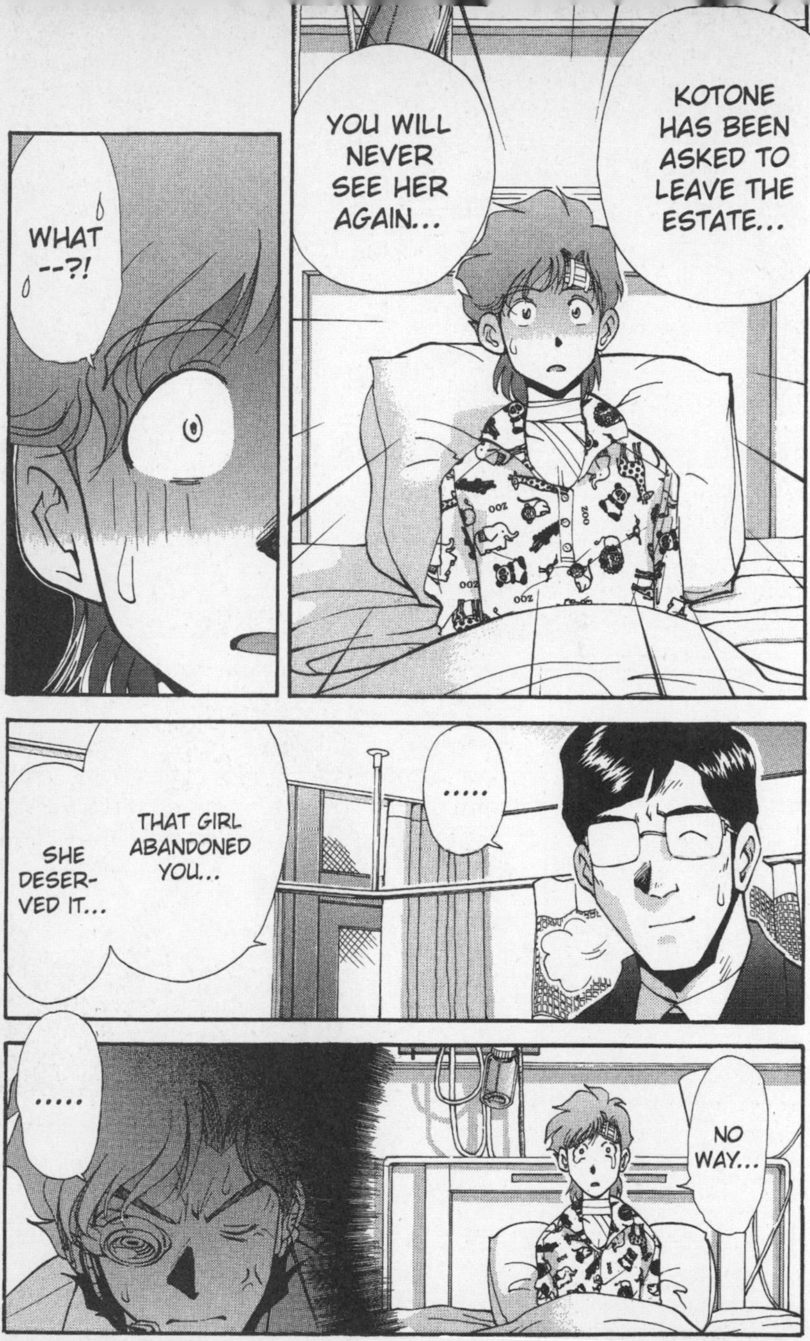
KOTONE HAS BEEN ASKED TO LEAVE THE ESTATE...
YOU WILL NEVER SEE HER AGAIN...
WHAT --?!
.....
THAT GIRL ABANDONED YOU...
SHE DESERVED IT...
NO WAY...
.....

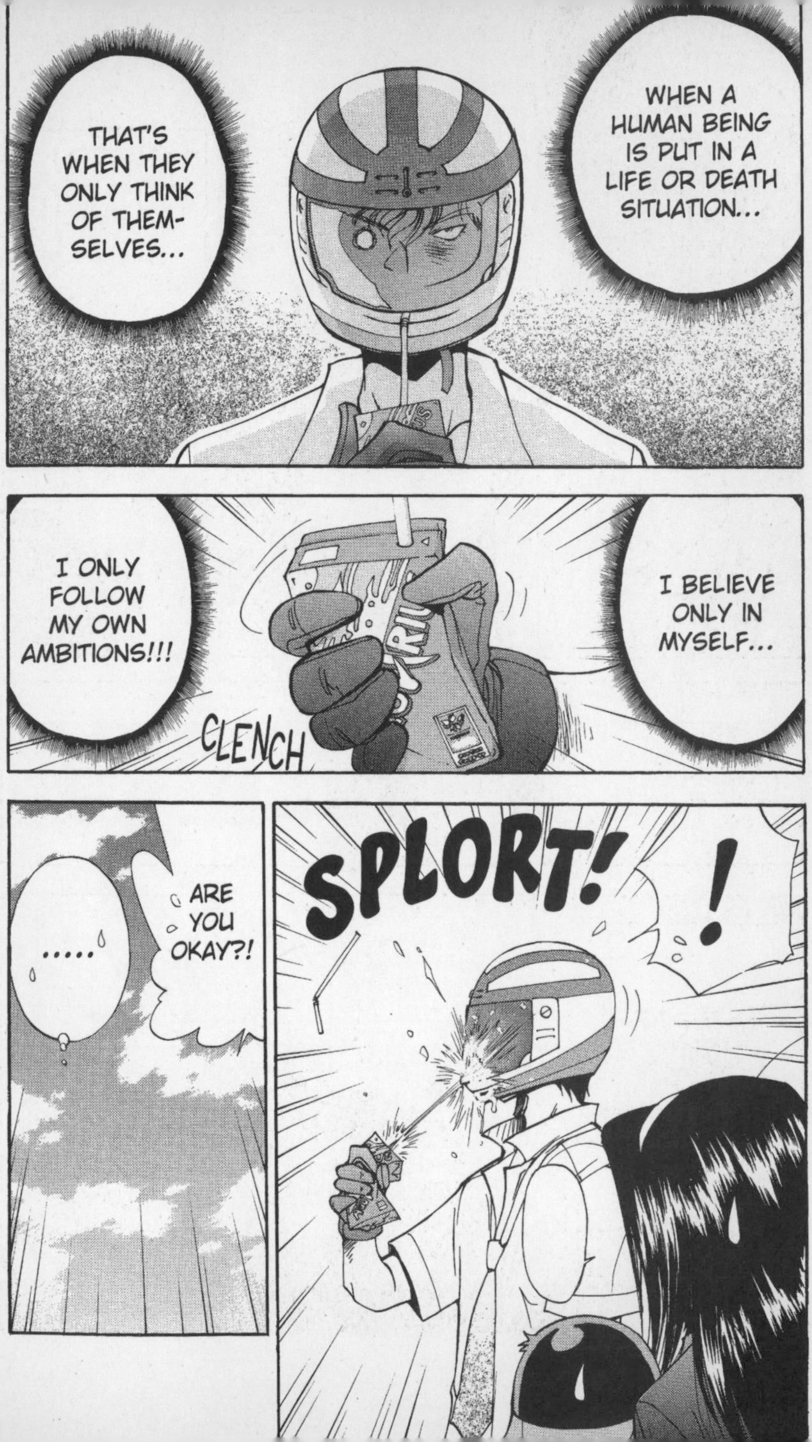
WHEN A HUMAN BEING IS PUT IN A LIFE OR DEATH SITUATION...
THAT'S WHEN THEY ONLY THINK OF THEM-SELVES...
I BELIEVE ONLY IN MYSELF...
I ONLY FOLLOW MY OWN AMBITIONS!!!
CLENCH
SPLORT!
!
ARE YOU OKAY?!
.....

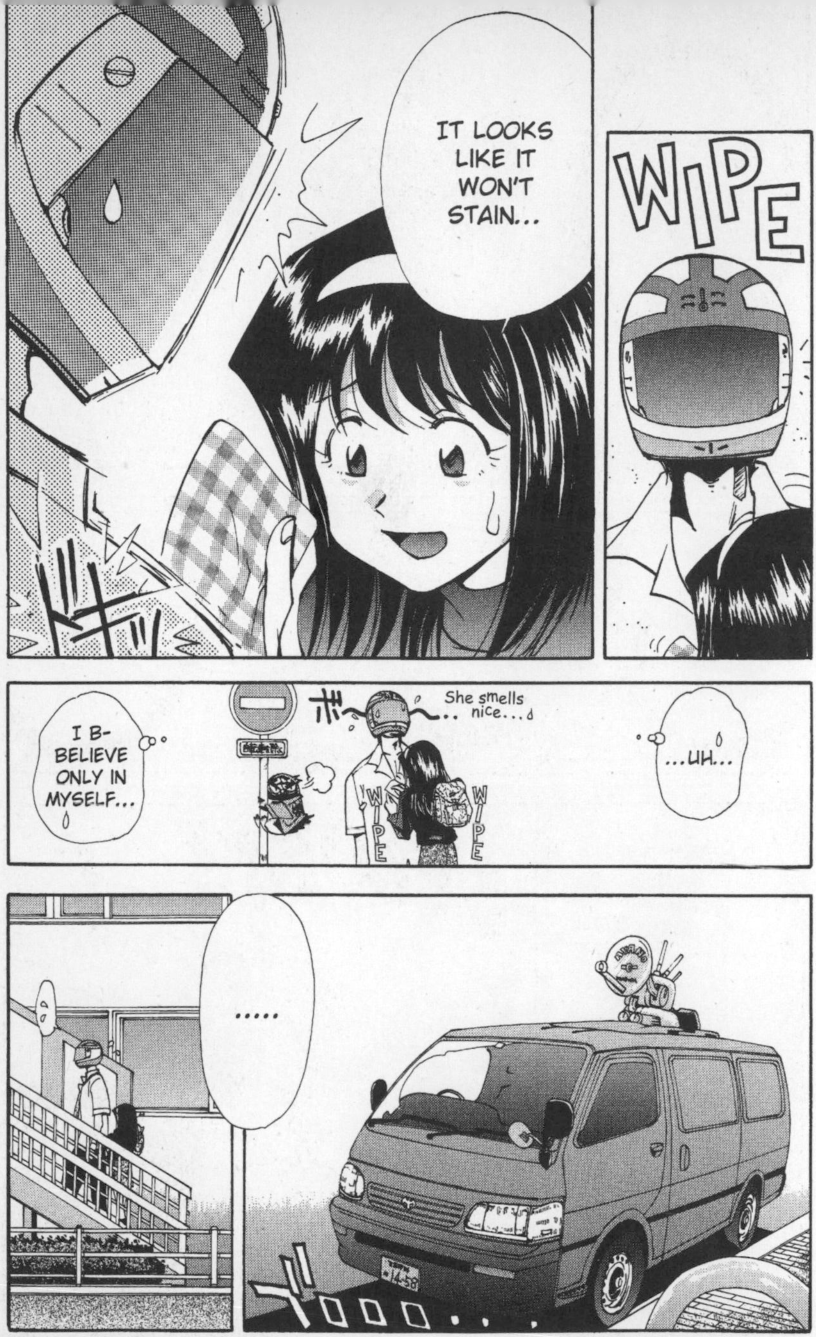
WIPE
IT LOOKS LIKE IT WON'T STAIN...
...UH...
She smells nice...
WIPE
WIPE
I B-BELIEVE ONLY IN MYSELF...
.....

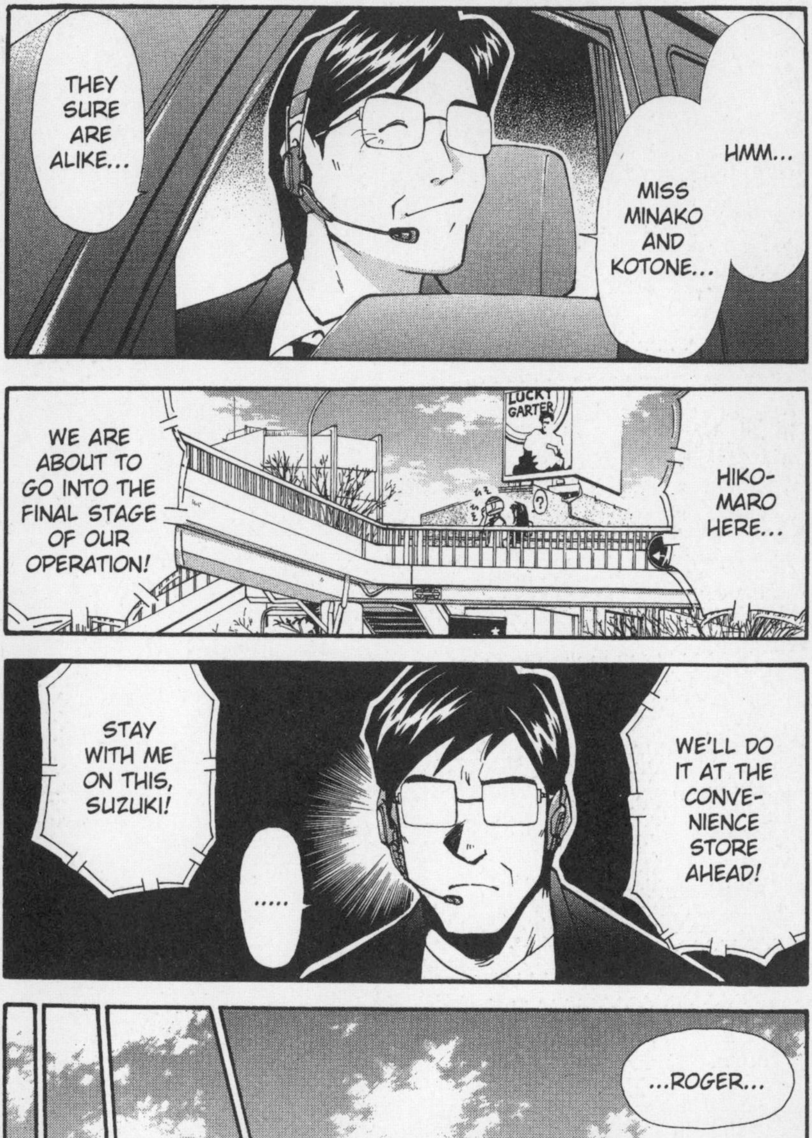
HMM... MISS MINAKO AND KOTONE...
THEY SURE ARE ALIKE...
LUCKY GARTER
HIKO-MARO HERE...
WE ARE ABOUT TO GO INTO THE FINAL STAGE OF OUR OPERATION!
WE'LL DO IT AT THE CONVE-NIENCE STORE AHEAD!
STAY WITH ME ON THIS, SUZUKI!
.....
...ROGER...

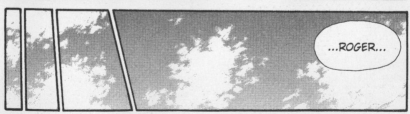

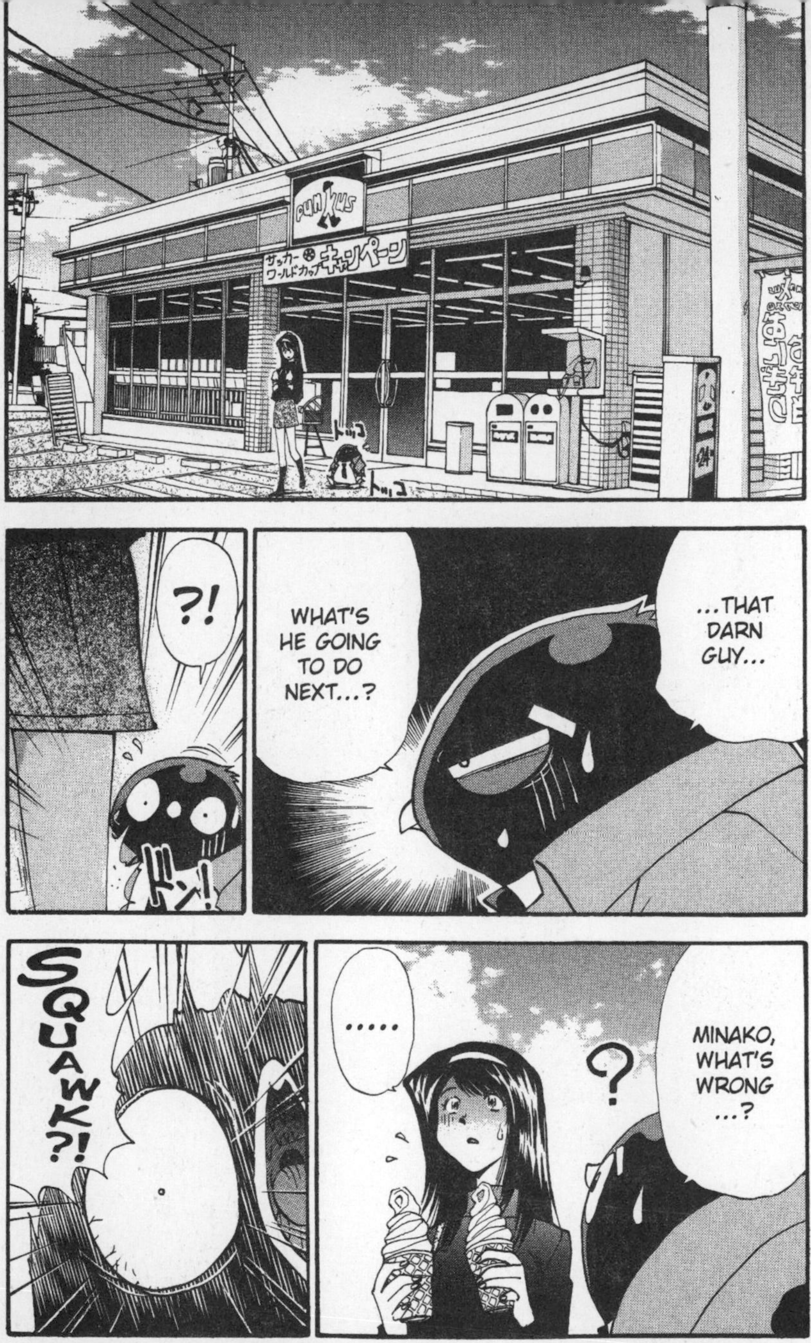
サッカー
ワールドカップ
キャンペーン
...THAT DARN GUY...
WHAT'S HE GOING TO DO NEXT...?
?!
ドン!
MINAKO, WHAT'S WRONG ...?
?
.....
SQUAWK?!

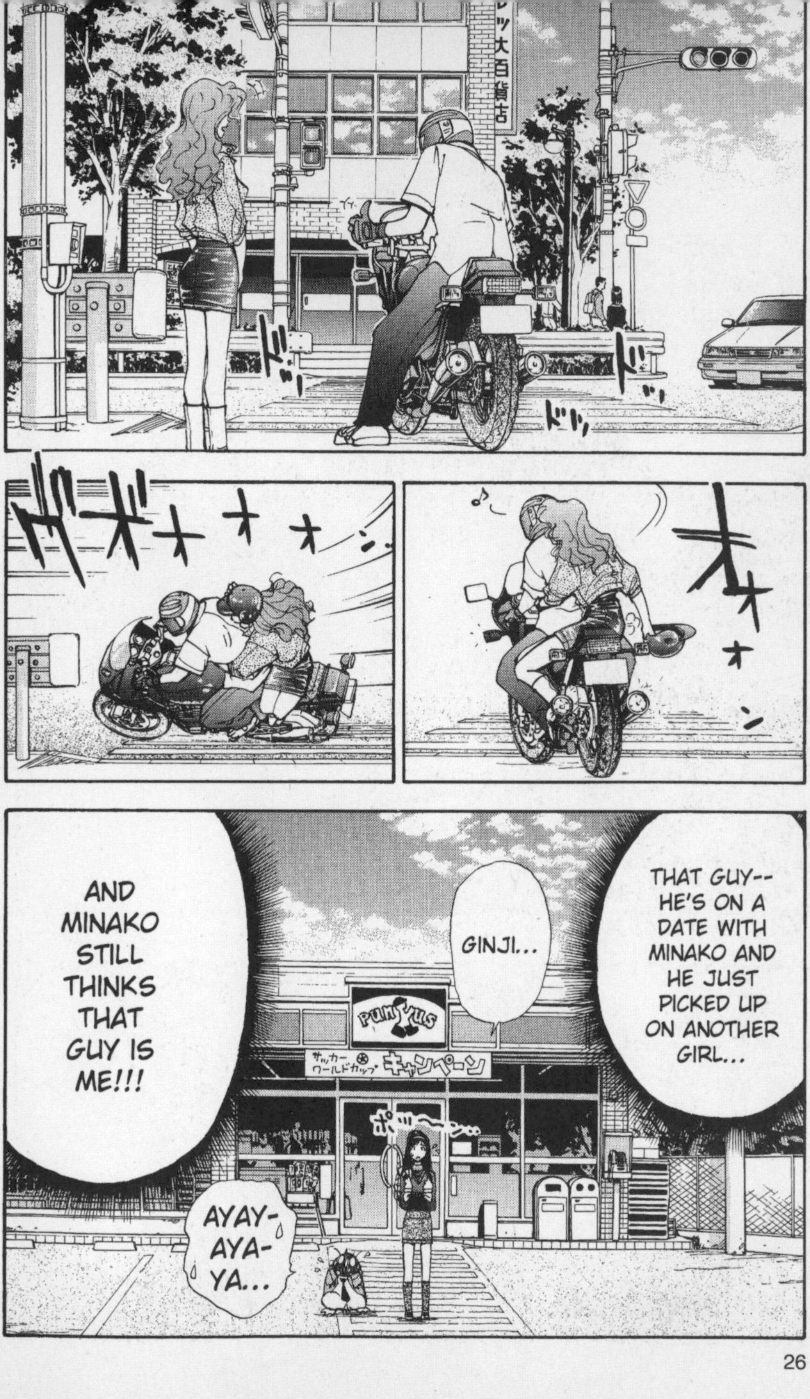
ドッ
ドッ
ドッ
オォォン
ヴオォォォン…
THAT GUY-- HE'S ON A DATE WITH MINAKO AND HE JUST PICKED UP ON ANOTHER GIRL...
GINJI...
AND MINAKO STILL THINKS THAT GUY IS ME!!!
PUNYUS
サッカーワールドカップ キャンペーン
ポッ〜〜ン…
AYAY-AYAYA-YA...

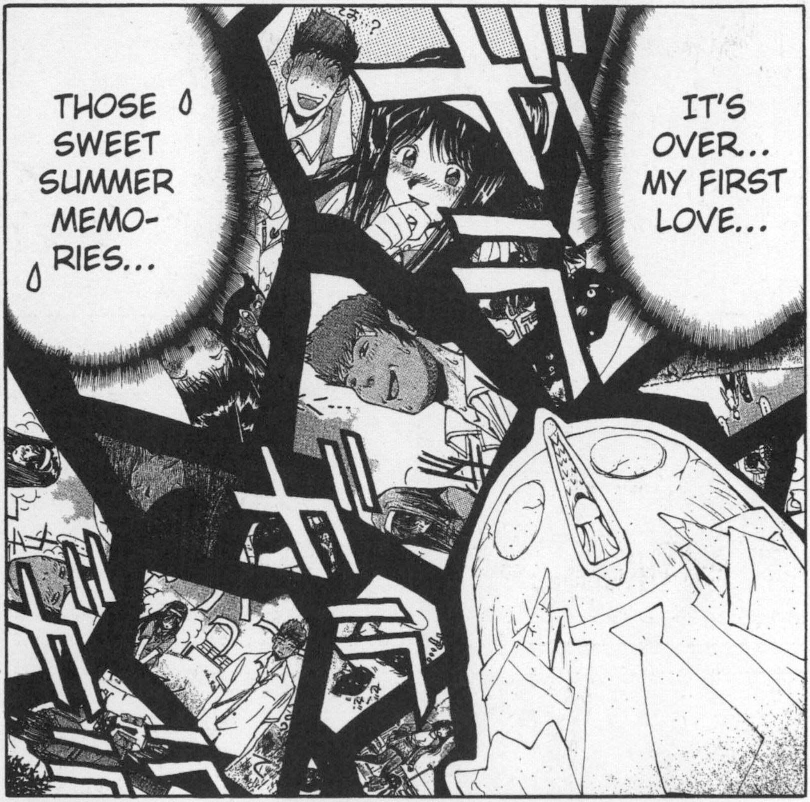
IT'S OVER... MY FIRST LOVE...
THOSE SWEET SUMMER MEMO-RIES...

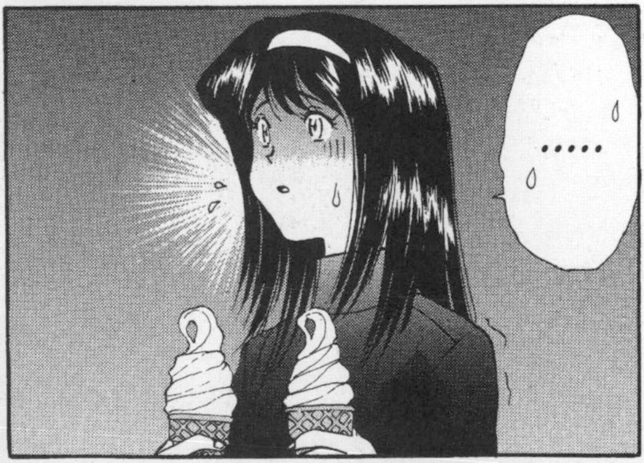
.....

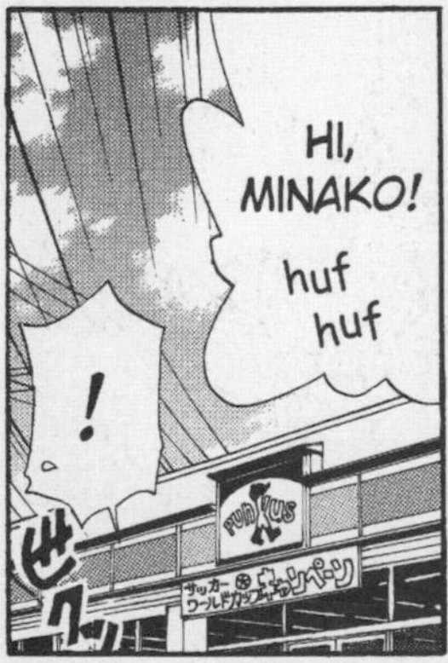
HI, MINAKO!
huf huf
!

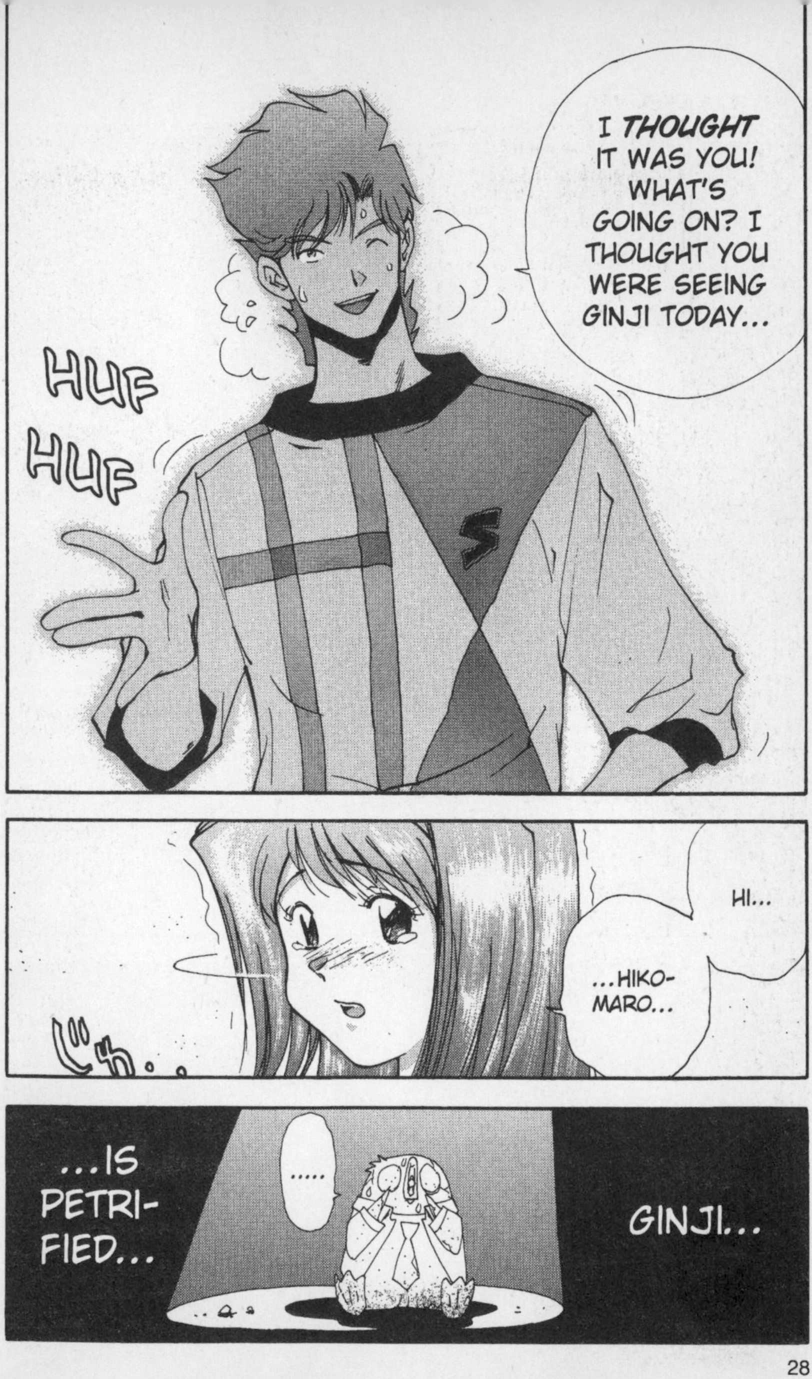
I THOUGHT IT WAS YOU! WHAT'S GOING ON? I THOUGHT YOU WERE SEEING GINJI TODAY...
HUF HUF
HI... ...HIKO-MARO...
じわ。。
GINJI...
.....
...IS PETRI-FIED...

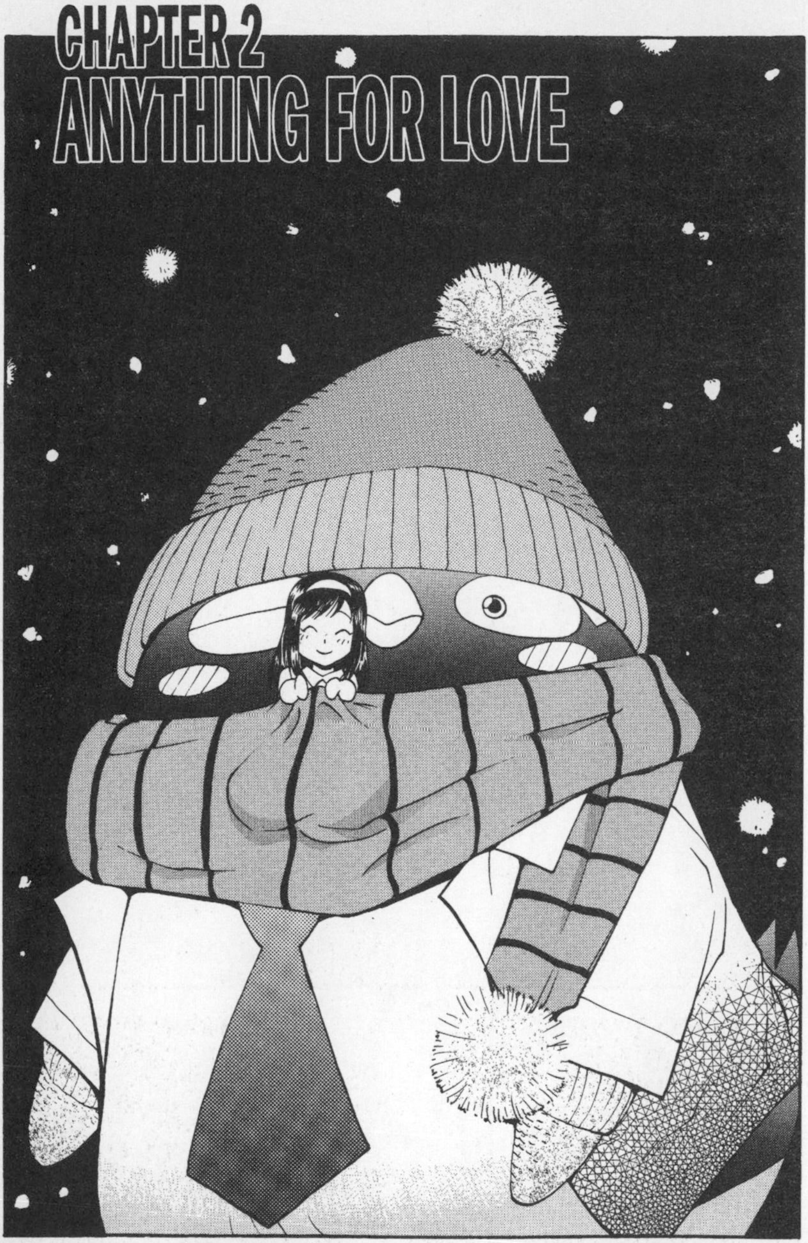
CHAPTER 2
ANYTHING FOR LOVE

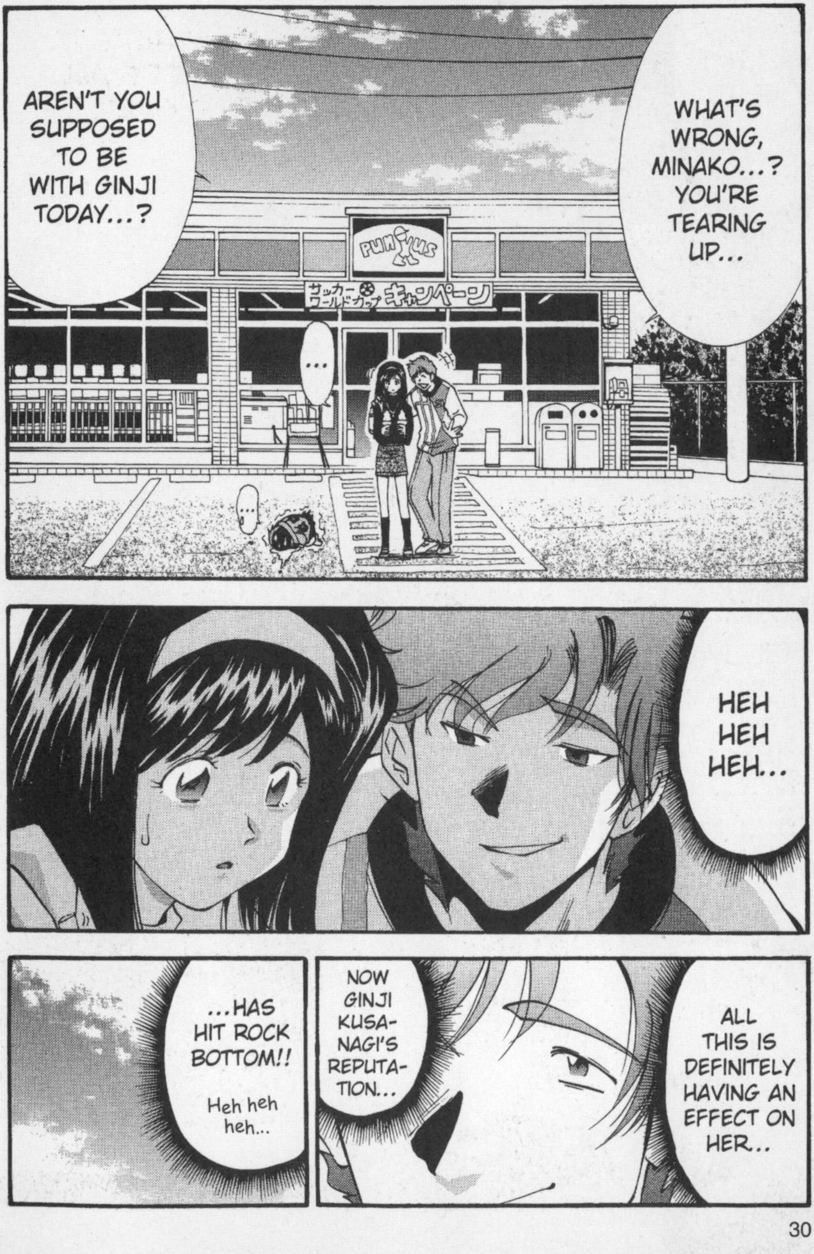
WHAT'S WRONG, MINAKO...? YOU'RE TEARING UP...
AREN'T YOU SUPPOSED TO BE WITH GINJI TODAY...?
サッカー ワールドカップ キャンペーン
...
...
HEH HEH HEH...
ALL THIS IS DEFINITELY HAVING AN EFFECT ON HER...
NOW GINJI KUSA-NAGI'S REPUTA-TION...
...HAS HIT ROCK BOTTOM!!
Heh heh heh...

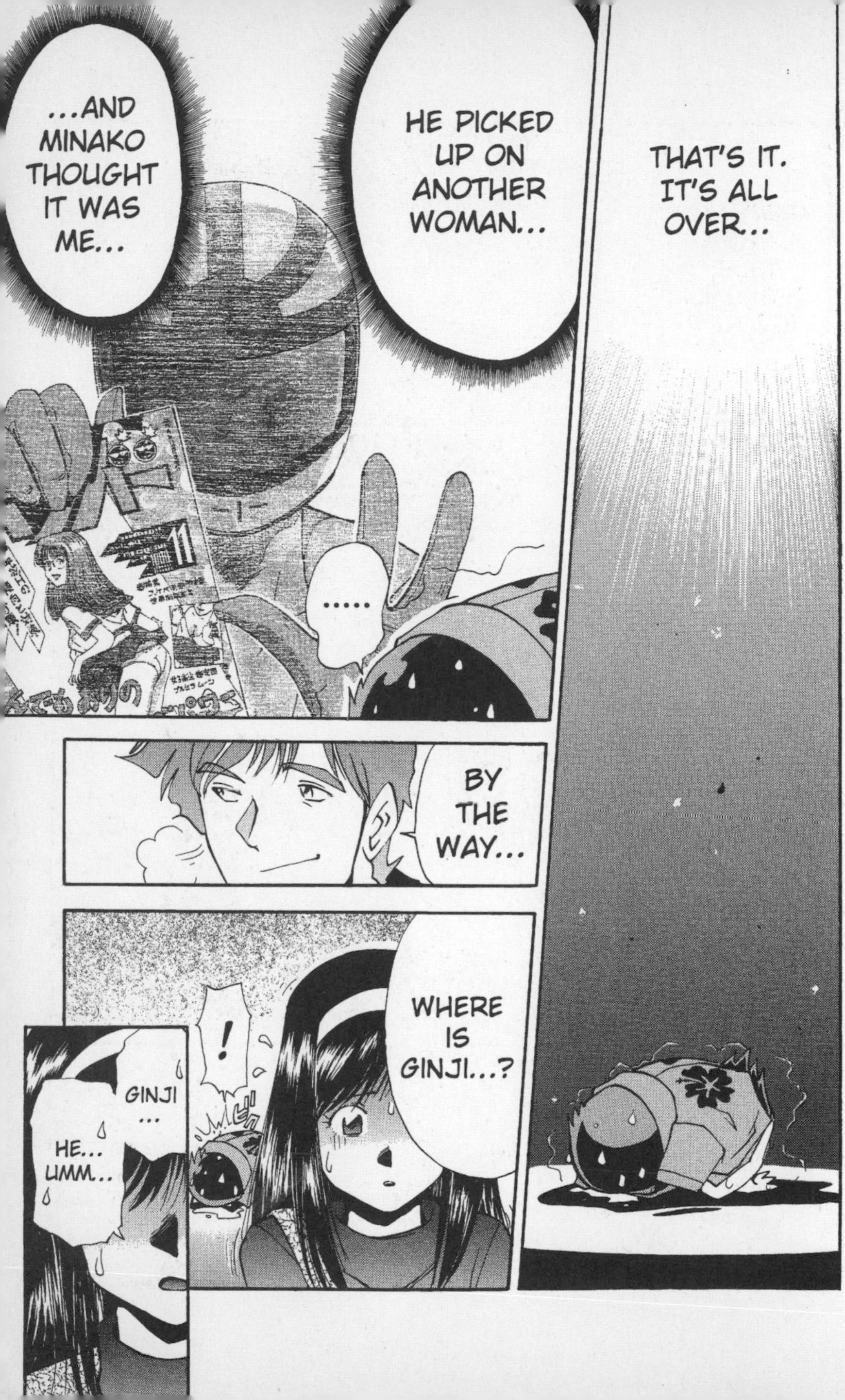
THAT'S IT. IT'S ALL OVER...
HE PICKED UP ON ANOTHER WOMAN...
...AND MINAKO THOUGHT IT WAS ME...
.....
BY THE WAY...
WHERE IS GINJI...?
!
GINJI ...
HE... UMM...

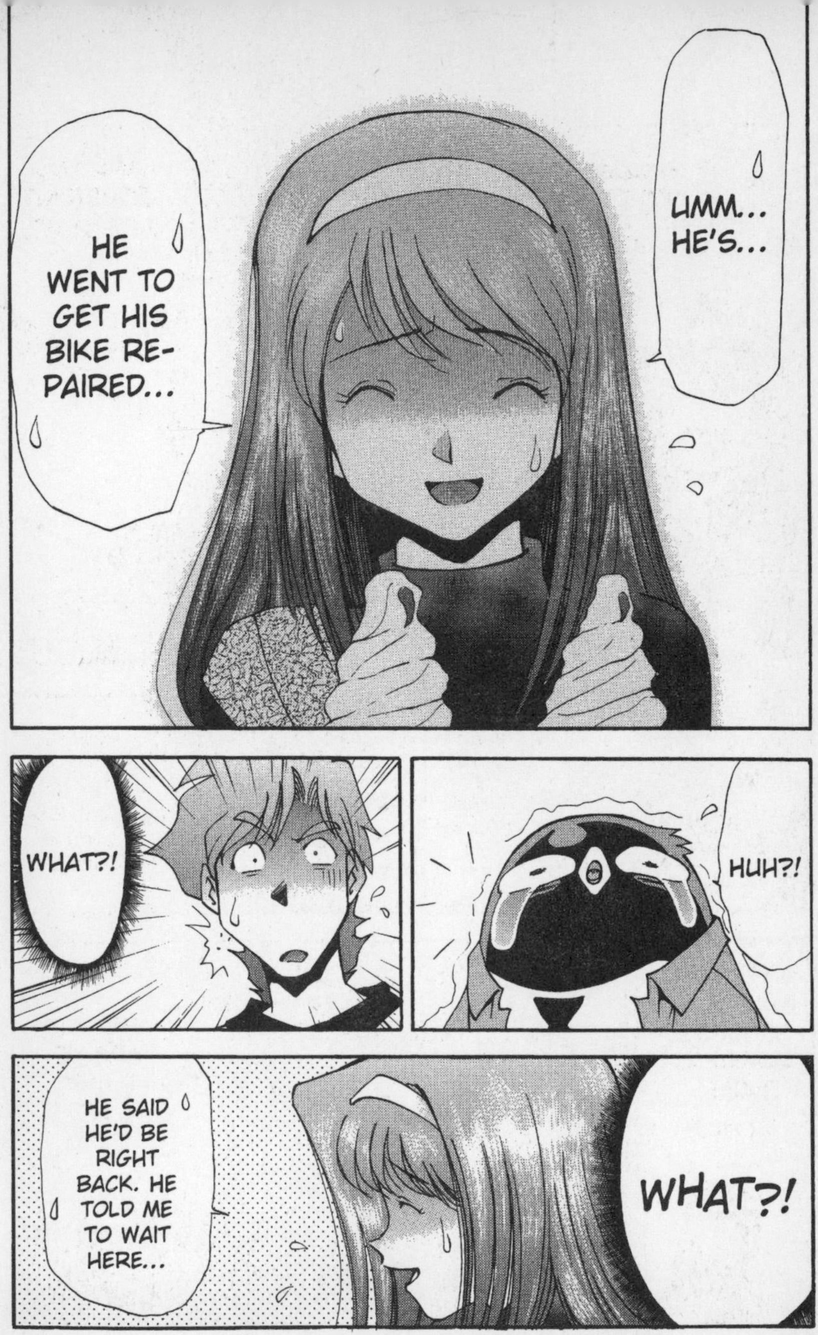
UMM... HE'S...
HE WENT TO GET HIS BIKE RE-PAIRED...
HUH?!
WHAT?!
WHAT?!
HE SAID HE'D BE RIGHT BACK. HE TOLD ME TO WAIT HERE...

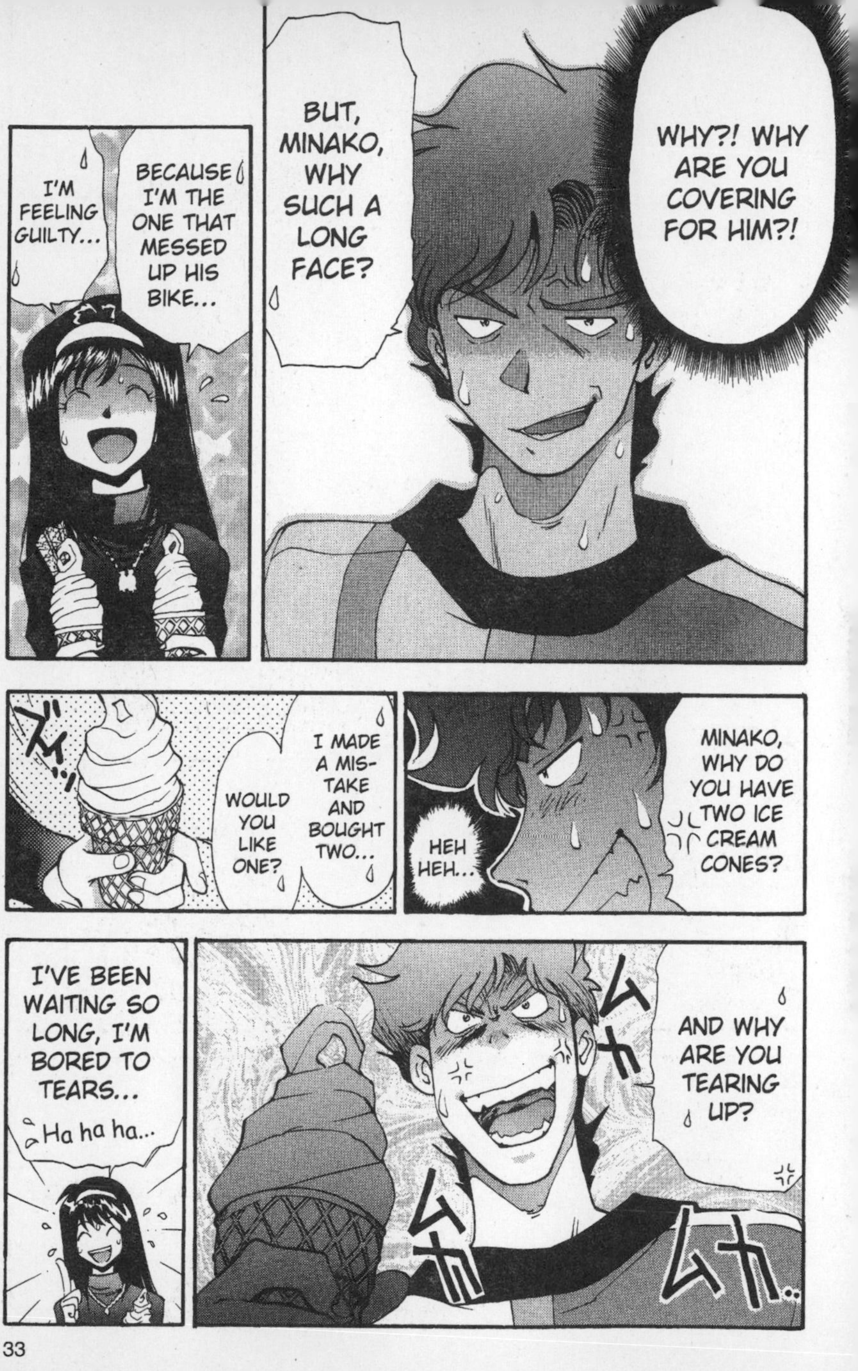
WHY?! WHY ARE YOU COVERING FOR HIM?!
BUT, MINAKO, WHY SUCH A LONG FACE?
BECAUSE I'M THE ONE THAT MESSED UP HIS BIKE...
I'M FEELING GUILTY...
MINAKO, WHY DO YOU HAVE TWO ICE CREAM CONES?
HEH HEH...
I MADE A MIS-TAKE AND BOUGHT TWO...
WOULD YOU LIKE ONE?
AND WHY ARE YOU TEARING UP?
ムカ
ムカ
ムカ..
I'VE BEEN WAITING SO LONG, I'M BORED TO TEARS...
Ha ha ha...

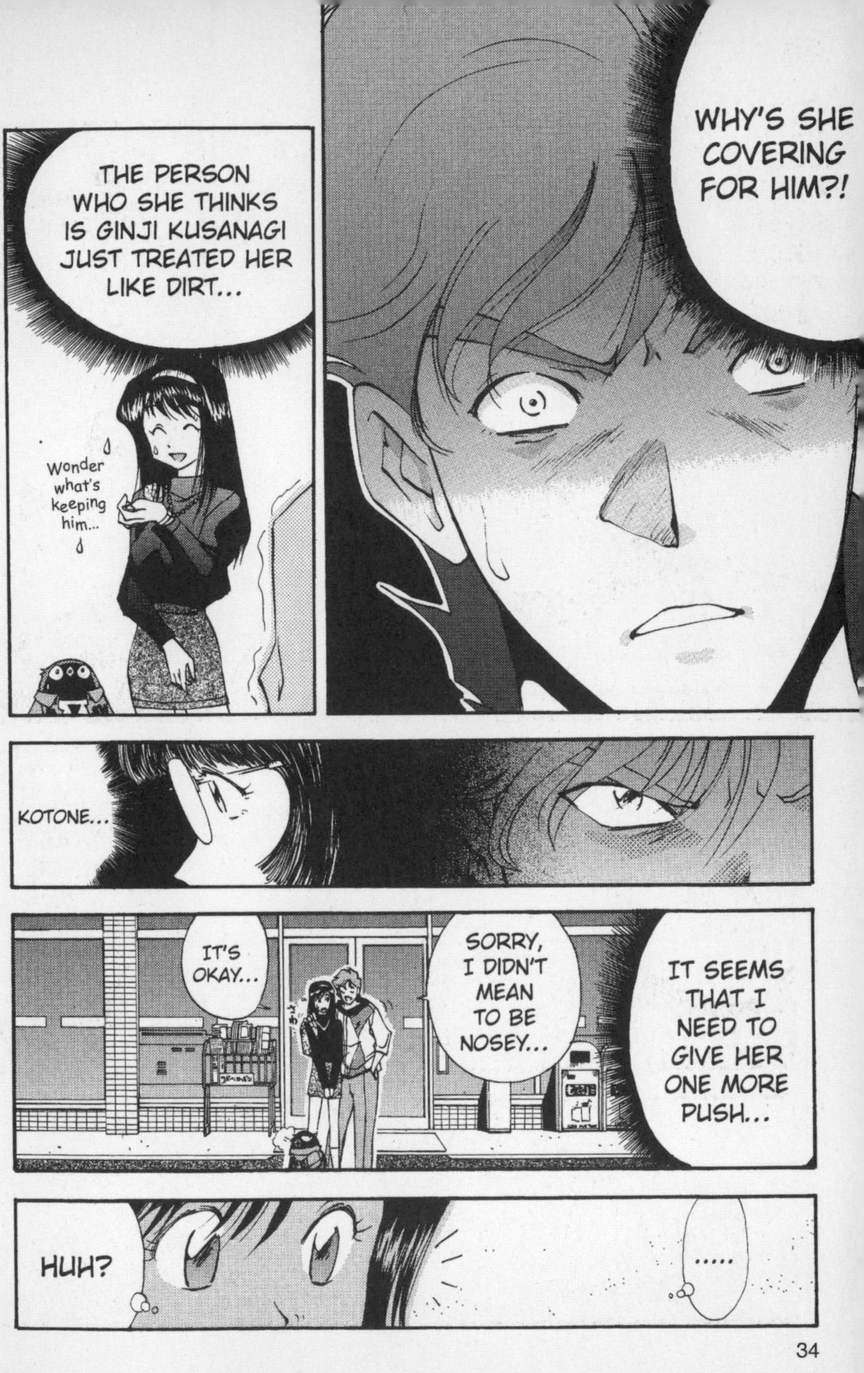
WHY'S SHE COVERING FOR HIM?!
THE PERSON WHO SHE THINKS IS GINJI KUSANAGI JUST TREATED HER LIKE DIRT...
Wonder what's keeping him...
KOTONE...
IT SEEMS THAT I NEED TO GIVE HER ONE MORE PUSH...
SORRY, I DIDN'T MEAN TO BE NOSEY...
IT'S OKAY...
.....
HUH?

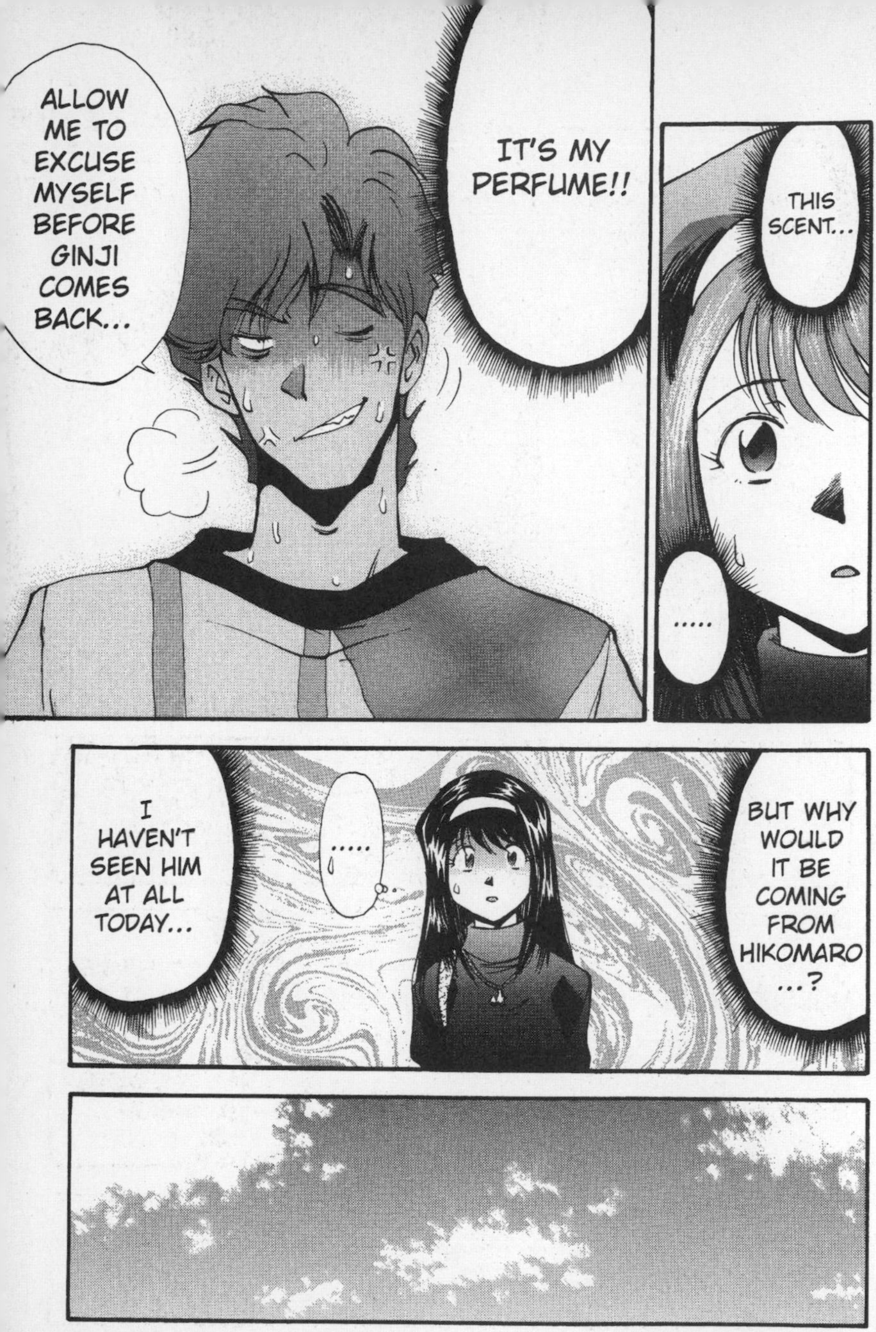
THIS SCENT...
.....
IT'S MY PERFUME!!
ALLOW ME TO EXCUSE MYSELF BEFORE GINJI COMES BACK...
BUT WHY WOULD IT BE COMING FROM HIKOMARO ...?
.....
I HAVEN'T SEEN HIM AT ALL TODAY...

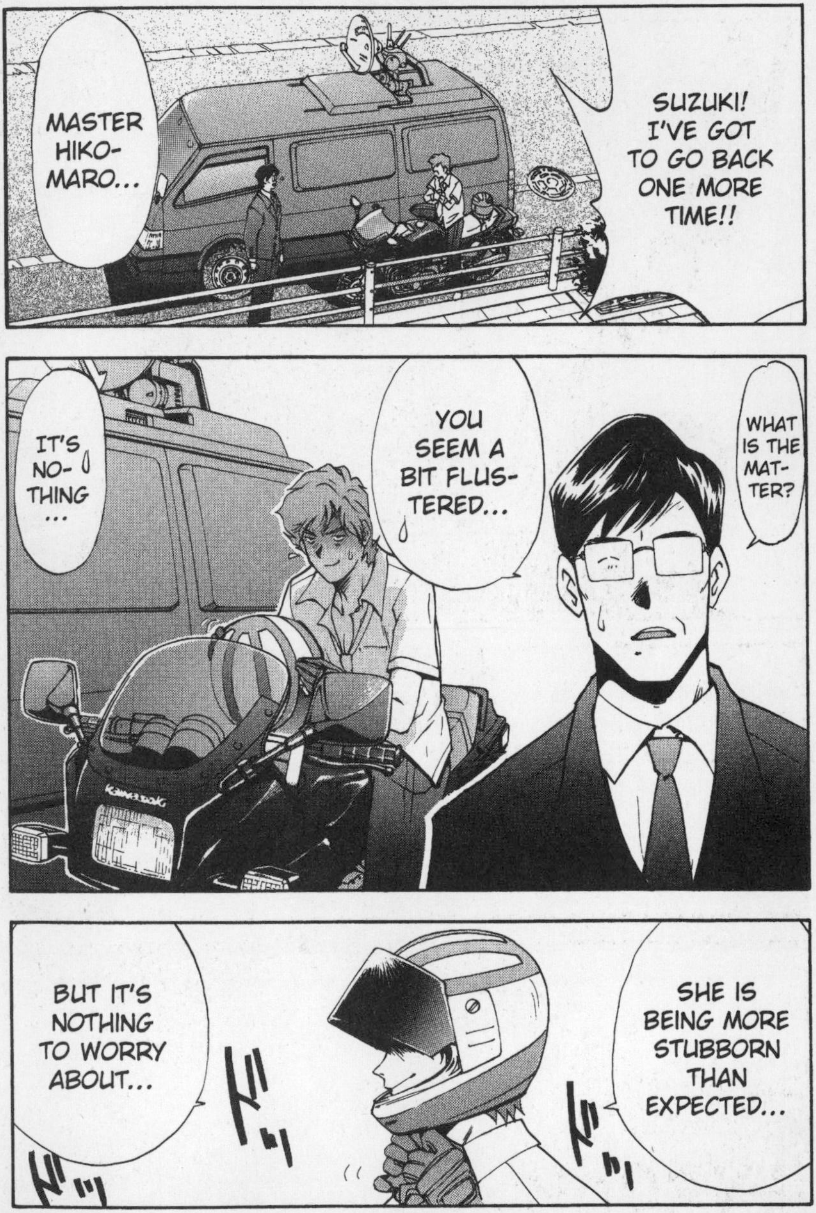
SUZUKI! I'VE GOT TO GO BACK ONE MORE TIME!!
MASTER HIKO-MARO...
WHAT IS THE MAT-TER?
YOU SEEM A BIT FLUS-TERED...
IT'S NO-THING...
SHE IS BEING MORE STUBBORN THAN EXPECTED...
ドッ
ドッ
BUT IT'S NOTHING TO WORRY ABOUT...
ドッ

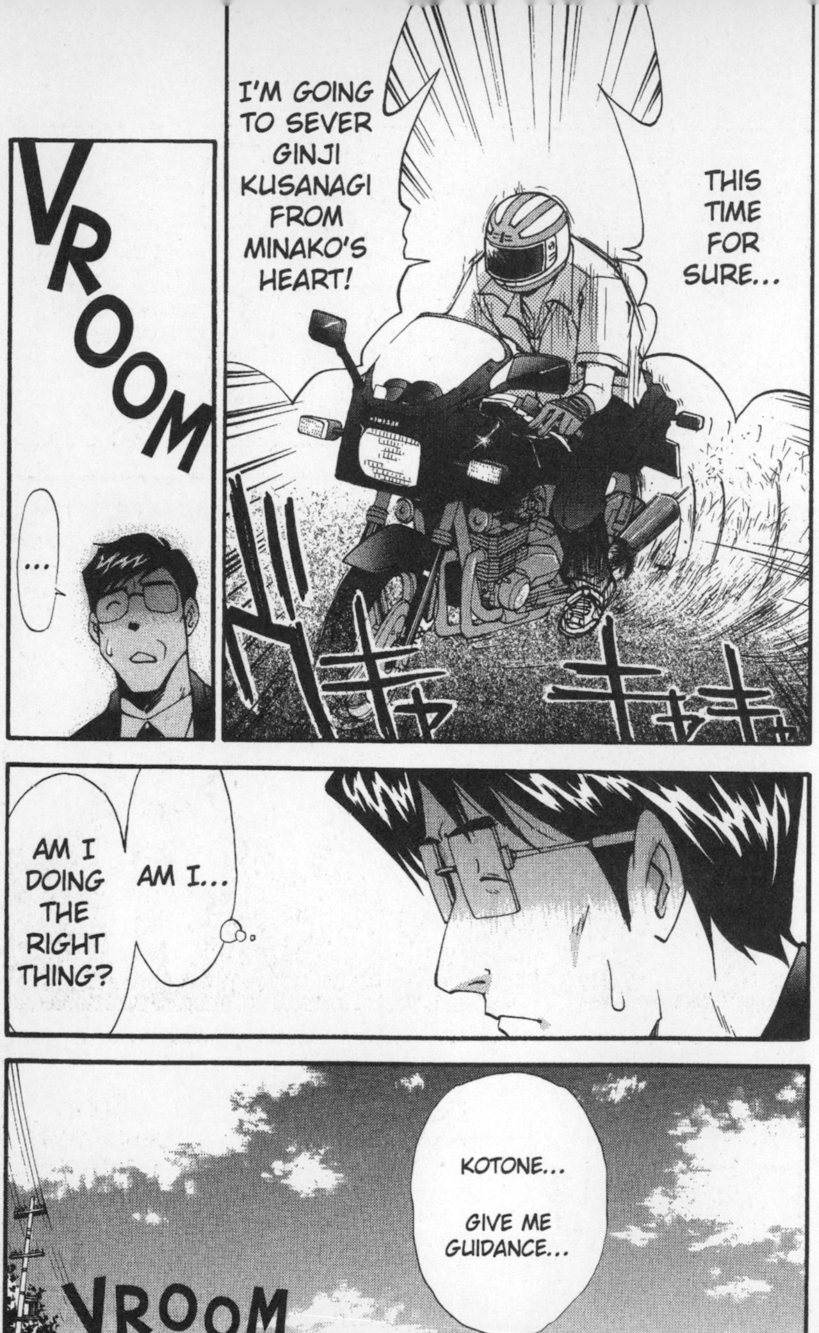
THIS TIME FOR SURE...
I'M GOING TO SEVER GINJI KUSANAGI FROM MINAKO'S HEART!
VROOM
...
AM I...
AM I DOING THE RIGHT THING?
KOTONE...
GIVE ME GUIDANCE...
VROOM

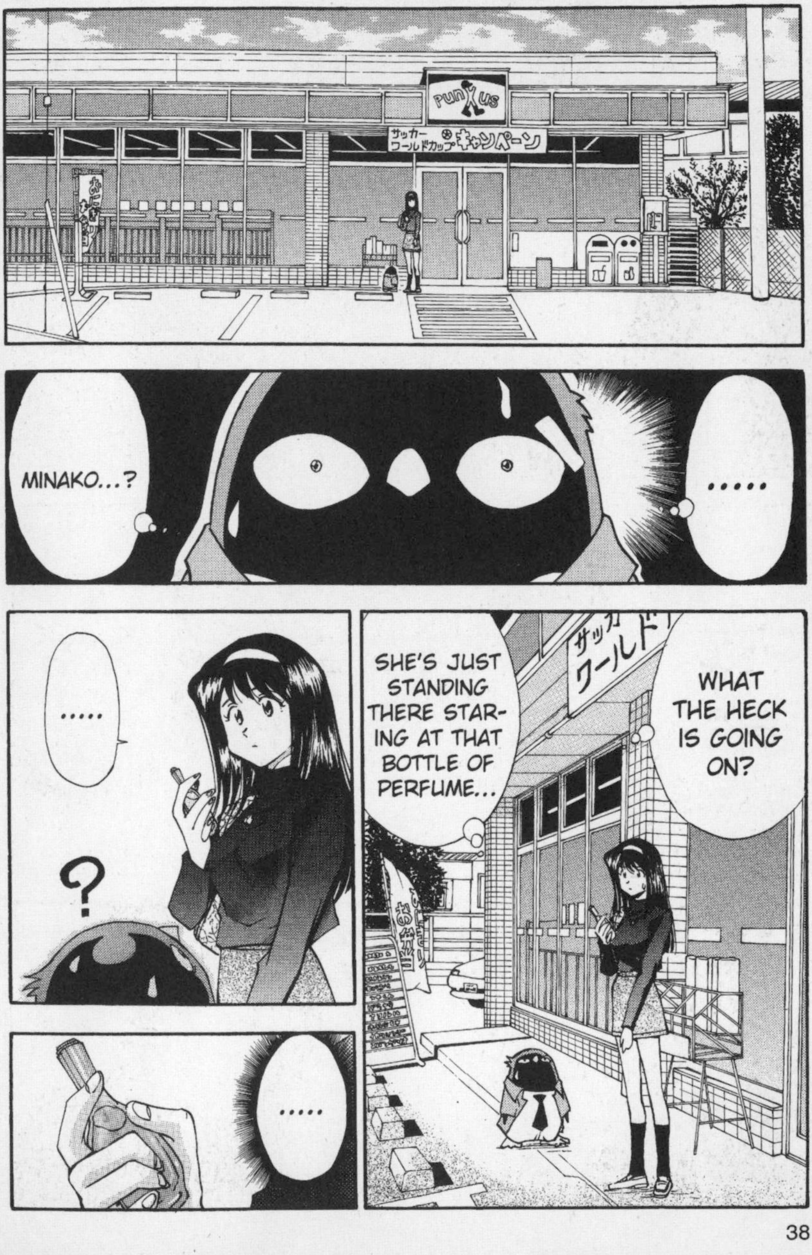
サッカー ワールドカップ キャンペーン
.....
MINAKO...?
WHAT THE HECK IS GOING ON?
SHE'S JUST STANDING THERE STAR-ING AT THAT BOTTLE OF PERFUME...
.....
?
.....

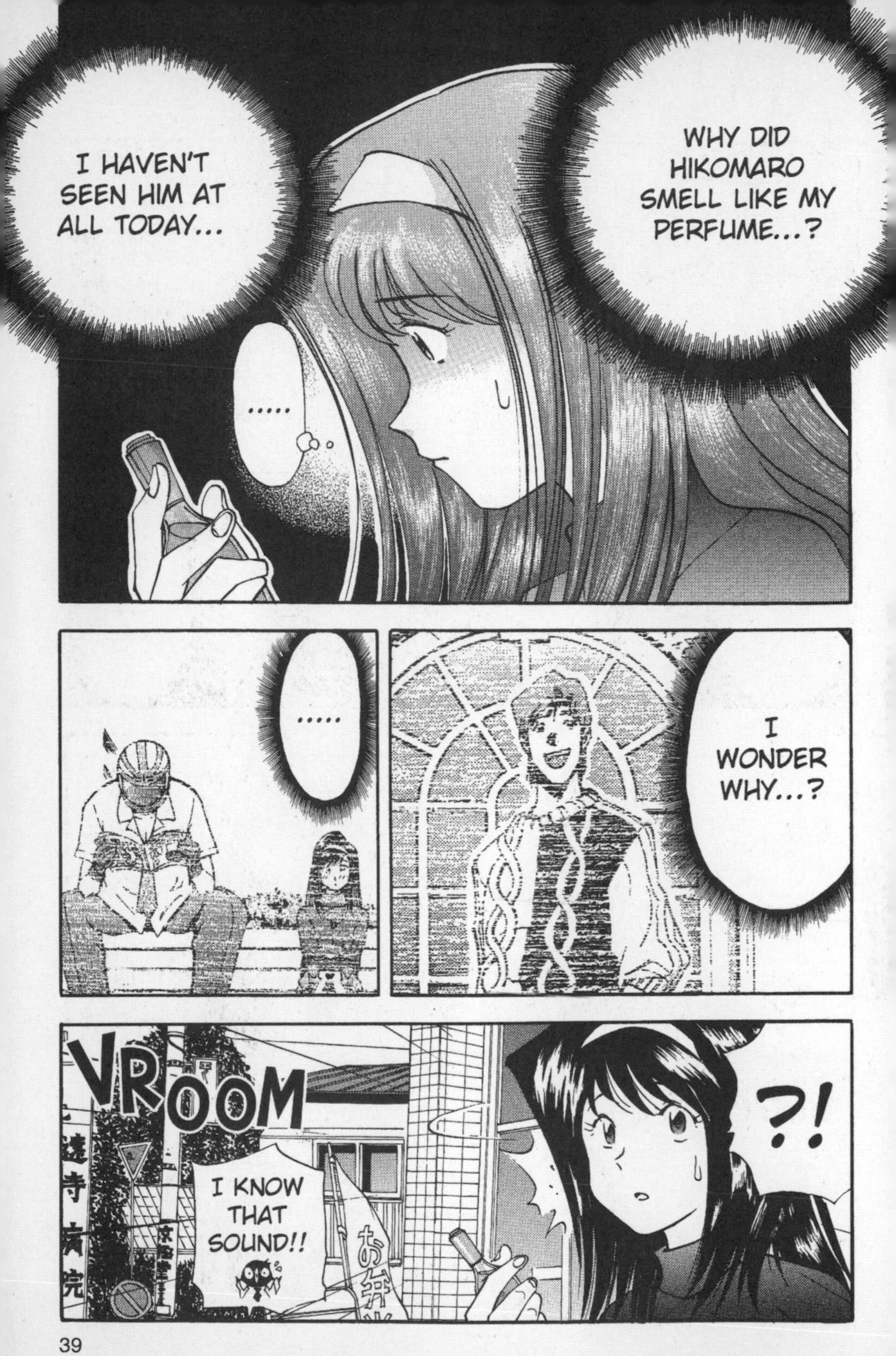
WHY DID HIKOMARO SMELL LIKE MY PERFUME...?
I HAVEN'T SEEN HIM AT ALL TODAY...
.....
I WONDER WHY...?
.....
?!
I KNOW THAT SOUND!!
VROOM

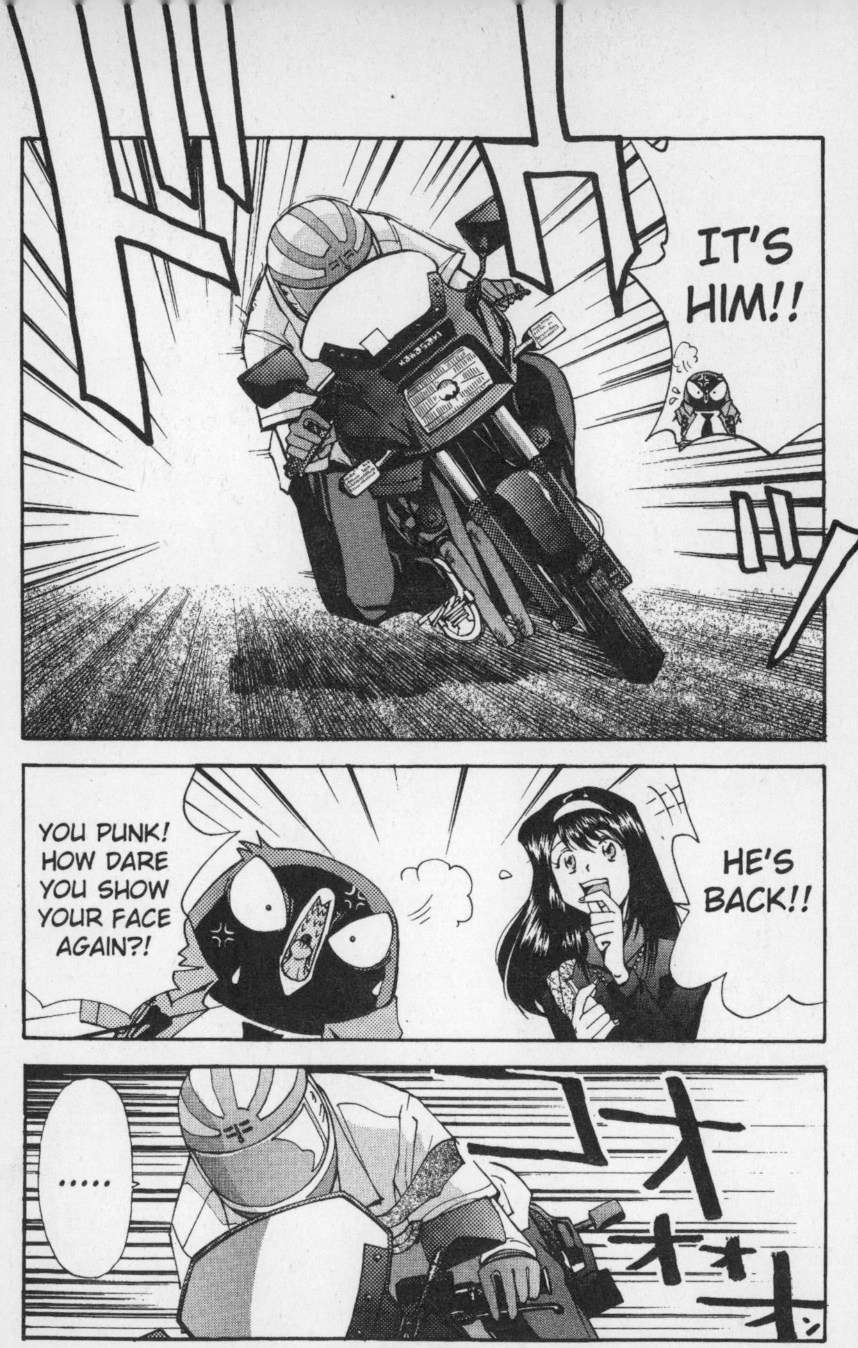
IT'S HIM!!
HE'S BACK!!
YOU PUNK! HOW DARE YOU SHOW YOUR FACE AGAIN?!
.....

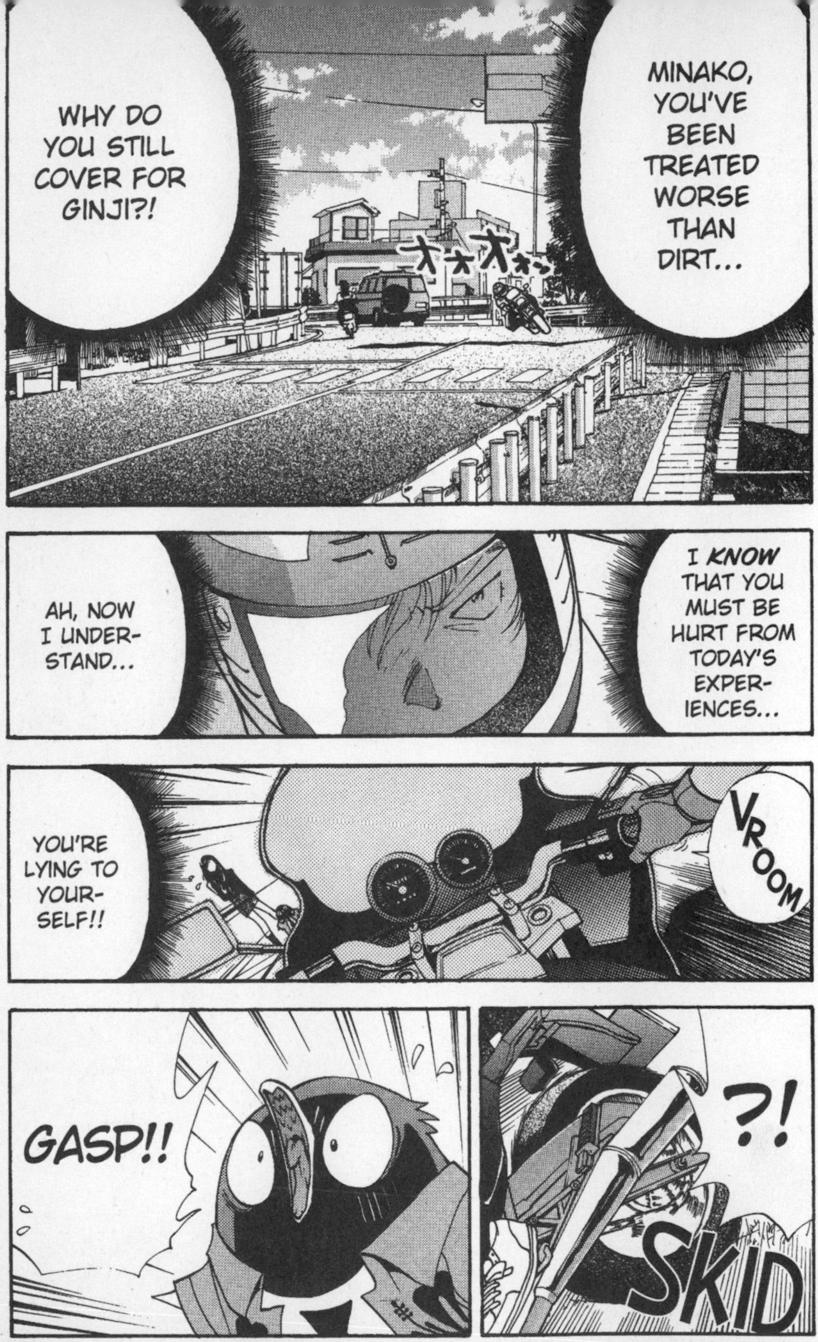
MINAKO, YOU'VE BEEN TREATED WORSE THAN DIRT...
WHY DO YOU STILL COVER FOR GINJI?!
I KNOW THAT YOU MUST BE HURT FROM TODAY'S EXPER-IENCES...
AH, NOW I UNDER-STAND...
VROOM
YOU'RE LYING TO YOUR-SELF!!
?!
SKID
GASP!!

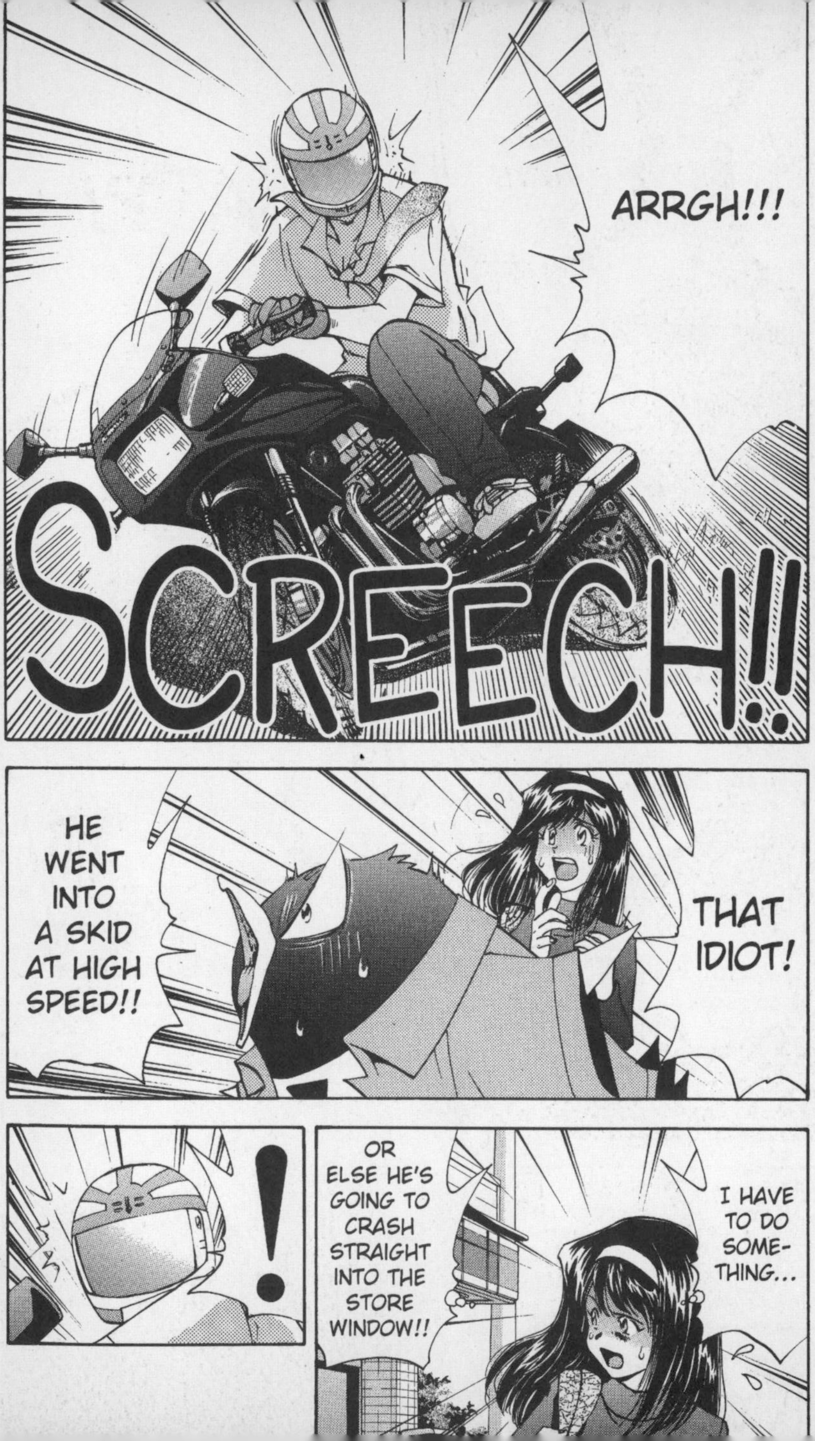
ARRGH!!!
SCREECH!!
THAT IDIOT!
HE WENT INTO A SKID AT HIGH SPEED!!
I HAVE TO DO SOME-THING...
OR ELSE HE'S GOING TO CRASH STRAIGHT INTO THE STORE WINDOW!!
!

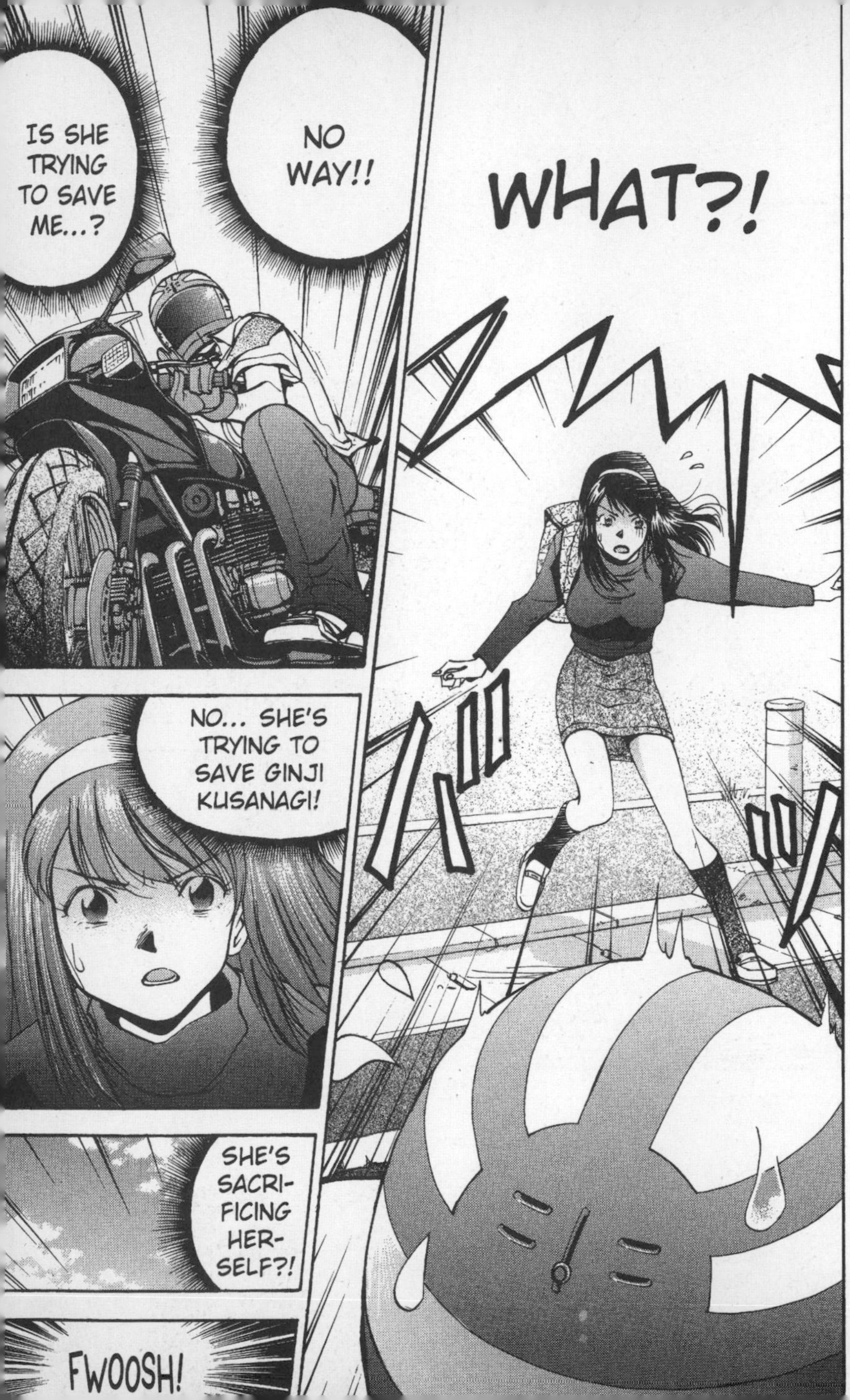
WHAT?!
NO WAY!!
IS SHE TRYING TO SAVE ME...?
NO... SHE'S TRYING TO SAVE GINJI KUSANAGI!
SHE'S SACRI-FICING HER-SELF?!
FWOOSH!

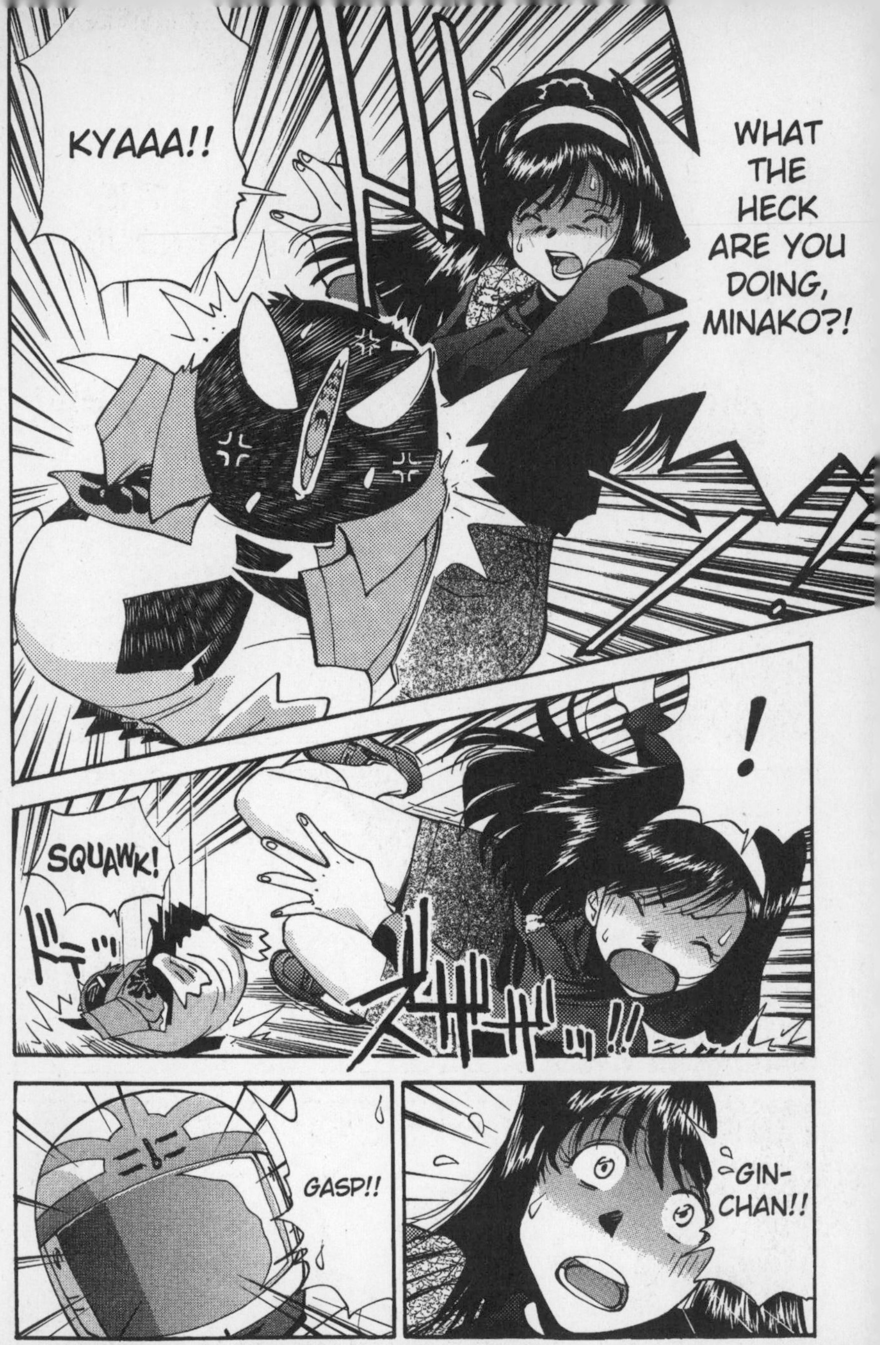
WHAT THE HECK ARE YOU DOING, MINAKO?!
KYAAA!!
!
SQUAWK!
GIN-CHAN!!
GASP!!

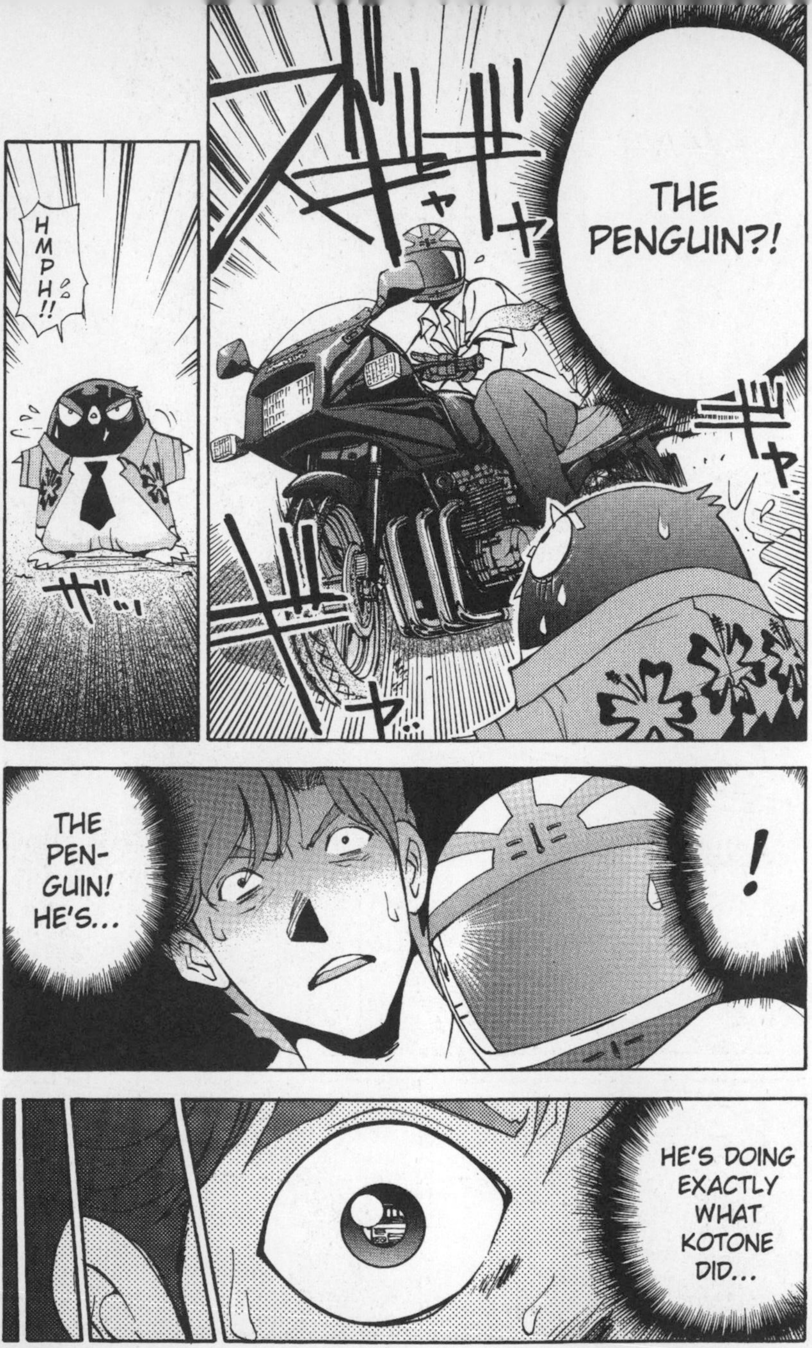
THE PENGUIN?!
HMPH!!
THE PEN-GUIN! HE'S...
!
HE'S DOING EXACTLY WHAT KOTONE DID...

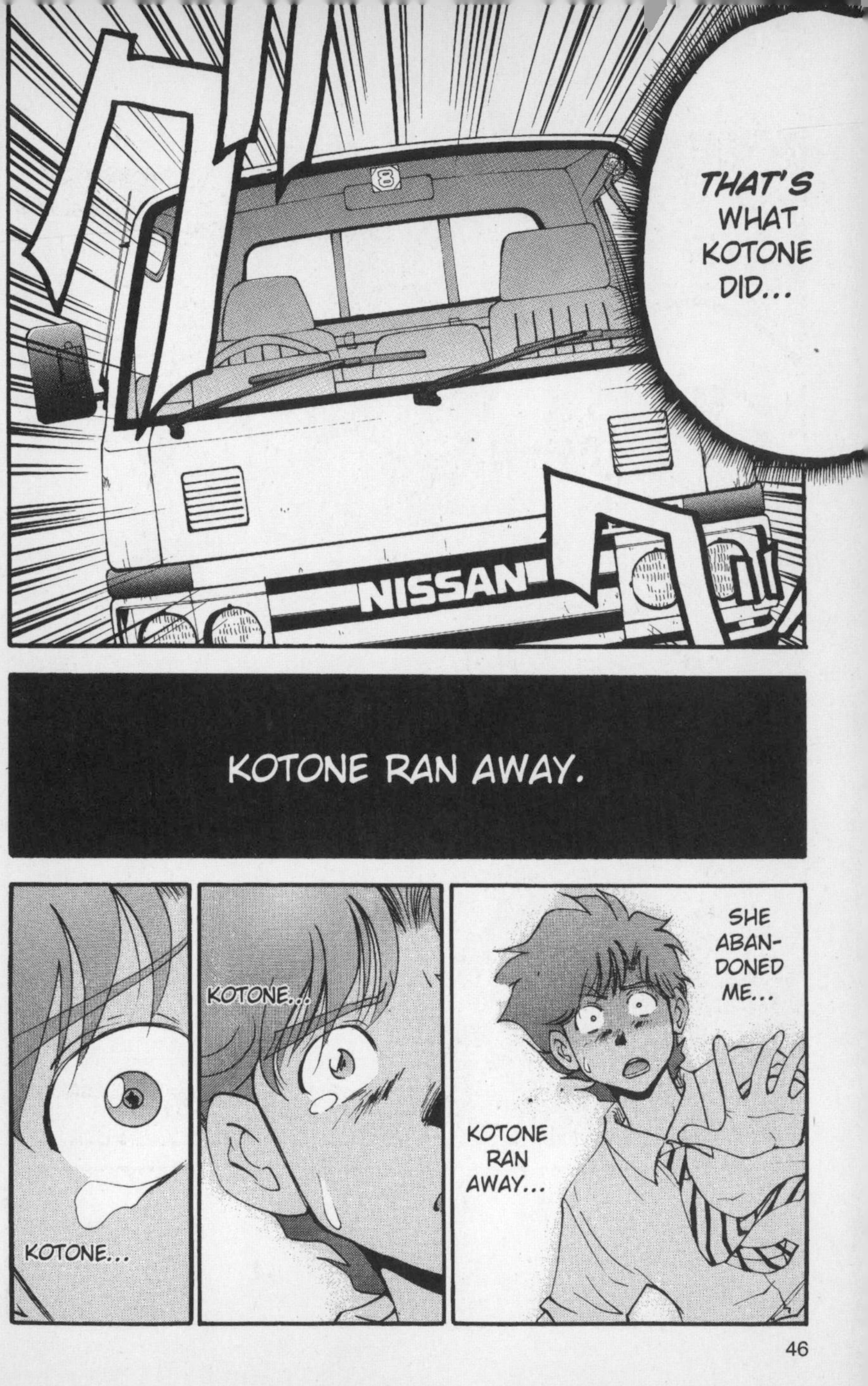
THAT'S WHAT KOTONE DID...
NISSAN
KOTONE RAN AWAY.
SHE ABAN-DONED ME...
KOTONE RAN AWAY...
KOTONE...
KOTONE...

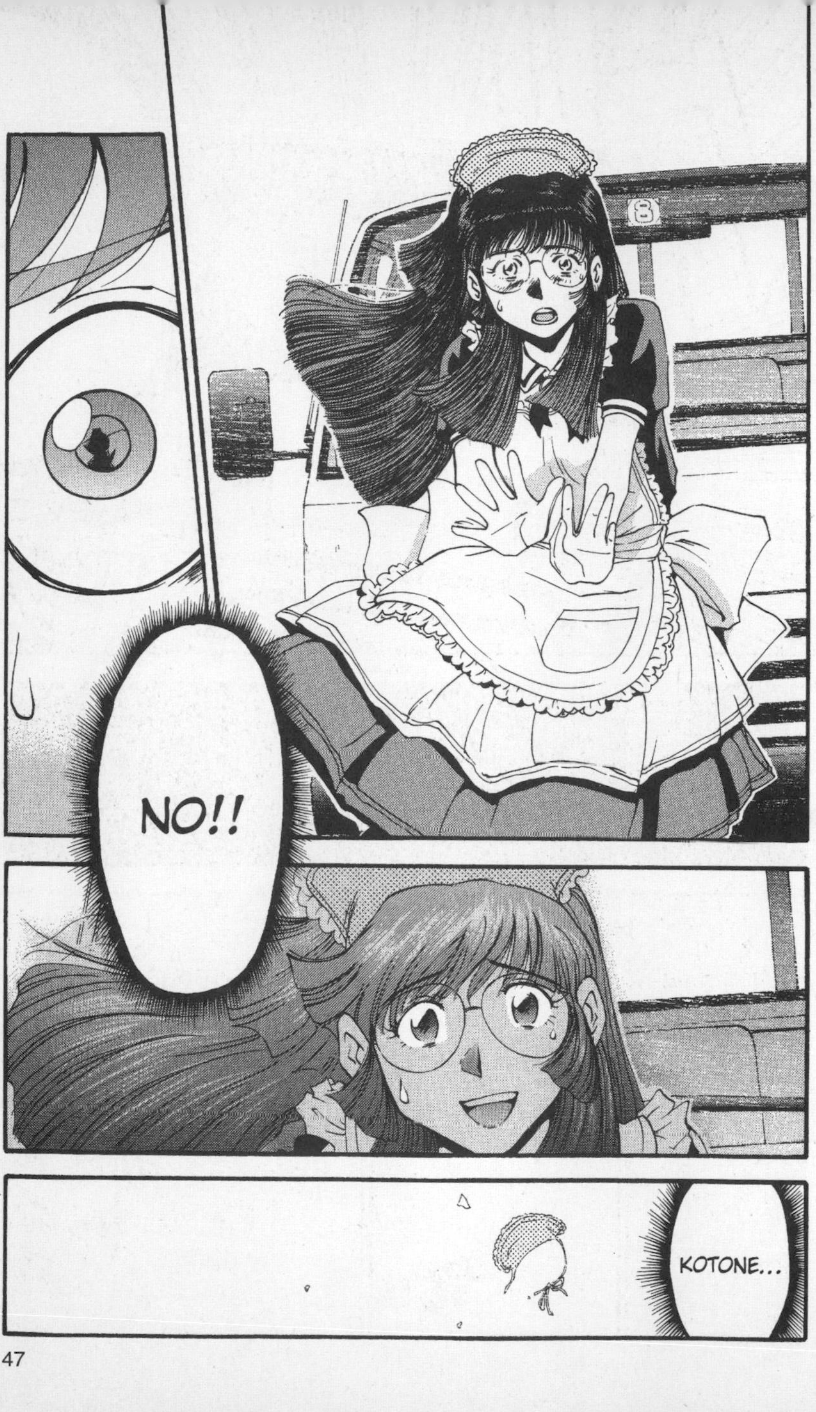
NO!!
KOTONE...

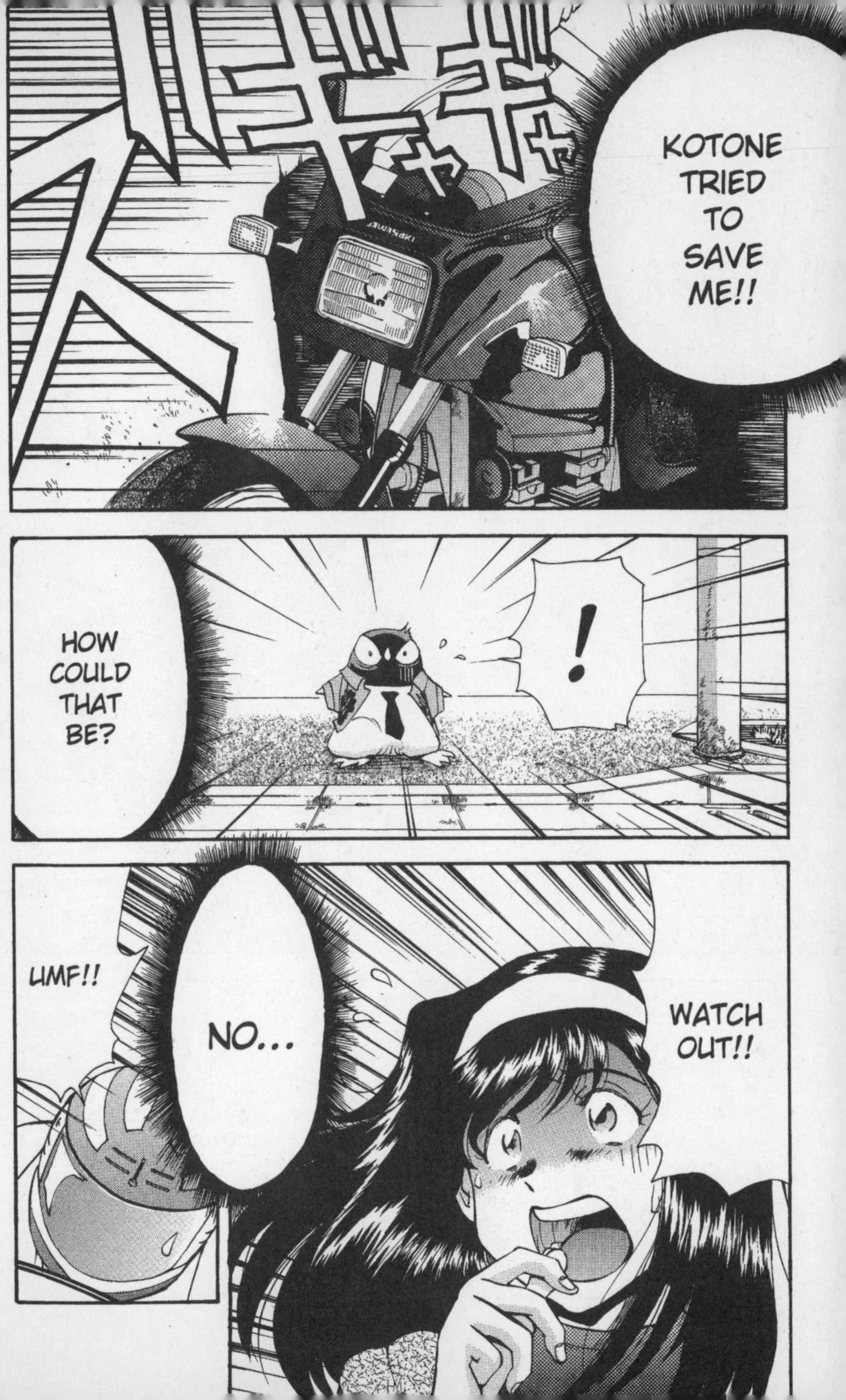
KOTONE TRIED TO SAVE ME!!
!
HOW COULD THAT BE?
WATCH OUT!!
NO...
UMF!!

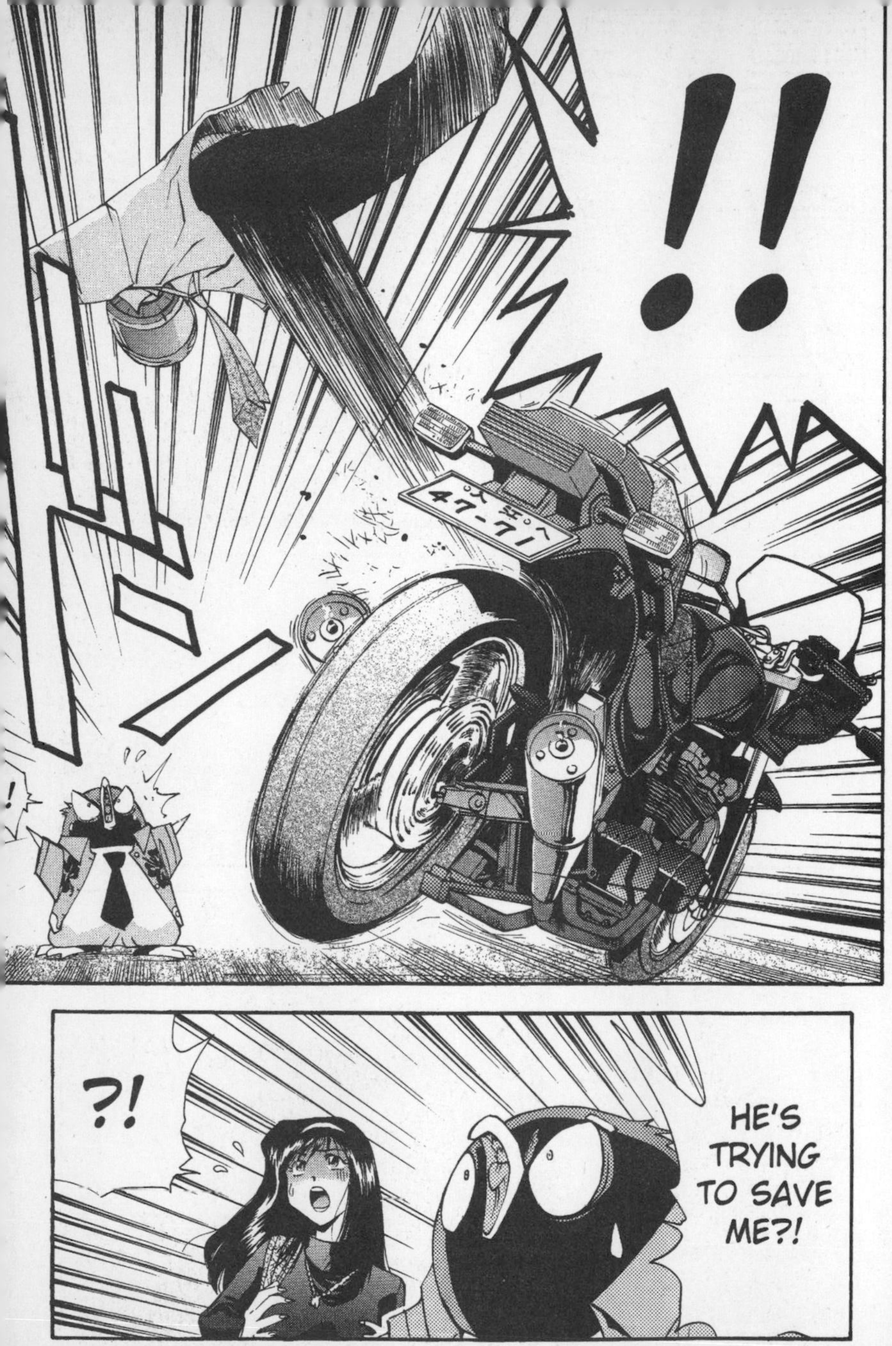
!!
!
HE'S TRYING TO SAVE ME?!
?!

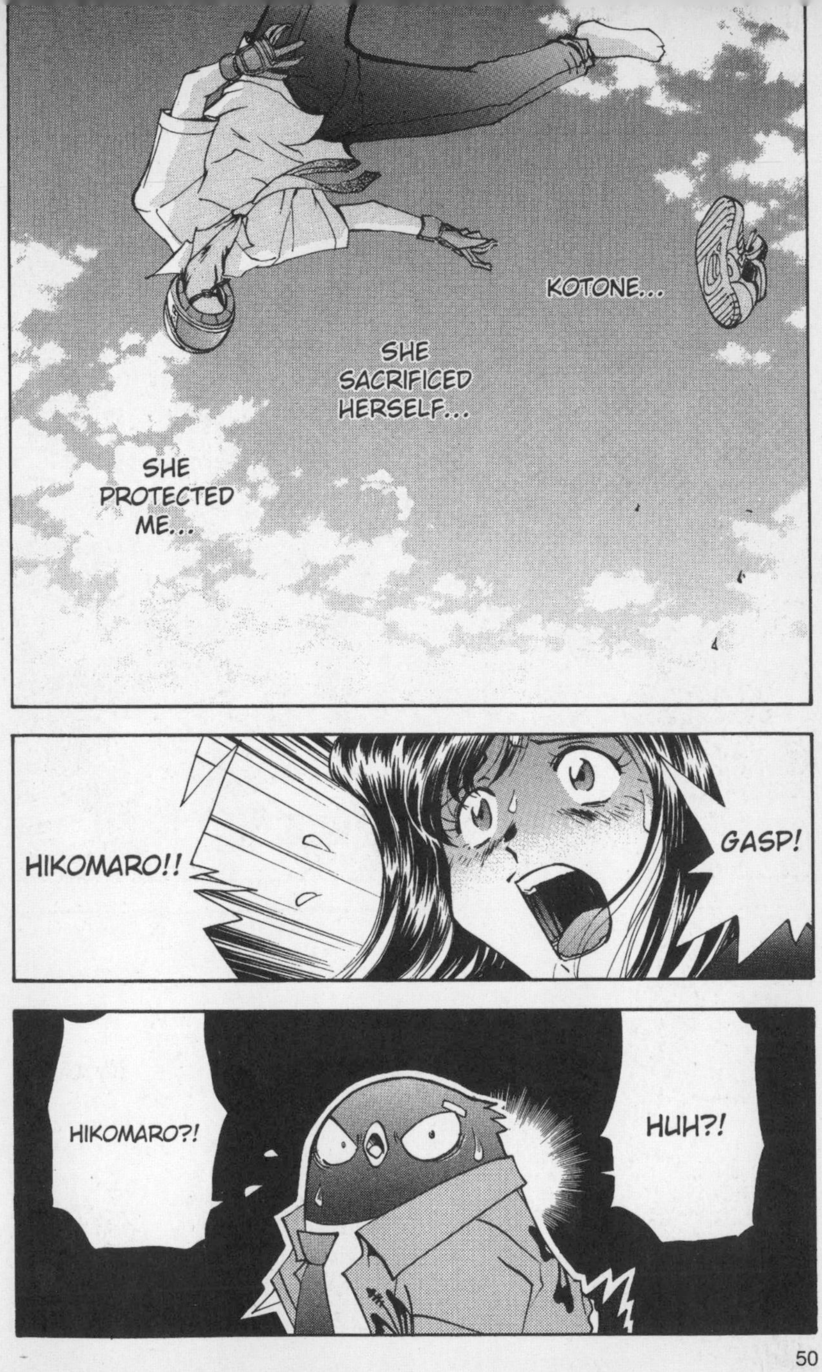
KOTONE...
SHE SACRIFICED HERSELF...
SHE PROTECTED ME...
GASP!
HIKOMARO!!
HUH?!
HIKOMARO?!

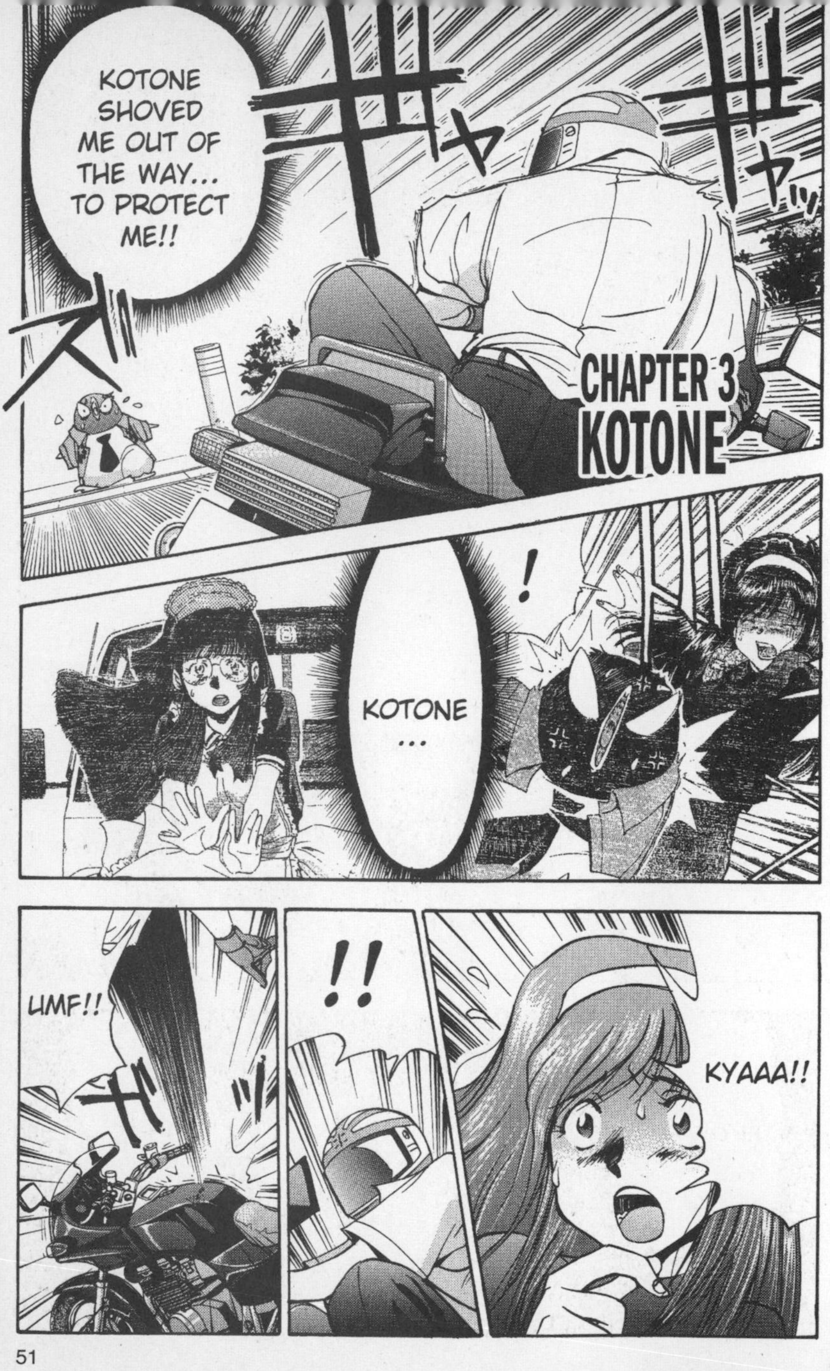
KOTONE SHOVED ME OUT OF THE WAY... TO PROTECT ME!!
CHAPTER 3
KOTONE
!
KOTONE ...
KYAAA!!
!!
UMF!!

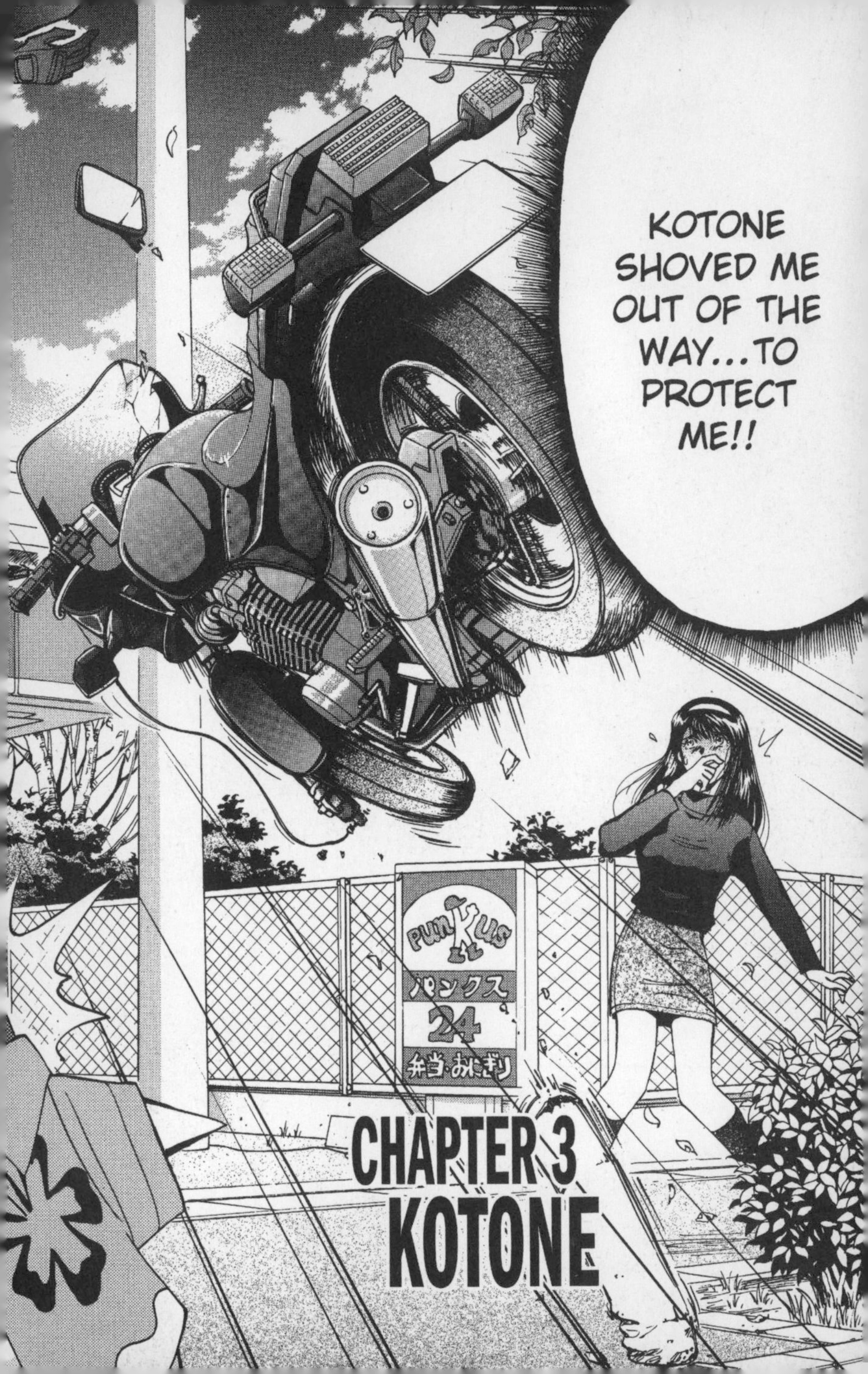
KOTONE SHOVED ME OUT OF THE WAY...TO PROTECT ME!!
PUNKUS
パンクス
24
弁当・おにぎり
CHAPTER 3
KOTONE

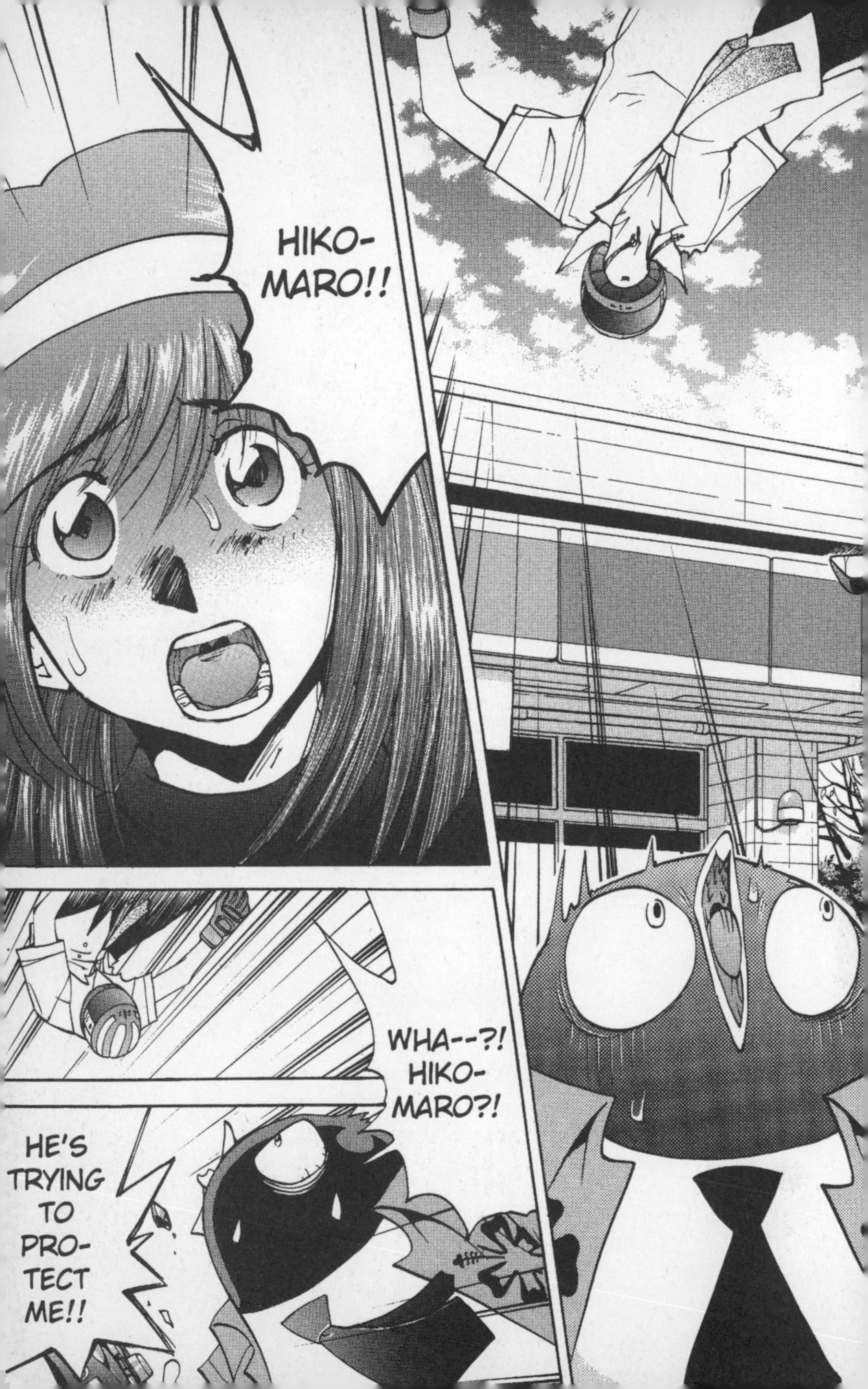
HIKO-MARO!!
WHA--?! HIKO-MARO?!
HE'S TRYING TO PROTECT ME!!

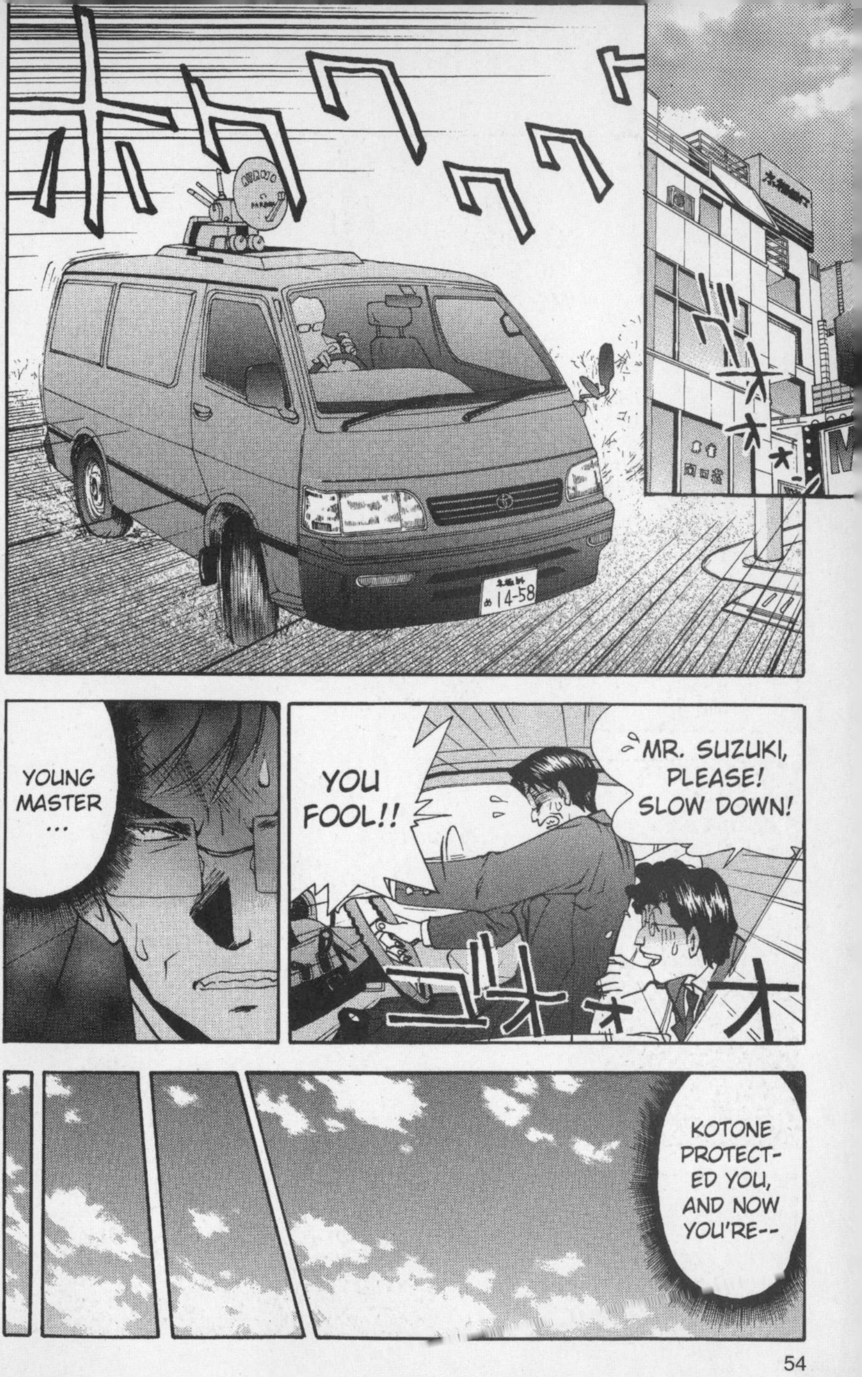
MR. SUZUKI, PLEASE! SLOW DOWN!
YOU FOOL!!
YOUNG MASTER ...
KOTONE PROTECTED YOU, AND NOW YOU'RE--

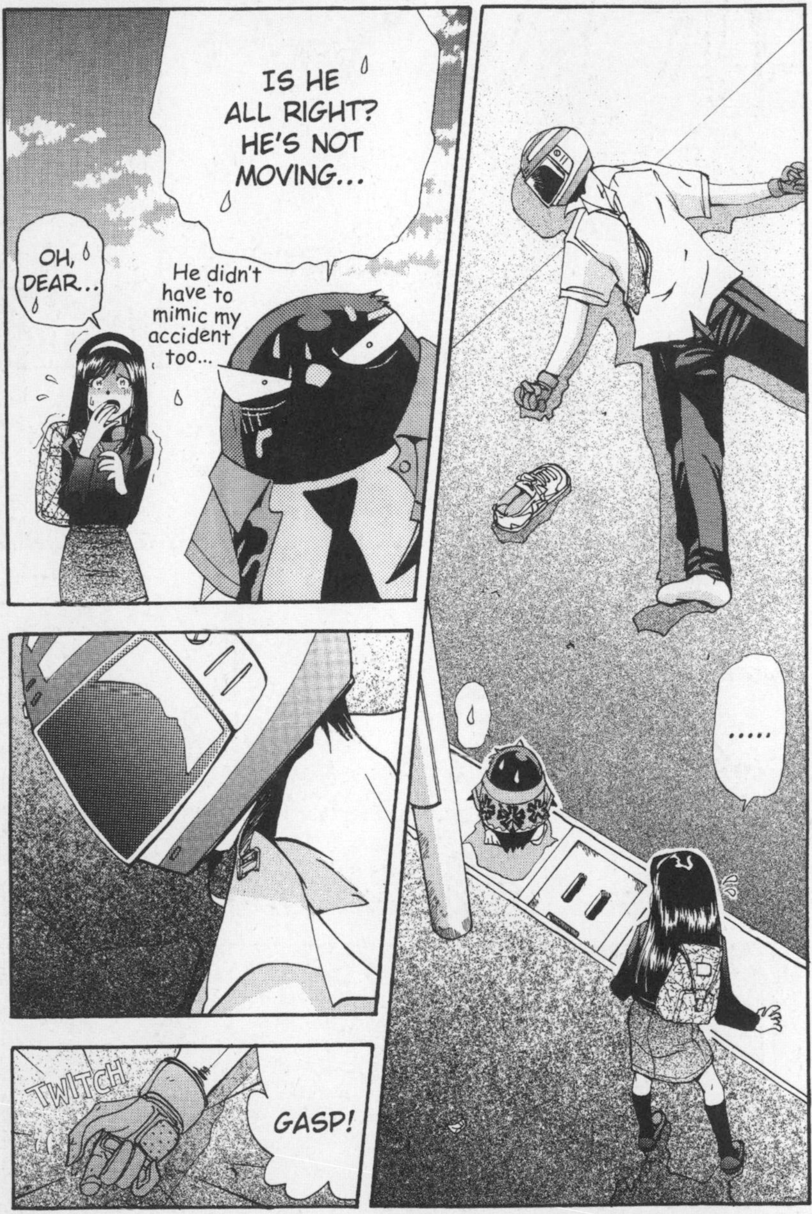

.....
IS HE ALL RIGHT? HE'S NOT MOVING...
OH, DEAR...
He didn't have to mimic my accident too...
GASP!
TWITCH

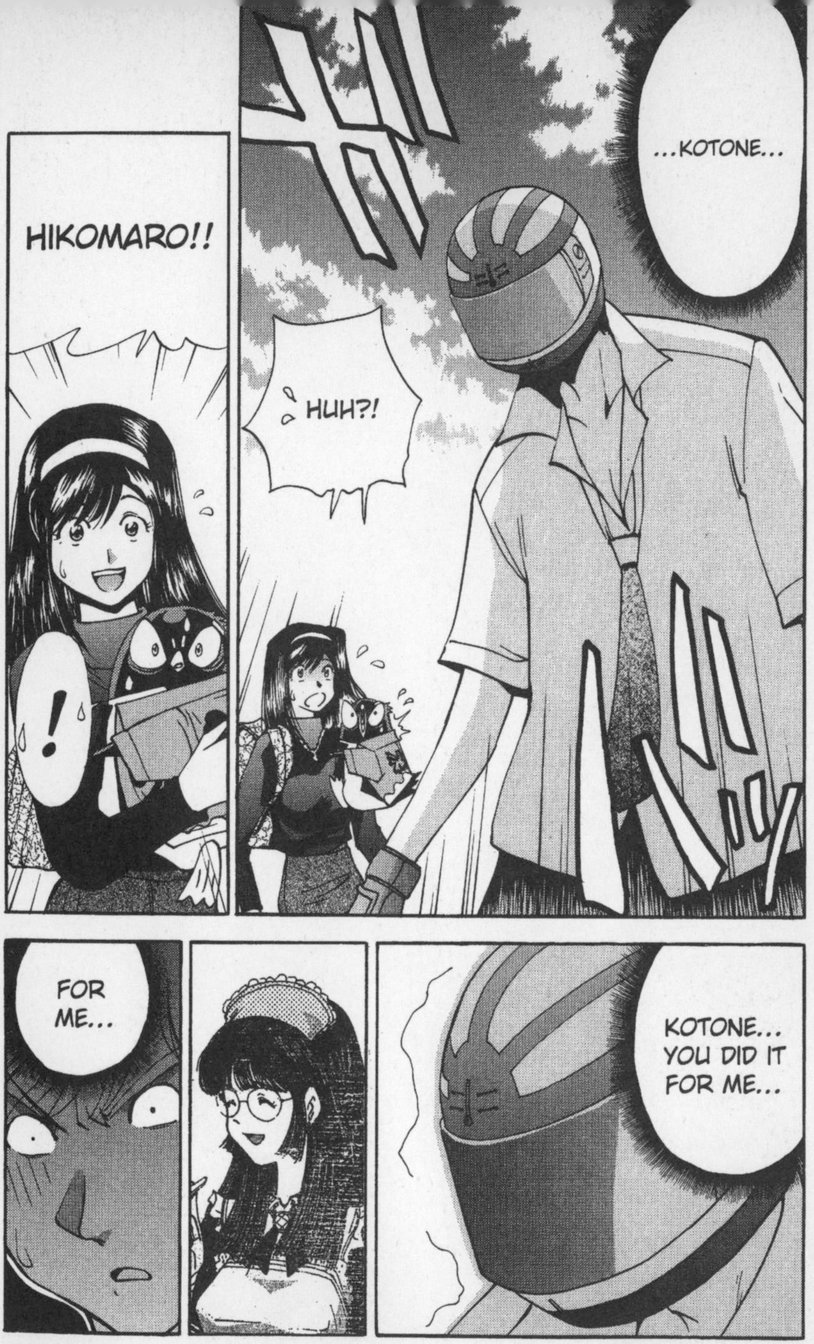
...KOTONE...
HUH?!
HIKOMARO!!
!
KOTONE... YOU DID IT FOR ME...
FOR ME...

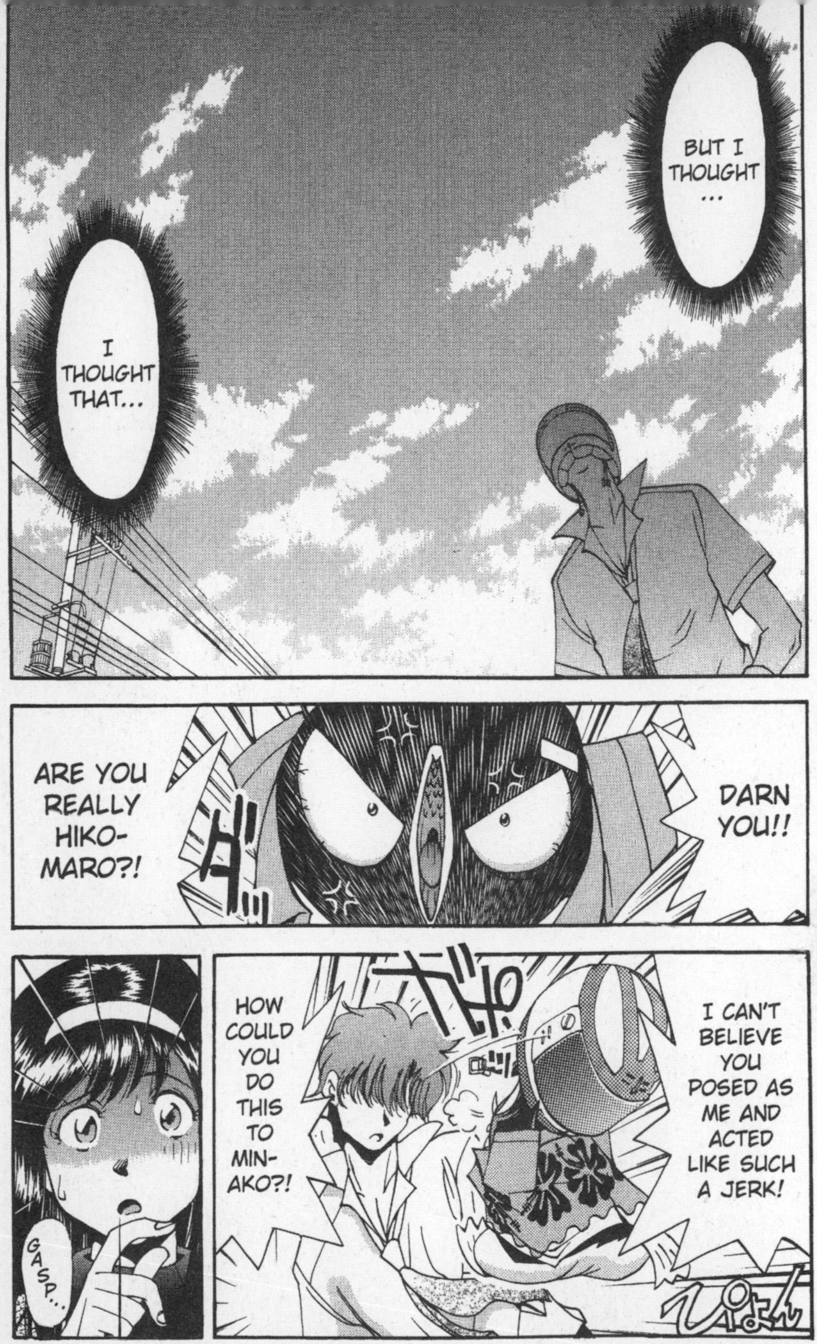
BUT I THOUGHT ...
I THOUGHT THAT...
DARN YOU!!
ARE YOU REALLY HIKO-MARO?!
I CAN'T BELIEVE YOU POSED AS ME AND ACTED LIKE SUCH A JERK!
HOW COULD YOU DO THIS TO MIN-AKO?!
ぴょん
GASP...

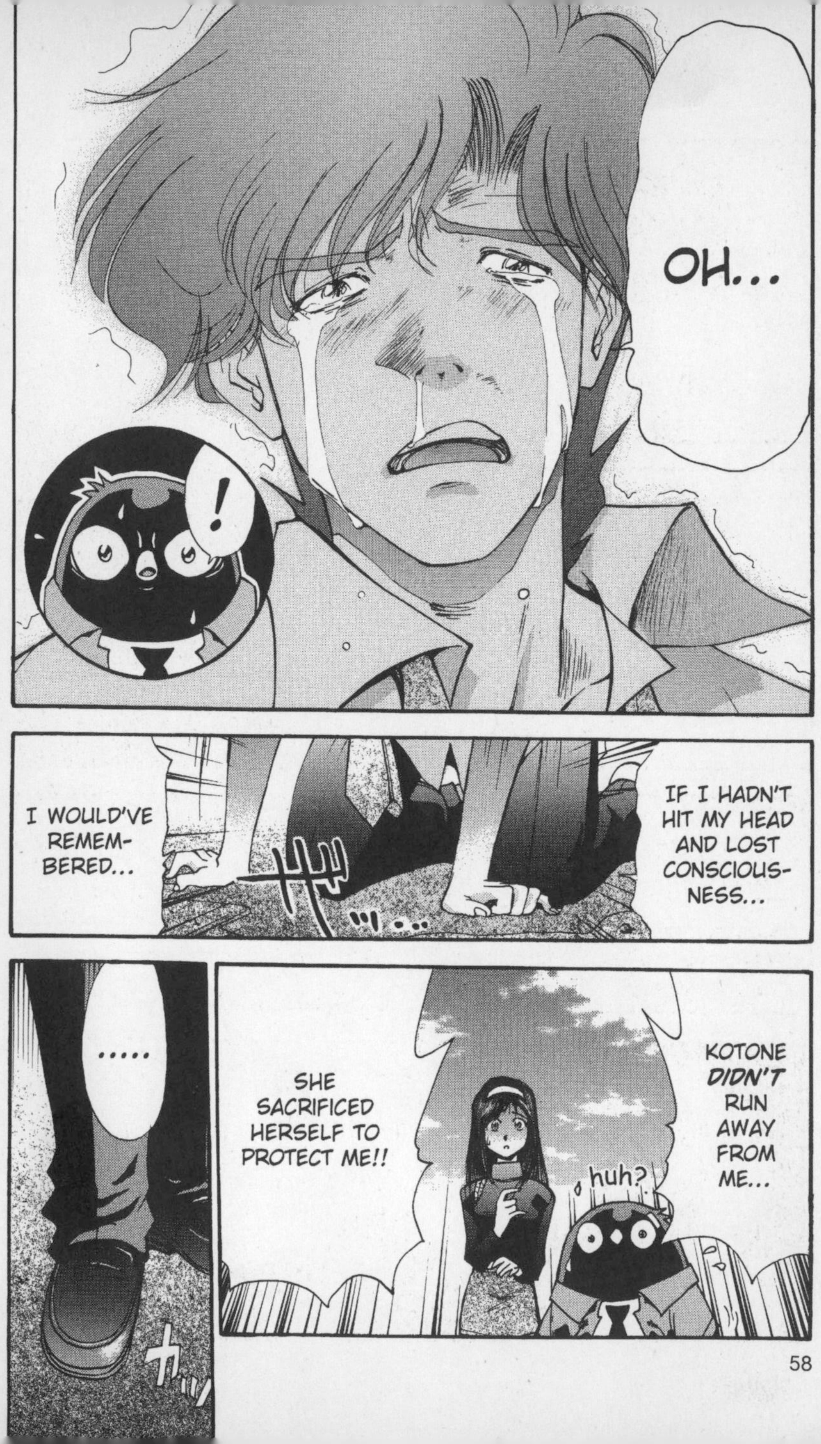
OH...
!
IF I HADN'T HIT MY HEAD AND LOST CONSCIOUS-NESS...
I WOULD'VE REMEM-BERED...
KOTONE *DIDN'T* RUN AWAY FROM ME...
huh?
SHE SACRIFICED HERSELF TO PROTECT ME!!
.....

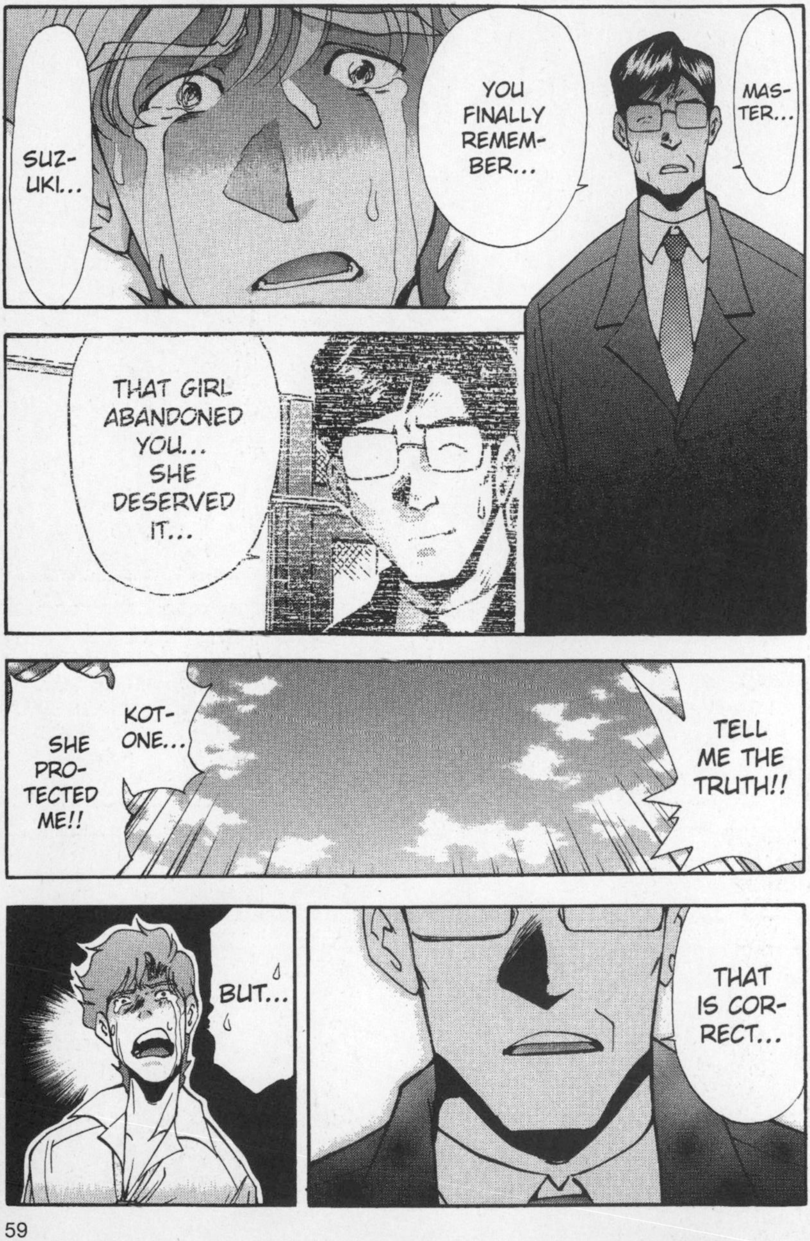
MAS-TER...
YOU FINALLY REMEM-BER...
SUZ-UKI...
THAT GIRL ABANDONED YOU... SHE DESERVED IT...
TELL ME THE TRUTH!!
KOT-ONE...
SHE PRO-TECTED ME!!
THAT IS COR-RECT...
BUT...

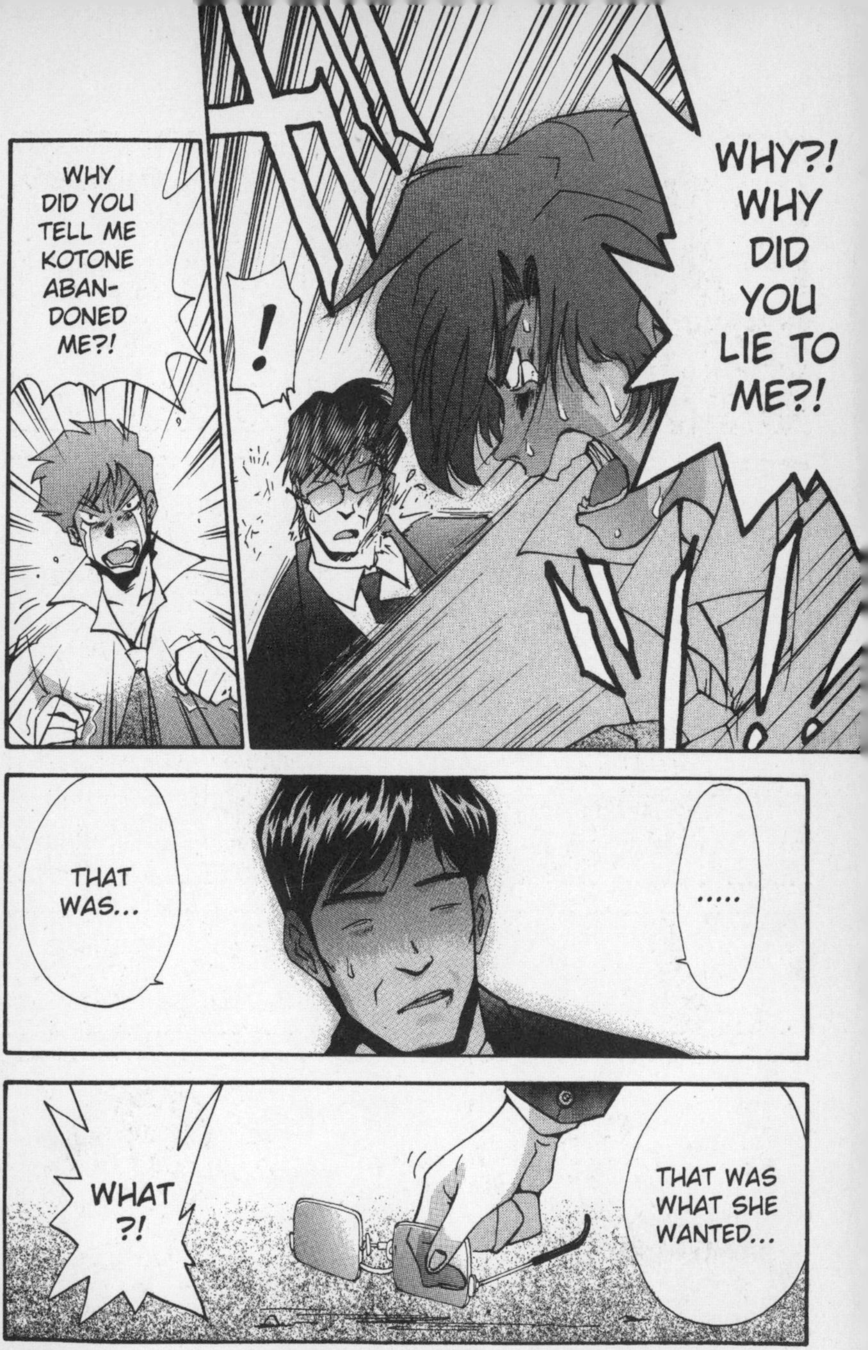
WHY?! WHY DID YOU LIE TO ME?!
!
WHY DID YOU TELL ME KOTONE ABAN-DONED ME?!
.....
THAT WAS...
THAT WAS WHAT SHE WANTED...
WHAT ?!

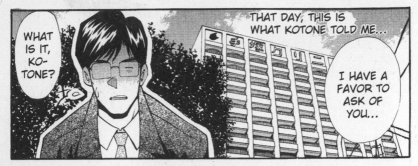

THAT DAY, THIS IS WHAT KOTONE TOLD ME...
I HAVE A FAVOR TO ASK OF YOU...
WHAT IS IT, KO-TONE?
DON'T TELL MASTER HIKOMARO WHAT HAPPENED TO ME...
PLEASE DON'T TELL HIM...
PLEASE ...
TELL HIM THAT I RAN AWAY...
.....
BUT WHY...?
HE WON'T BE ABLE TO VISIT YOU...
And, umm...
.....
sepia

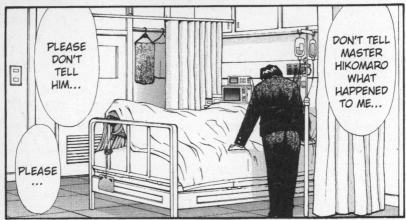

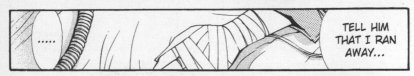

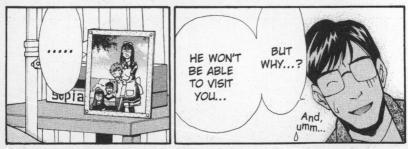

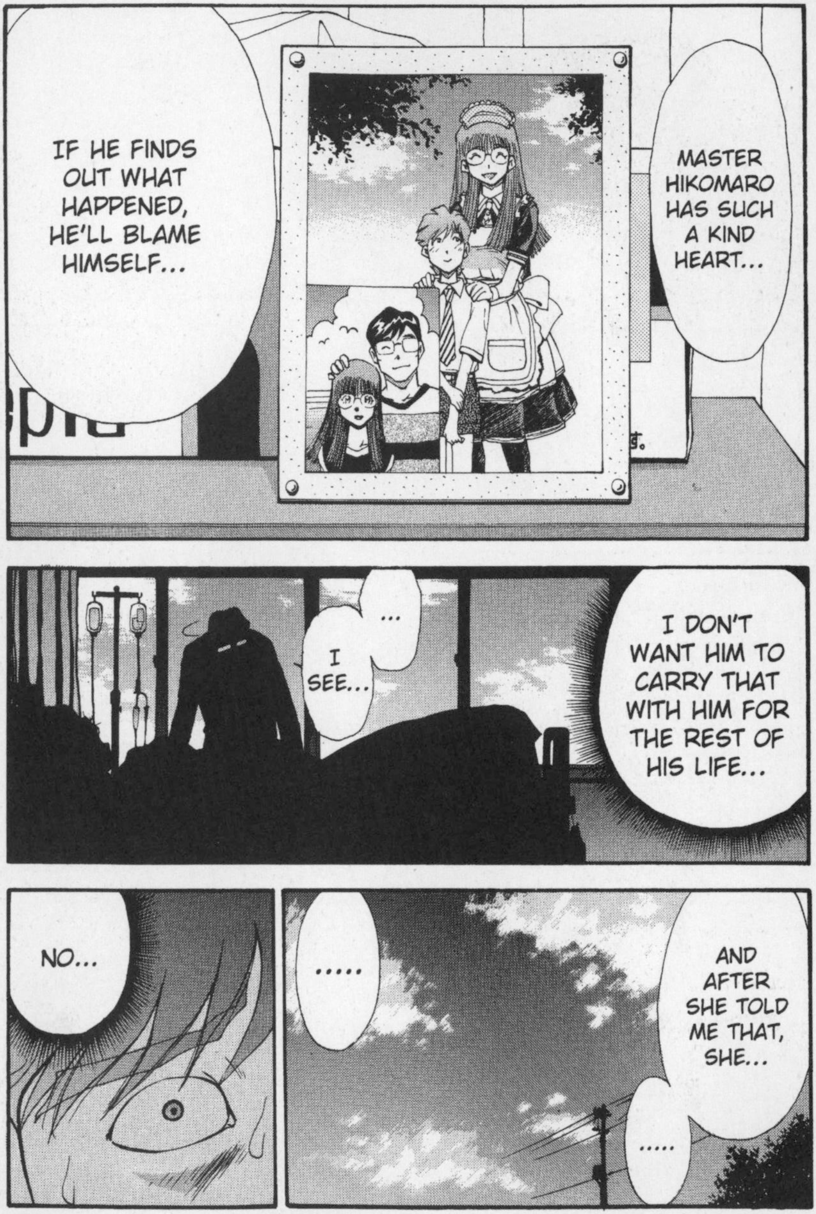
MASTER HIKOMARO HAS SUCH A KIND HEART...
IF HE FINDS OUT WHAT HAPPENED, HE'LL BLAME HIMSELF...
I DON'T WANT HIM TO CARRY THAT WITH HIM FOR THE REST OF HIS LIFE...
...
I SEE...
AND AFTER SHE TOLD ME THAT, SHE...
.....
.....
NO...

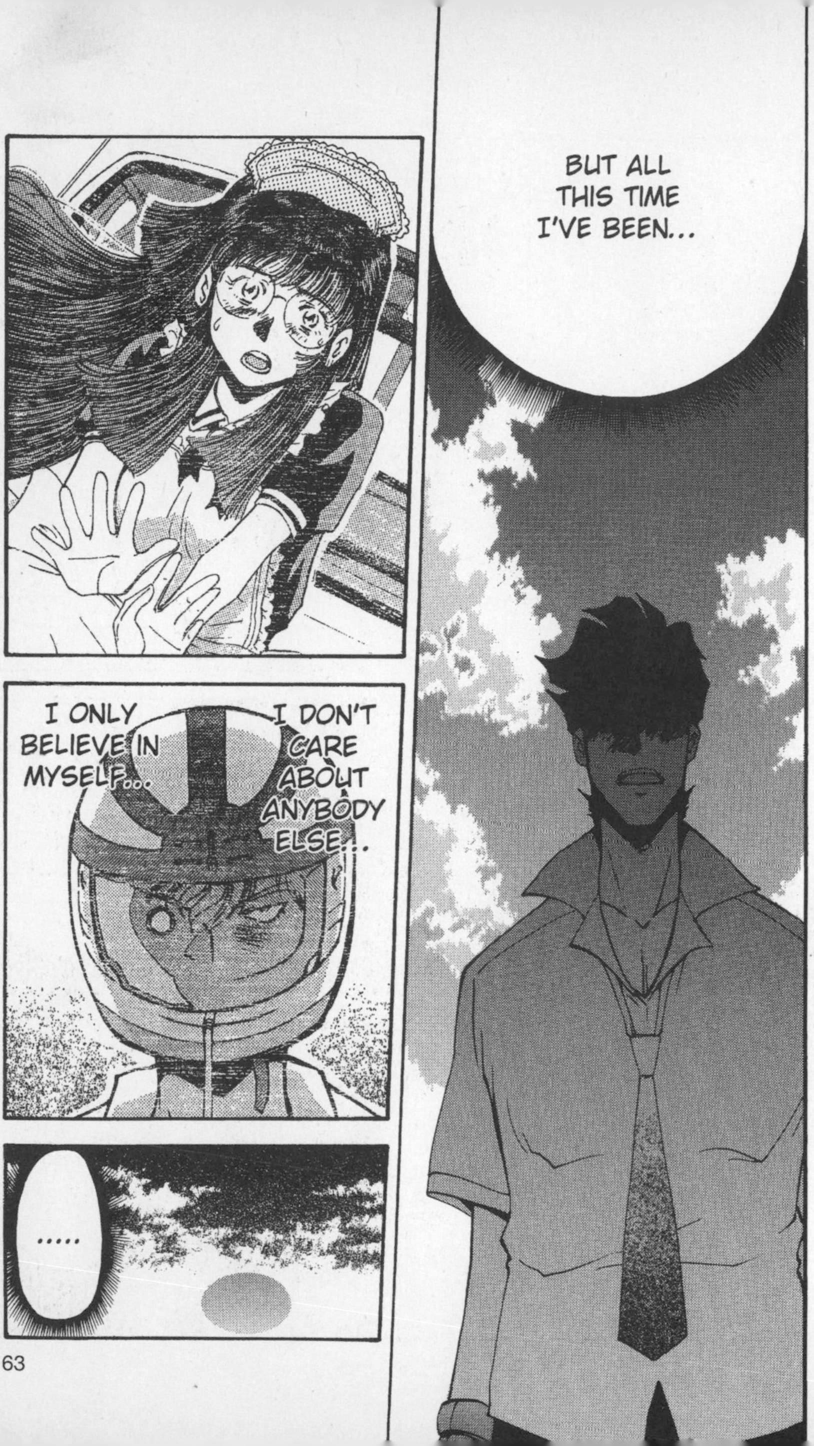
BUT ALL THIS TIME I'VE BEEN...
I DON'T CARE ABOUT ANYBODY ELSE...
I ONLY BELIEVE IN MYSELF...
.....

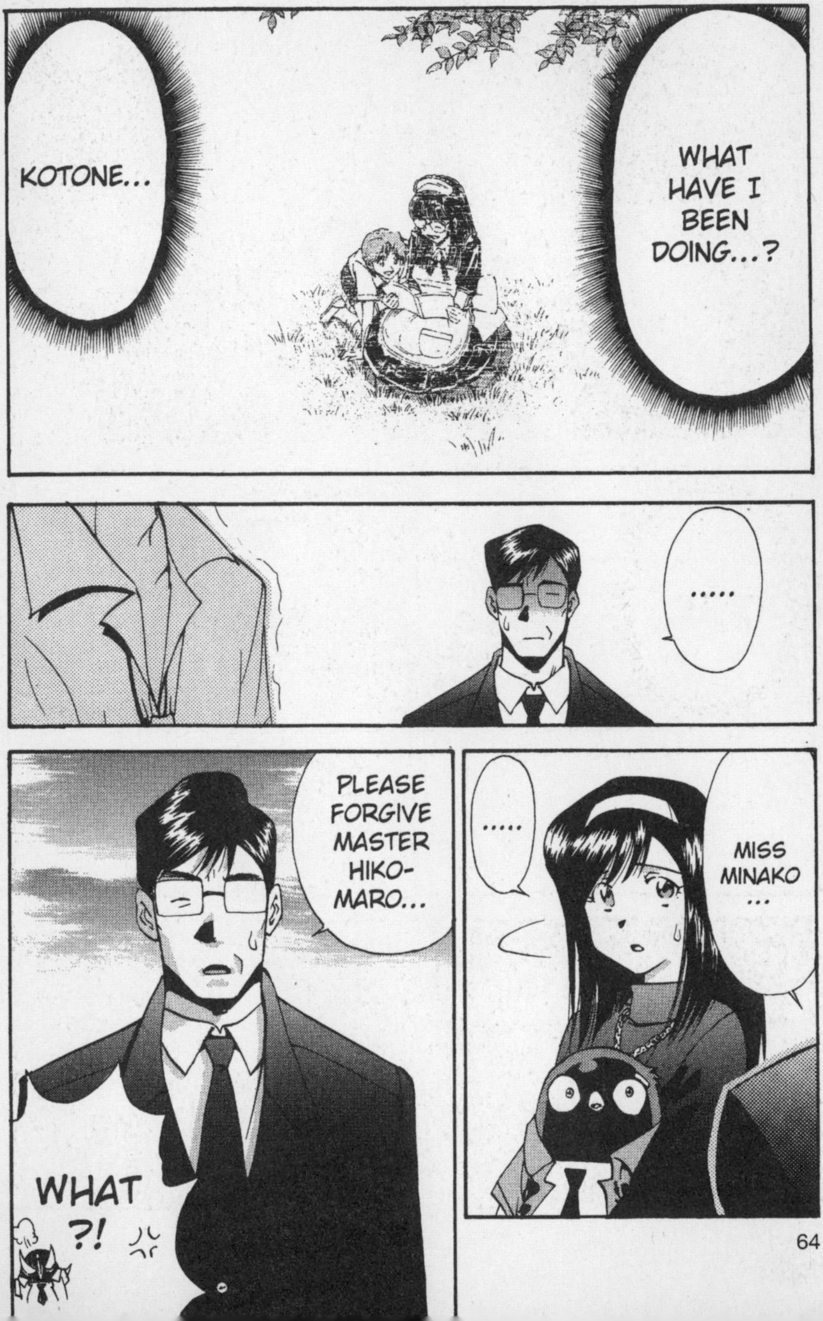
WHAT HAVE I BEEN DOING...?
KOTONE...
.....
MISS MINAKO ...
.....
PLEASE FORGIVE MASTER HIKO-MARO...
WHAT ?!

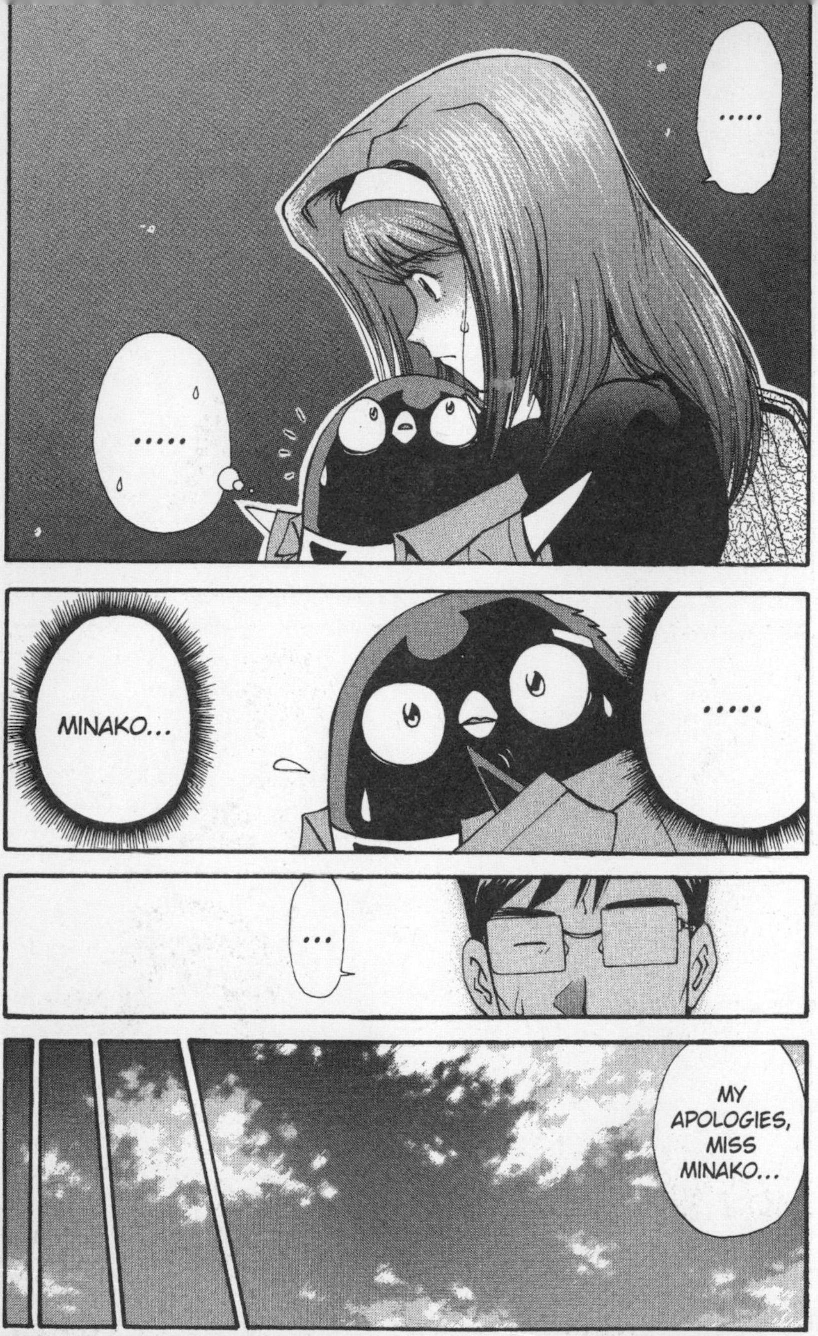
.....
.....
.....
MINAKO...
...
MY APOLOGIES, MISS MINAKO...

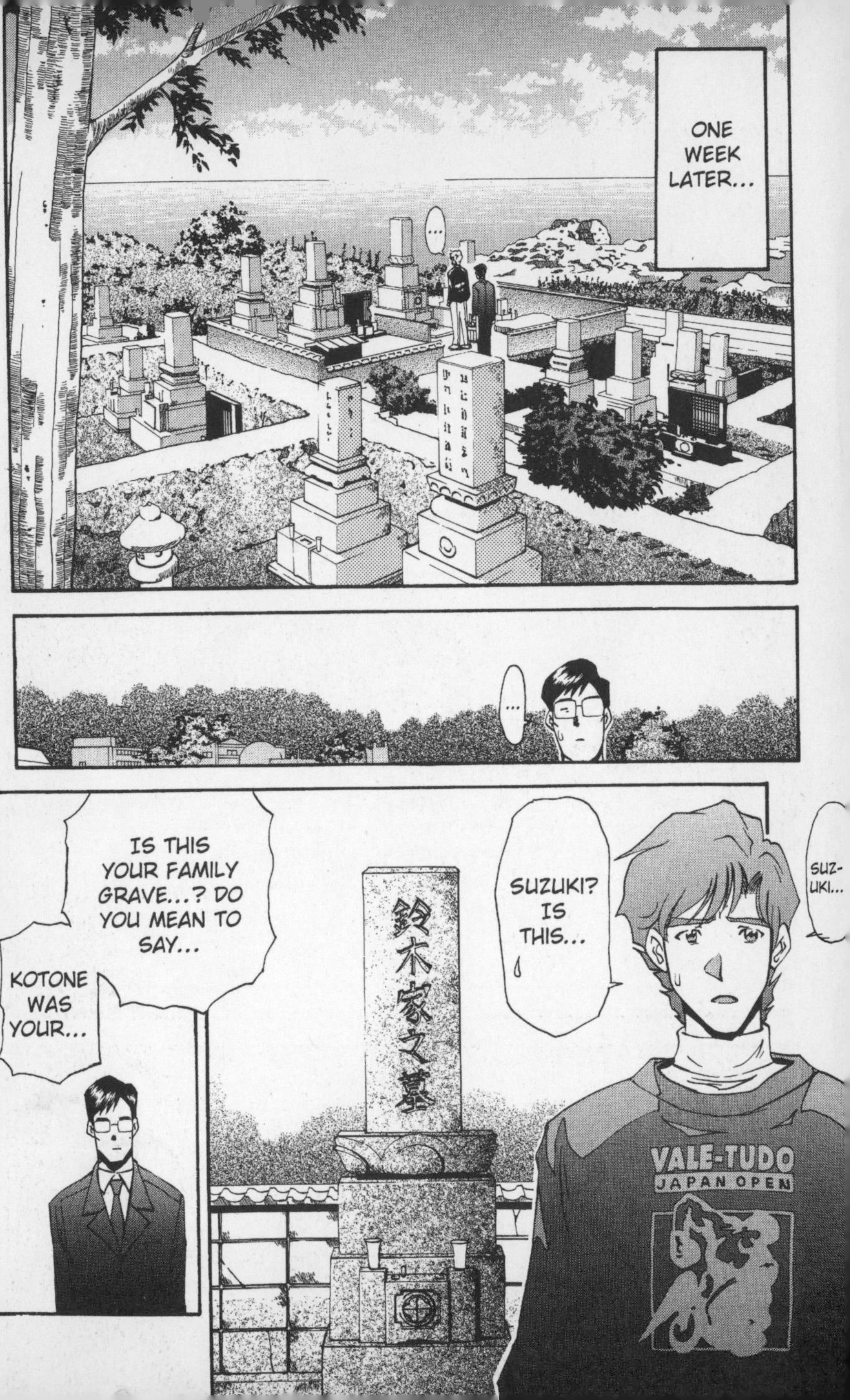
ONE WEEK LATER...
...
...
SUZ-UKI...
SUZUKI? IS THIS...
IS THIS YOUR FAMILY GRAVE...? DO YOU MEAN TO SAY...
KOTONE WAS YOUR...
鈴木家之墓
VALE-TUDO
JAPAN OPEN

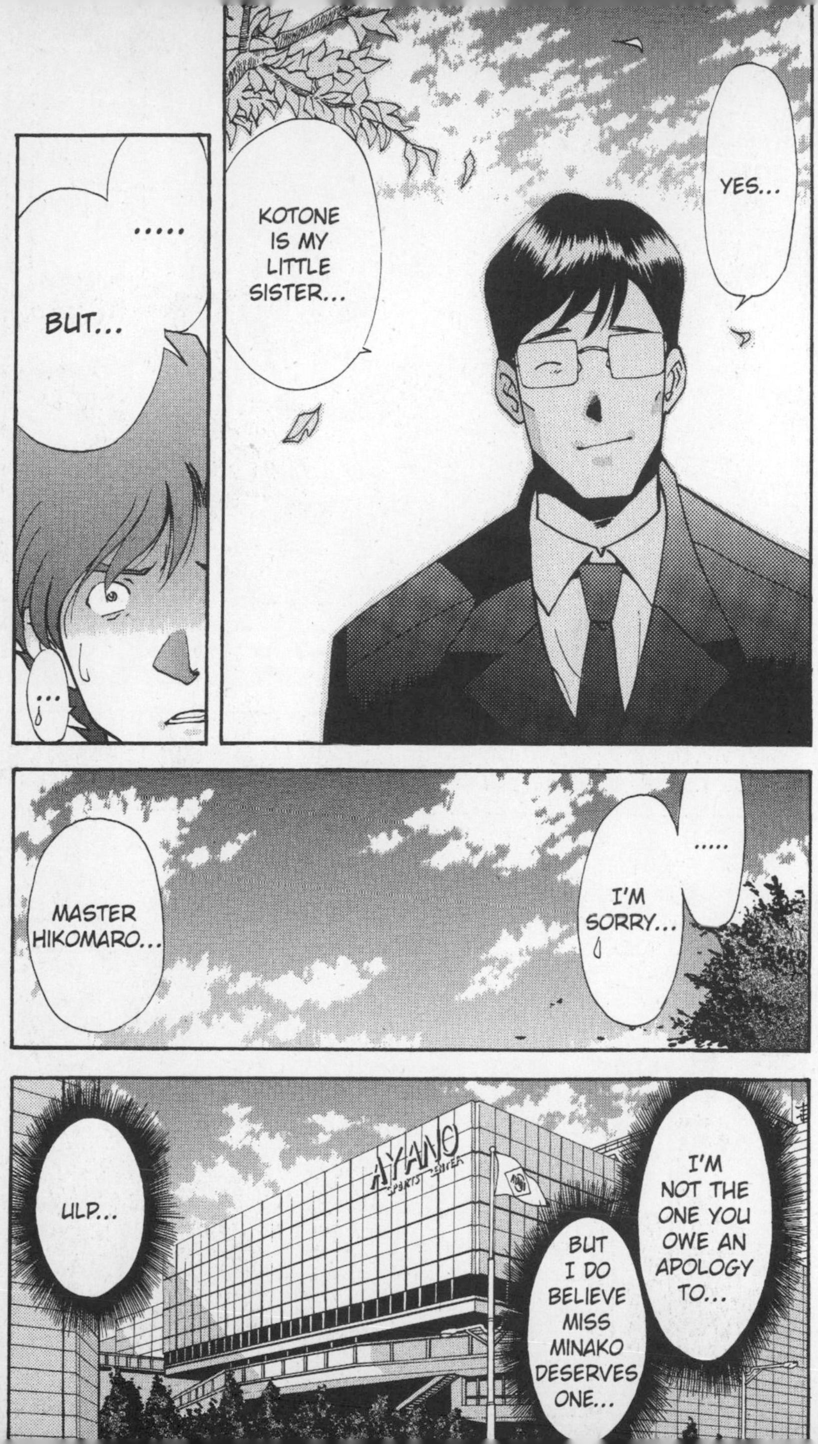
YES...
KOTONE IS MY LITTLE SISTER...
.....
BUT...
...
.....
I'M SORRY...
MASTER HIKOMARO...
AYANO
I'M NOT THE ONE YOU OWE AN APOLOGY TO...
BUT I DO BELIEVE MISS MINAKO DESERVES ONE...
ULP...

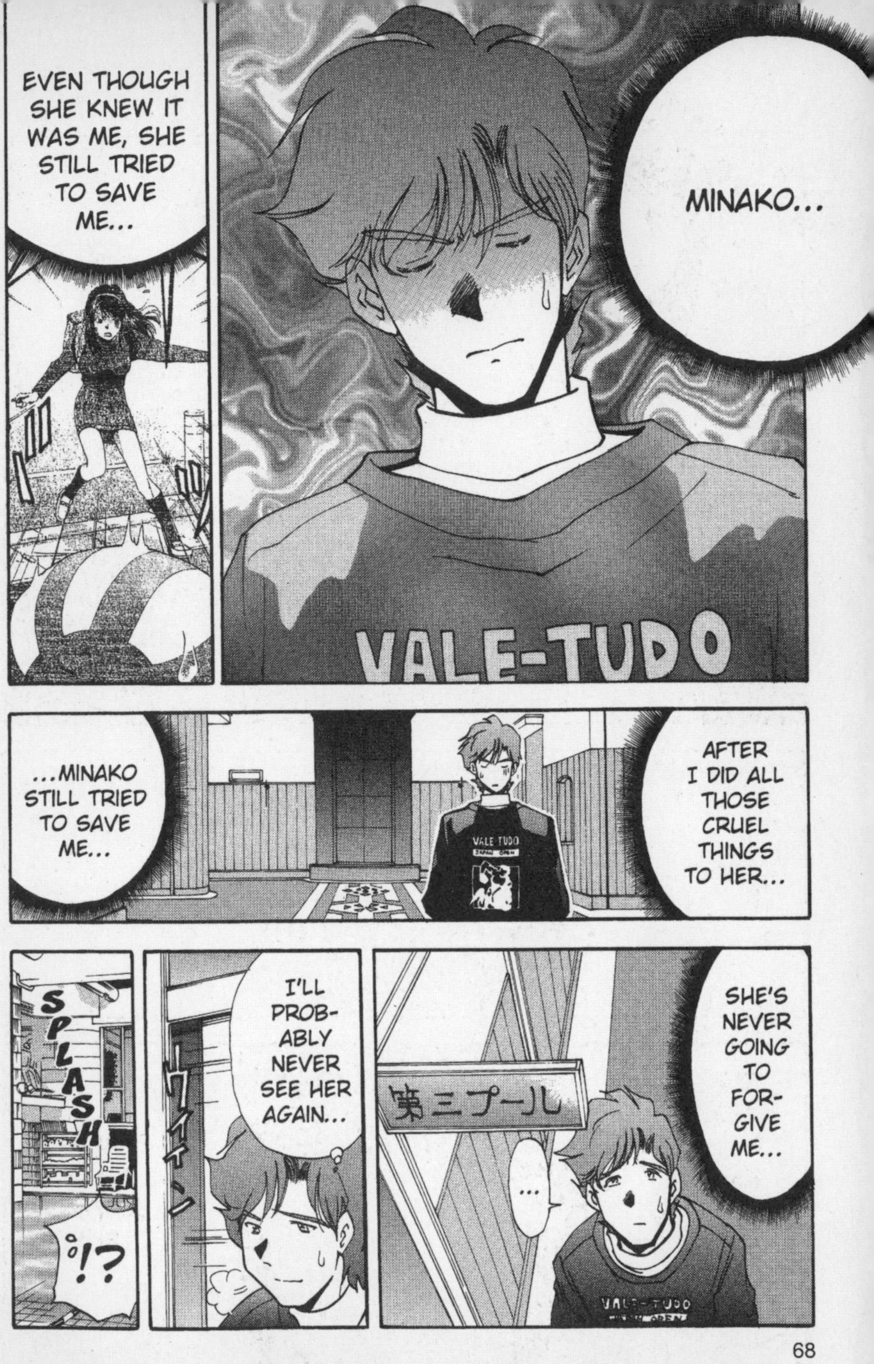
MINAKO...
EVEN THOUGH SHE KNEW IT WAS ME, SHE STILL TRIED TO SAVE ME...
VALE-TUDO
AFTER I DID ALL THOSE CRUEL THINGS TO HER...
...MINAKO STILL TRIED TO SAVE ME...
VALE-TUDO
SHE'S NEVER GOING TO FOR-GIVE ME...
第三プール
...
I'LL PROB-ABLY NEVER SEE HER AGAIN...
SPLASH
!?

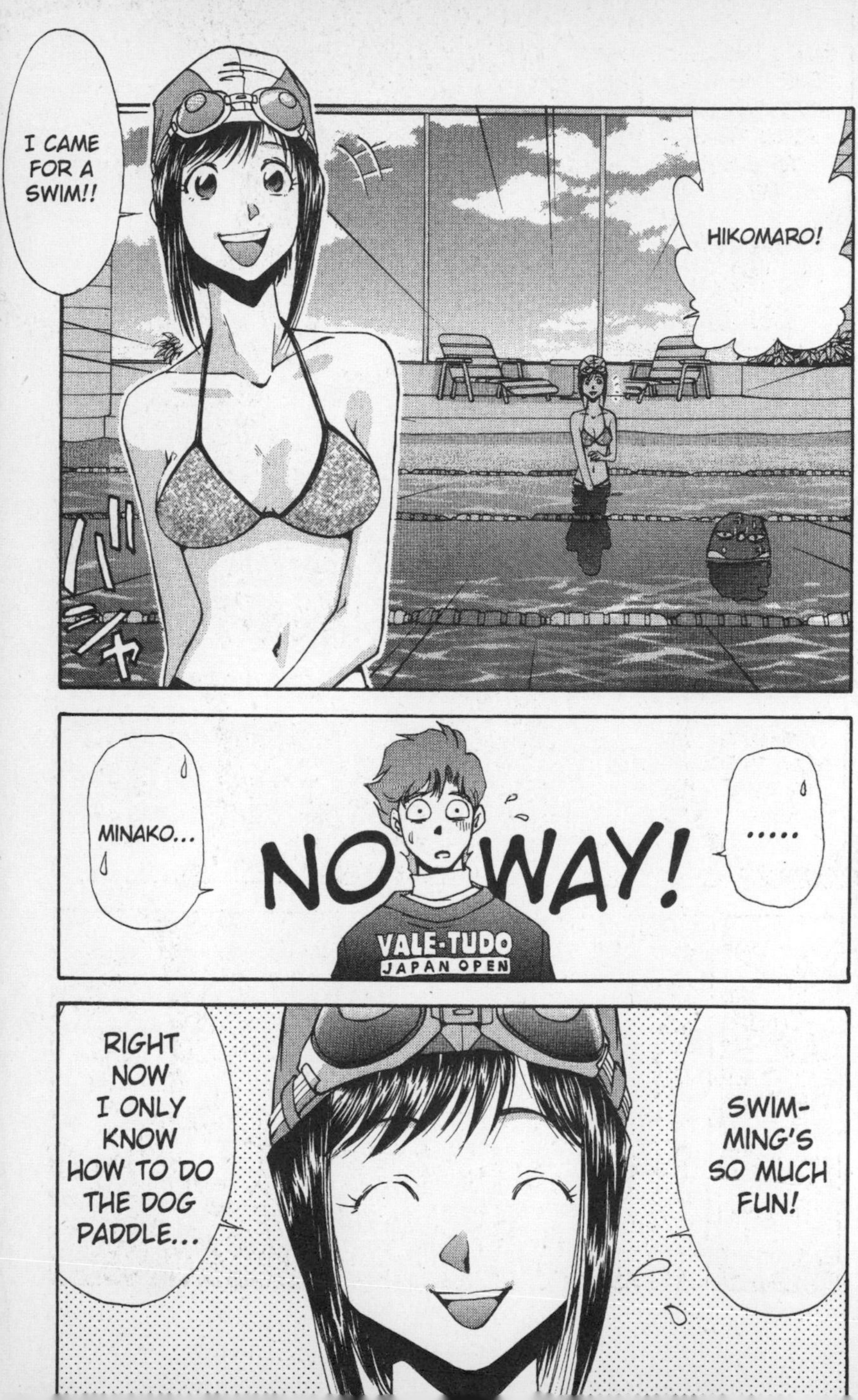
HIKOMARO!
I CAME FOR A SWIM!!
.....
NO WAY!
VALE-TUDO JAPAN OPEN
MINAKO...
SWIM-MING'S SO MUCH FUN!
RIGHT NOW I ONLY KNOW HOW TO DO THE DOG PADDLE...

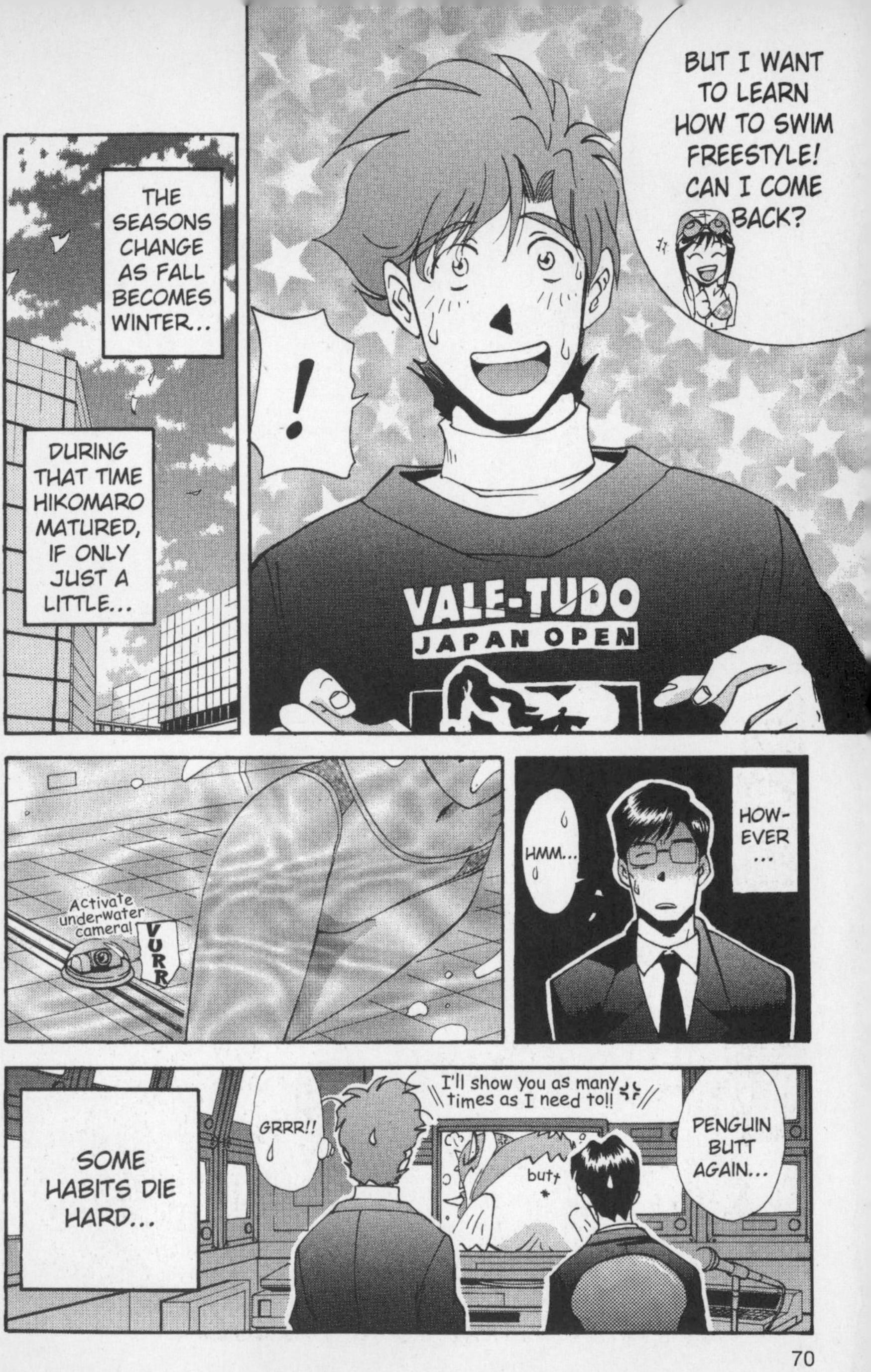
BUT I WANT TO LEARN HOW TO SWIM FREESTYLE! CAN I COME BACK?
!
THE SEASONS CHANGE AS FALL BECOMES WINTER...
DURING THAT TIME HIKOMARO MATURED, IF ONLY JUST A LITTLE...
HOW-EVER ...
HMM...
Activate underwater camera!
VURR
PENGUIN BUTT AGAIN...
I'll show you as many times as I need to!!
butt
GRRR!!
SOME HABITS DIE HARD...

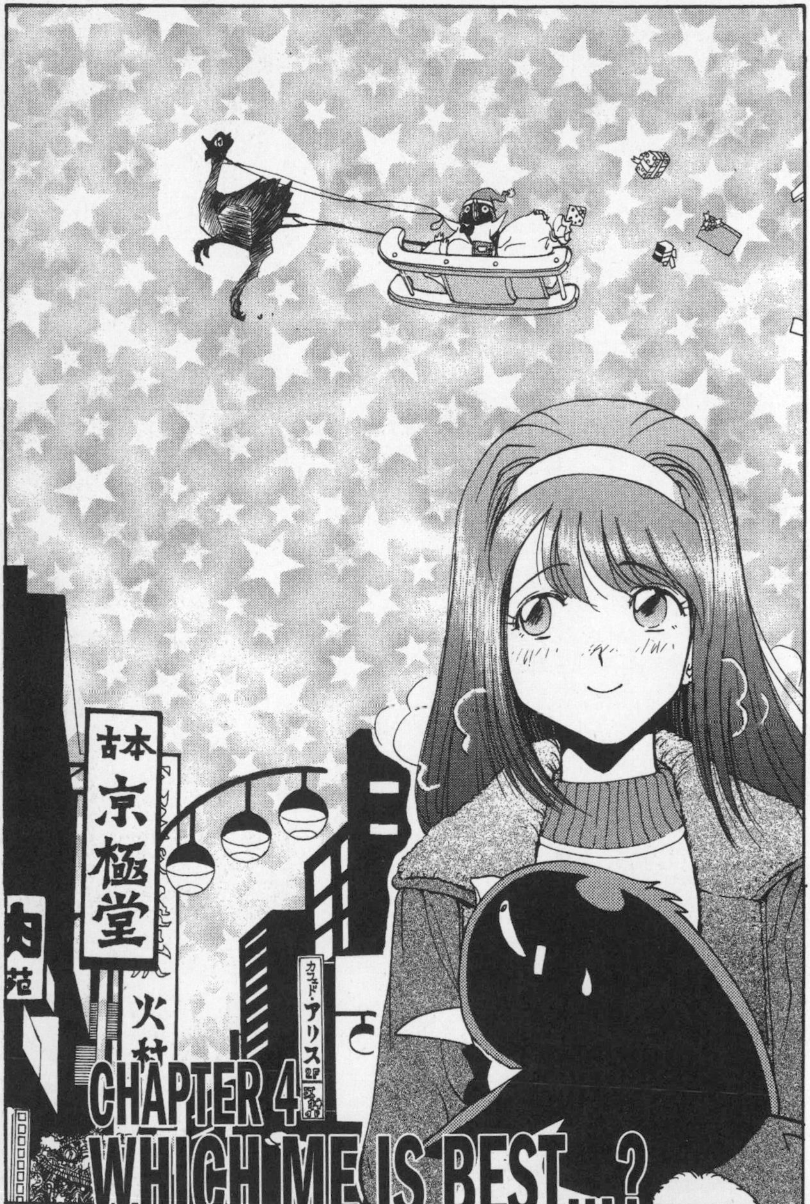
古本
京極堂
火村
カフェド・アリス
CHAPTER 4
WHICH ME IS BEST...?

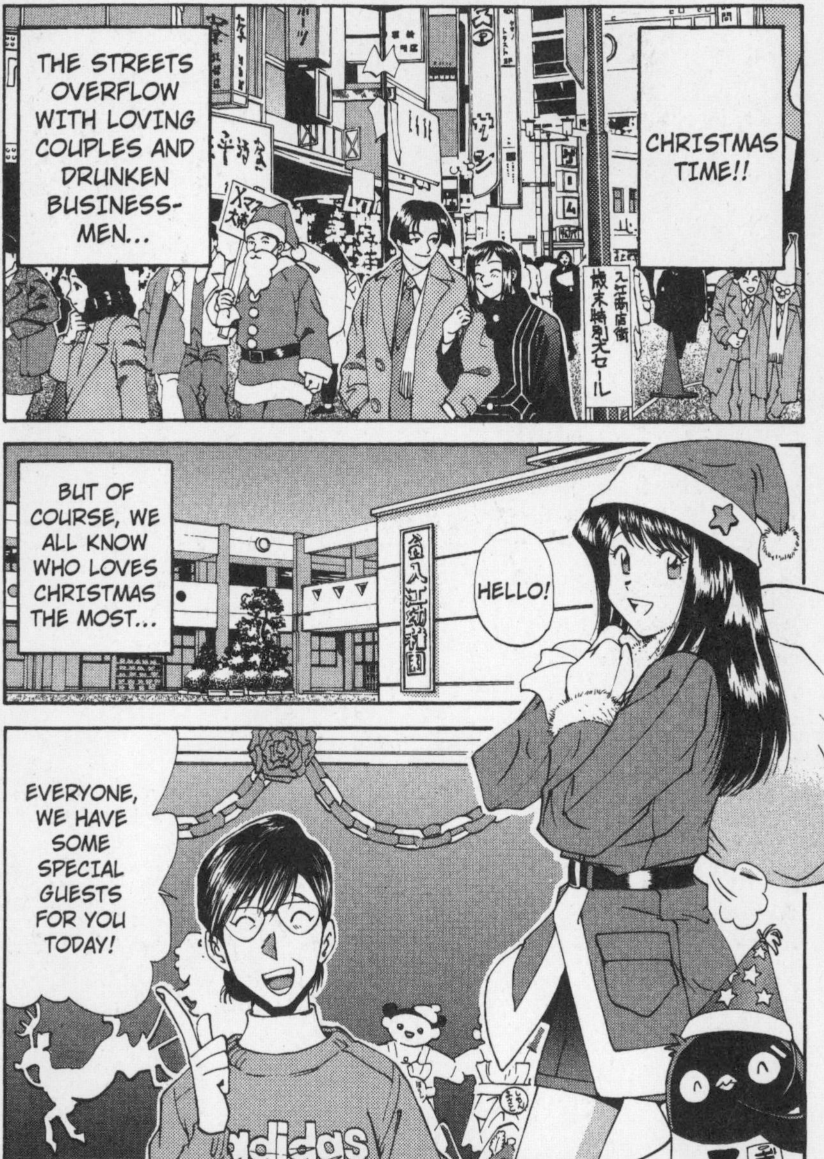
CHRISTMAS TIME!!
THE STREETS OVERFLOW WITH LOVING COUPLES AND DRUNKEN BUSINESS-MEN...
BUT OF COURSE, WE ALL KNOW WHO LOVES CHRISTMAS THE MOST...
HELLO!
EVERYONE, WE HAVE SOME SPECIAL GUESTS FOR YOU TODAY!

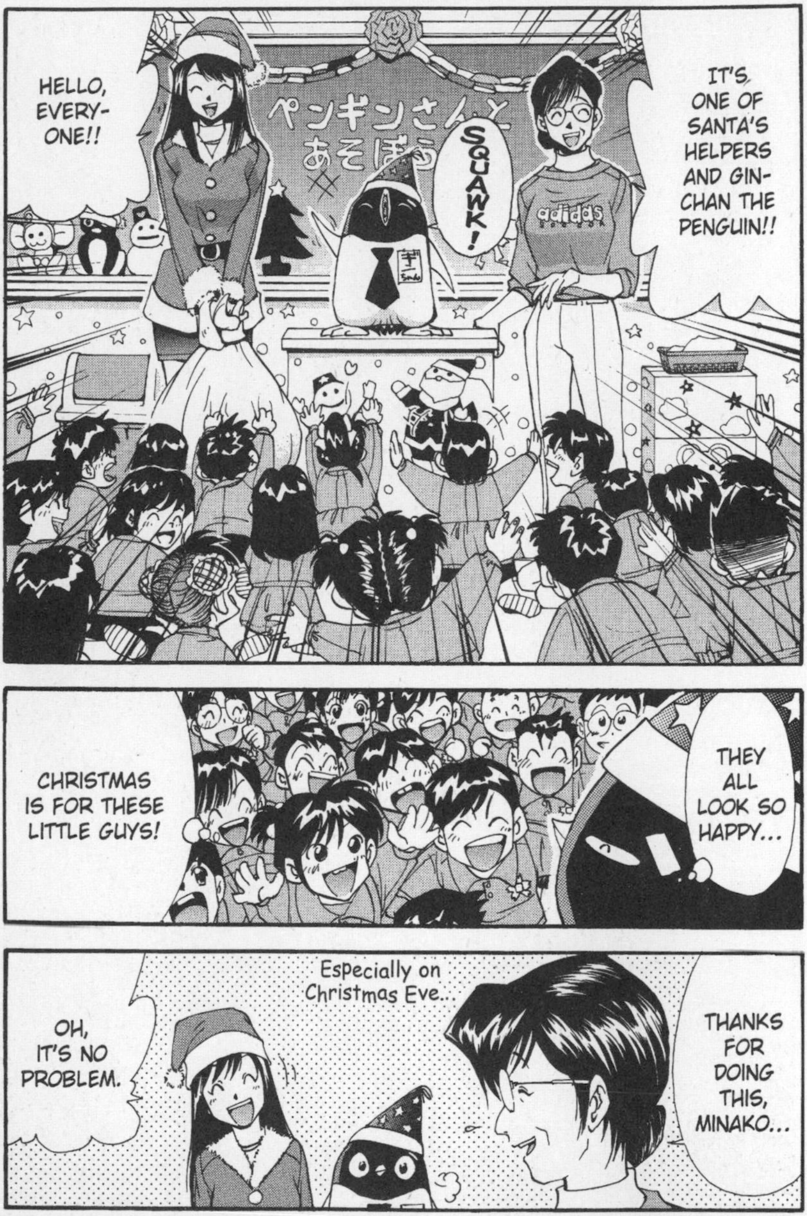
IT'S ONE OF SANTA'S HELPERS AND GIN-CHAN THE PENGUIN!!
SQUAWK!
ペンギンさんと
あそぼう
HELLO, EVERY-ONE!!
THEY ALL LOOK SO HAPPY...
CHRISTMAS IS FOR THESE LITTLE GUYS!
THANKS FOR DOING THIS, MINAKO...
Especially on Christmas Eve...
OH, IT'S NO PROBLEM.

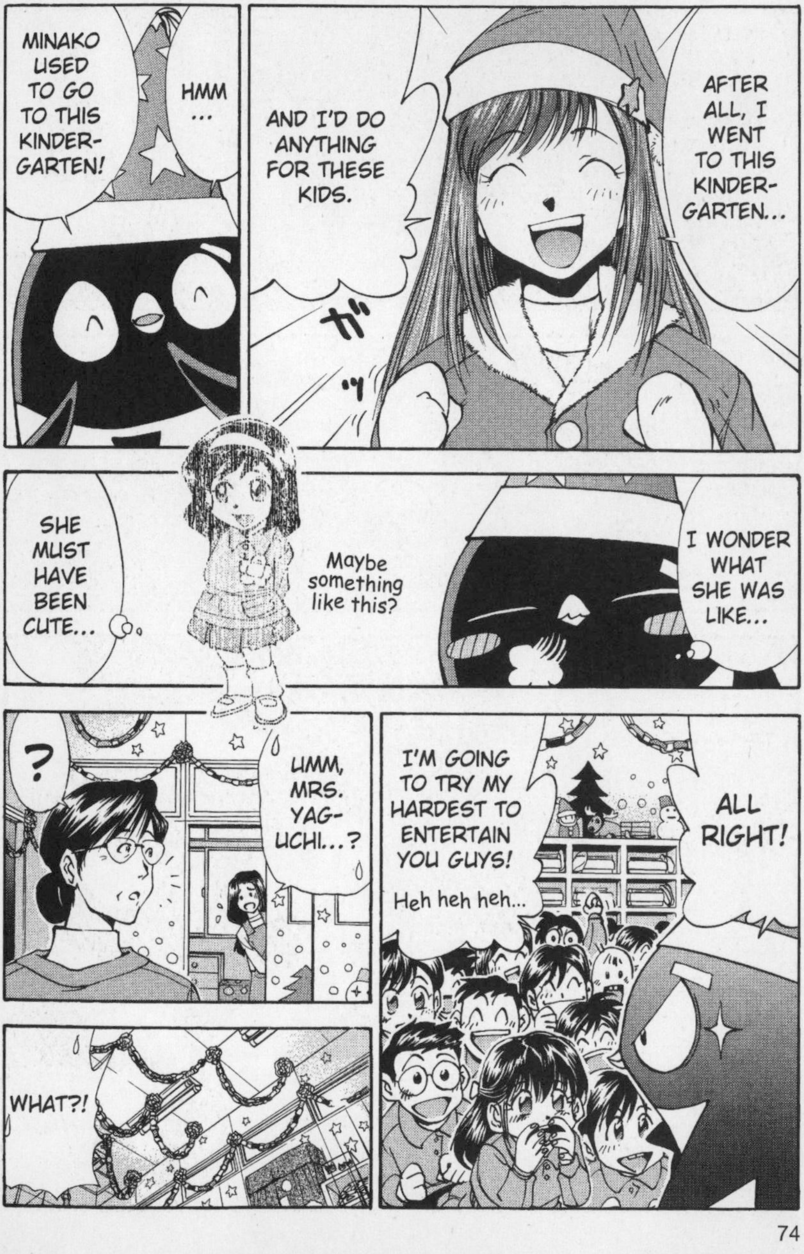
AFTER ALL, I WENT TO THIS KINDER-GARTEN...
AND I'D DO ANYTHING FOR THESE KIDS.
ガッ
HMM ...
MINAKO USED TO GO TO THIS KINDER-GARTEN!
I WONDER WHAT SHE WAS LIKE...
Maybe something like this?
SHE MUST HAVE BEEN CUTE...
ALL RIGHT!
I'M GOING TO TRY MY HARDEST TO ENTERTAIN YOU GUYS!
Heh heh heh...
UMM, MRS. YAG-UCHI...?
?
WHAT?!

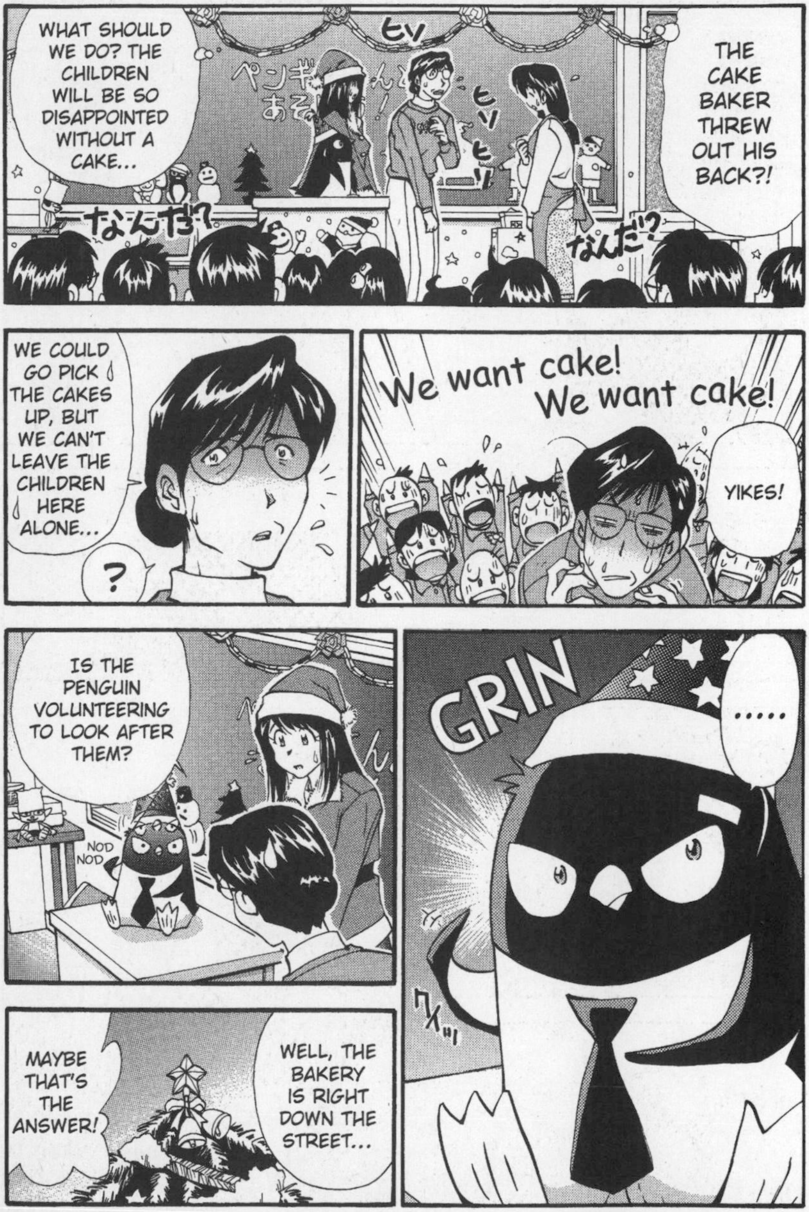
THE CAKE BAKER THREW OUT HIS BACK?!
ヒソ
ヒソ ヒソ
WHAT SHOULD WE DO? THE CHILDREN WILL BE SO DISAPPOINTED WITHOUT A CAKE...
なんだ!?
なんだ!?
We want cake! We want cake!
YIKES!
WE COULD GO PICK THE CAKES UP, BUT WE CAN'T LEAVE THE CHILDREN HERE ALONE...
?
.....
GRIN
IS THE PENGUIN VOLUNTEERING TO LOOK AFTER THEM?
NOD NOD
WELL, THE BAKERY IS RIGHT DOWN THE STREET...
MAYBE THAT'S THE ANSWER!

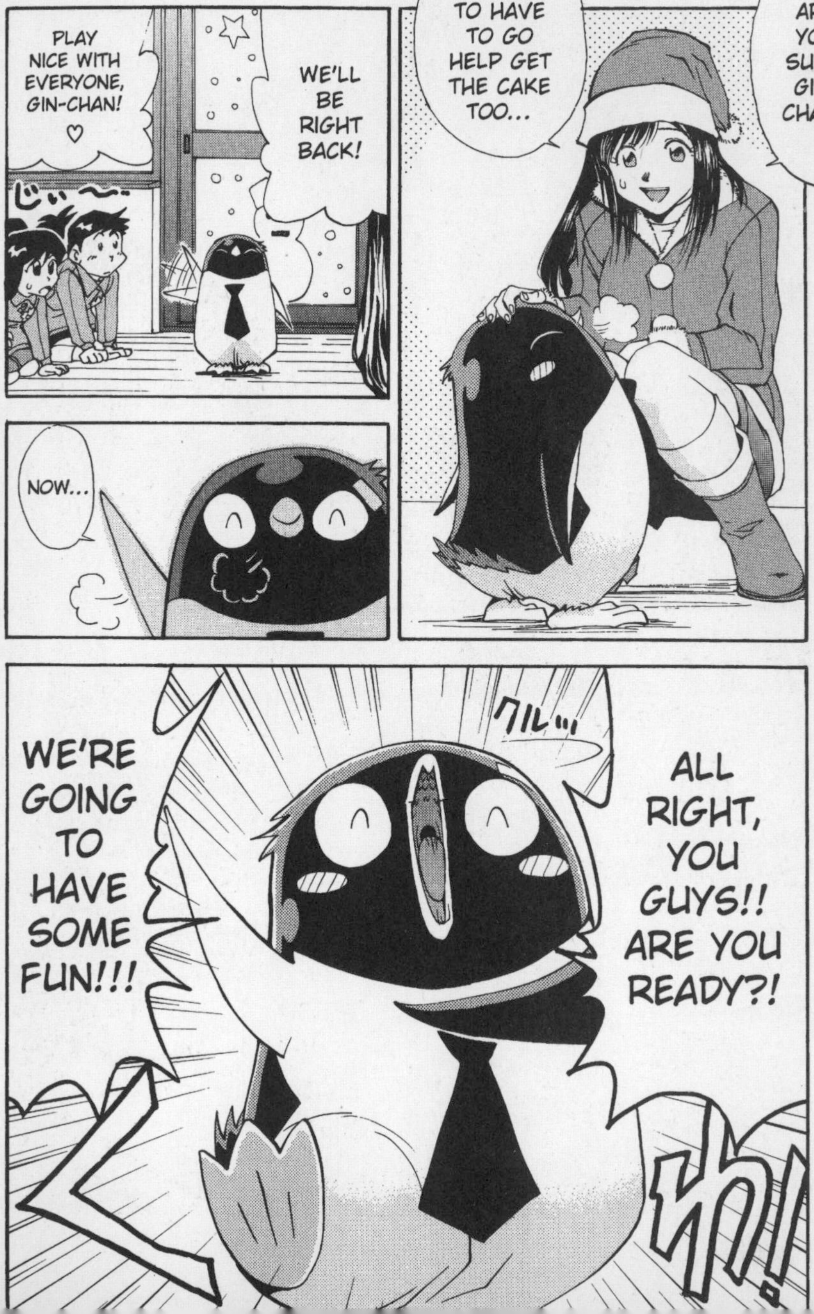
ARE YOU SURE, GIN-CHAN?
I'M GOING TO HAVE TO GO HELP GET THE CAKE TOO...
WE'LL BE RIGHT BACK!
PLAY NICE WITH EVERYONE, GIN-CHAN! ♡
じぃ〜
NOW...
クル…
ALL RIGHT, YOU GUYS!! ARE YOU READY?!
WE'RE GOING TO HAVE SOME FUN!!!
わ!

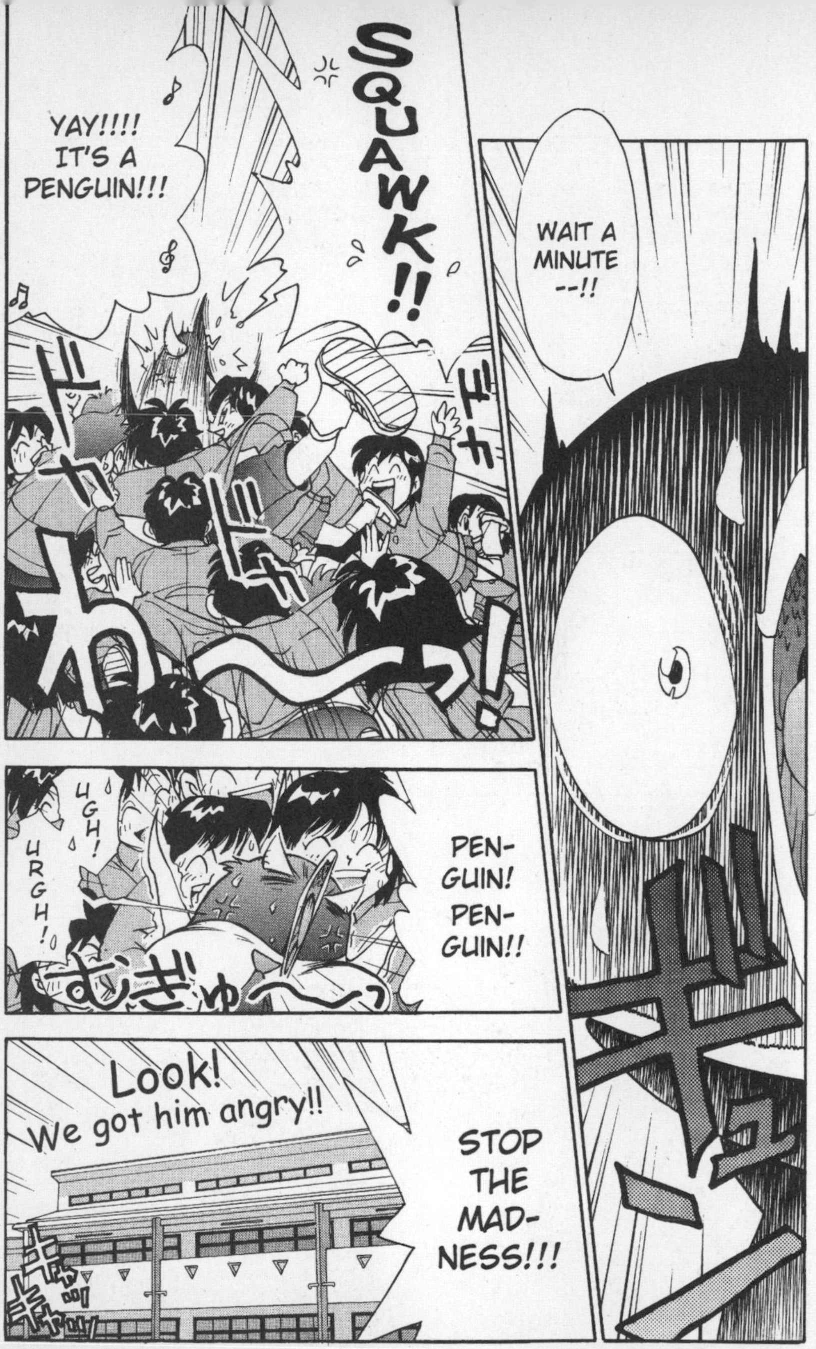
WAIT A MINUTE --!!
YAY!!!! IT'S A PENGUIN!!!
SQUAWK!!
PEN-GUIN! PEN-GUIN!!
UGH!
URGH!
むぎゅ〜〜っ
STOP THE MAD-NESS!!!
Look! We got him angry!!

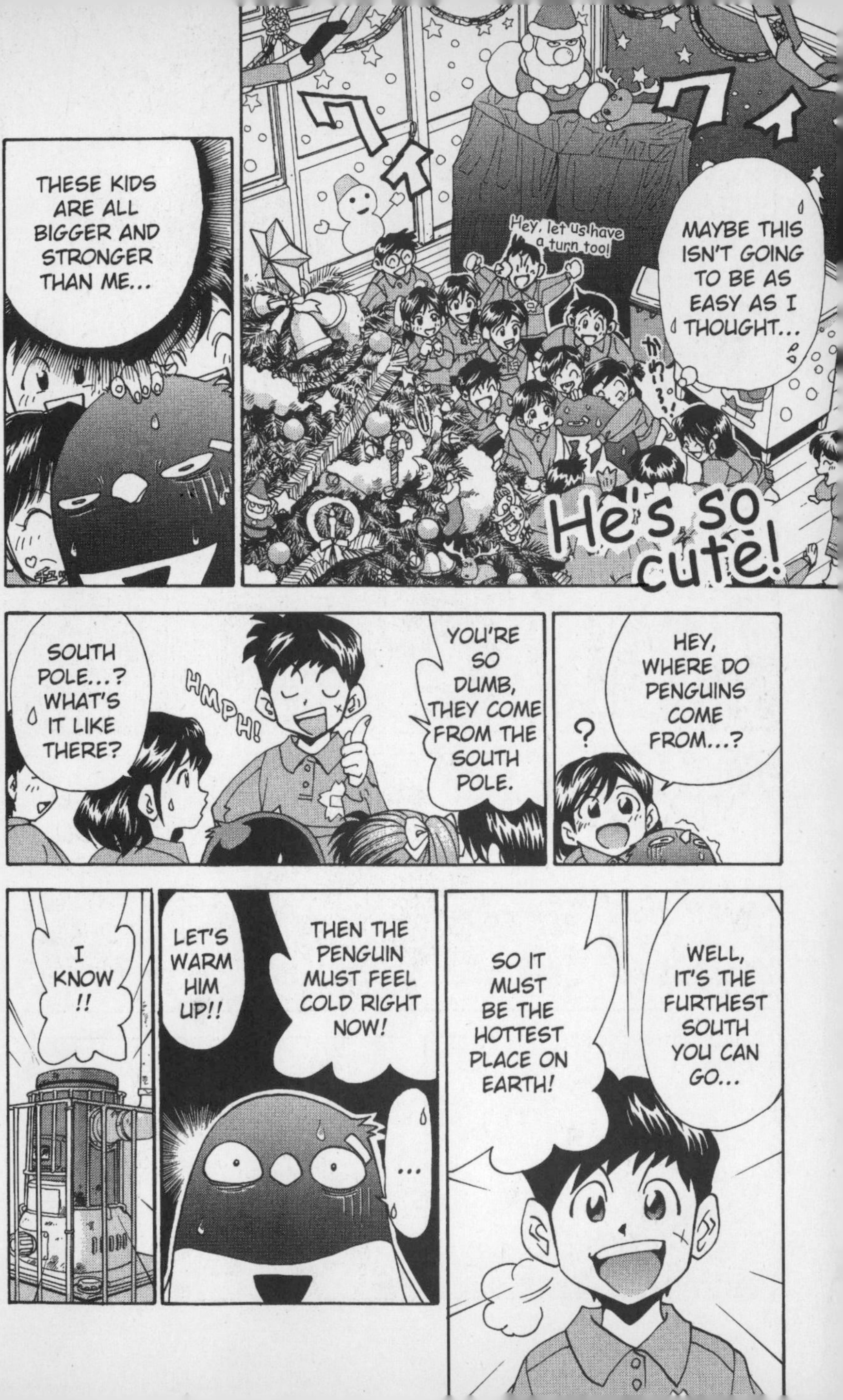
ワイ
MAYBE THIS ISN'T GOING TO BE AS EASY AS I THOUGHT...
ワイ
Hey, let us have a turn too!
He's so cute!
THESE KIDS ARE ALL BIGGER AND STRONGER THAN ME...
HEY, WHERE DO PENGUINS COME FROM...?
?
YOU'RE SO DUMB, THEY COME FROM THE SOUTH POLE.
HMPH!
SOUTH POLE...? WHAT'S IT LIKE THERE?
WELL, IT'S THE FURTHEST SOUTH YOU CAN GO...
SO IT MUST BE THE HOTTEST PLACE ON EARTH!
THEN THE PENGUIN MUST FEEL COLD RIGHT NOW!
LET'S WARM HIM UP!!
...
I KNOW!!

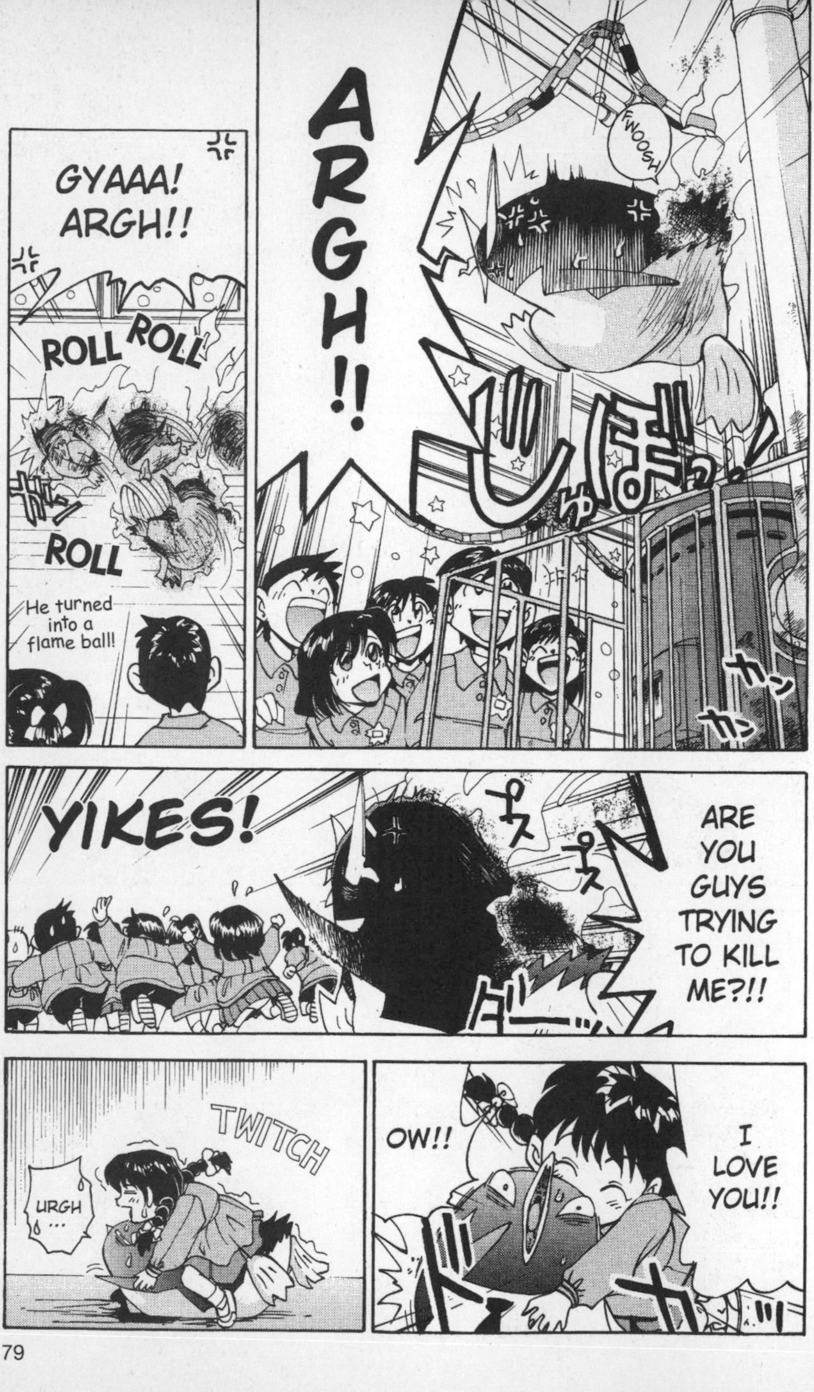
FWOOSH
ARGH!!
GYAAA! ARGH!!
ROLL ROLL
ROLL
He turned into a flame ball!
ARE YOU GUYS TRYING TO KILL ME?!!
YIKES!
I LOVE YOU!!
OW!!
TWITCH
URGH ...

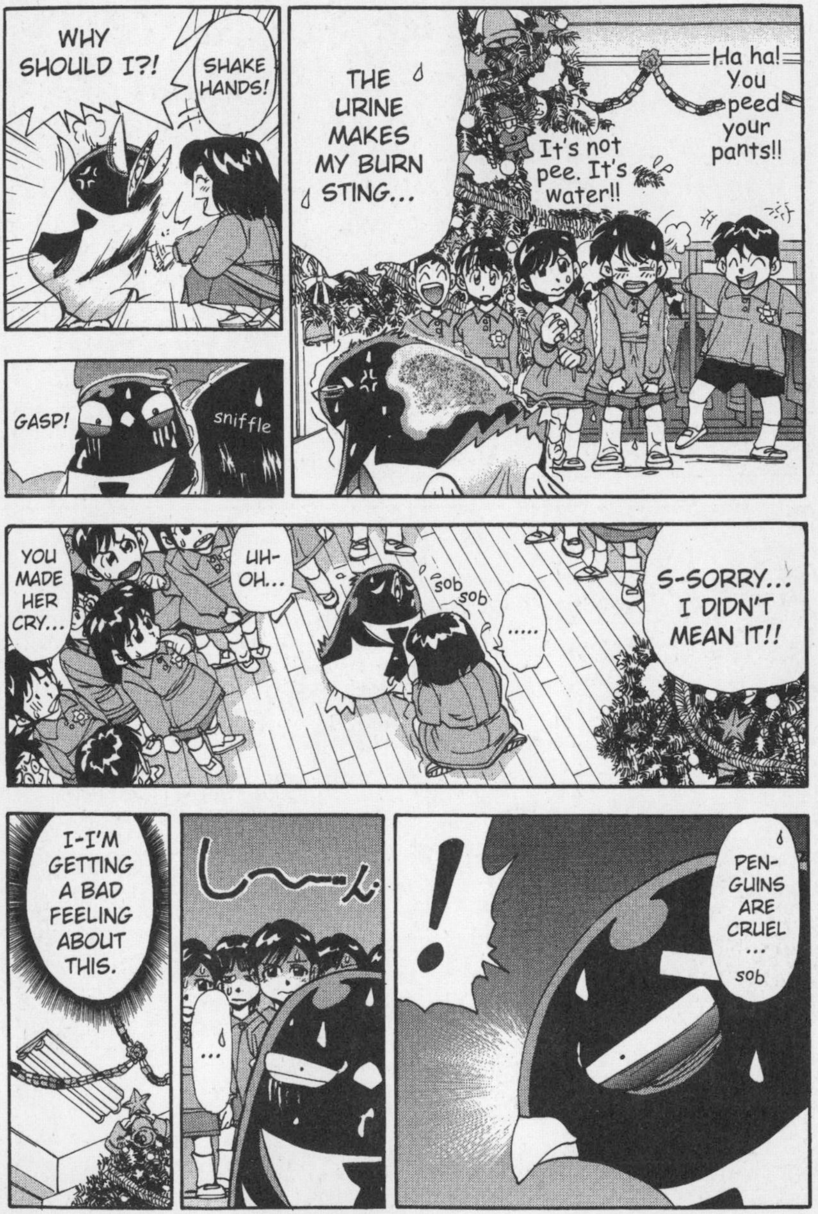
Ha ha! You peed your pants!!
It's not pee. It's water!!
THE URINE MAKES MY BURN STING...
SHAKE HANDS!
WHY SHOULD I?!
sniffle
GASP!
S-SORRY... I DIDN'T MEAN IT!!
sob sob
.....
UH-OH...
YOU MADE HER CRY...
PEN-GUINS ARE CRUEL ... sob
!
しーーん
...
I-I'M GETTING A BAD FEELING ABOUT THIS.

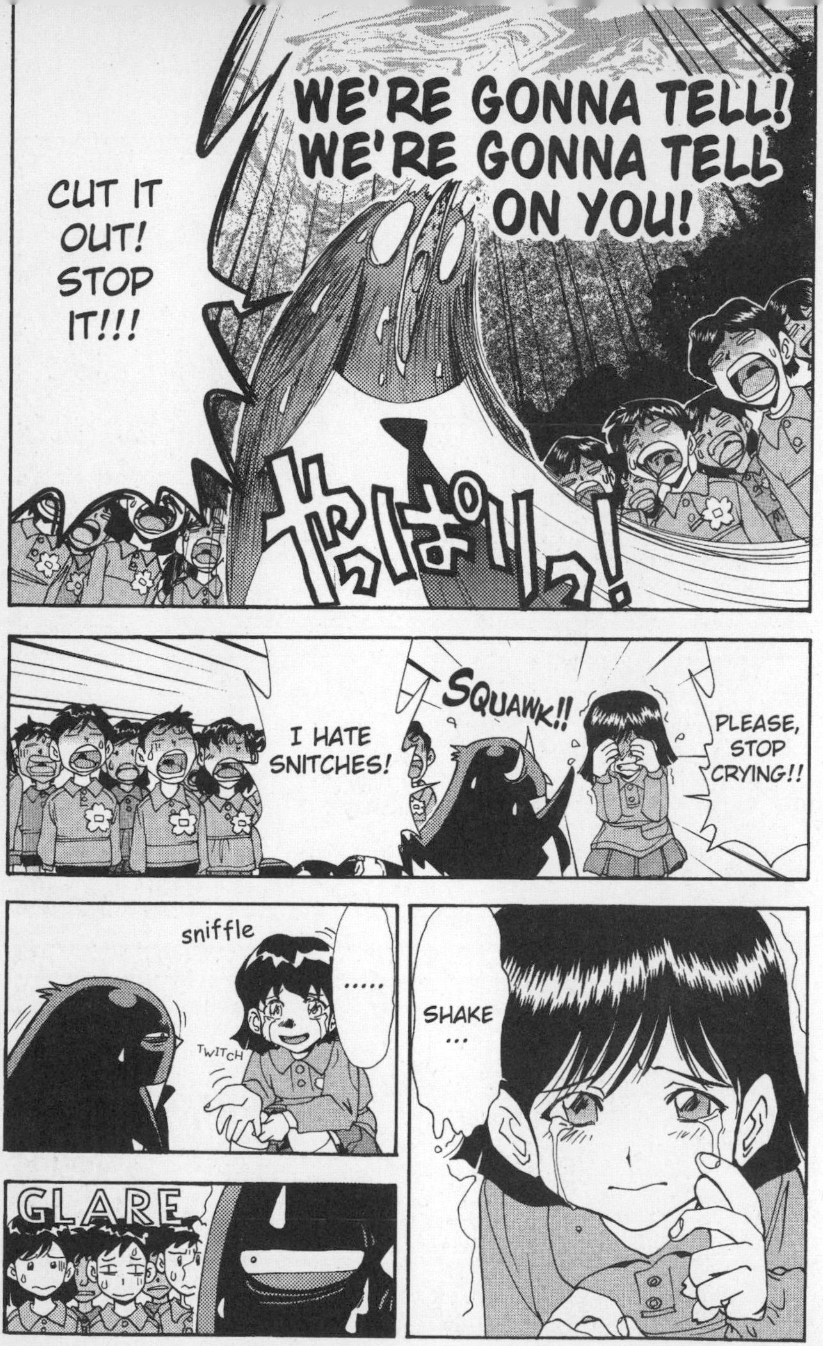
WE'RE GONNA TELL! WE'RE GONNA TELL ON YOU!
CUT IT OUT! STOP IT!!!
ちゃぽりっ!
PLEASE, STOP CRYING!!
SQUAWK!!
I HATE SNITCHES!
SHAKE ...
......
sniffle
TWITCH
GLARE

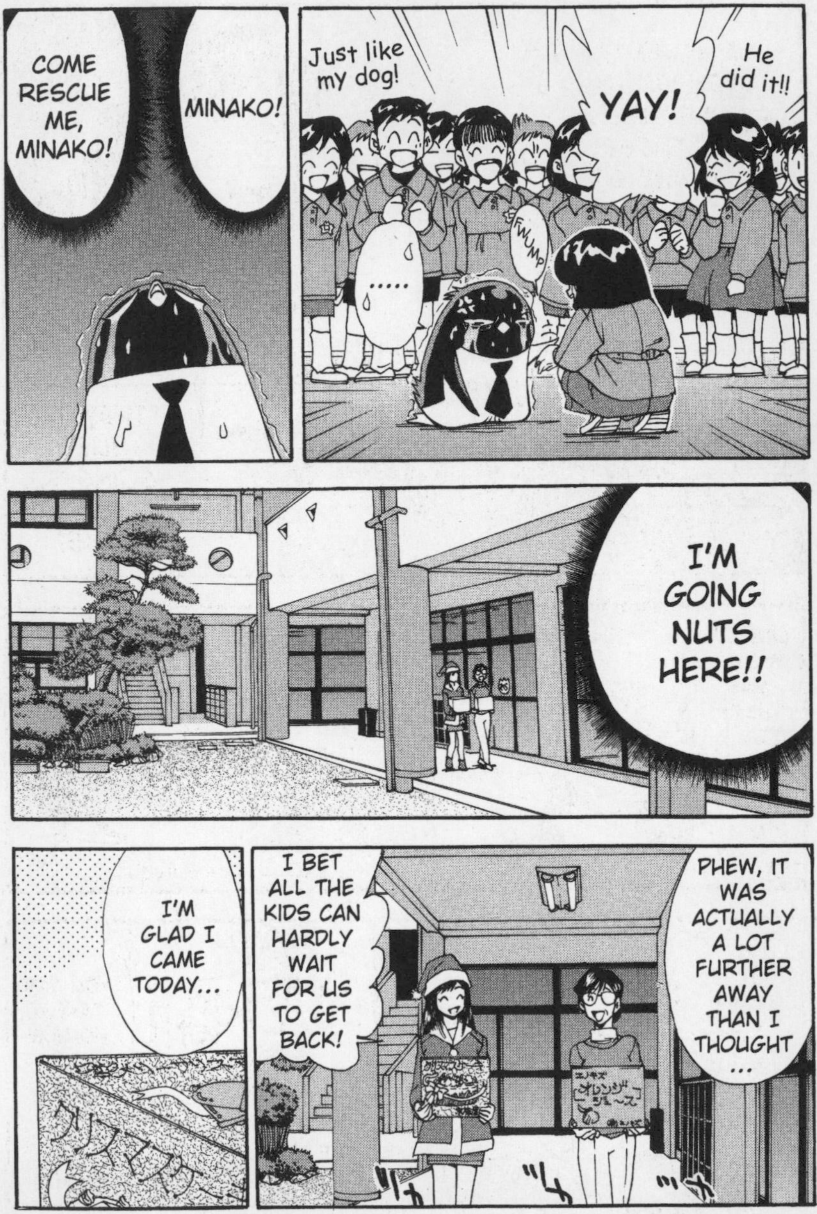
He did it!!
YAY!
Just like my dog!
FWUMP
.....
MINAKO!
COME RESCUE ME, MINAKO!
I'M GOING NUTS HERE!!
PHEW, IT WAS ACTUALLY A LOT FURTHER AWAY THAN I THOUGHT ...
I BET ALL THE KIDS CAN HARDLY WAIT FOR US TO GET BACK!
I'M GLAD I CAME TODAY...

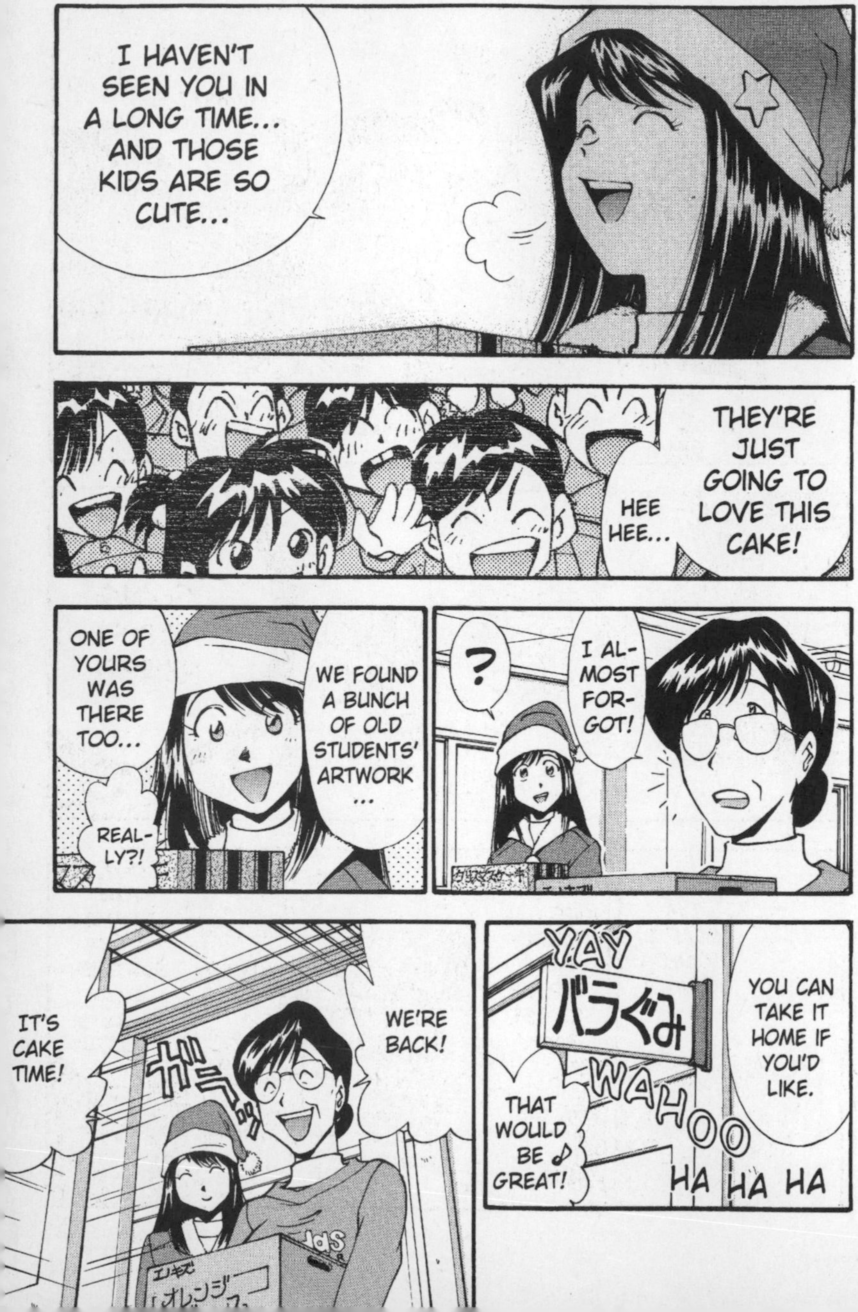
I HAVEN'T SEEN YOU IN A LONG TIME... AND THOSE KIDS ARE SO CUTE...
THEY'RE JUST GOING TO LOVE THIS CAKE!
HEE HEE...
I AL-MOST FOR-GOT!
?
WE FOUND A BUNCH OF OLD STUDENTS' ARTWORK ...
ONE OF YOURS WAS THERE TOO...
REAL-LY?!
YOU CAN TAKE IT HOME IF YOU'D LIKE.
YAY
バラぐみ
WAHOO
THAT WOULD BE ♪ GREAT!
HA HA HA
WE'RE BACK!
ガラ
IT'S CAKE TIME!

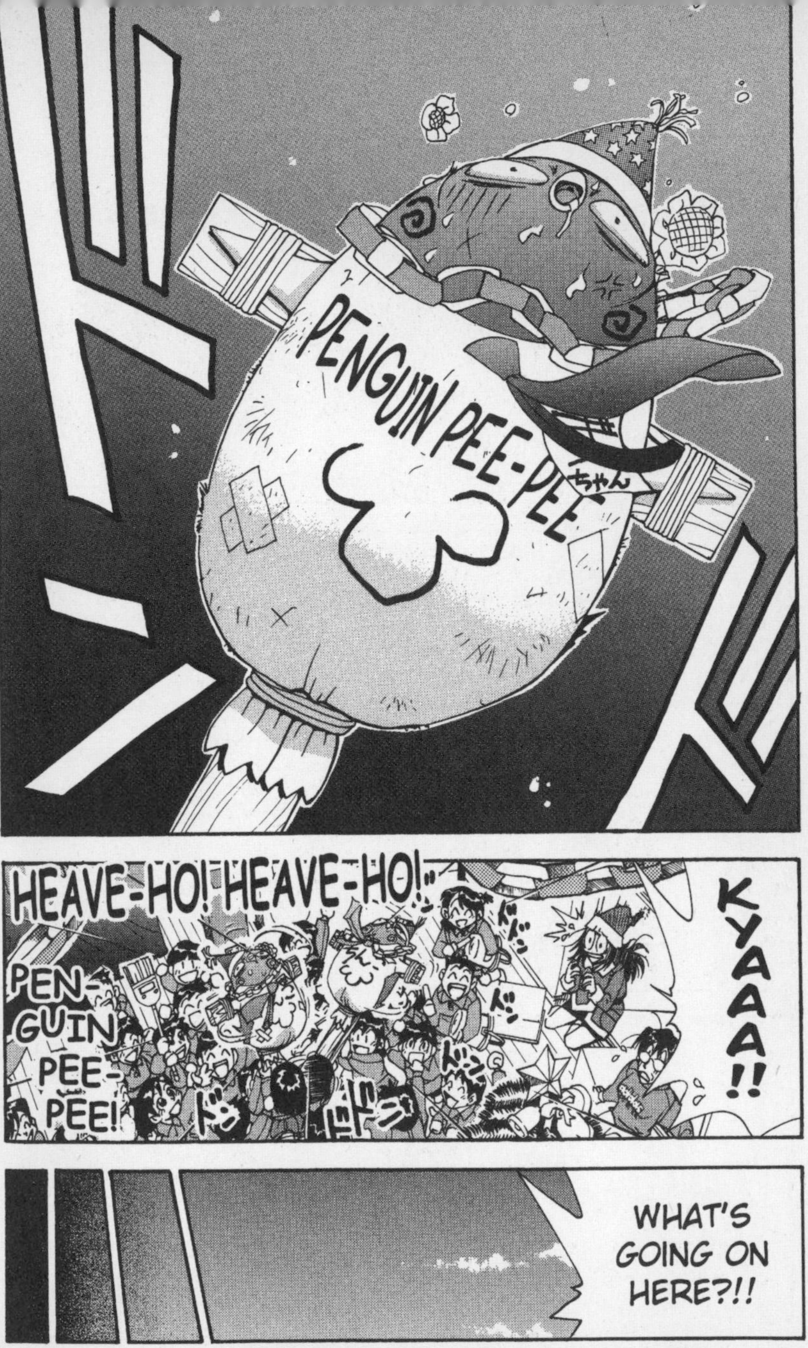
PENGUIN PEE-PEE
ちゃん
HEAVE-HO! HEAVE-HO!
KYAAAA!!
PEN-GUIN PEE-PEE!
WHAT'S GOING ON HERE?!!

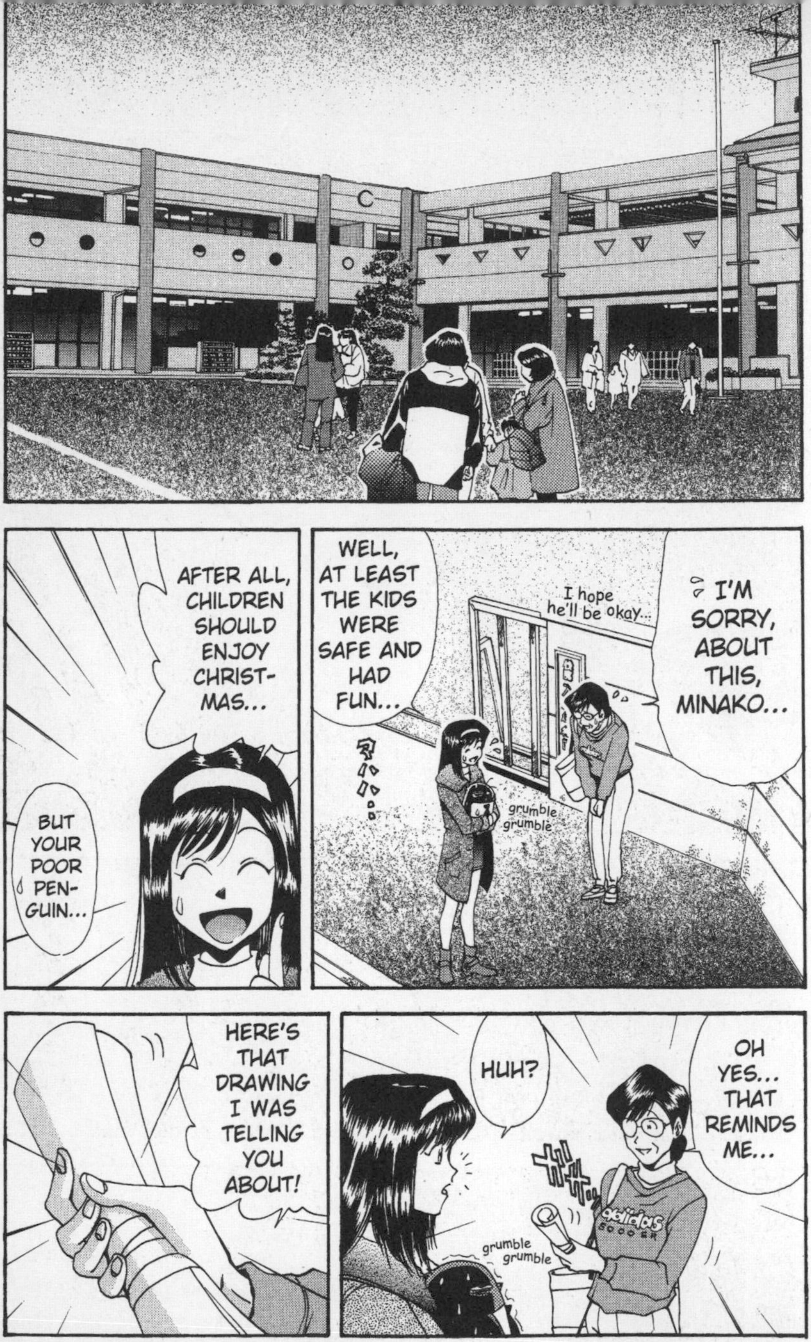
I'M SORRY, ABOUT THIS, MINAKO...
I hope he'll be okay...
WELL, AT LEAST THE KIDS WERE SAFE AND HAD FUN...
grumble grumble
AFTER ALL, CHILDREN SHOULD ENJOY CHRIST-MAS...
BUT YOUR POOR PEN-GUIN...
OH YES... THAT REMINDS ME...
HUH?
grumble grumble
HERE'S THAT DRAWING I WAS TELLING YOU ABOUT!

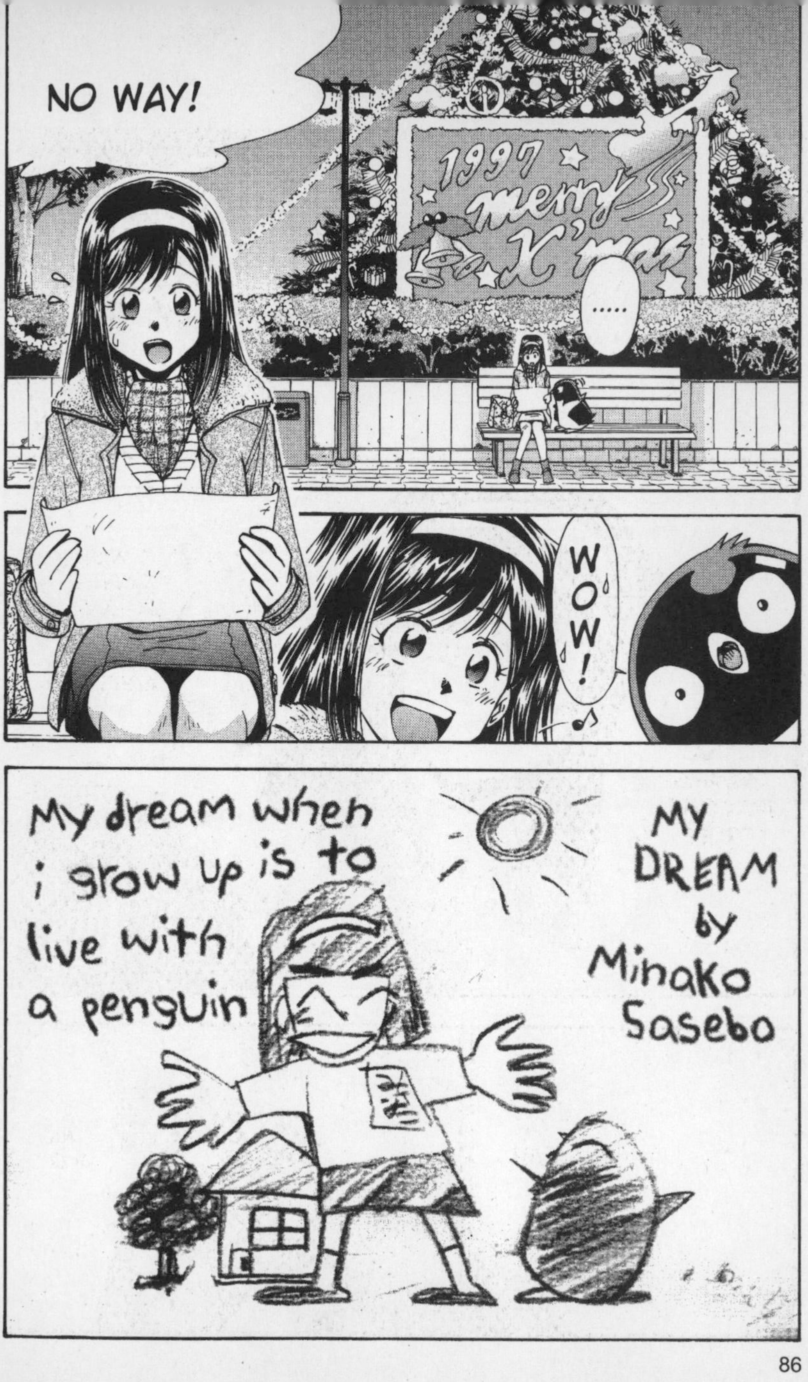
1997 merry X'mas
......
NO WAY!
WOW!
My dream when i grow up is to live with a penguin
MY DREAM by Minako Sasebo

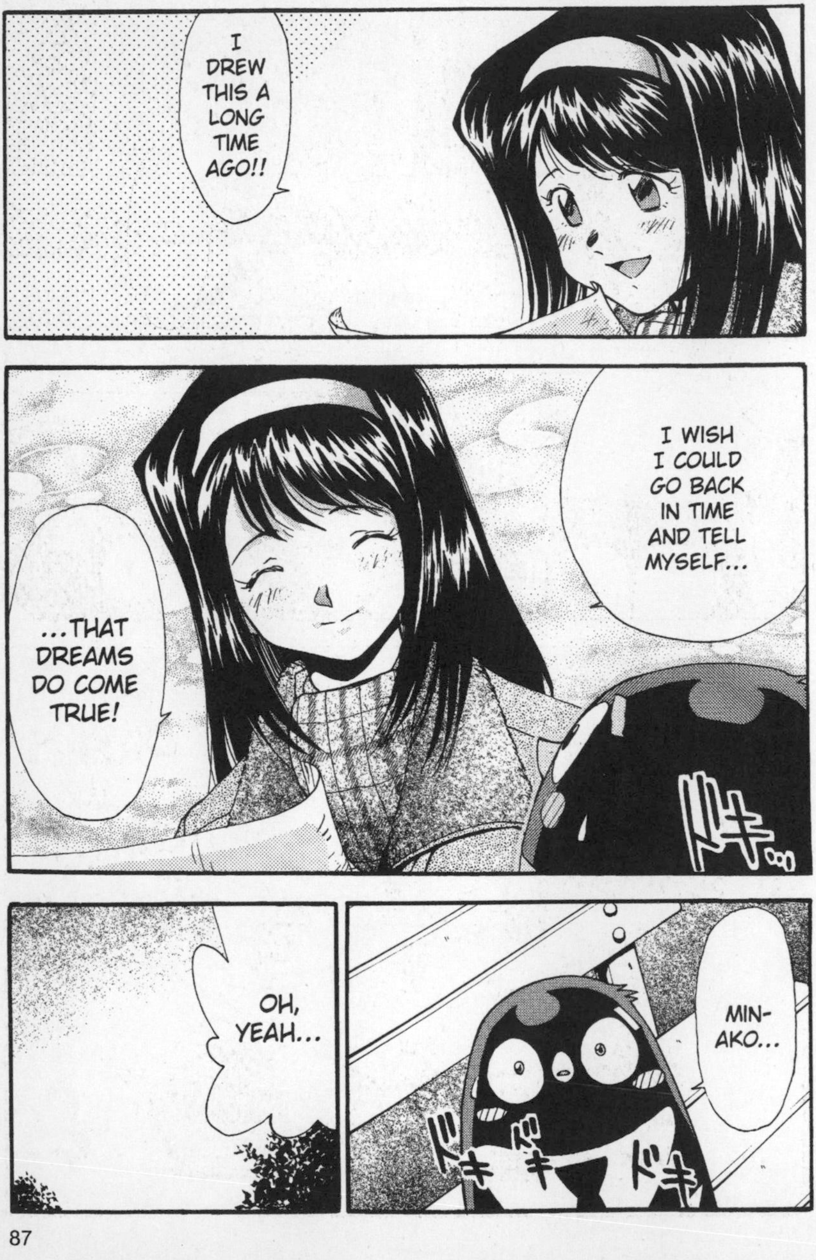
I DREW THIS A LONG TIME AGO!!
I WISH I COULD GO BACK IN TIME AND TELL MYSELF...
...THAT DREAMS DO COME TRUE!
MIN-AKO...
OH, YEAH...

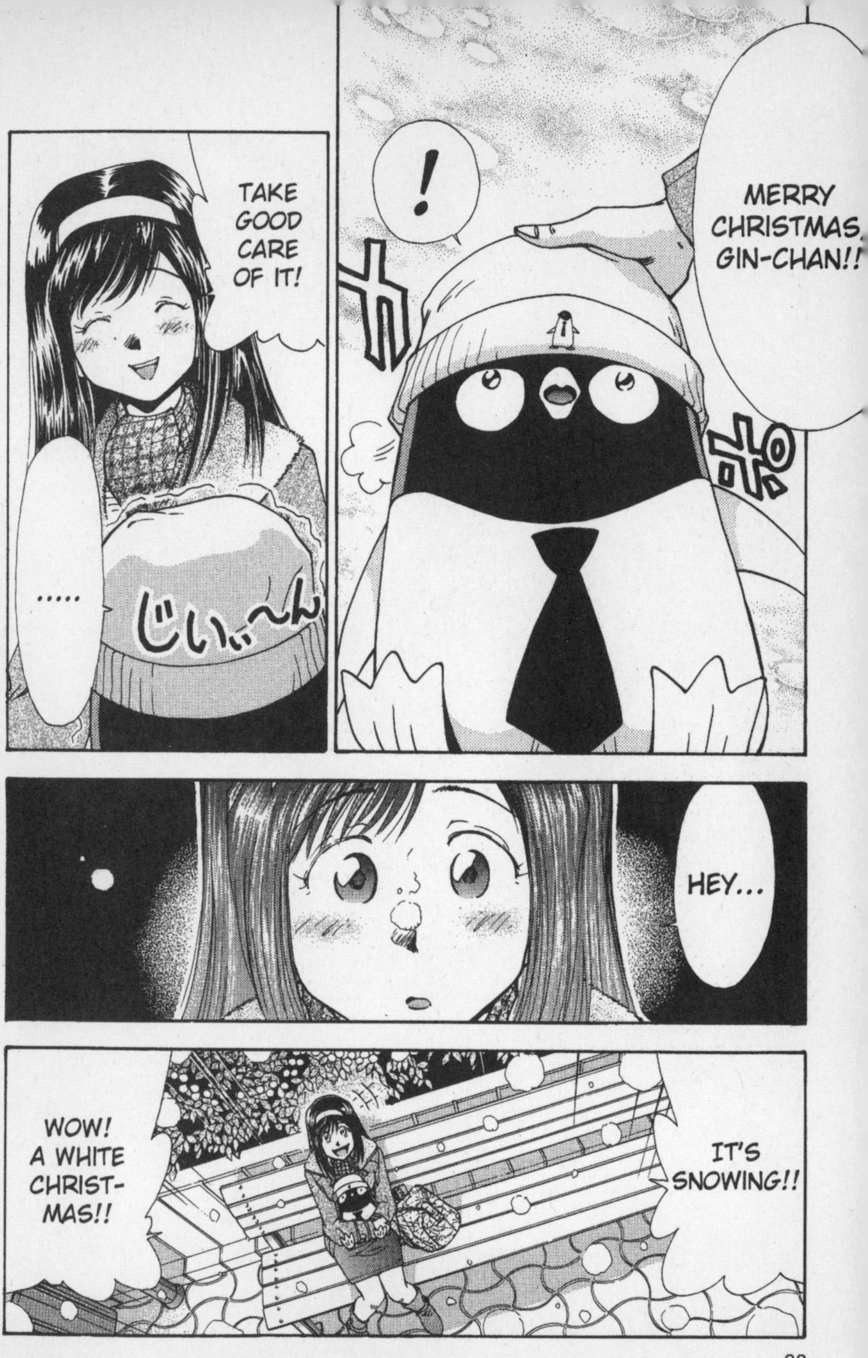
MERRY CHRISTMAS GIN-CHAN!!
!
TAKE GOOD CARE OF IT!
.....
じぃ~ん
HEY...
IT'S SNOWING!!
WOW! A WHITE CHRIST-MAS!!

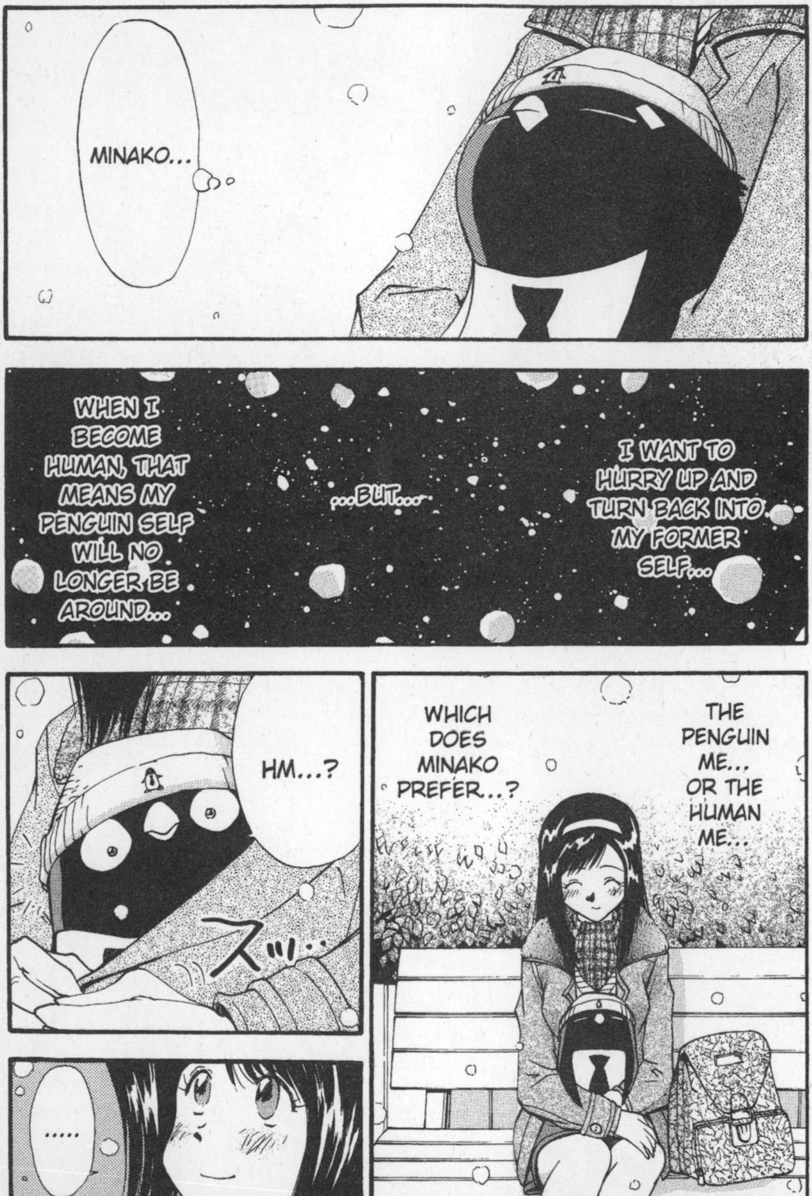
MINAKO...
I WANT TO HURRY UP AND TURN BACK INTO MY FORMER SELF...
...BUT...
WHEN I BECOME HUMAN, THAT MEANS MY PENGUIN SELF WILL NO LONGER BE AROUND...
THE PENGUIN ME... OR THE HUMAN ME...
WHICH DOES MINAKO PREFER...?
HM...?
スッ..
.....

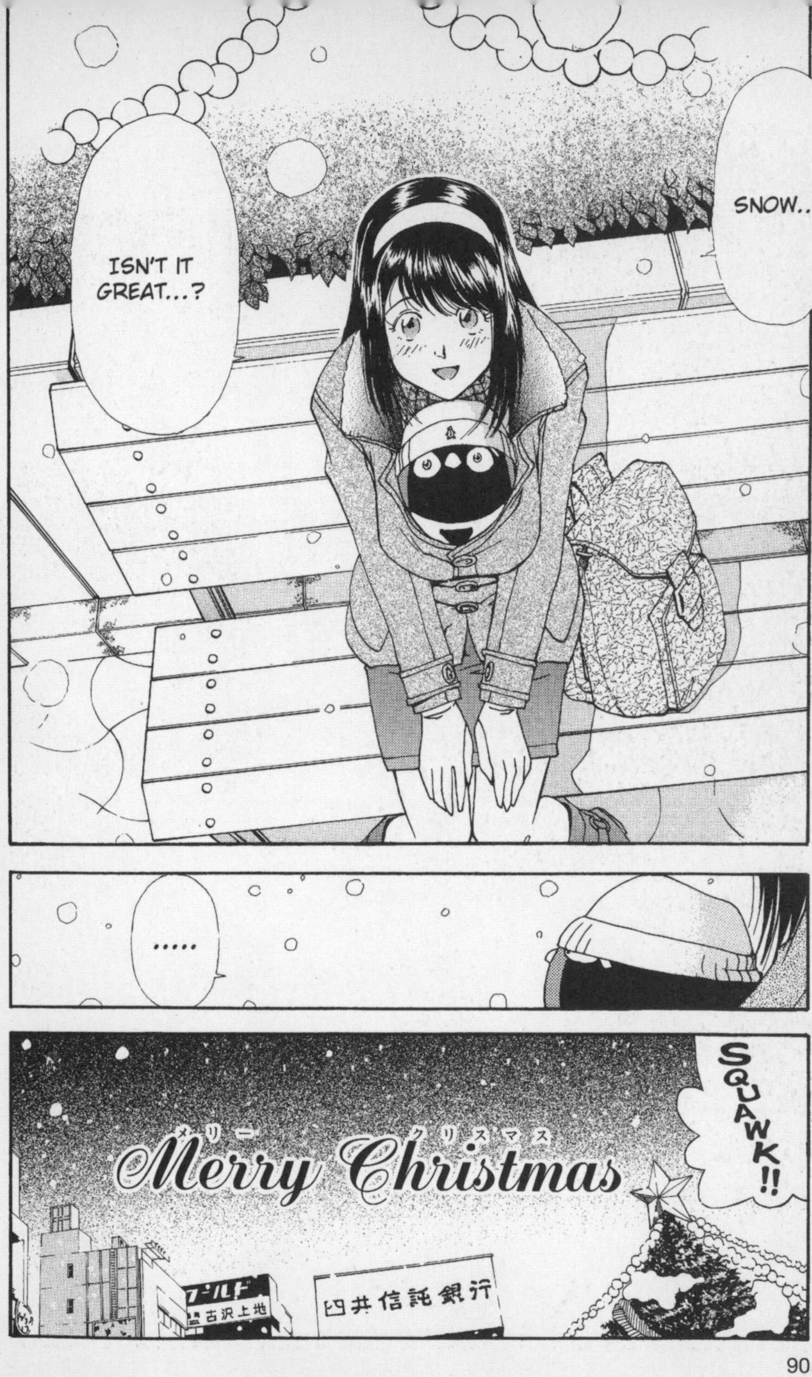
SNOW...
ISN'T IT GREAT...?
.....
SQUAWK!!
メリー クリスマス
Merry Christmas
ワールド
古沢上地
四井信託銀行

CHAPTER 5
HEAVEN, HEAR MY CALL...

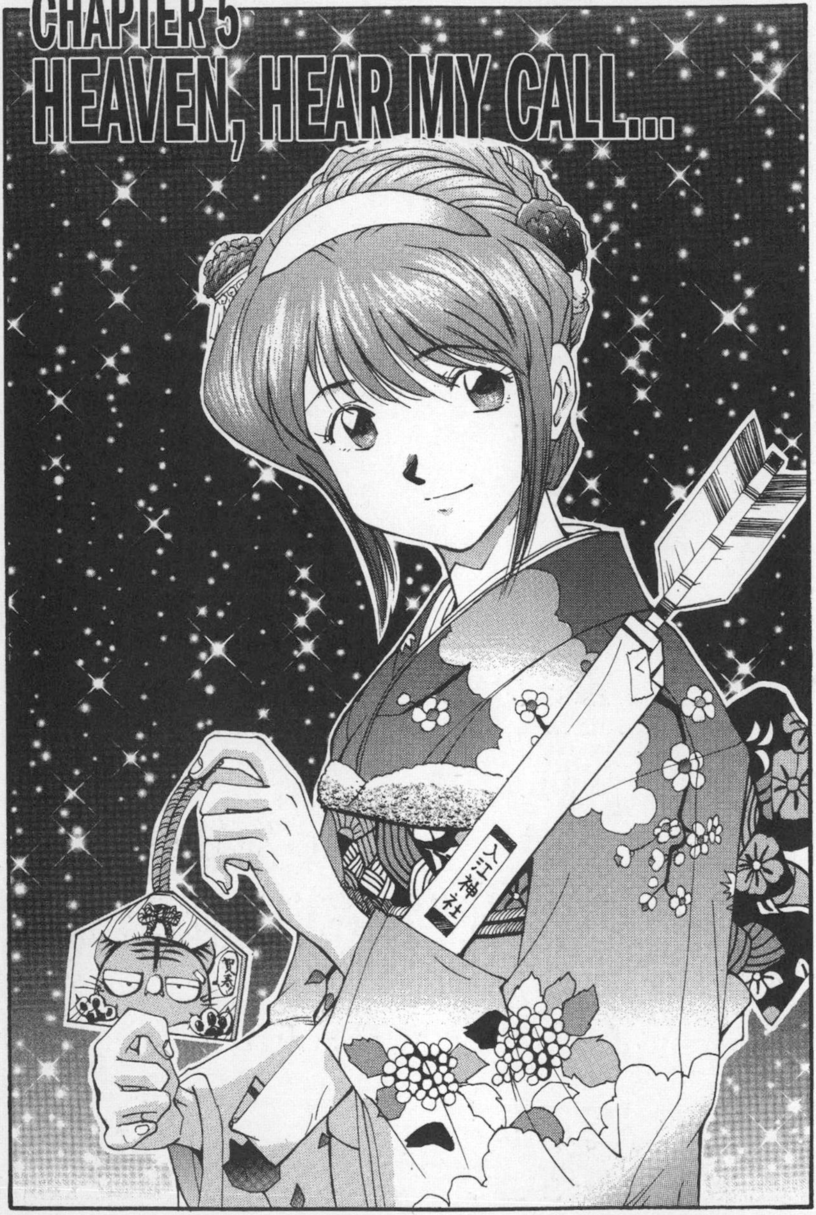
入江神社

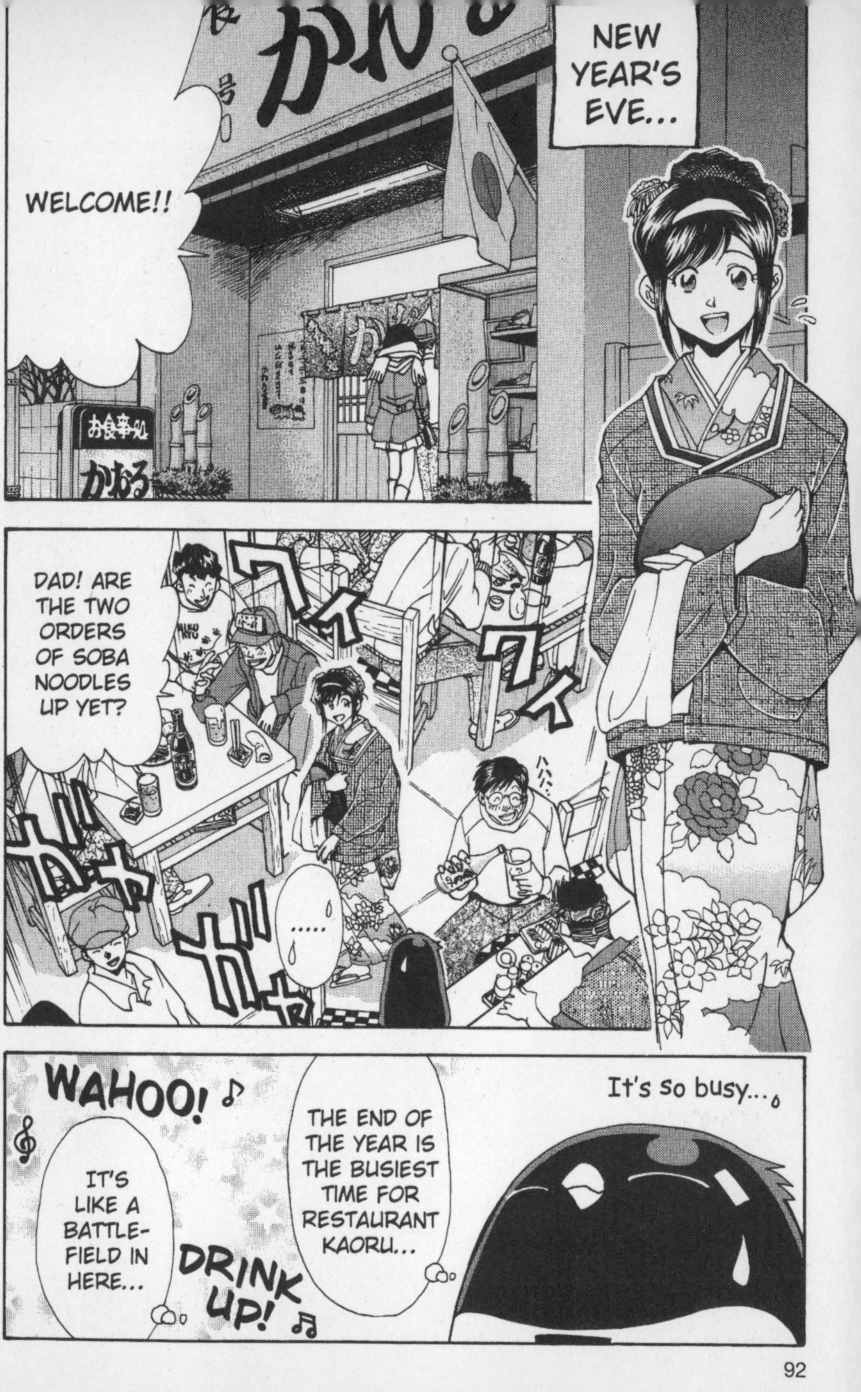
NEW YEAR'S EVE...
WELCOME!!
お食事処
かおる
DAD! ARE THE TWO ORDERS OF SOBA NOODLES UP YET?
ワイワイ
ガヤガヤ
.....
It's so busy...
THE END OF THE YEAR IS THE BUSIEST TIME FOR RESTAURANT KAORU...
IT'S LIKE A BATTLE-FIELD IN HERE...
WAHOO!
DRINK UP!

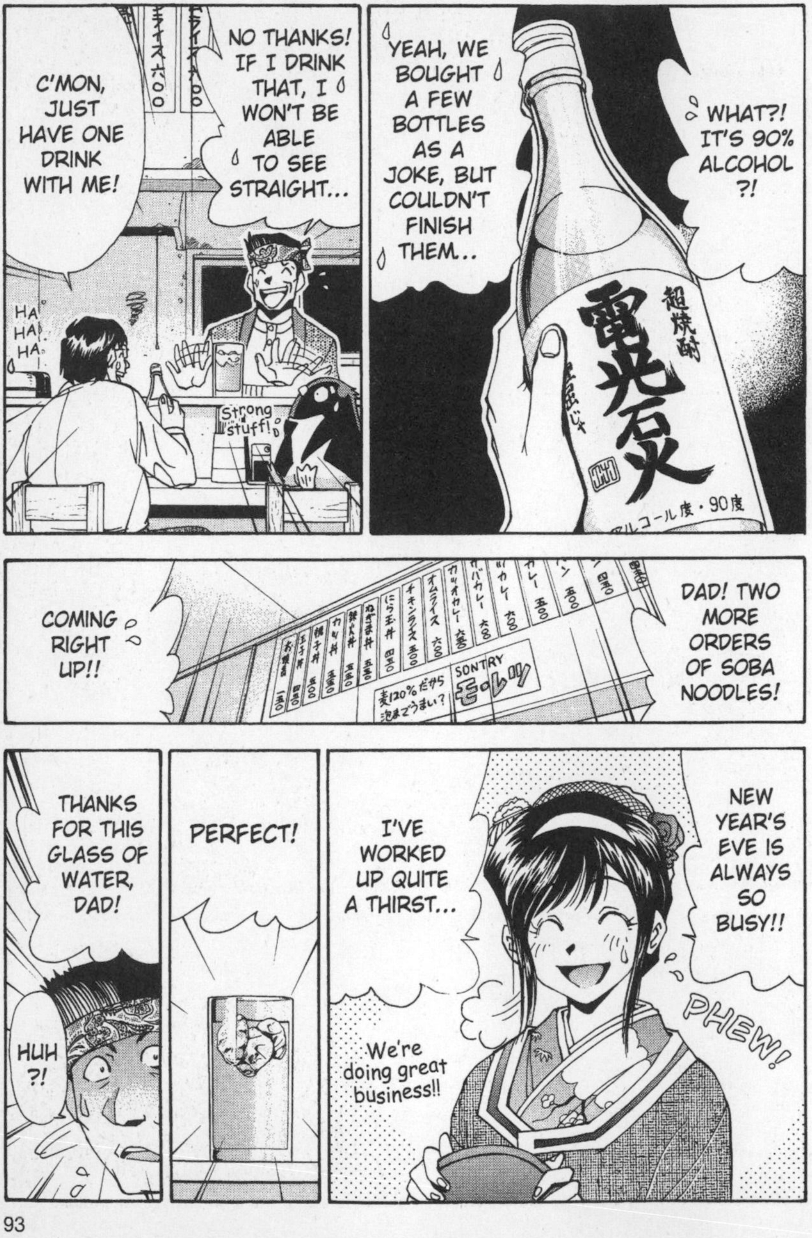
WHAT?! IT'S 90% ALCOHOL ?!
YEAH, WE BOUGHT A FEW BOTTLES AS A JOKE, BUT COULDN'T FINISH THEM...
超焼酎
電光石火
アルコール度・90度
NO THANKS! IF I DRINK THAT, I WON'T BE ABLE TO SEE STRAIGHT...
C'MON, JUST HAVE ONE DRINK WITH ME!
HA HA HA
Strong stuff!
DAD! TWO MORE ORDERS OF SOBA NOODLES!
COMING RIGHT UP!!
NEW YEAR'S EVE IS ALWAYS SO BUSY!!
I'VE WORKED UP QUITE A THIRST...
PHEW!
We're doing great business!!
PERFECT!
THANKS FOR THIS GLASS OF WATER, DAD!
HUH ?!

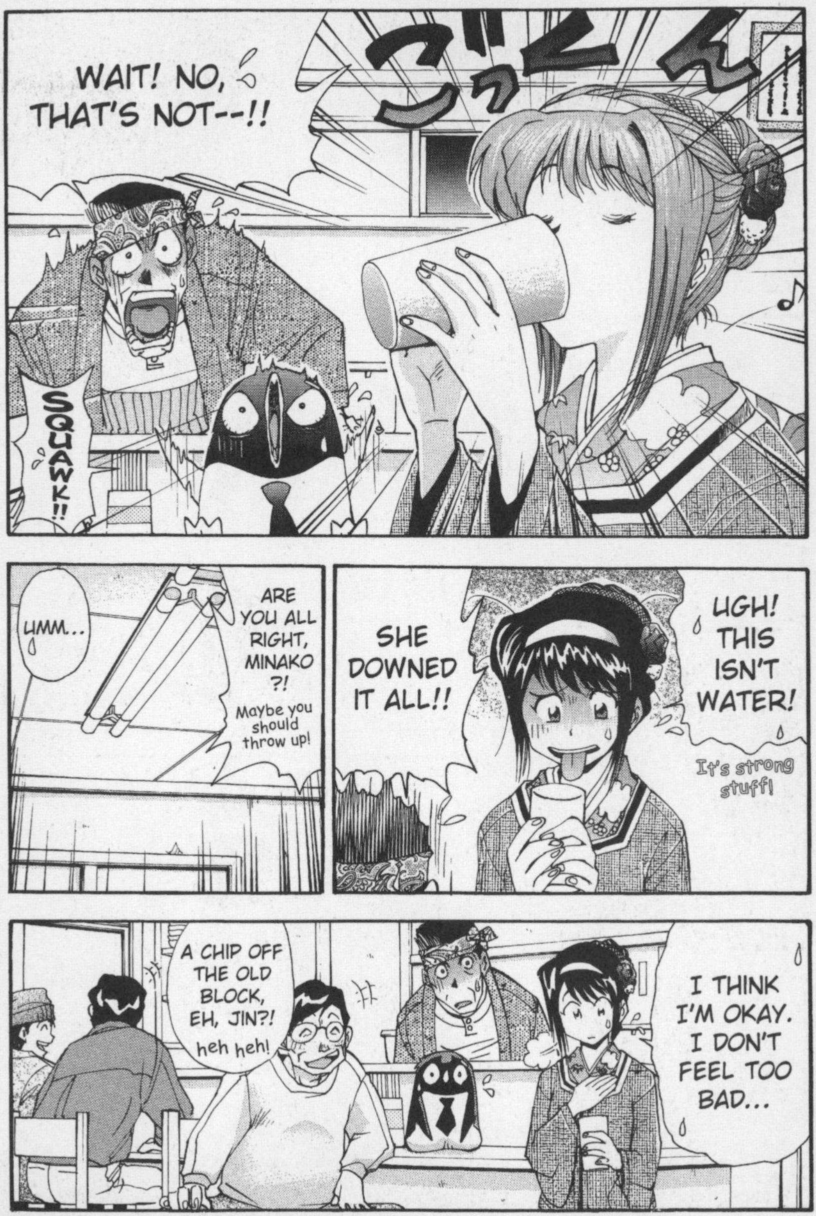
WAIT! NO, THAT'S NOT--!!
SQUAWK!!
UGH! THIS ISN'T WATER!
It's strong stuff!
SHE DOWNED IT ALL!!
ARE YOU ALL RIGHT, MINAKO?!
Maybe you should throw up!
UMM...
I THINK I'M OKAY. I DON'T FEEL TOO BAD...
A CHIP OFF THE OLD BLOCK, EH, JIN?!
heh heh!

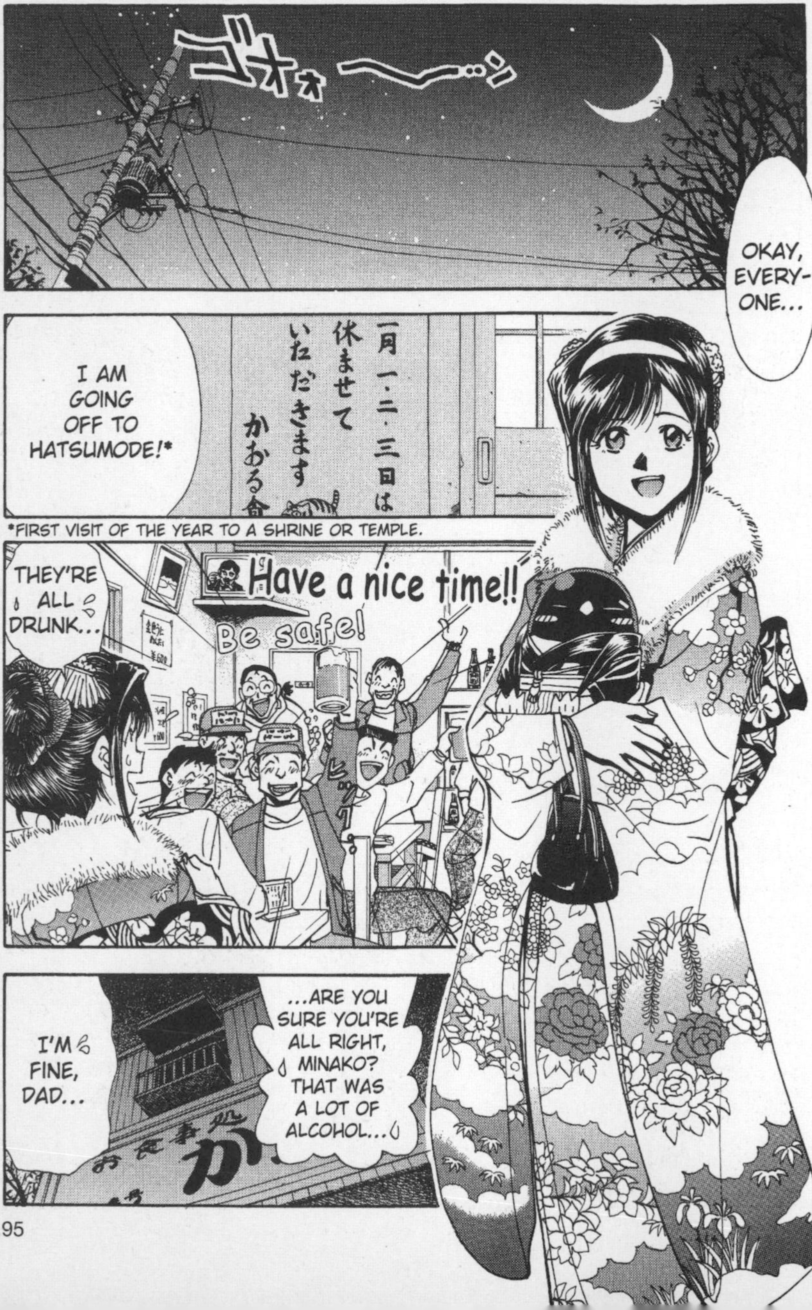
ゴォォ〜〜ン
OKAY, EVERY-ONE...
一月一・二・三日は
休ませて
いただきます
かおる
I AM GOING OFF TO HATSUMODE!*
*FIRST VISIT OF THE YEAR TO A SHRINE OR TEMPLE.
Have a nice time!!
THEY'RE ALL DRUNK...
Be safe!
...ARE YOU SURE YOU'RE ALL RIGHT, MINAKO? THAT WAS A LOT OF ALCOHOL...
I'M FINE, DAD...

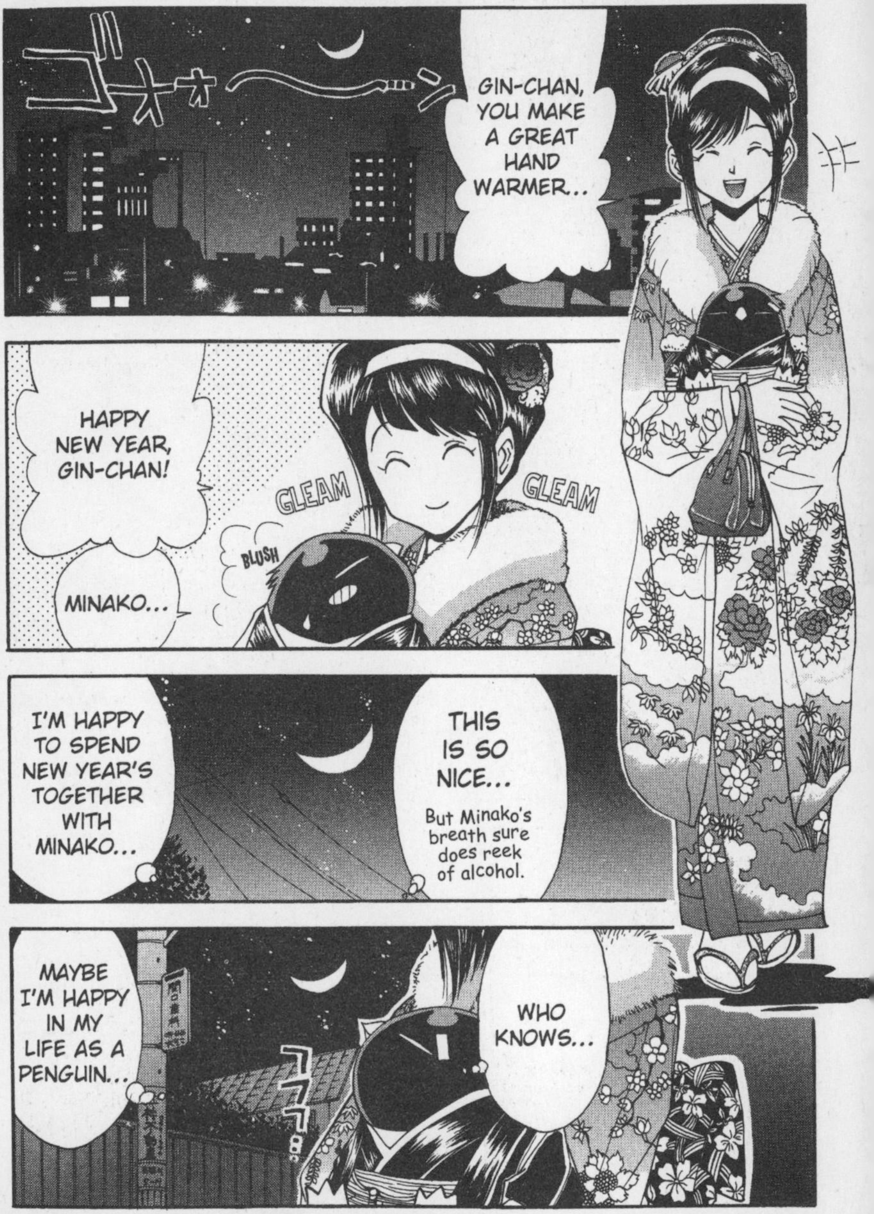
GIN-CHAN, YOU MAKE A GREAT HAND WARMER...
HAPPY NEW YEAR, GIN-CHAN!
GLEAM
GLEAM
MINAKO...
BLUSH
THIS IS SO NICE...
But Minako's breath sure does reek of alcohol.
I'M HAPPY TO SPEND NEW YEAR'S TOGETHER WITH MINAKO...
WHO KNOWS...
MAYBE I'M HAPPY IN MY LIFE AS A PENGUIN...

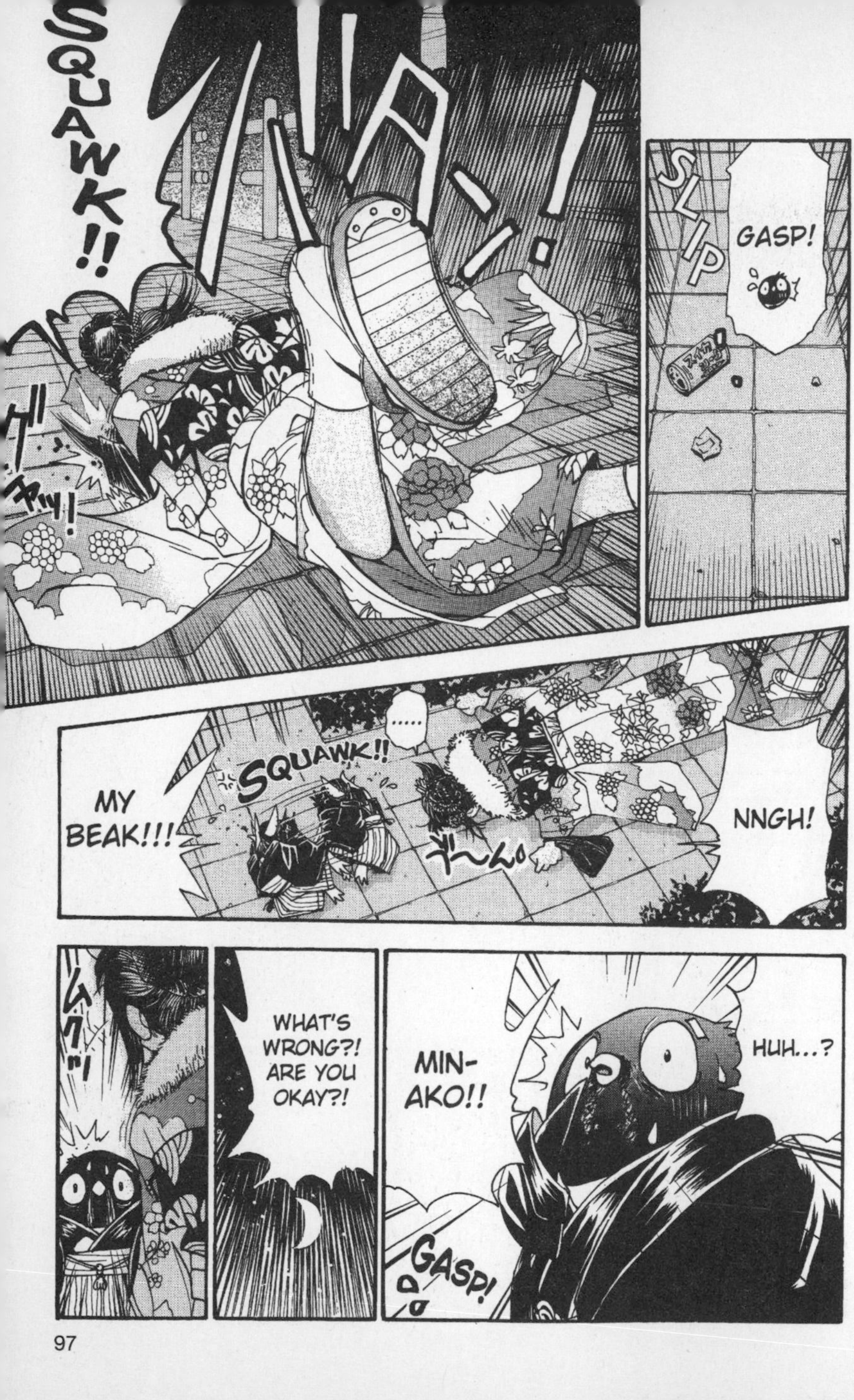
SLIP
GASP!
SQUAWK!!
NNGH!
......
SQUAWK!!
MY BEAK!!!
HUH...?
MIN-AKO!!
GASP!
WHAT'S WRONG?! ARE YOU OKAY?!

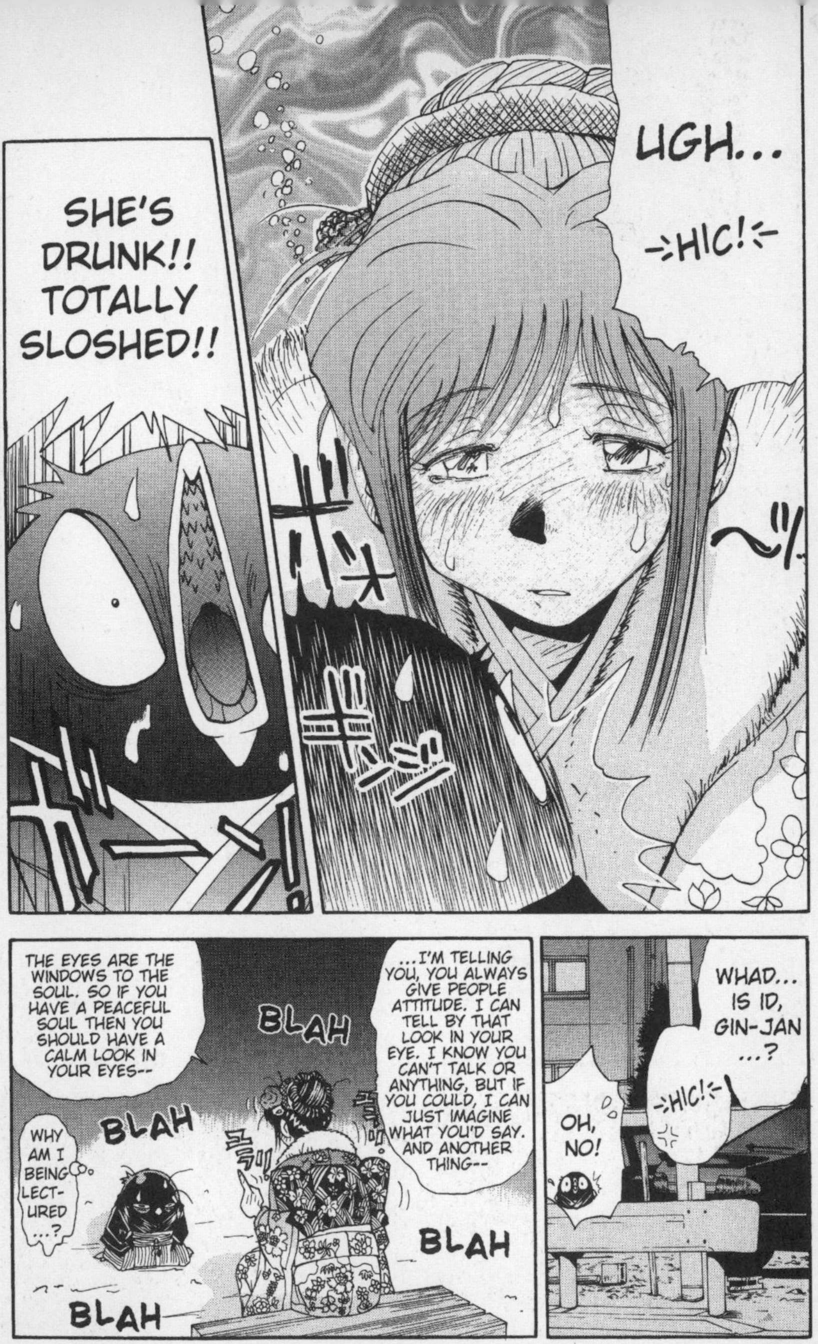
UGH...
HIC!
SHE'S DRUNK!! TOTALLY SLOSHED!!
WHAD... IS ID, GIN-JAN ...?
HIC!
OH, NO!
...I'M TELLING YOU, YOU ALWAYS GIVE PEOPLE ATTITUDE. I CAN TELL BY THAT LOOK IN YOUR EYE. I KNOW YOU CAN'T TALK OR ANYTHING, BUT IF YOU COULD, I CAN JUST IMAGINE WHAT YOU'D SAY. AND ANOTHER THING--
BLAH
THE EYES ARE THE WINDOWS TO THE SOUL. SO IF YOU HAVE A PEACEFUL SOUL THEN YOU SHOULD HAVE A CALM LOOK IN YOUR EYES--
BLAH
BLAH
WHY AM I BEING LECT-URED ...?
BLAH

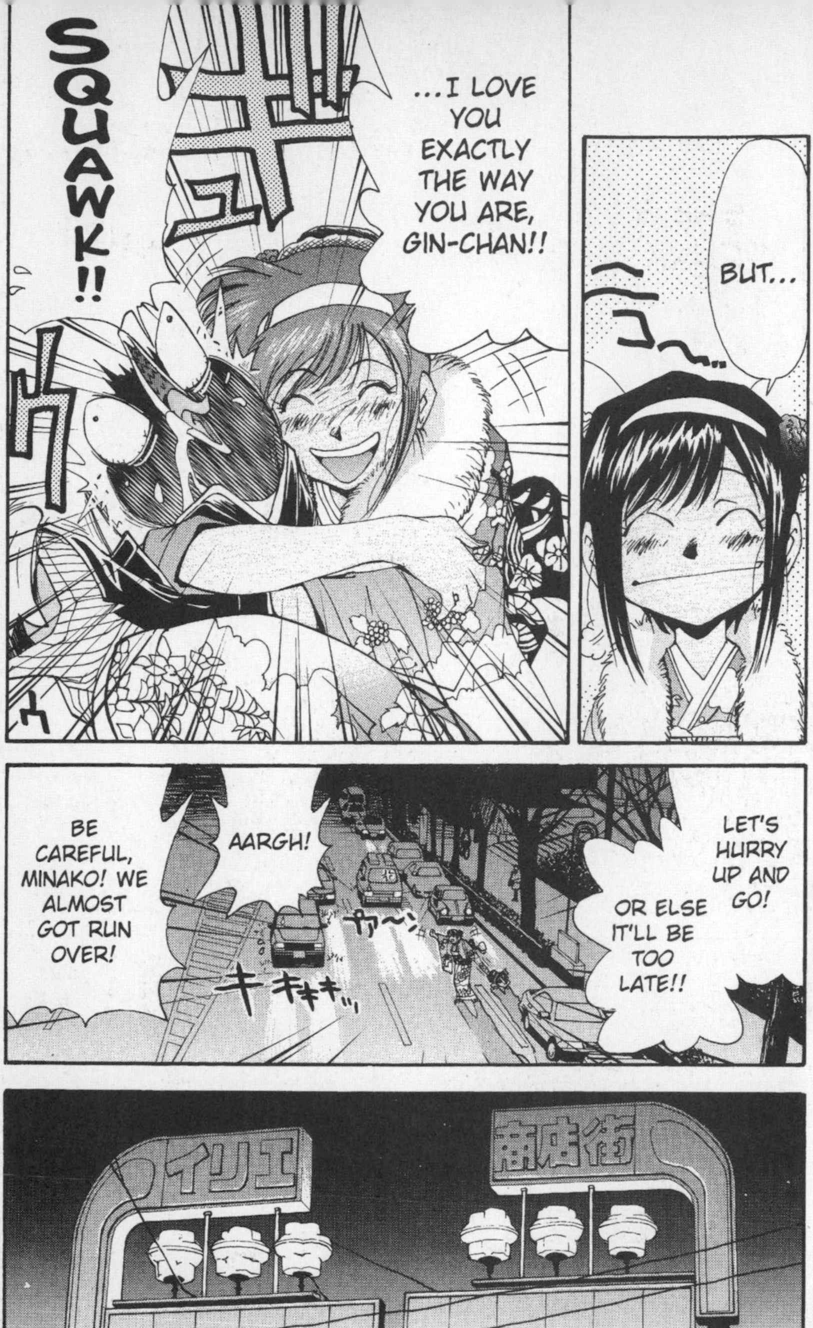
BUT...
...I LOVE YOU EXACTLY THE WAY YOU ARE, GIN-CHAN!!
SQUAWK!!
LET'S HURRY UP AND GO!
OR ELSE IT'LL BE TOO LATE!!
AARGH!
BE CAREFUL, MINAKO! WE ALMOST GOT RUN OVER!
イリエ
商店街

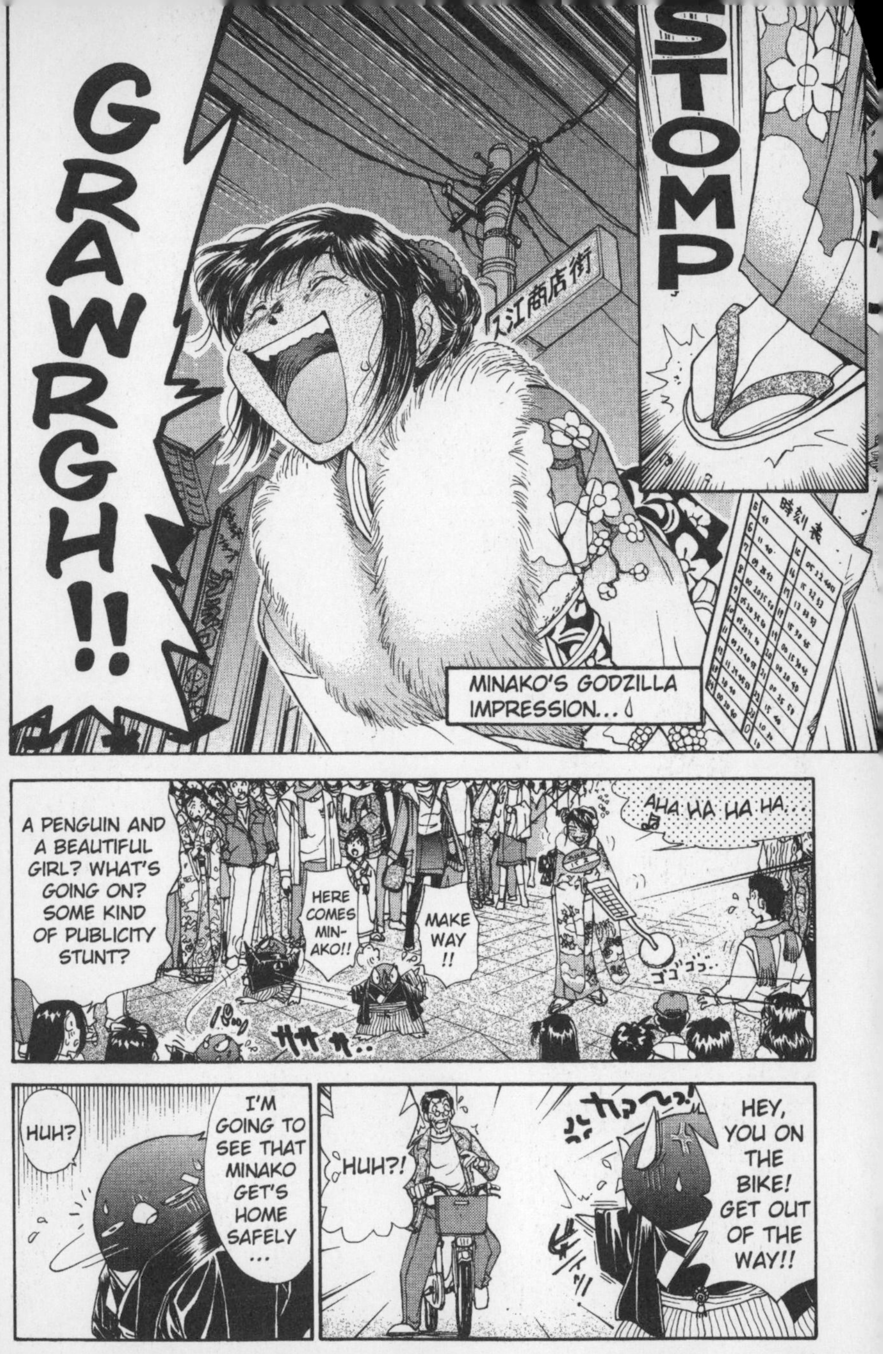
STOMP
GRAWRGH!!
入江商店街
時刻表
MINAKO'S GODZILLA IMPRESSION...♪
AHA HA HA HA...♪
MAKE WAY !!
HERE COMES MIN-AKO!!
A PENGUIN AND A BEAUTIFUL GIRL? WHAT'S GOING ON? SOME KIND OF PUBLICITY STUNT?
HEY, YOU ON THE BIKE! GET OUT OF THE WAY!!
HUH?!
I'M GOING TO SEE THAT MINAKO GET'S HOME SAFELY ...
HUH?

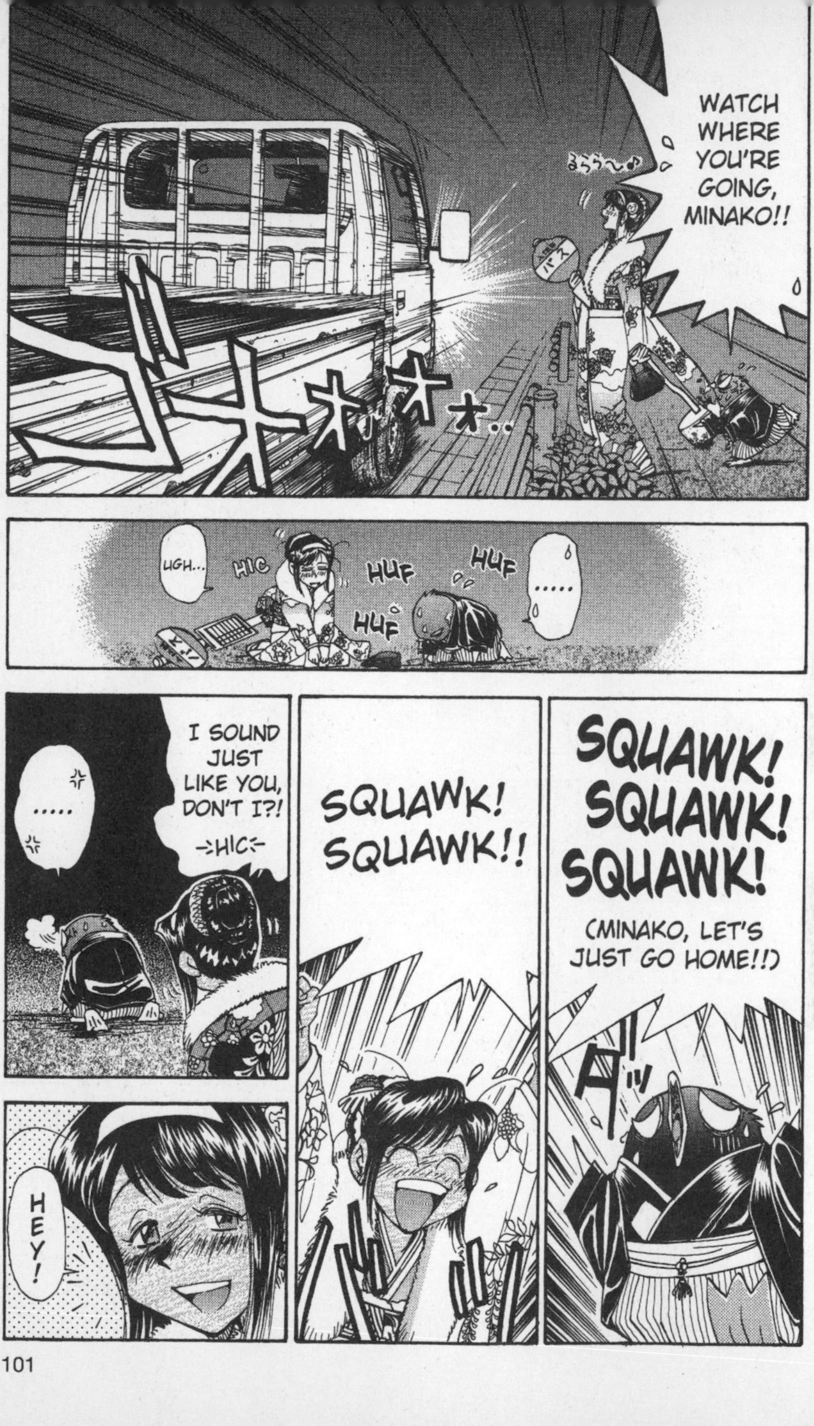
WATCH WHERE YOU'RE GOING, MINAKO!!
......
HUF
HUF
HUF
HIC
UGH...
SQUAWK! SQUAWK! SQUAWK!
(MINAKO, LET'S JUST GO HOME!!)
SQUAWK! SQUAWK!!
I SOUND JUST LIKE YOU, DON'T I?!
HIC
.....
HEY!

IT'S MUSASHI!!

WHAT A GREAT WAY TO START THE NEW YEAR! I'VE ALREADY MANAGED TO PICK UP THIS CHICK, AND SHE'S REALLY HOT!

HEH HEH HEH!

WHAT'S THE BIG IDEA?!

SQUAWK!

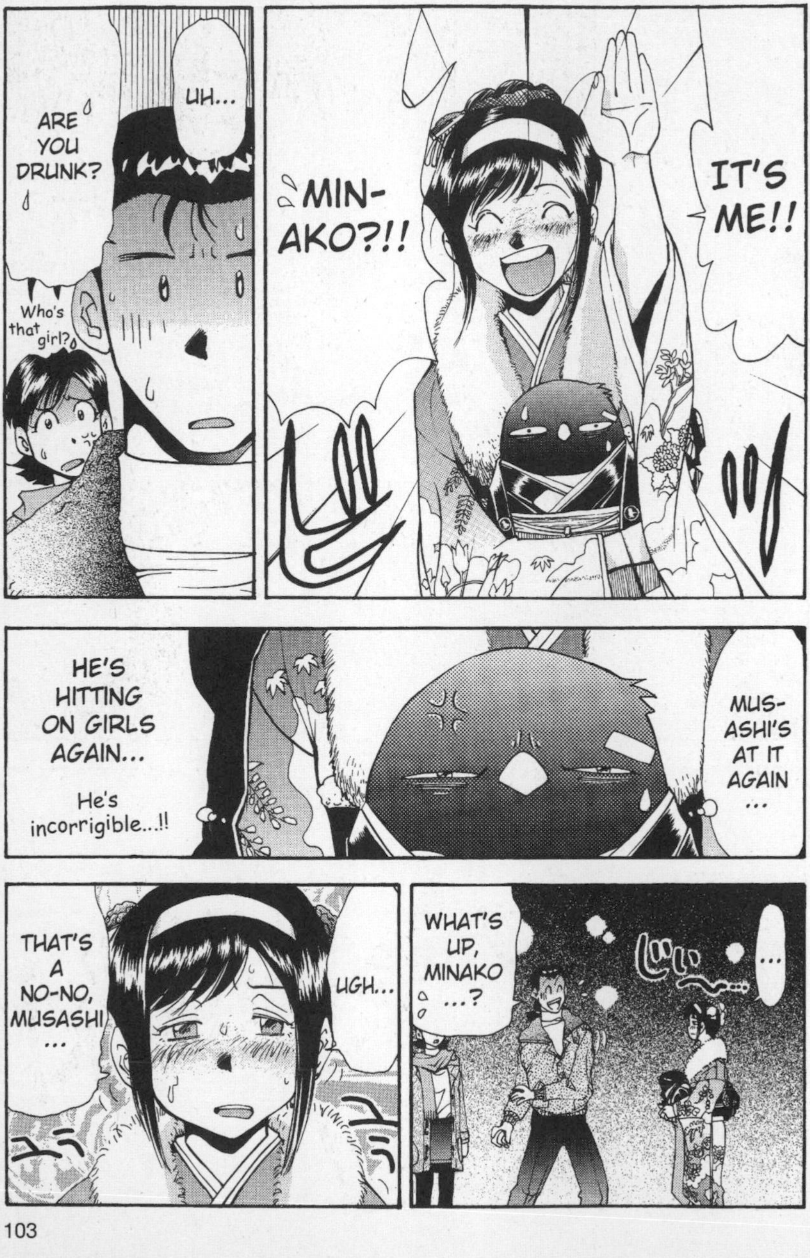
IT'S ME!!
MIN-AKO?!!
UH...
ARE YOU DRUNK?
Who's that girl?
MUS-ASHI'S AT IT AGAIN ...
HE'S HITTING ON GIRLS AGAIN...
He's incorrigible...!!
...
WHAT'S UP, MINAKO ...?
UGH...
THAT'S A NO-NO, MUSASHI ...

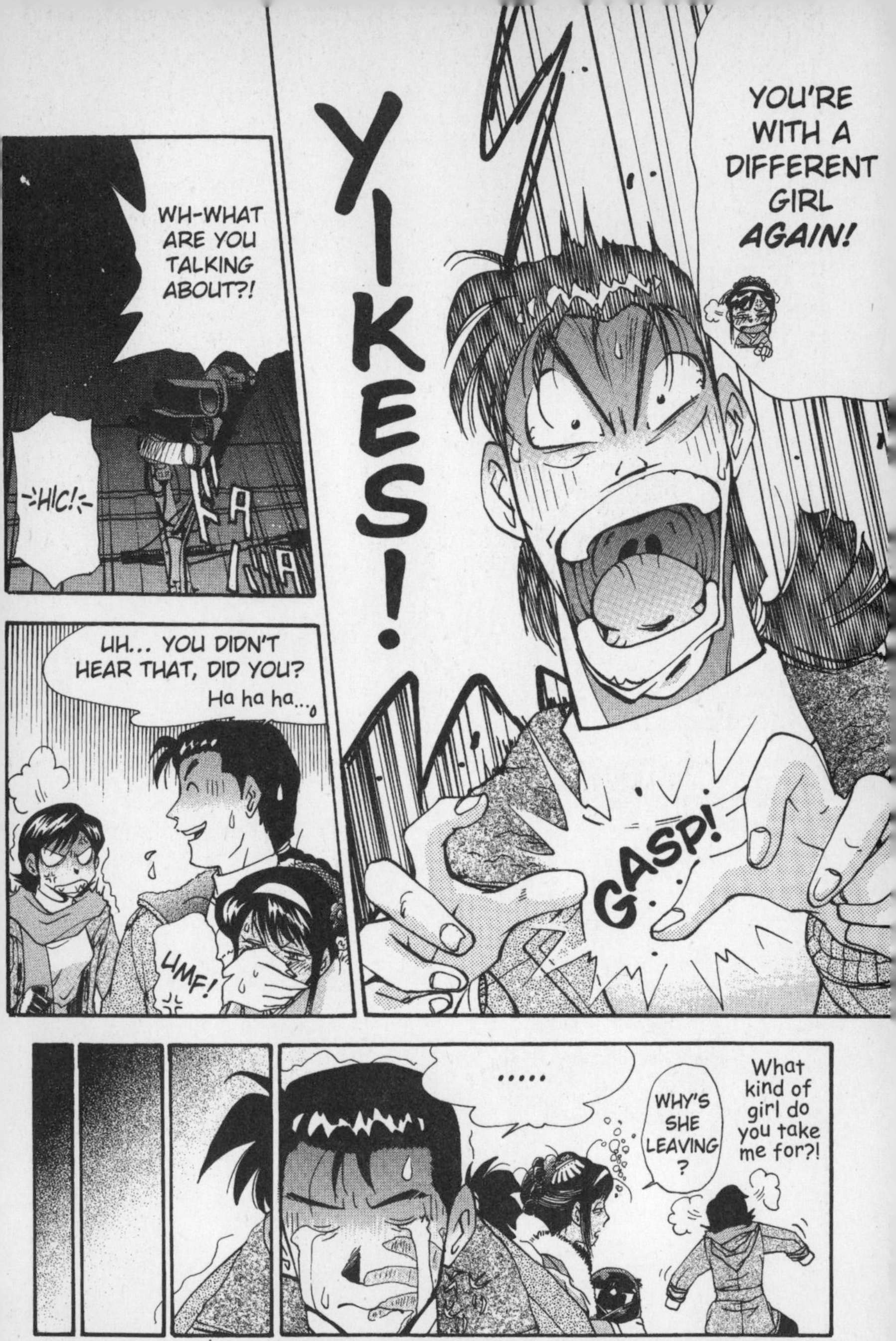
YOU'RE WITH A DIFFERENT GIRL AGAIN!
YIKES!
GASP!
WH-WHAT ARE YOU TALKING ABOUT?!
HIC!
UH... YOU DIDN'T HEAR THAT, DID YOU?
Ha ha ha...
UMF!
What kind of girl do you take me for?!
WHY'S SHE LEAVING?
.....

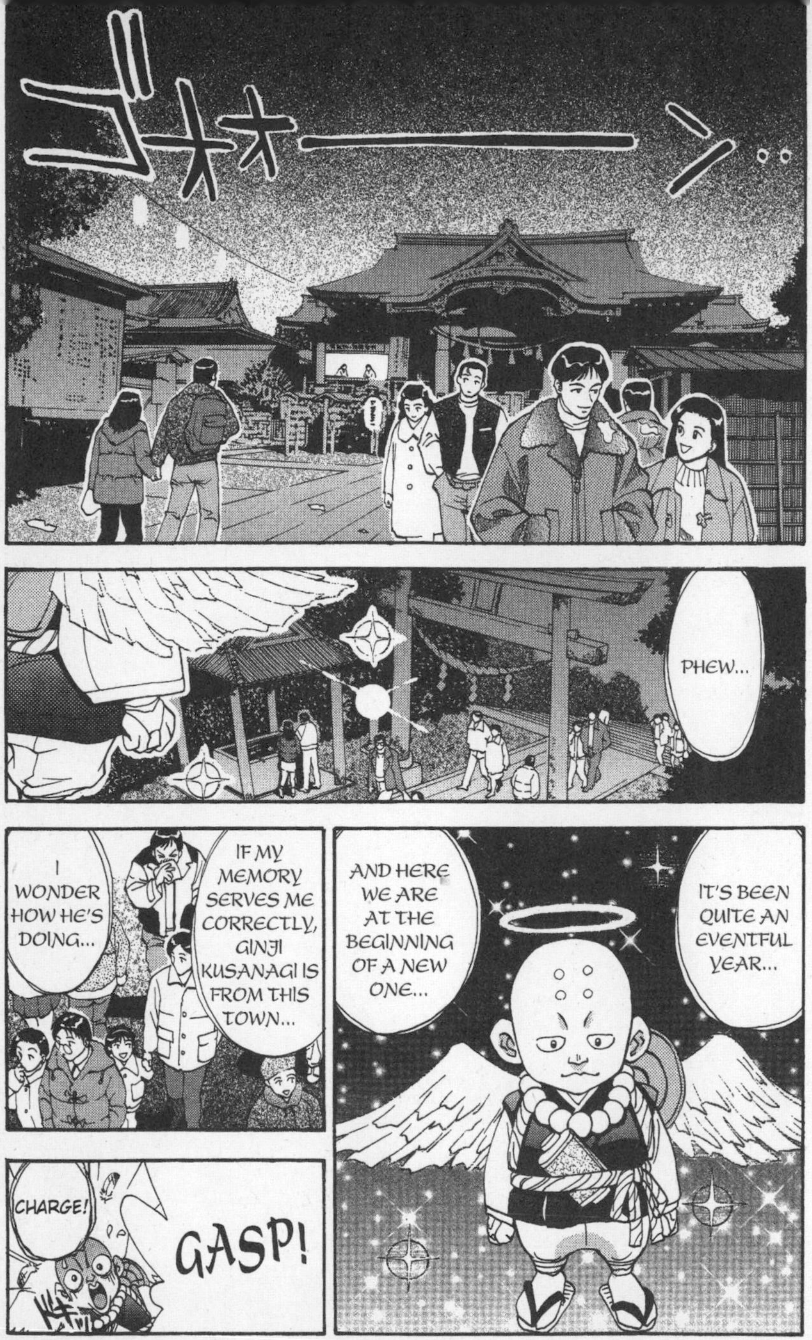
ゴォォーーン‥
PHEW...
IT'S BEEN QUITE AN EVENTFUL YEAR...
AND HERE WE ARE AT THE BEGINNING OF A NEW ONE...
IF MY MEMORY SERVES ME CORRECTLY, GINJI KUSANAGI IS FROM THIS TOWN...
I WONDER HOW HE'S DOING...
CHARGE!
GASP!

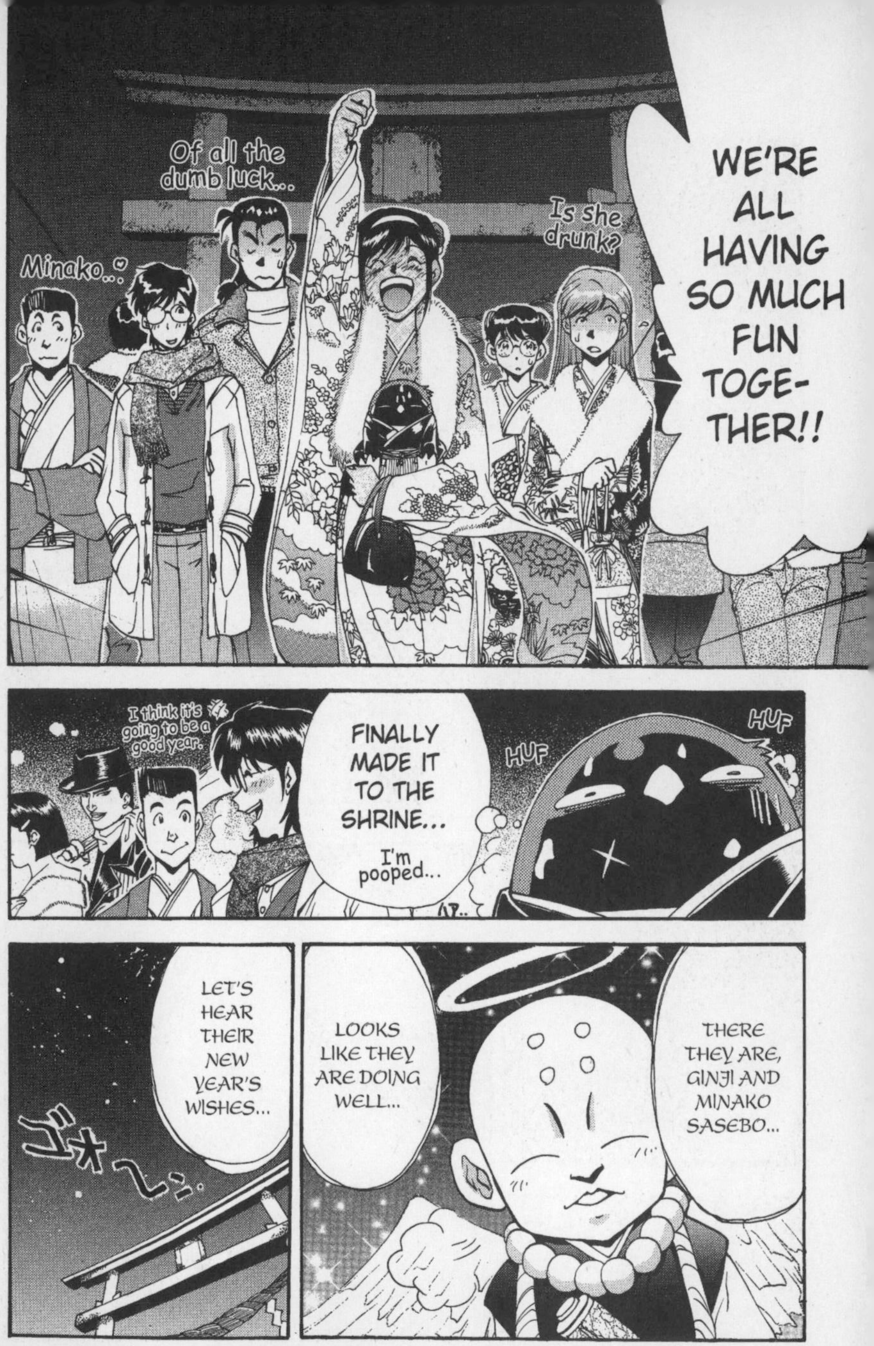
WE'RE ALL HAVING SO MUCH FUN TOGE-THER!!
Is she drunk?
Of all the dumb luck...
Minako..♡
HUF
HUF
FINALLY MADE IT TO THE SHRINE...
I'm pooped...
I think it's going to be a good year.
THERE THEY ARE, GINJI AND MINAKO SASEBO...
LOOKS LIKE THEY ARE DOING WELL...
LET'S HEAR THEIR NEW YEAR'S WISHES...
ゴオ〜ン

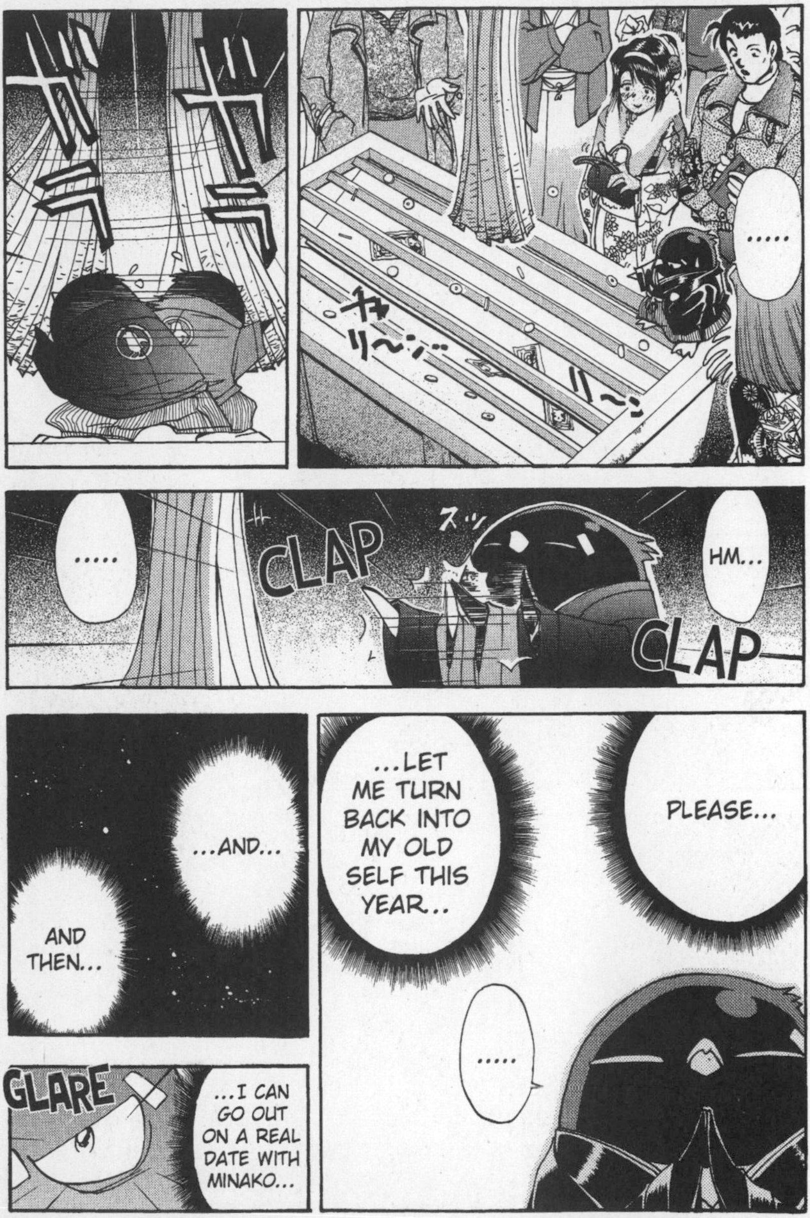
.....
HM...
CLAP
CLAP
.....
PLEASE...
...LET ME TURN BACK INTO MY OLD SELF THIS YEAR...
.....
...AND...
AND THEN...
GLARE
...I CAN GO OUT ON A REAL DATE WITH MINAKO...

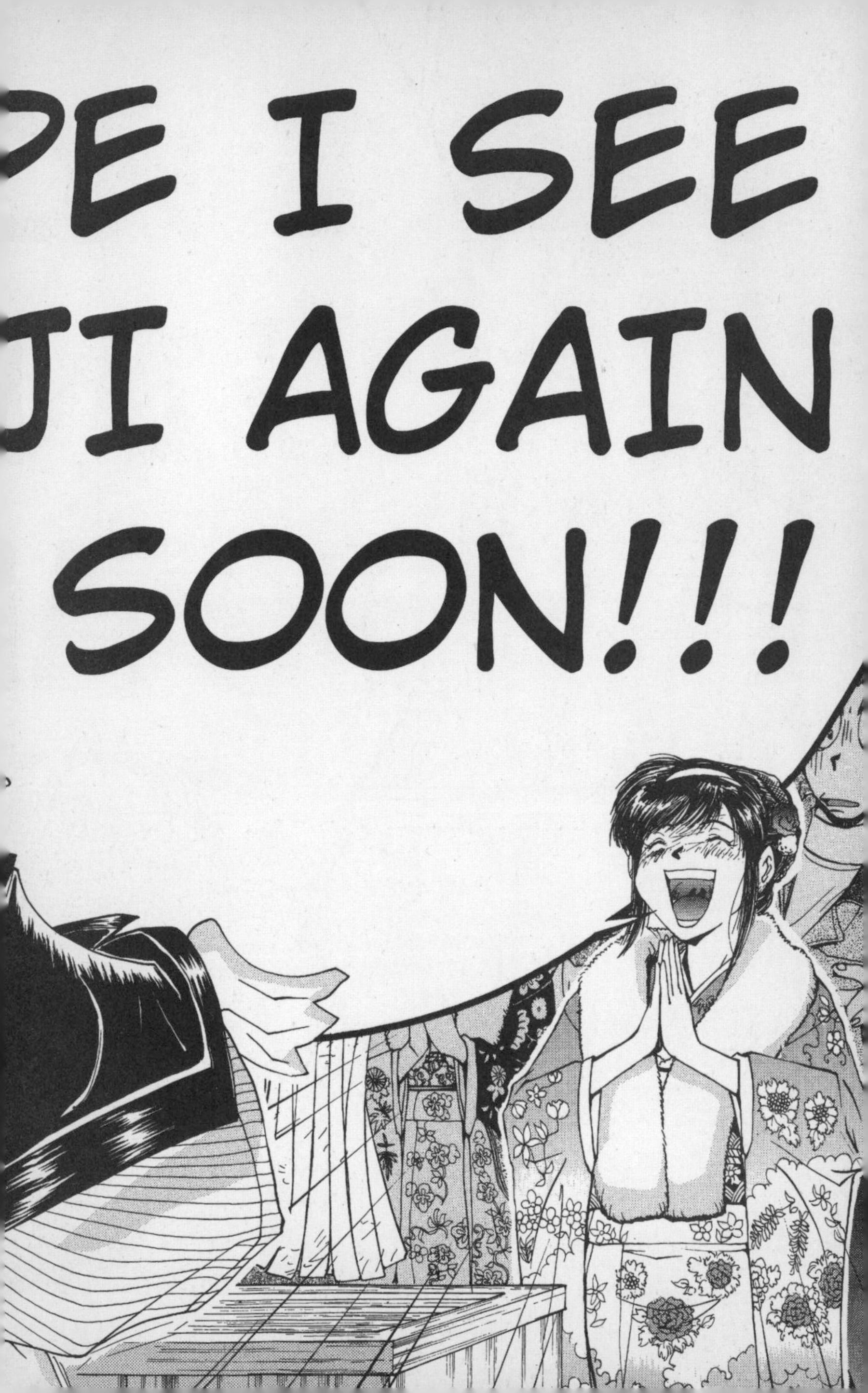
PE I SEE JI AGAIN SOON!!!

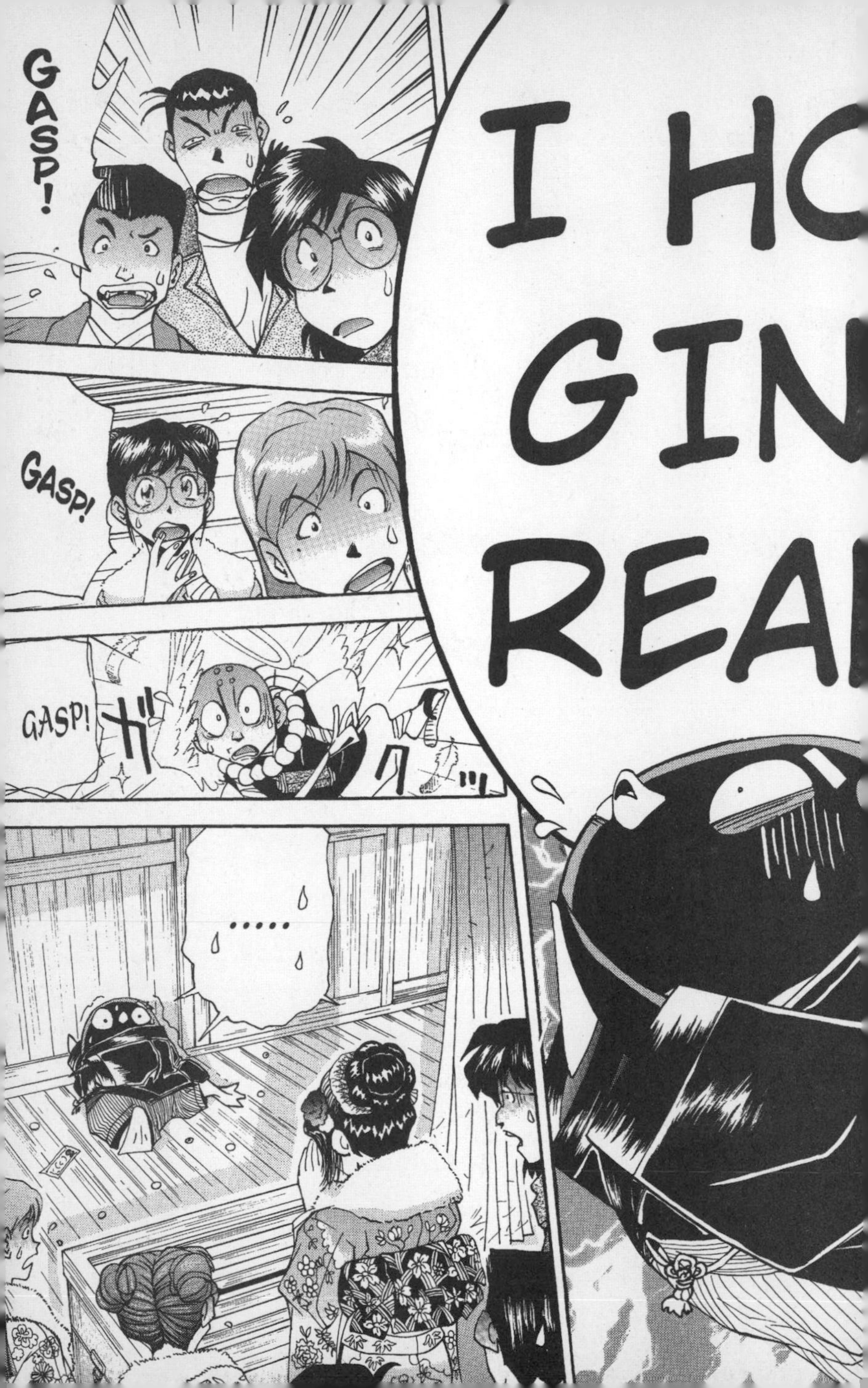
I HO
GIN
REA
GASP!
GASP!
GASP!
ガ!
クッ
.....

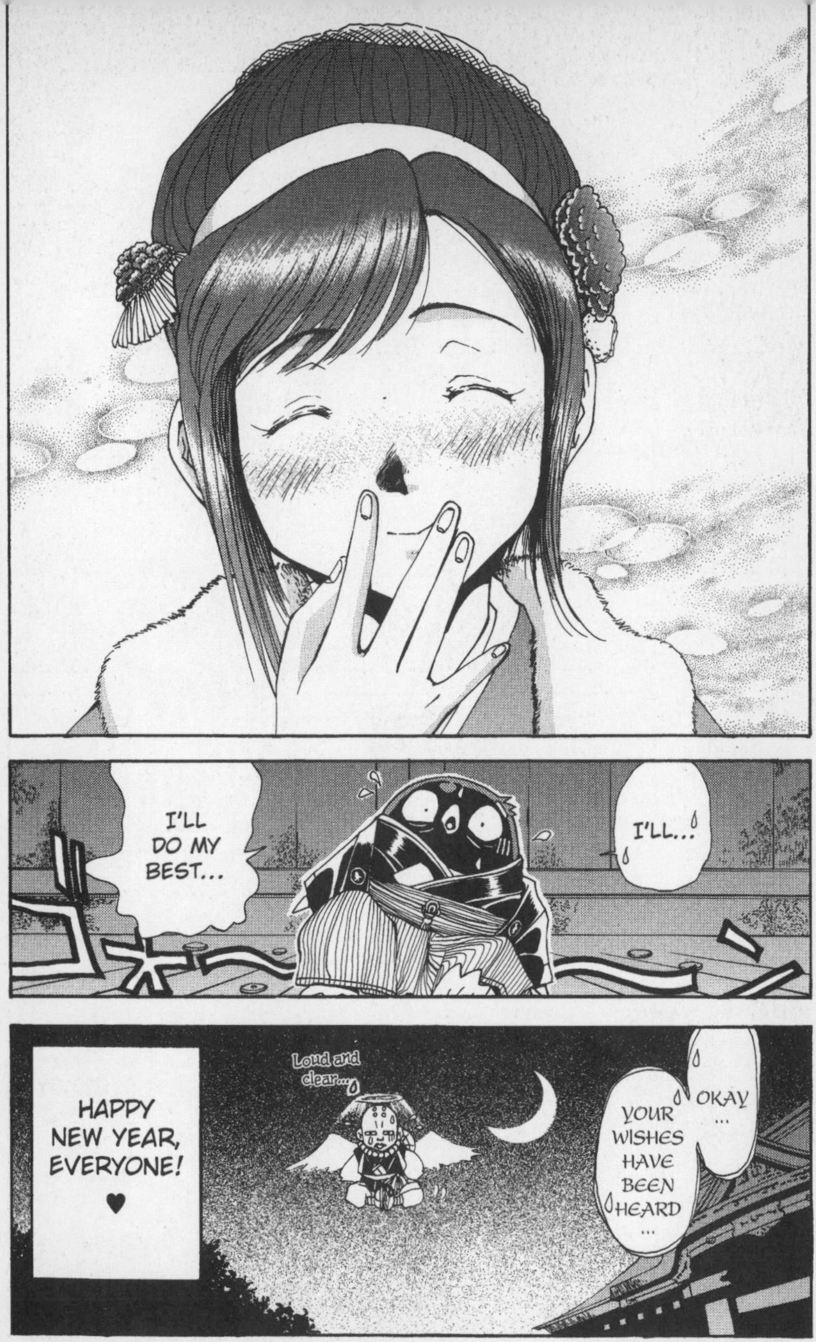
I'LL...!
I'LL DO MY BEST...
OKAY...
YOUR WISHES HAVE BEEN HEARD...
Loud and clear...
HAPPY NEW YEAR, EVERYONE! ♥

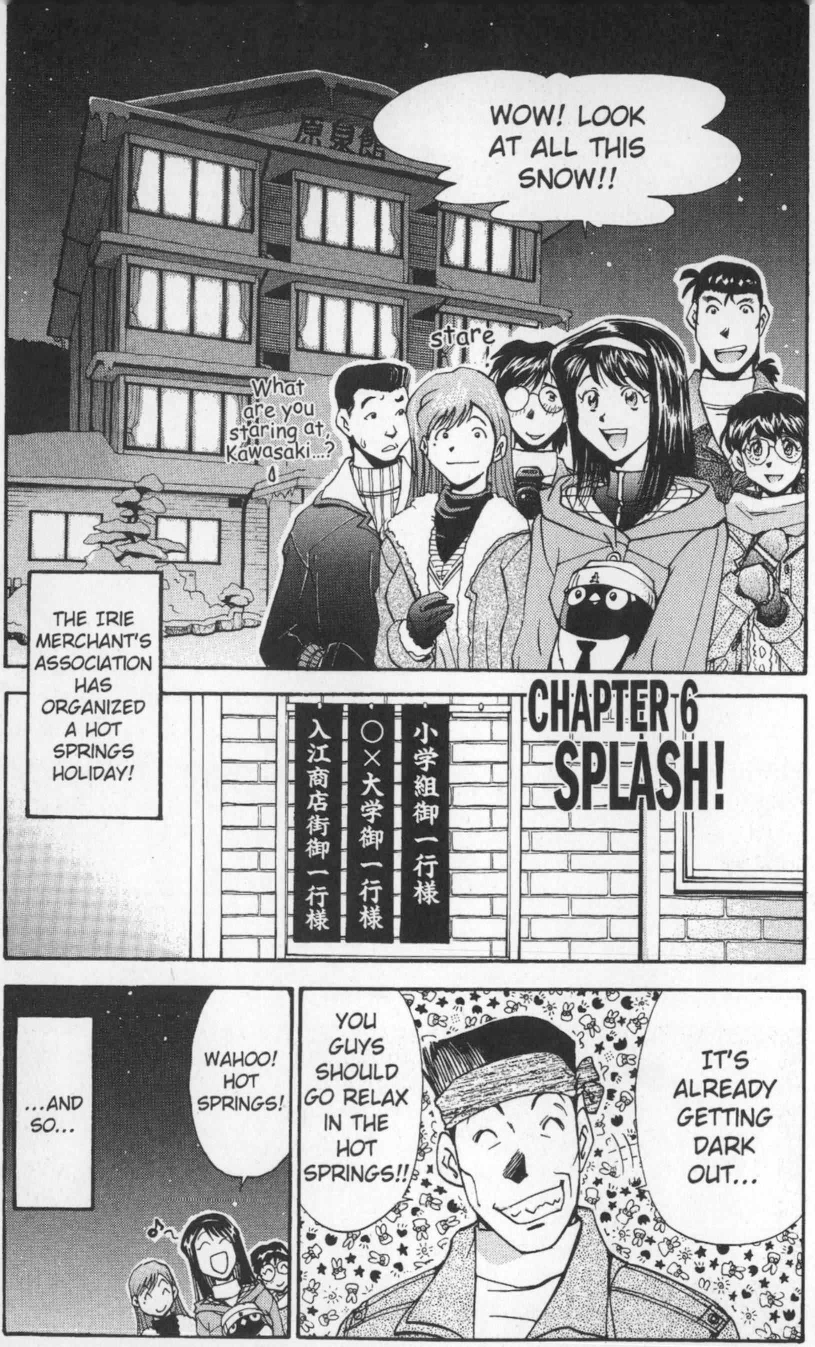
原泉館
WOW! LOOK AT ALL THIS SNOW!!
stare
What are you staring at, Kawasaki...?
THE IRIE MERCHANT'S ASSOCIATION HAS ORGANIZED A HOT SPRINGS HOLIDAY!
CHAPTER 6 SPLASH!
小学組御一行様
○×大学御一行様
入江商店街御一行様
IT'S ALREADY GETTING DARK OUT...
YOU GUYS SHOULD GO RELAX IN THE HOT SPRINGS!!
WAHOO! HOT SPRINGS!
...AND SO...

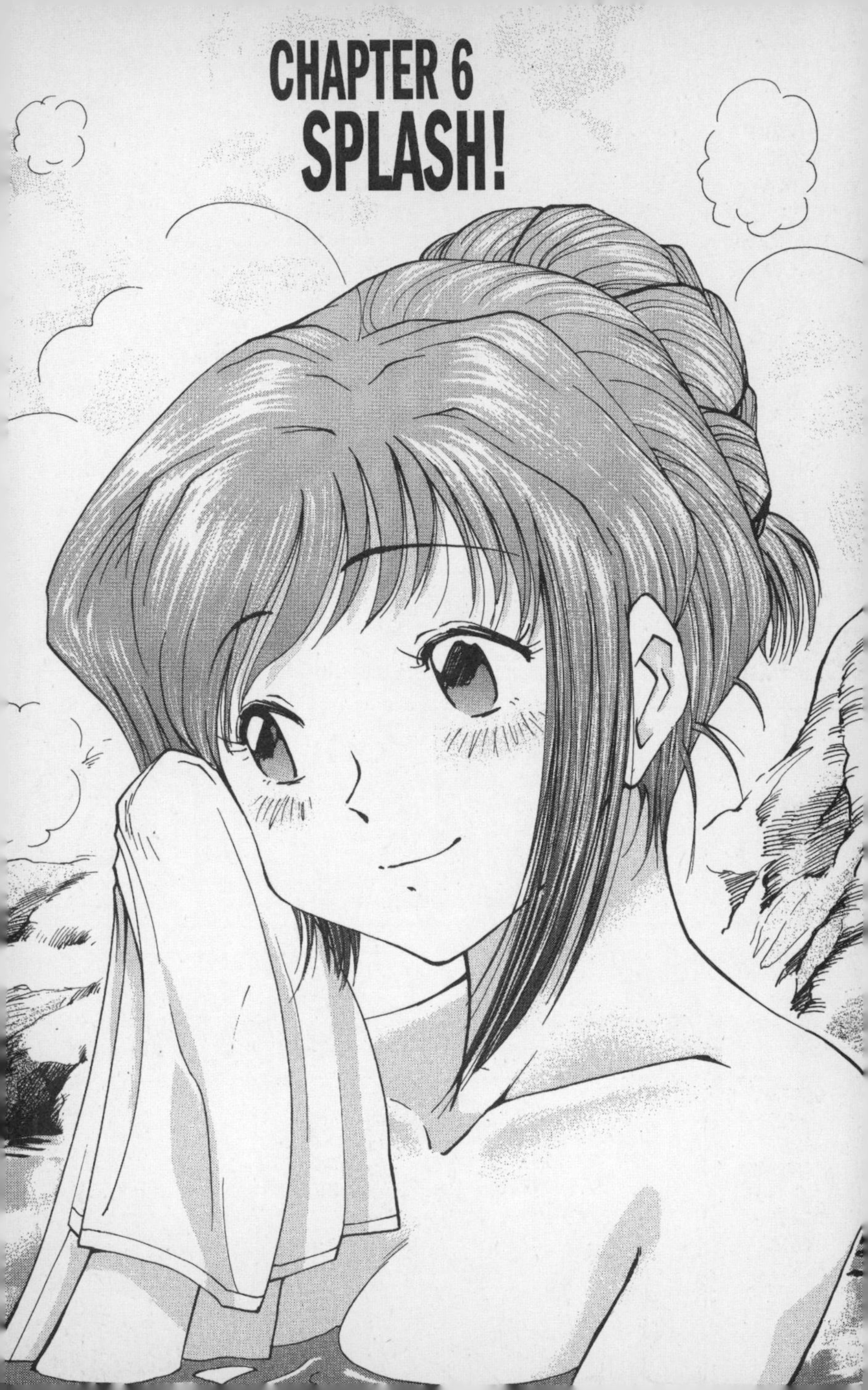
CHAPTER 6
SPLASH!

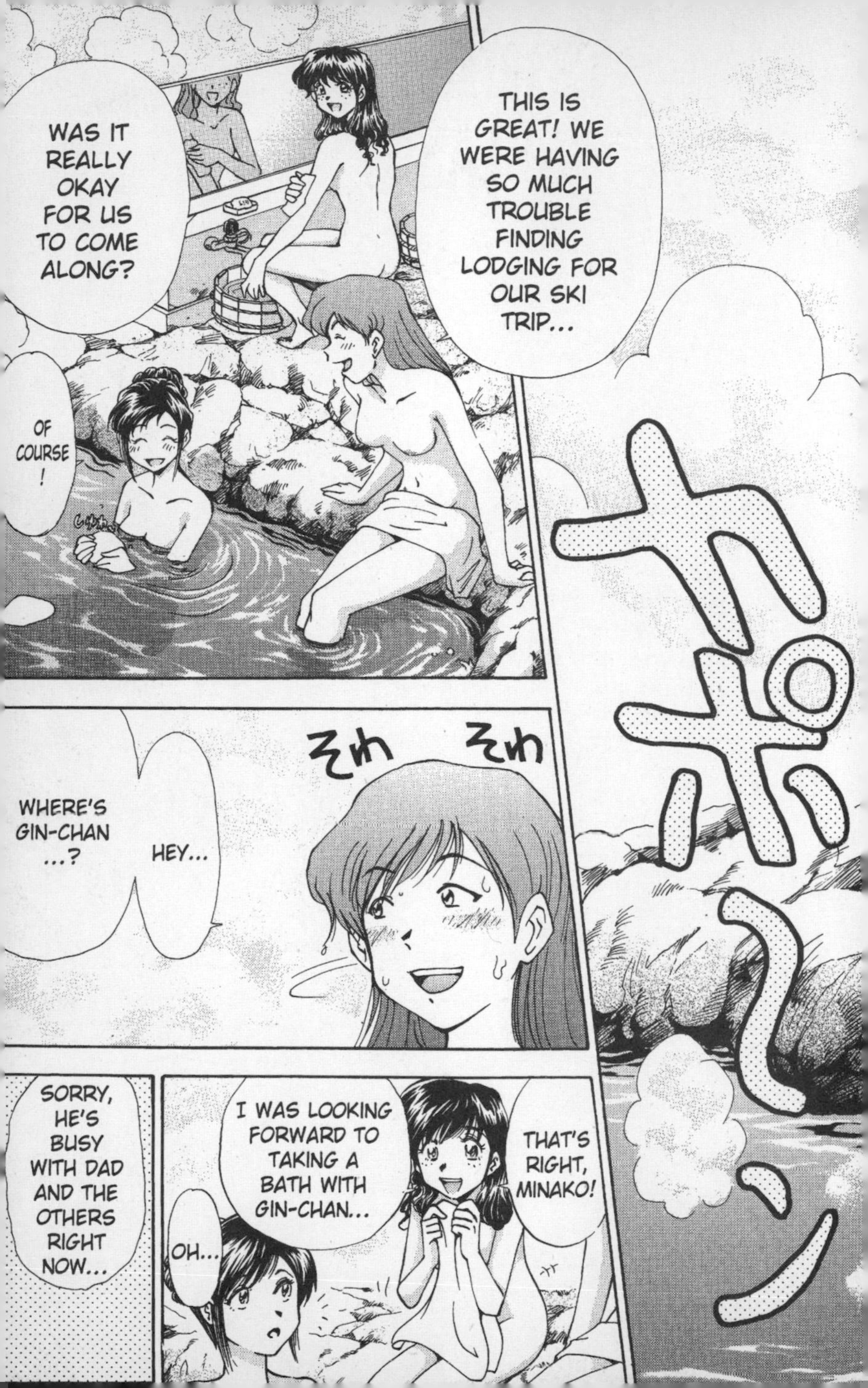
カポーン
THIS IS GREAT! WE WERE HAVING SO MUCH TROUBLE FINDING LODGING FOR OUR SKI TRIP...
WAS IT REALLY OKAY FOR US TO COME ALONG?
OF COURSE!
そわ そわ
HEY...
WHERE'S GIN-CHAN ...?
THAT'S RIGHT, MINAKO!
I WAS LOOKING FORWARD TO TAKING A BATH WITH GIN-CHAN...
OH...
SORRY, HE'S BUSY WITH DAD AND THE OTHERS RIGHT NOW...

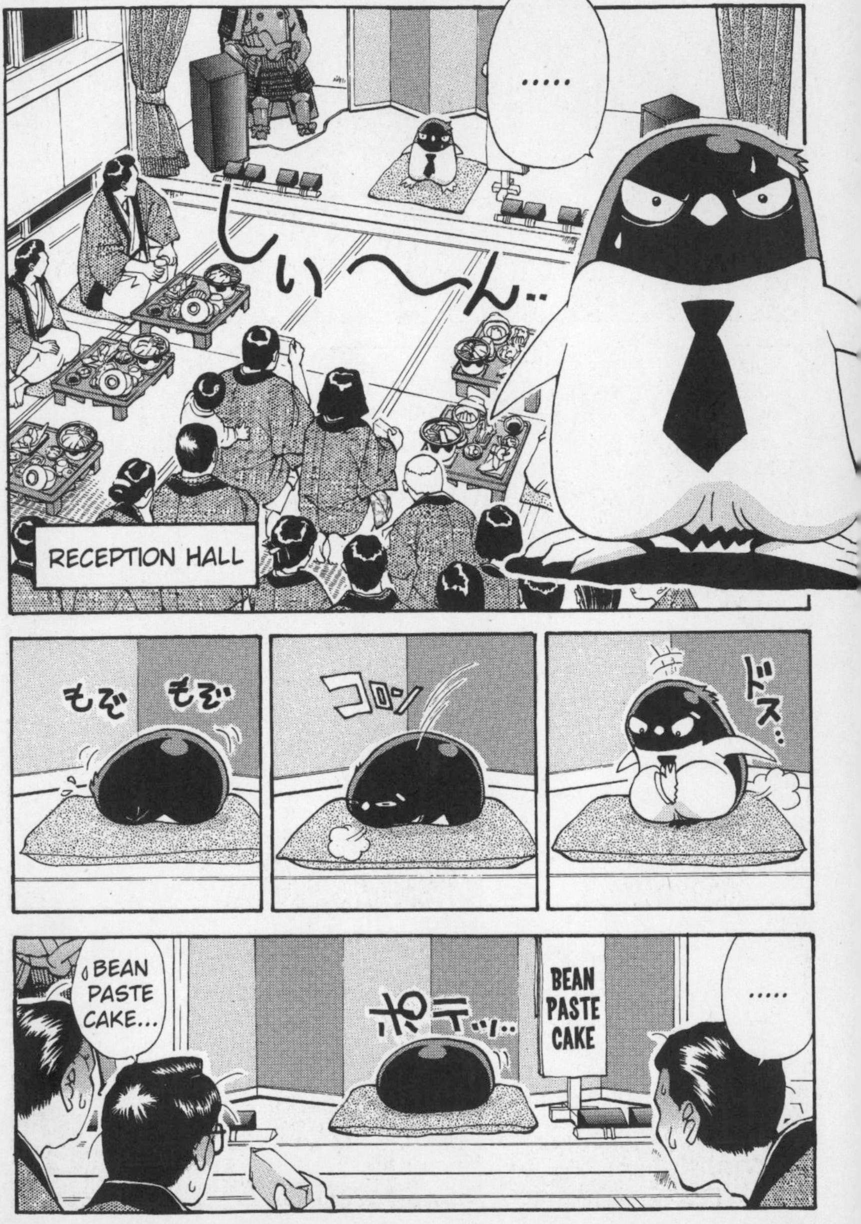
.....
しい〜ん..
RECEPTION HALL
ドス..
コロン
もぞ もぞ
.....
BEAN PASTE CAKE
ポテッ..
BEAN PASTE CAKE...

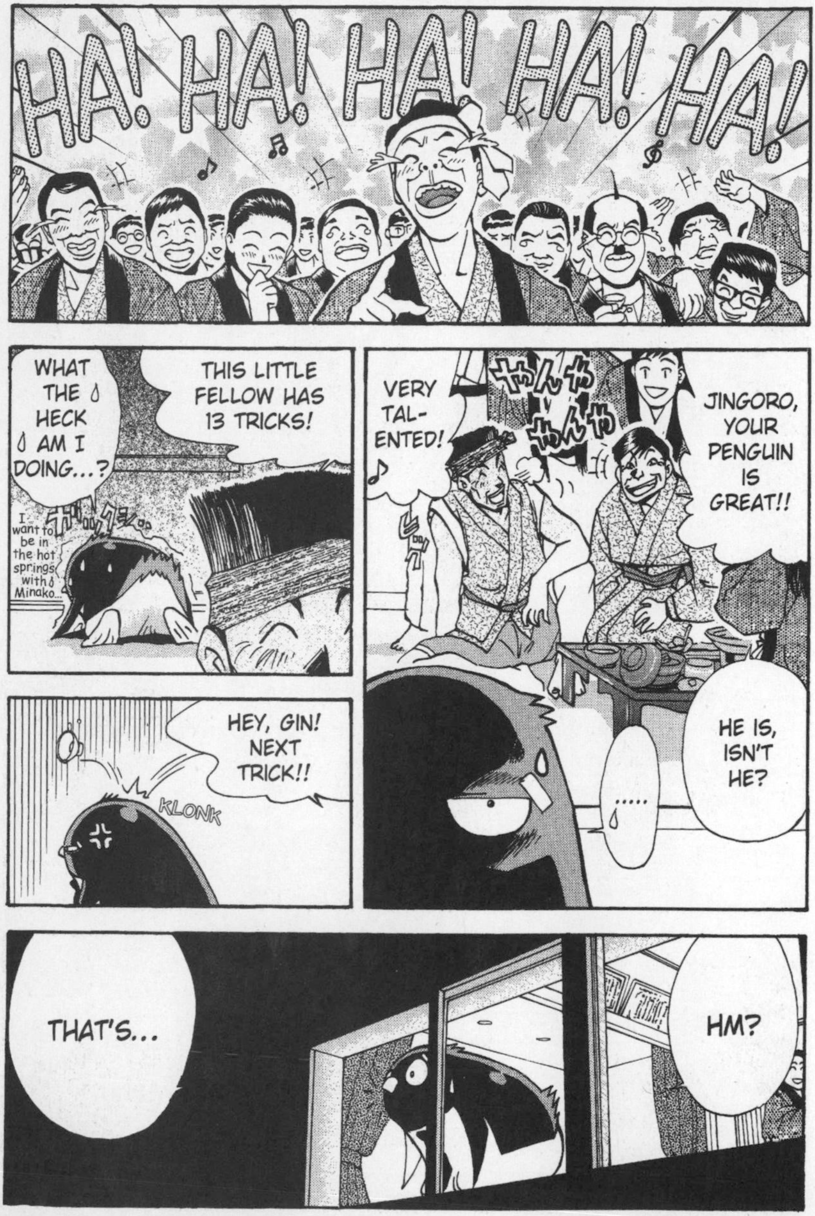
HA! HA! HA! HA! HA!
JINGORO, YOUR PENGUIN IS GREAT!!
やんや やんや
VERY TAL-ENTED!
HE IS, ISN'T HE?
.....
THIS LITTLE FELLOW HAS 13 TRICKS!
WHAT THE HECK AM I DOING...?
I want to be in the hot springs with Minako...
HEY, GIN! NEXT TRICK!!
KLONK
HM?
THAT'S...

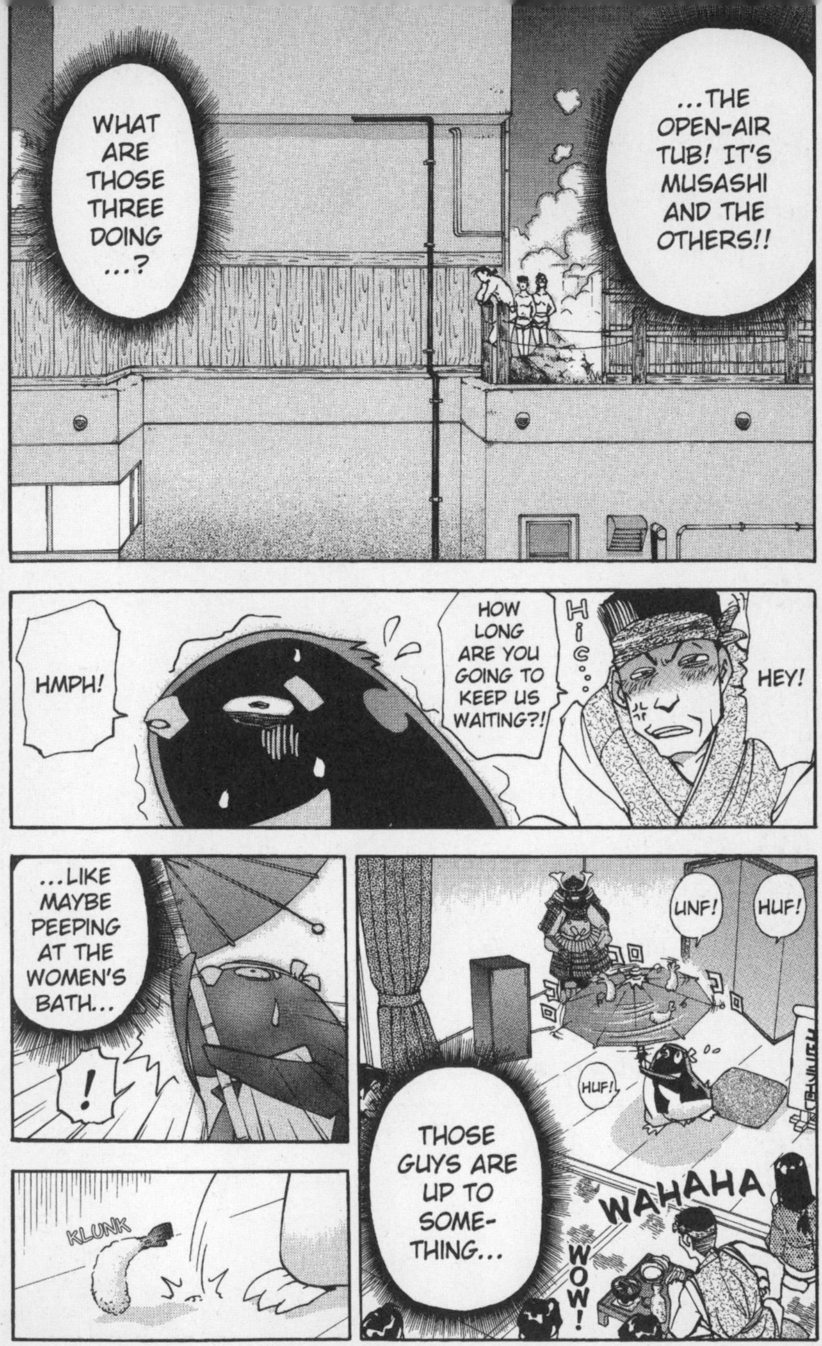
...THE OPEN-AIR TUB! IT'S MUSASHI AND THE OTHERS!!
WHAT ARE THOSE THREE DOING ...?
HEY!
Hic...
HOW LONG ARE YOU GOING TO KEEP US WAITING?!
HMPH!
UNF!
HUF!
HUF!
THOSE GUYS ARE UP TO SOME-THING...
WAHAHA
WOW!
...LIKE MAYBE PEEPING AT THE WOMEN'S BATH...
!
KLUNK

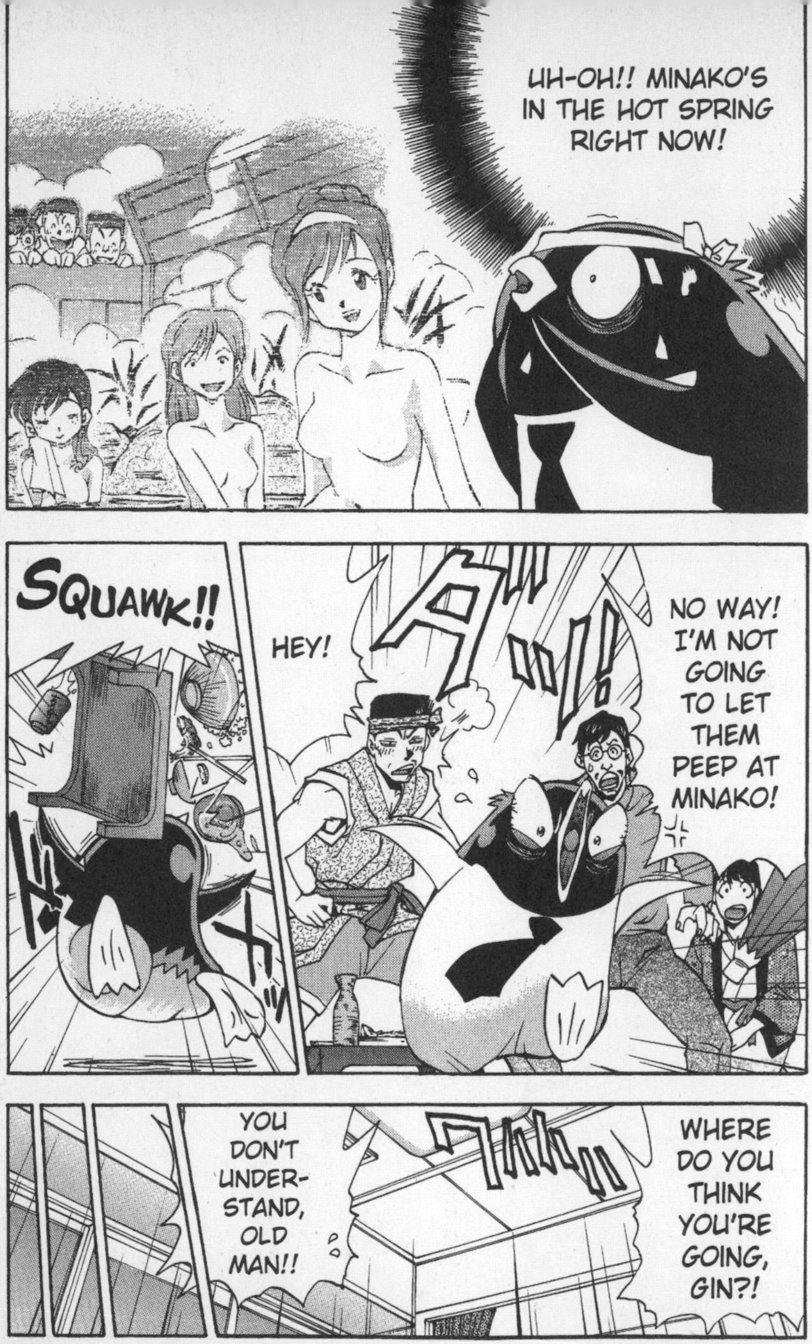
UH-OH!! MINAKO'S IN THE HOT SPRING RIGHT NOW!
NO WAY! I'M NOT GOING TO LET THEM PEEP AT MINAKO!
HEY!
SQUAWK!!
WHERE DO YOU THINK YOU'RE GOING, GIN?!
YOU DON'T UNDER-STAND, OLD MAN!!

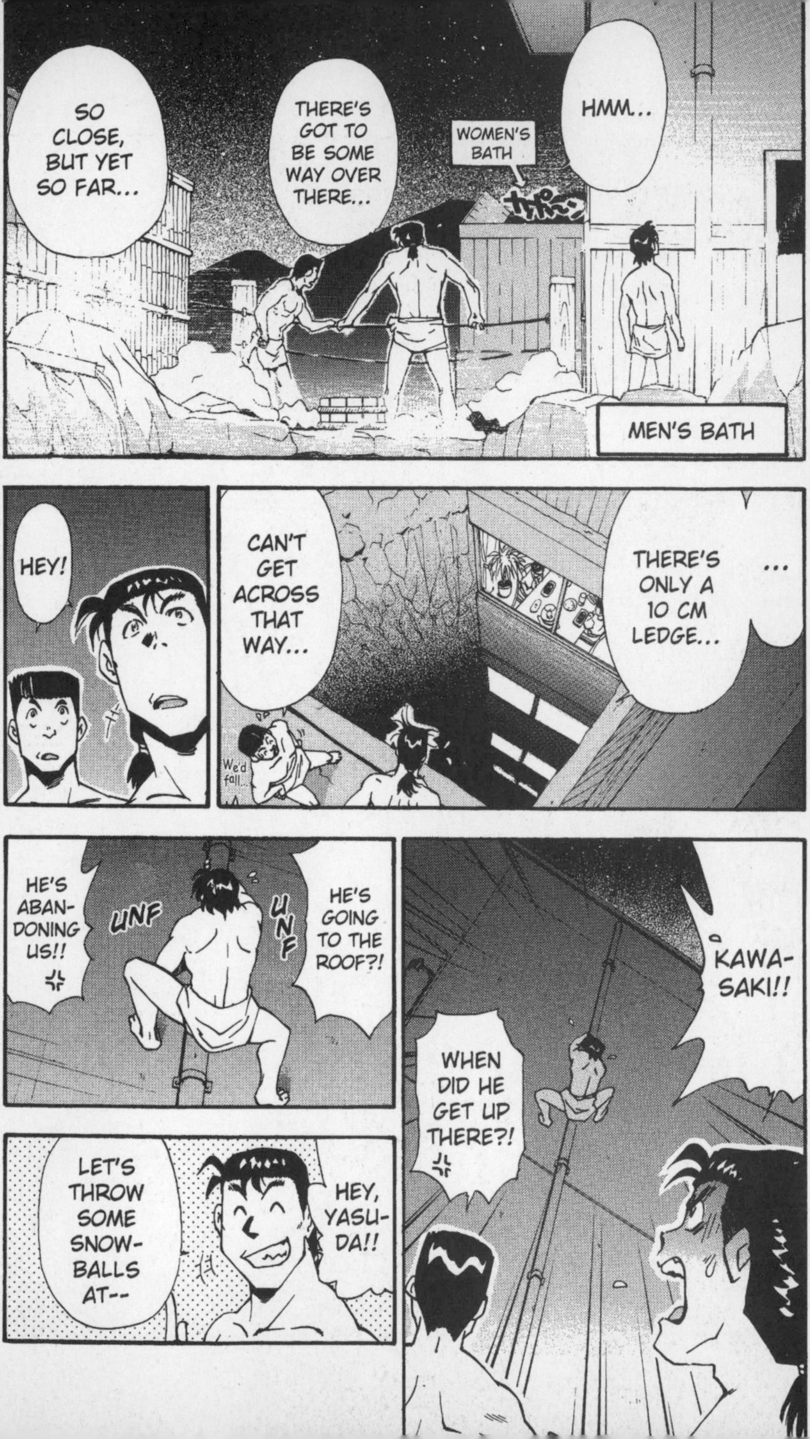
HMM...
WOMEN'S BATH
THERE'S GOT TO BE SOME WAY OVER THERE...
SO CLOSE, BUT YET SO FAR...
MEN'S BATH
...
THERE'S ONLY A 10 CM LEDGE...
CAN'T GET ACROSS THAT WAY...
We'd fall...
HEY!
KAWA-SAKI!!
WHEN DID HE GET UP THERE?!
HE'S GOING TO THE ROOF?!
UNF
UNF
HE'S ABAN-DONING US!!
HEY, YASU-DA!!
LET'S THROW SOME SNOW-BALLS AT--

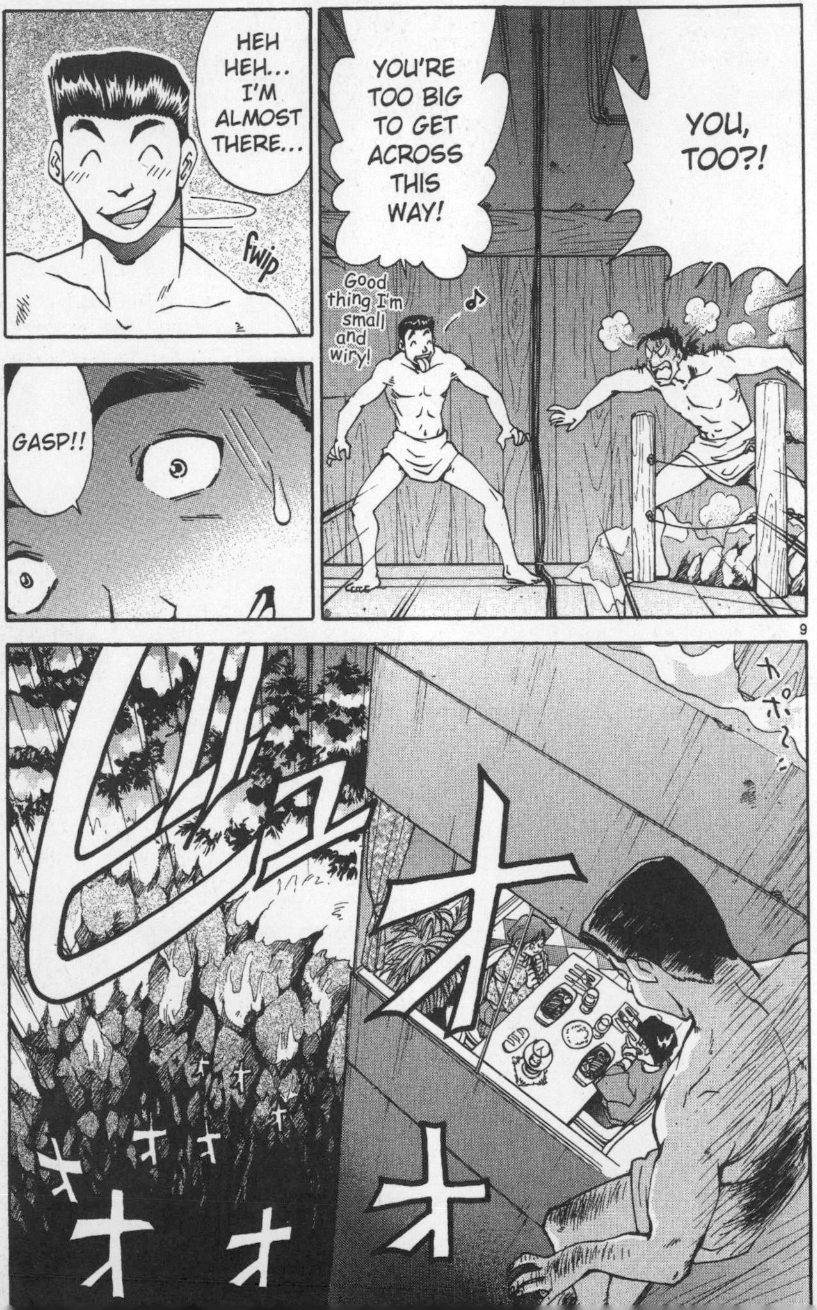
YOU, TOO?!
YOU'RE TOO BIG TO GET ACROSS THIS WAY!
Good thing I'm small and wiry!
HEH HEH... I'M ALMOST THERE...
fwip
GASP!!

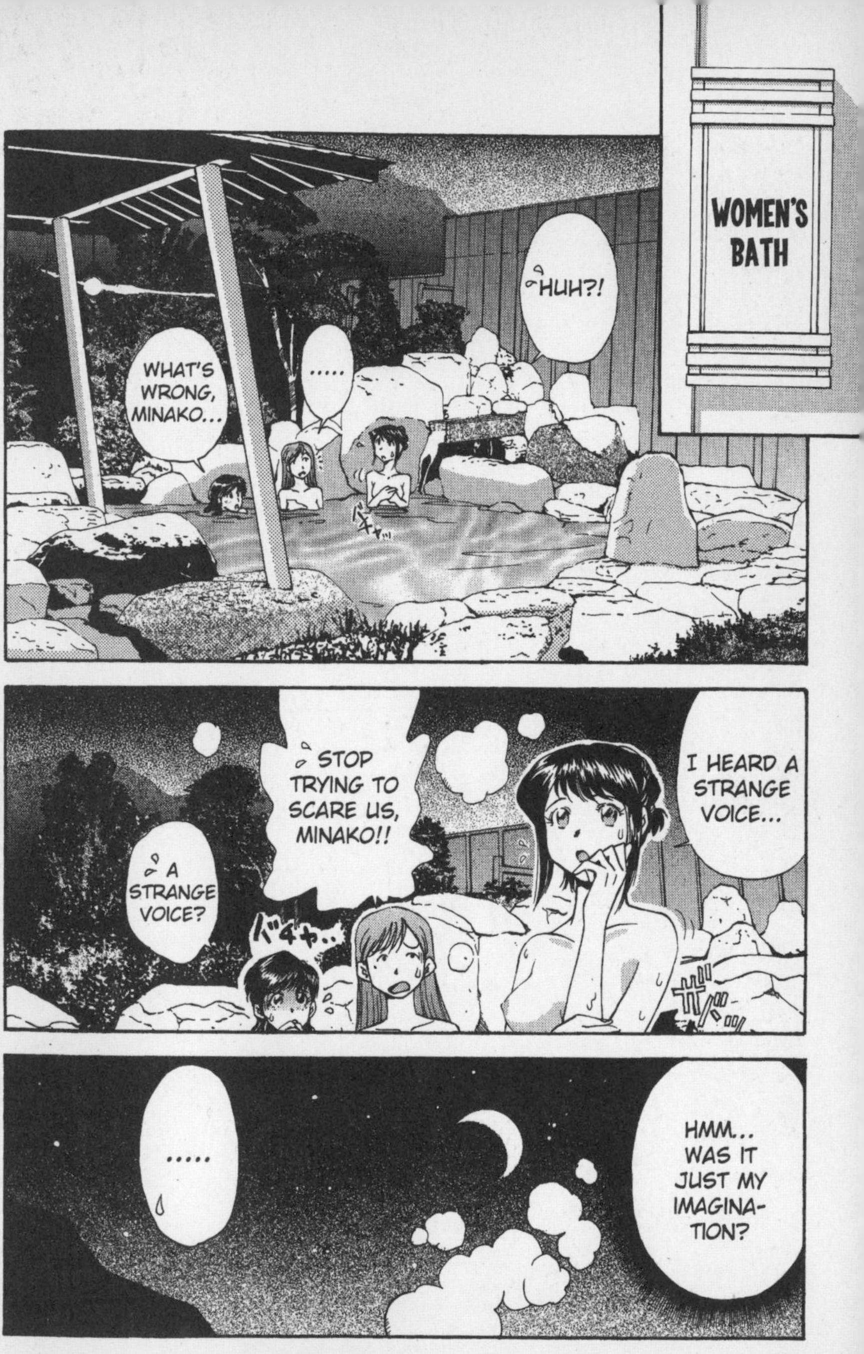
WOMEN'S BATH
HUH?!
.....
WHAT'S WRONG, MINAKO...
I HEARD A STRANGE VOICE...
STOP TRYING TO SCARE US, MINAKO!!
A STRANGE VOICE?
HMM... WAS IT JUST MY IMAGINATION?
.....

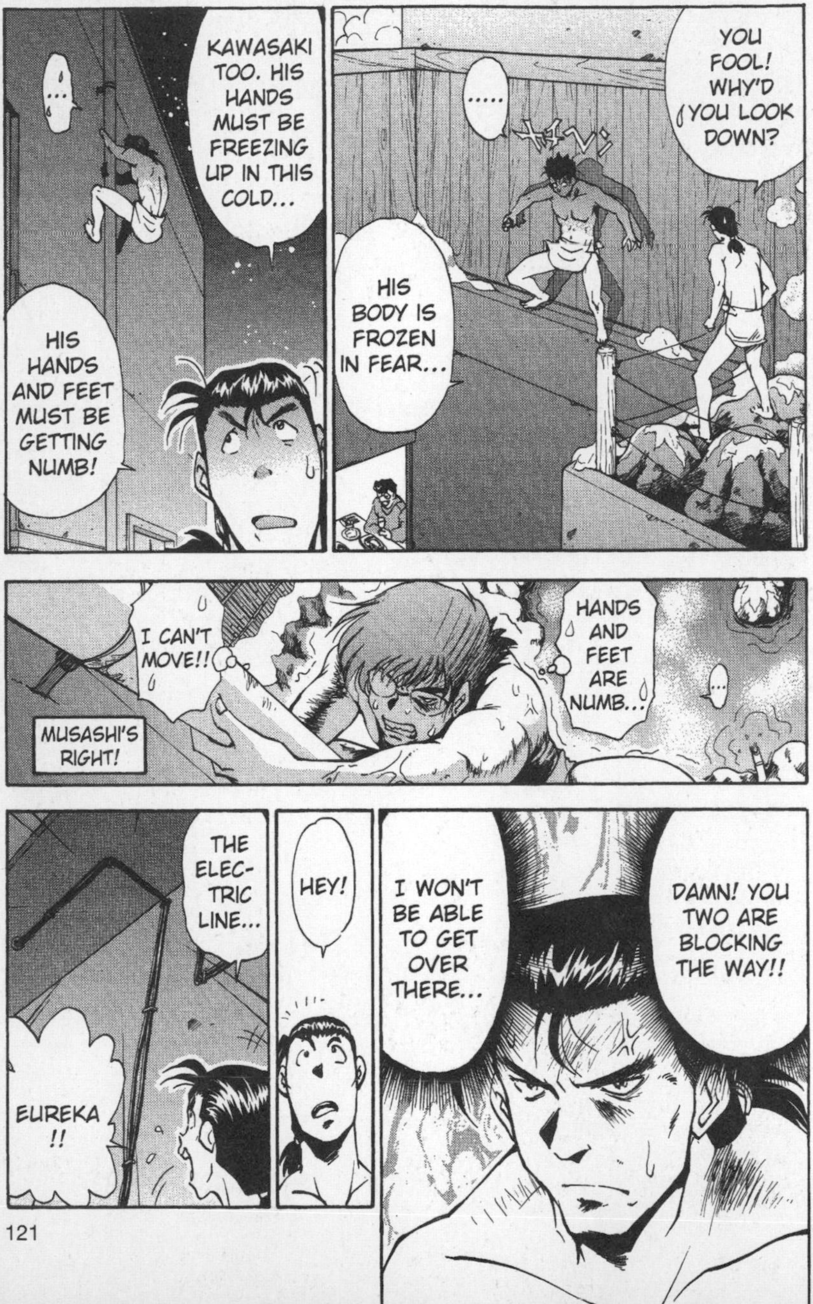
YOU FOOL! WHY'D YOU LOOK DOWN?
.....
HIS BODY IS FROZEN IN FEAR...
KAWASAKI TOO. HIS HANDS MUST BE FREEZING UP IN THIS COLD...
...
HIS HANDS AND FEET MUST BE GETTING NUMB!
HANDS AND FEET ARE NUMB...
...
I CAN'T MOVE!!
MUSASHI'S RIGHT!
DAMN! YOU TWO ARE BLOCKING THE WAY!!
I WON'T BE ABLE TO GET OVER THERE...
HEY!
THE ELEC-TRIC LINE...
EUREKA !!

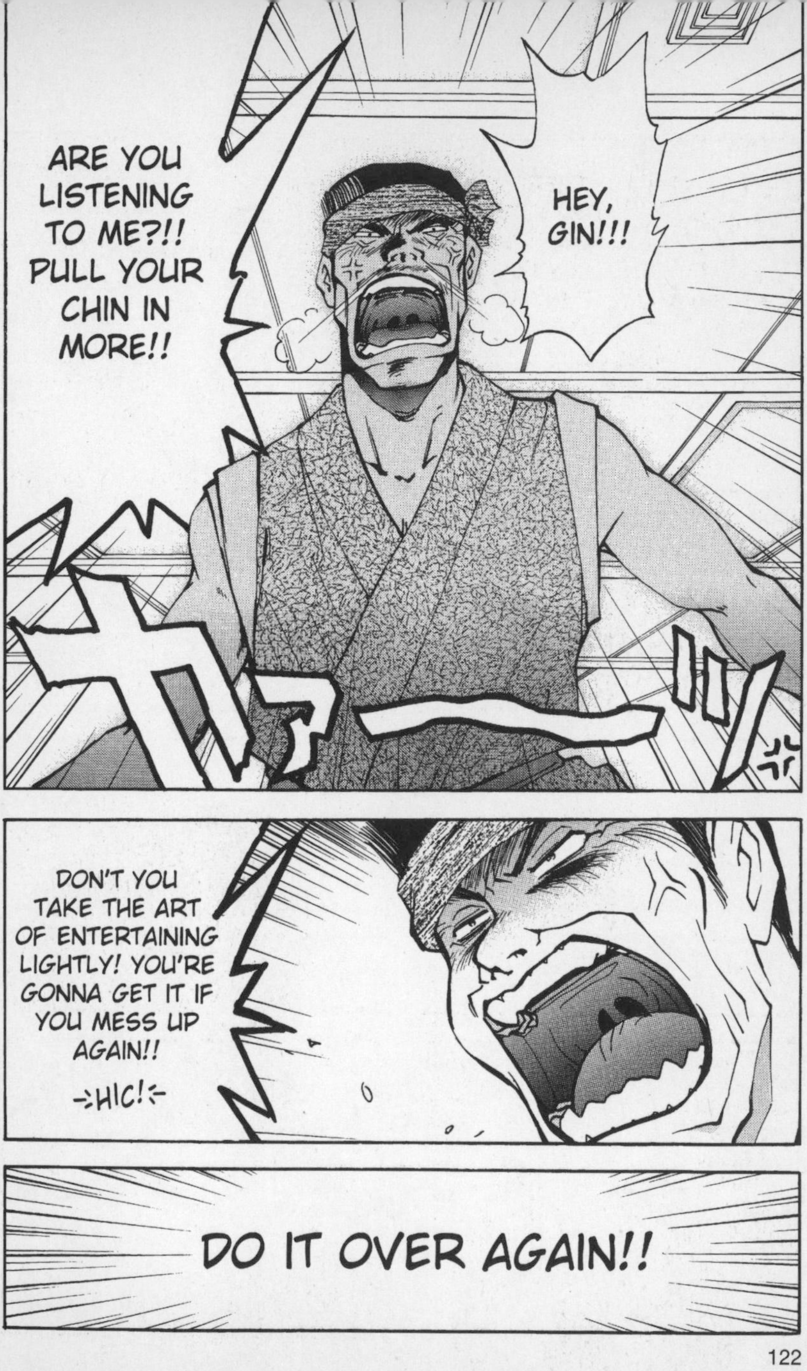
HEY, GIN!!!
ARE YOU LISTENING TO ME?!! PULL YOUR CHIN IN MORE!!
カァーッ
DON'T YOU TAKE THE ART OF ENTERTAINING LIGHTLY! YOU'RE GONNA GET IT IF YOU MESS UP AGAIN!!
-HIC!-
DO IT OVER AGAIN!!

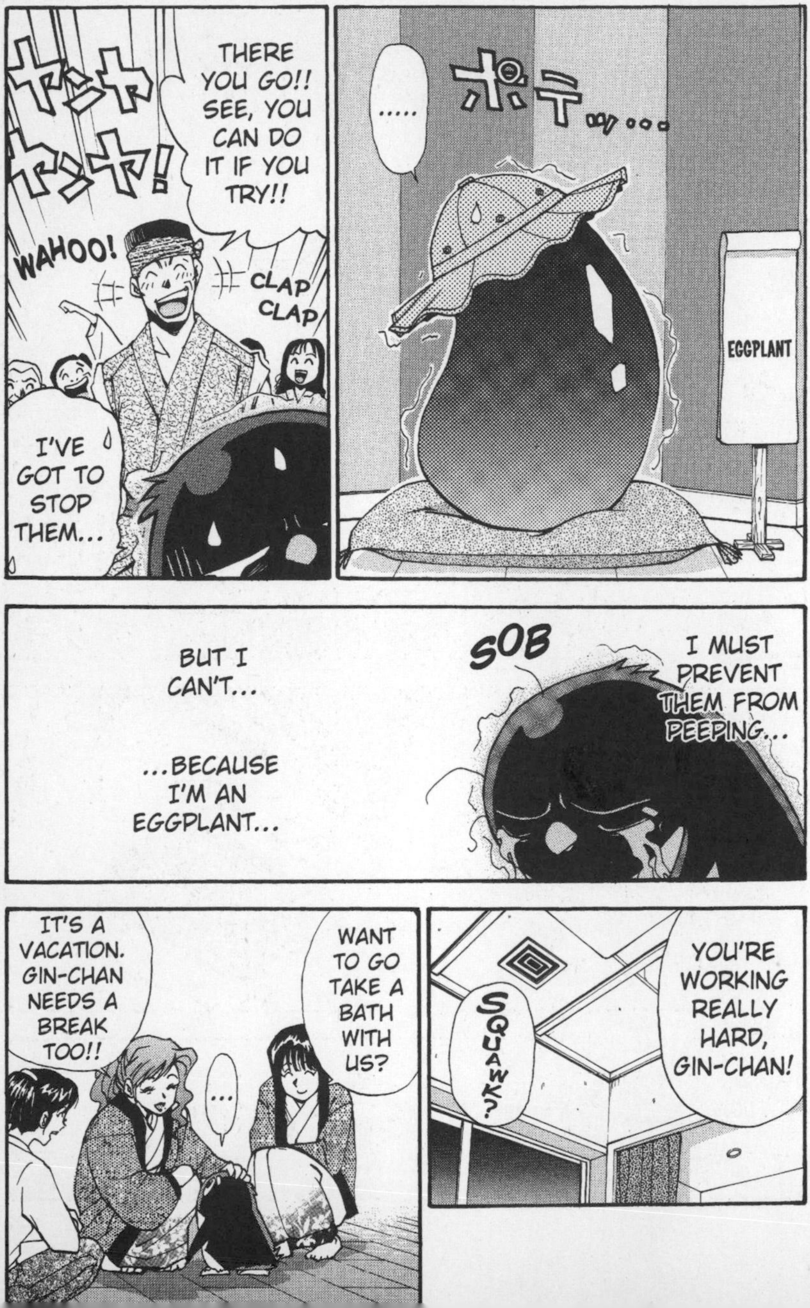
.....
ポテッ…
EGGPLANT
ヤンヤヤンヤ!
THERE YOU GO!! SEE, YOU CAN DO IT IF YOU TRY!!
WAHOO!
CLAP CLAP
I'VE GOT TO STOP THEM...
I MUST PREVENT THEM FROM PEEPING...
SOB
BUT I CAN'T...
...BECAUSE I'M AN EGGPLANT...
YOU'RE WORKING REALLY HARD, GIN-CHAN!
SQUAWK?
WANT TO GO TAKE A BATH WITH US?
...
IT'S A VACATION. GIN-CHAN NEEDS A BREAK TOO!!

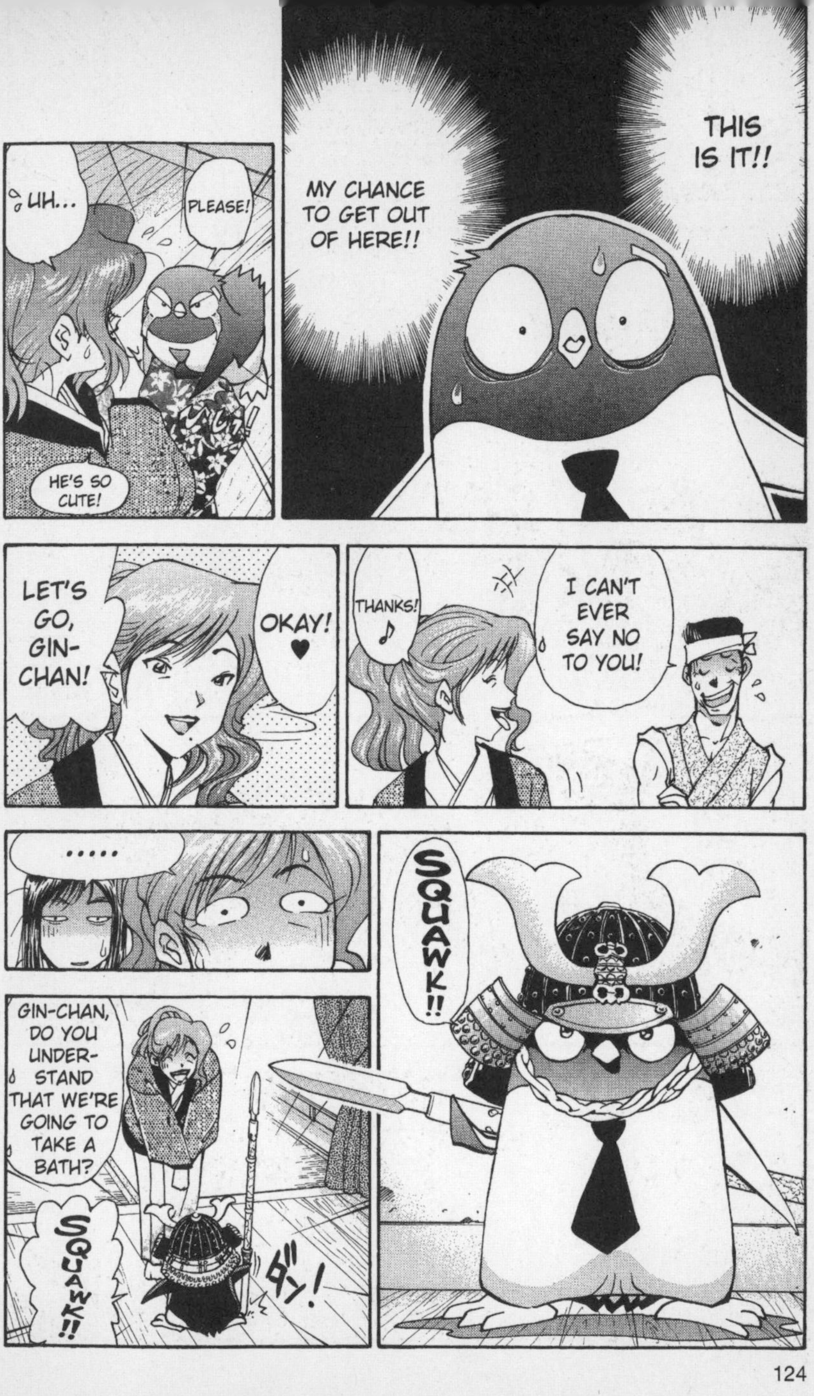

THIS IS IT!!
MY CHANCE TO GET OUT OF HERE!!
PLEASE!
UH...
HE'S SO CUTE!
I CAN'T EVER SAY NO TO YOU!
THANKS! ♪
OKAY! ♥
LET'S GO, GIN-CHAN!
SQUAWK!!
.....
GIN-CHAN, DO YOU UNDERSTAND THAT WE'RE GOING TO TAKE A BATH?
ダッ!
SQUAWK!!

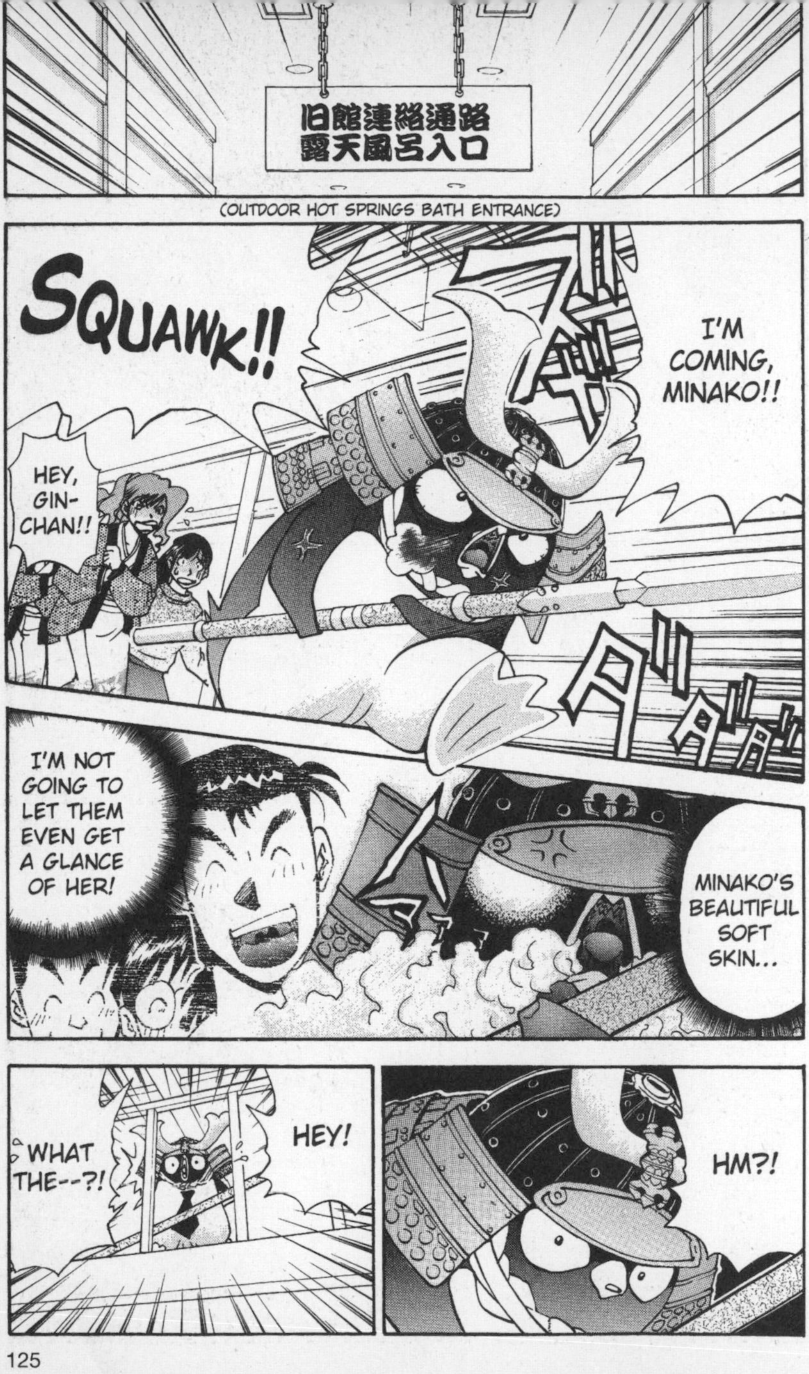
旧館連絡通路
露天風呂入口
(OUTDOOR HOT SPRINGS BATH ENTRANCE)
I'M COMING, MINAKO!!
SQUAWK!!
HEY, GIN-CHAN!!
MINAKO'S BEAUTIFUL SOFT SKIN...
I'M NOT GOING TO LET THEM EVEN GET A GLANCE OF HER!
HM?!
HEY!
WHAT THE--?!

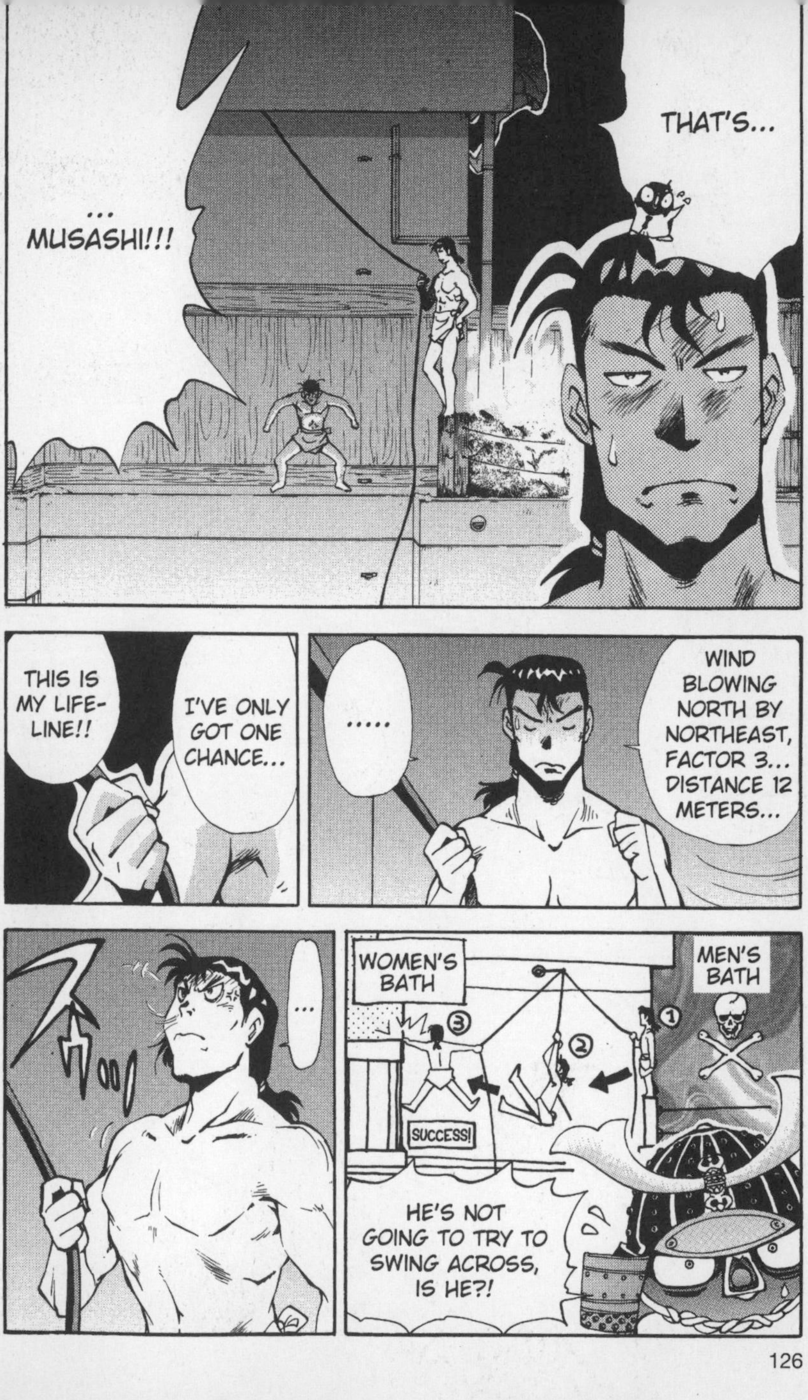
THAT'S...
... MUSASHI!!!
WIND BLOWING NORTH BY NORTHEAST, FACTOR 3... DISTANCE 12 METERS...
.....
I'VE ONLY GOT ONE CHANCE...
THIS IS MY LIFE-LINE!!
MEN'S BATH
WOMEN'S BATH
SUCCESS!
HE'S NOT GOING TO TRY TO SWING ACROSS, IS HE?!
...

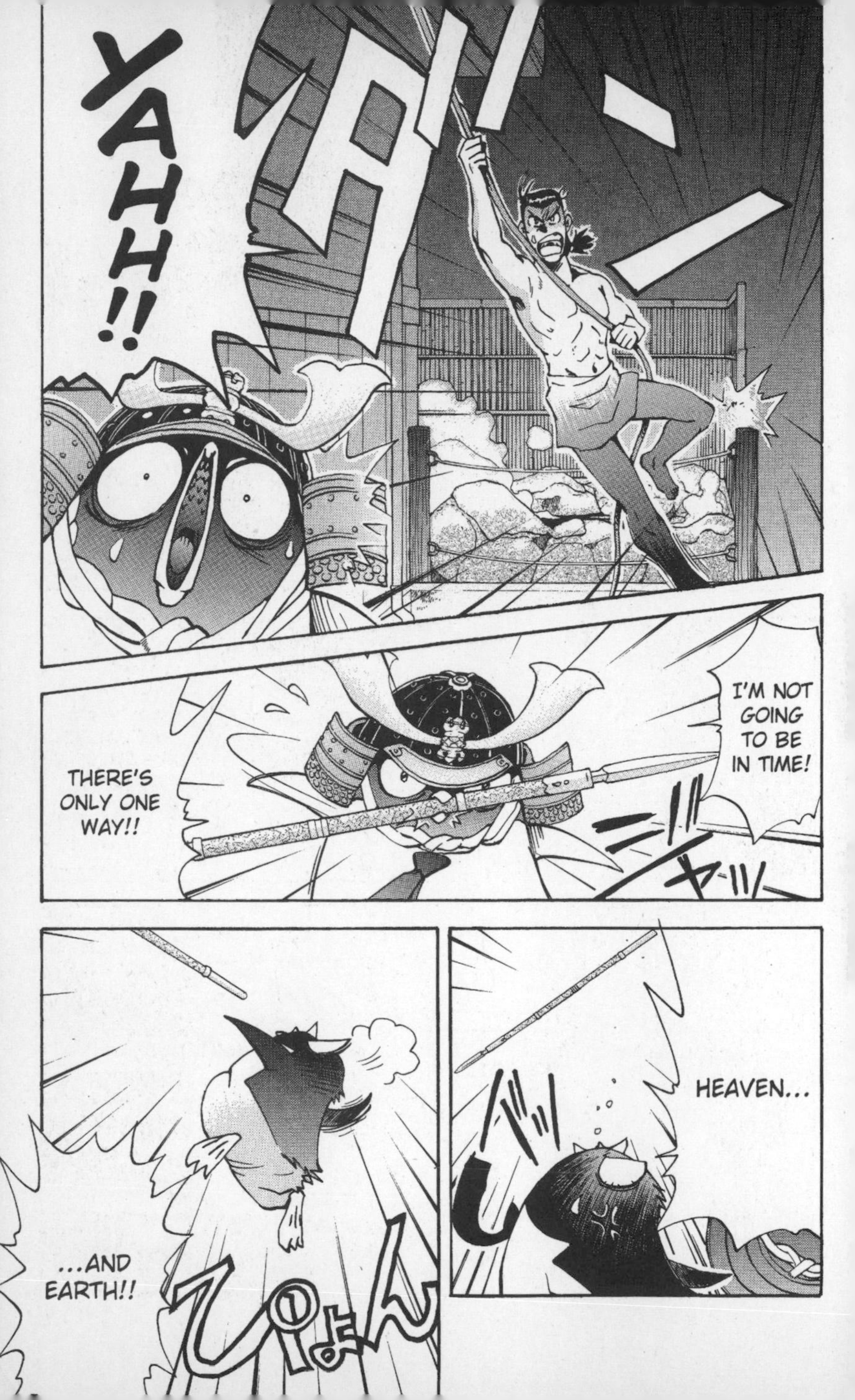
YAHHH!!
I'M NOT GOING TO BE IN TIME!
THERE'S ONLY ONE WAY!!
HEAVEN...
...AND EARTH!!

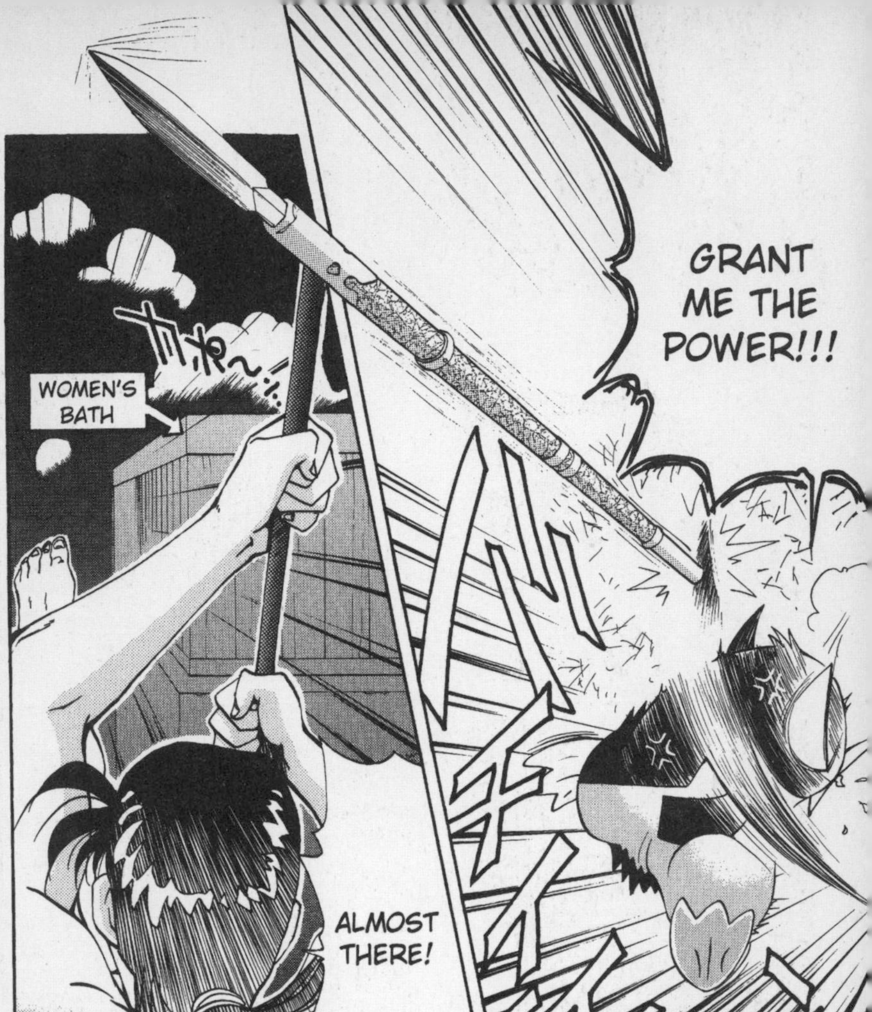
GRANT ME THE POWER!!!
WOMEN'S BATH
ALMOST THERE!

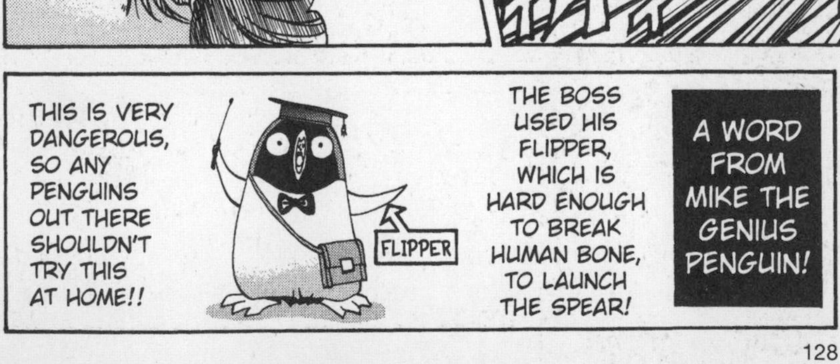
A WORD FROM MIKE THE GENIUS PENGUIN!
THE BOSS USED HIS FLIPPER, WHICH IS HARD ENOUGH TO BREAK HUMAN BONE, TO LAUNCH THE SPEAR!
FLIPPER
THIS IS VERY DANGEROUS, SO ANY PENGUINS OUT THERE SHOULDN'T TRY THIS AT HOME!!

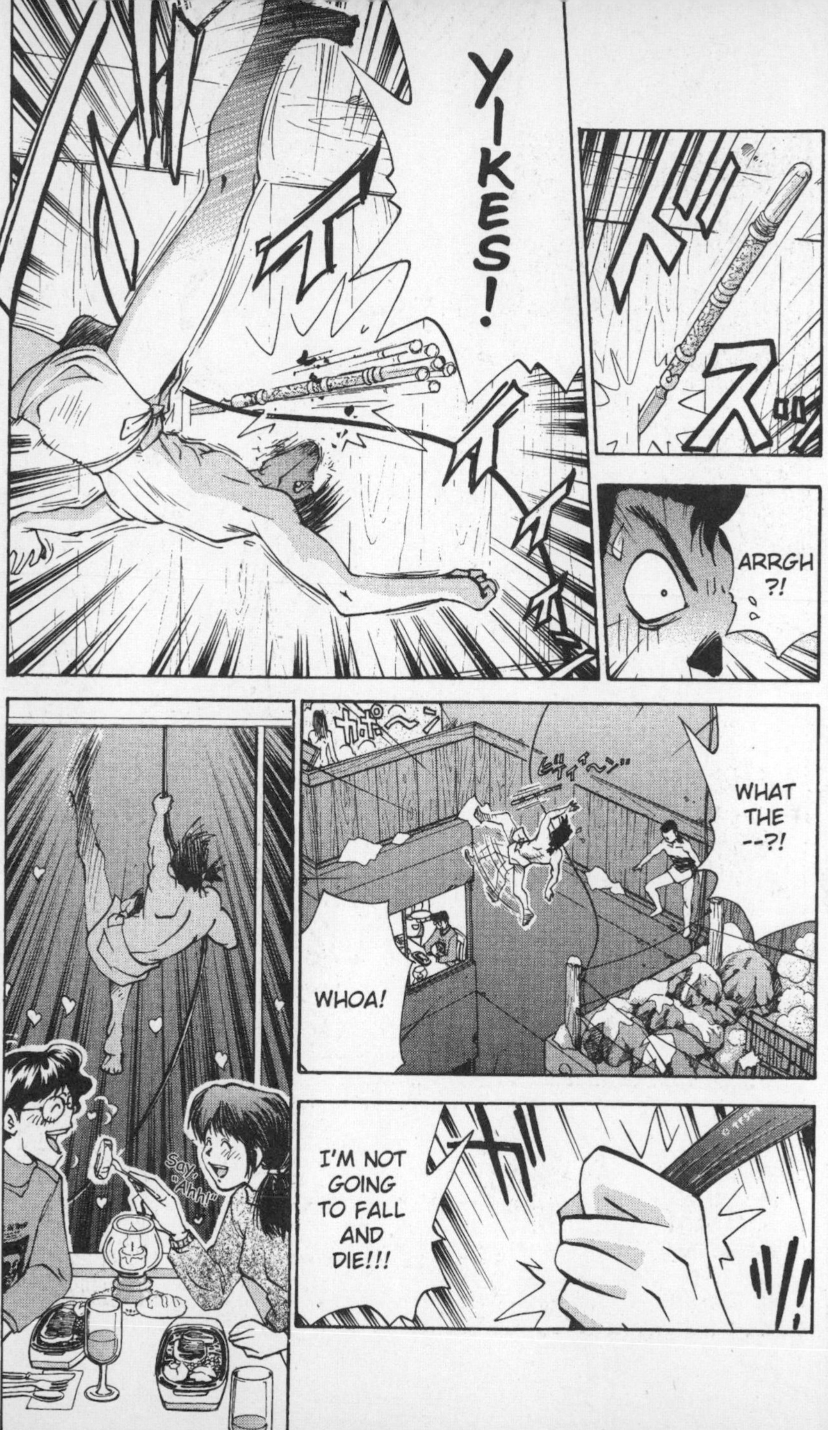
ARRGH ?!
YIKES!
WHAT THE --?!
WHOA!
I'M NOT GOING TO FALL AND DIE!!!
Say, "Ahh!"

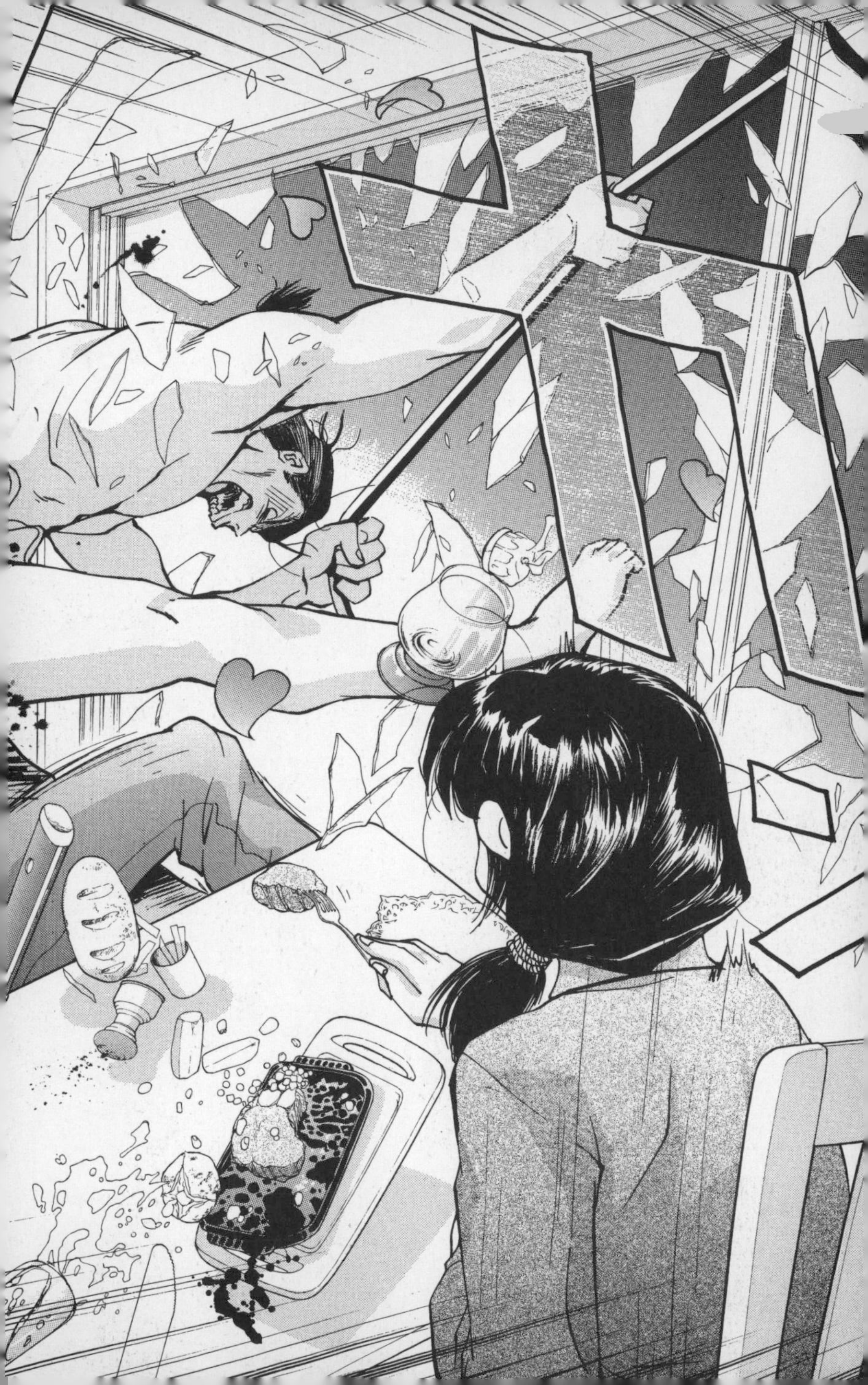

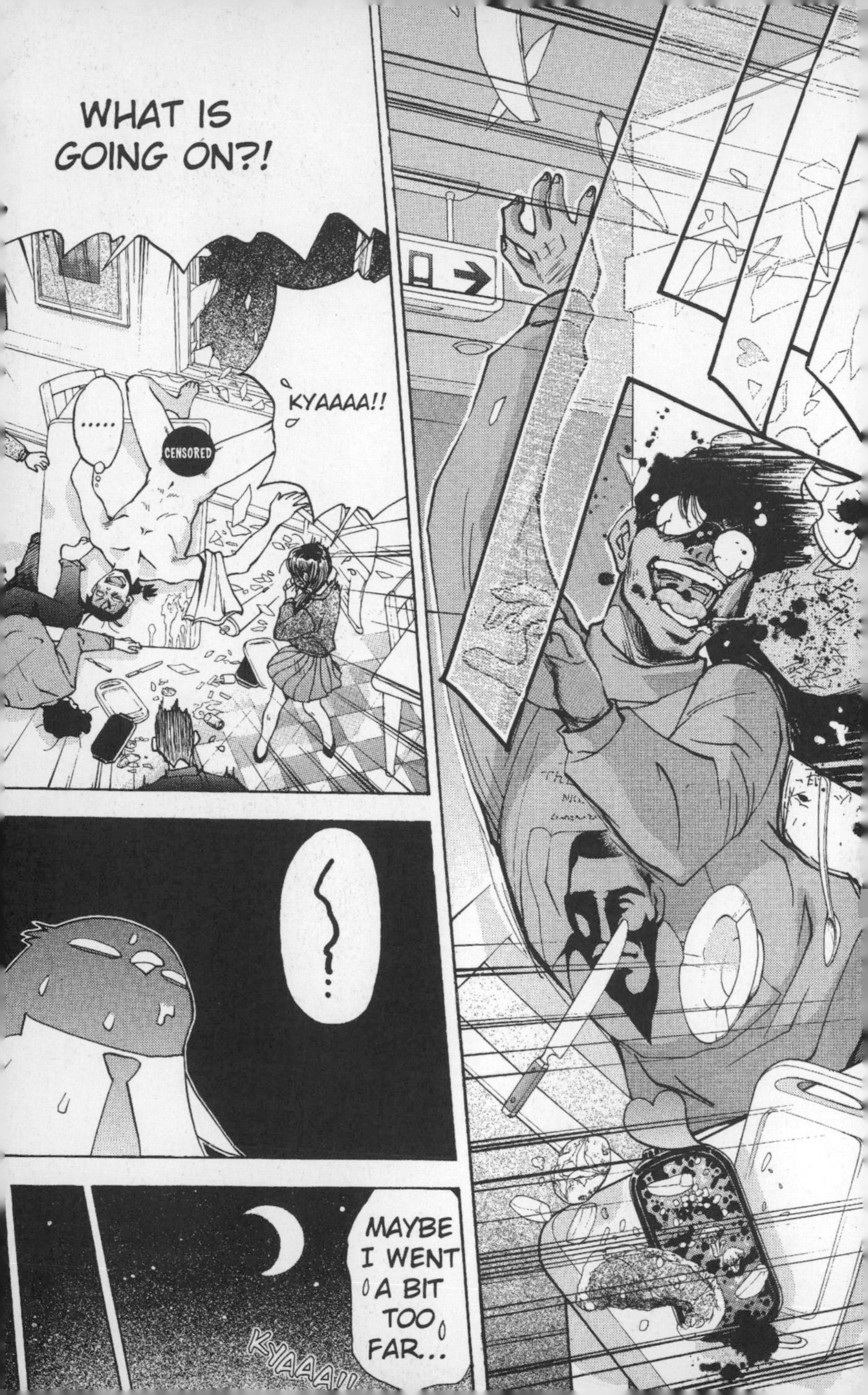
WHAT IS GOING ON?!
KYAAAA!!
......
CENSORED
MAYBE I WENT A BIT TOO FAR...
KYAAA!!

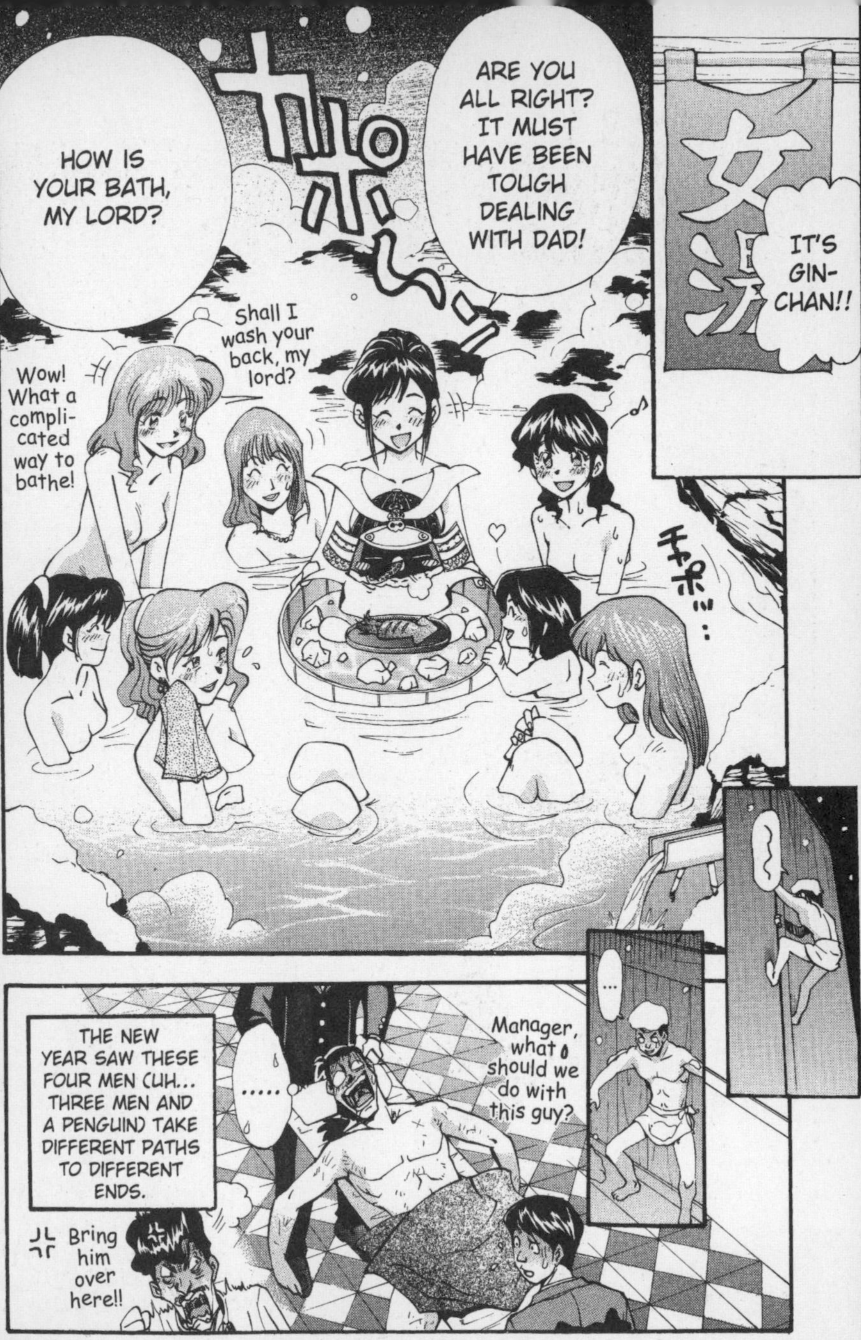
IT'S GIN-CHAN!!
ARE YOU ALL RIGHT? IT MUST HAVE BEEN TOUGH DEALING WITH DAD!
HOW IS YOUR BATH, MY LORD?
Shall I wash your back, my lord?
Wow! What a compli-cated way to bathe!
...
Manager, what should we do with this guy?
.....
THE NEW YEAR SAW THESE FOUR MEN (UH... THREE MEN AND A PENGUIN) TAKE DIFFERENT PATHS TO DIFFERENT ENDS.
Bring him over here!!

CHAPTER 7
BEWARE OF PENGUINS!!

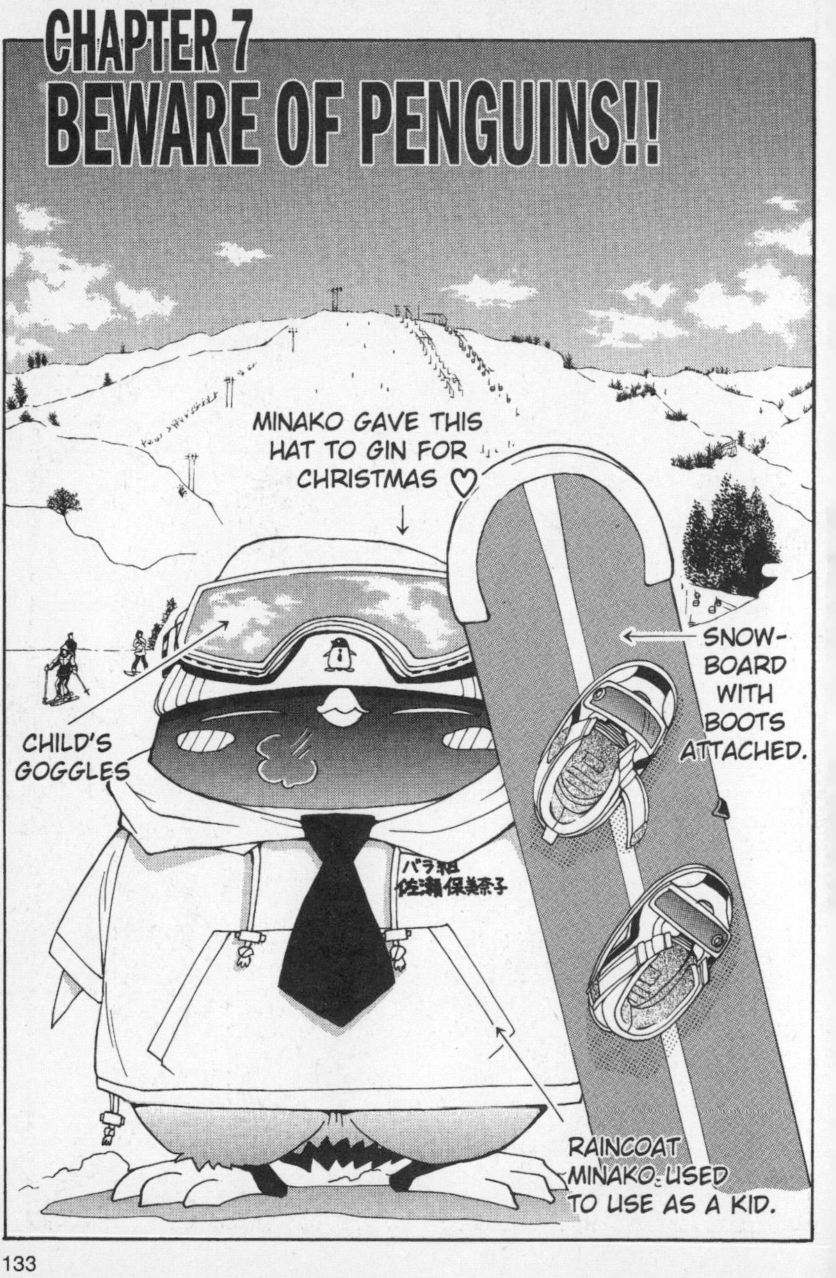
MINAKO GAVE THIS HAT TO GIN FOR CHRISTMAS ♡
SNOW-BOARD WITH BOOTS ATTACHED.
CHILD'S GOGGLES
バラ組
佐瀬保美奈子
RAINCOAT MINAKO USED TO USE AS A KID.

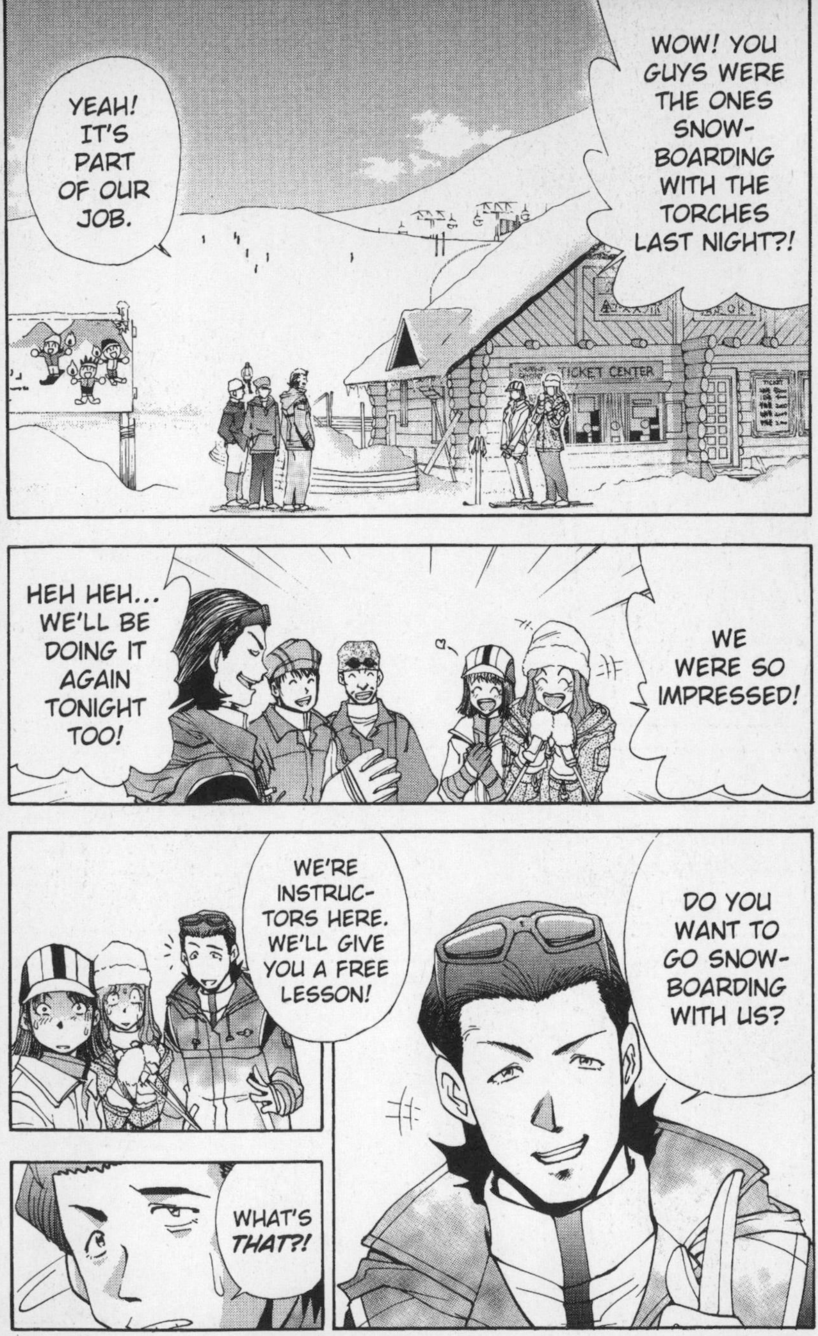
WOW! YOU GUYS WERE THE ONES SNOW-BOARDING WITH THE TORCHES LAST NIGHT?!
YEAH! IT'S PART OF OUR JOB.
TICKET CENTER
WE WERE SO IMPRESSED!
HEH HEH... WE'LL BE DOING IT AGAIN TONIGHT TOO!
DO YOU WANT TO GO SNOW-BOARDING WITH US?
WE'RE INSTRUC-TORS HERE. WE'LL GIVE YOU A FREE LESSON!
WHAT'S *THAT?!*

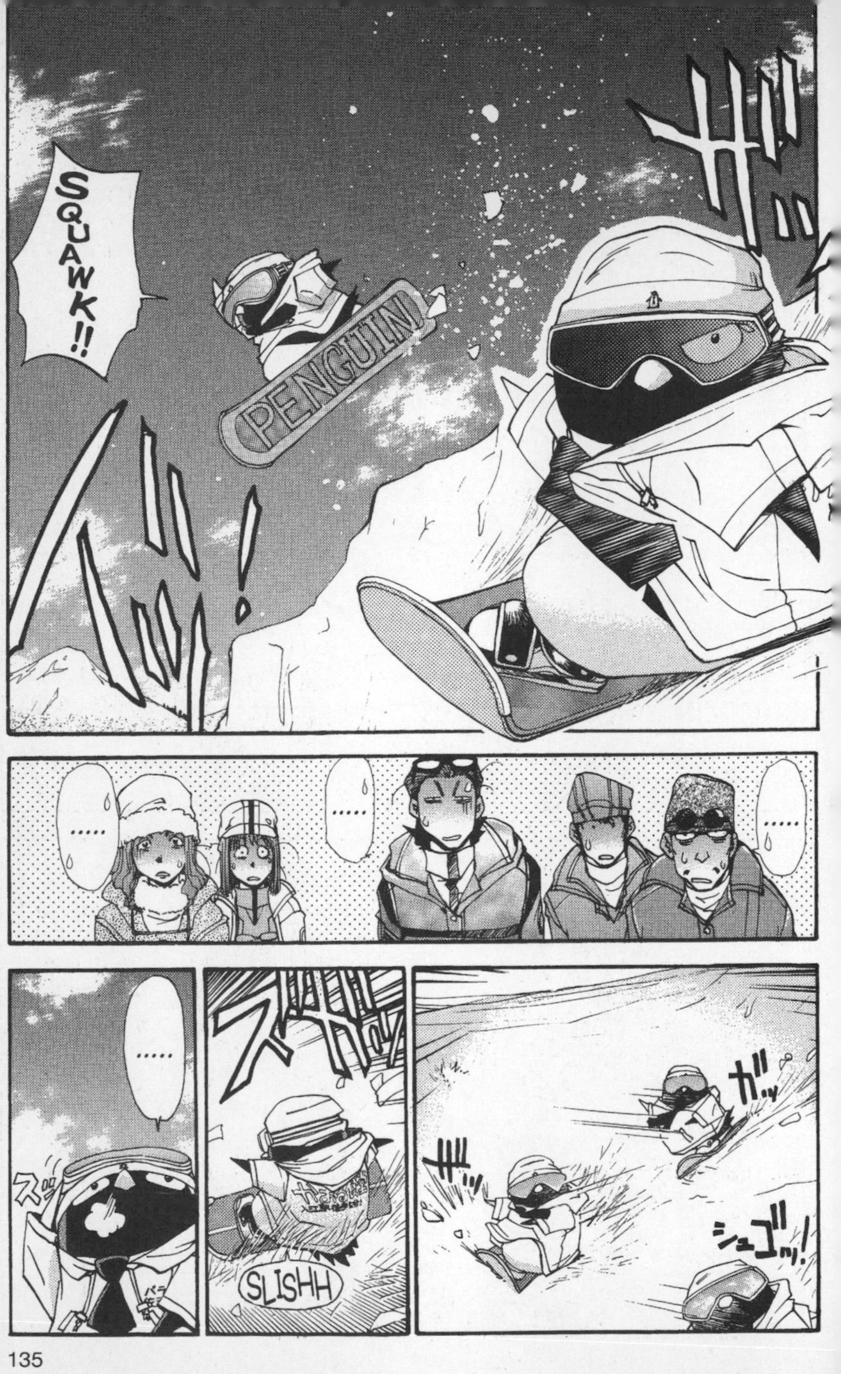
SQUAWK!!
.....
.....
.....
ガッ
ギッ
シュゴッ!
SLISHH
.....

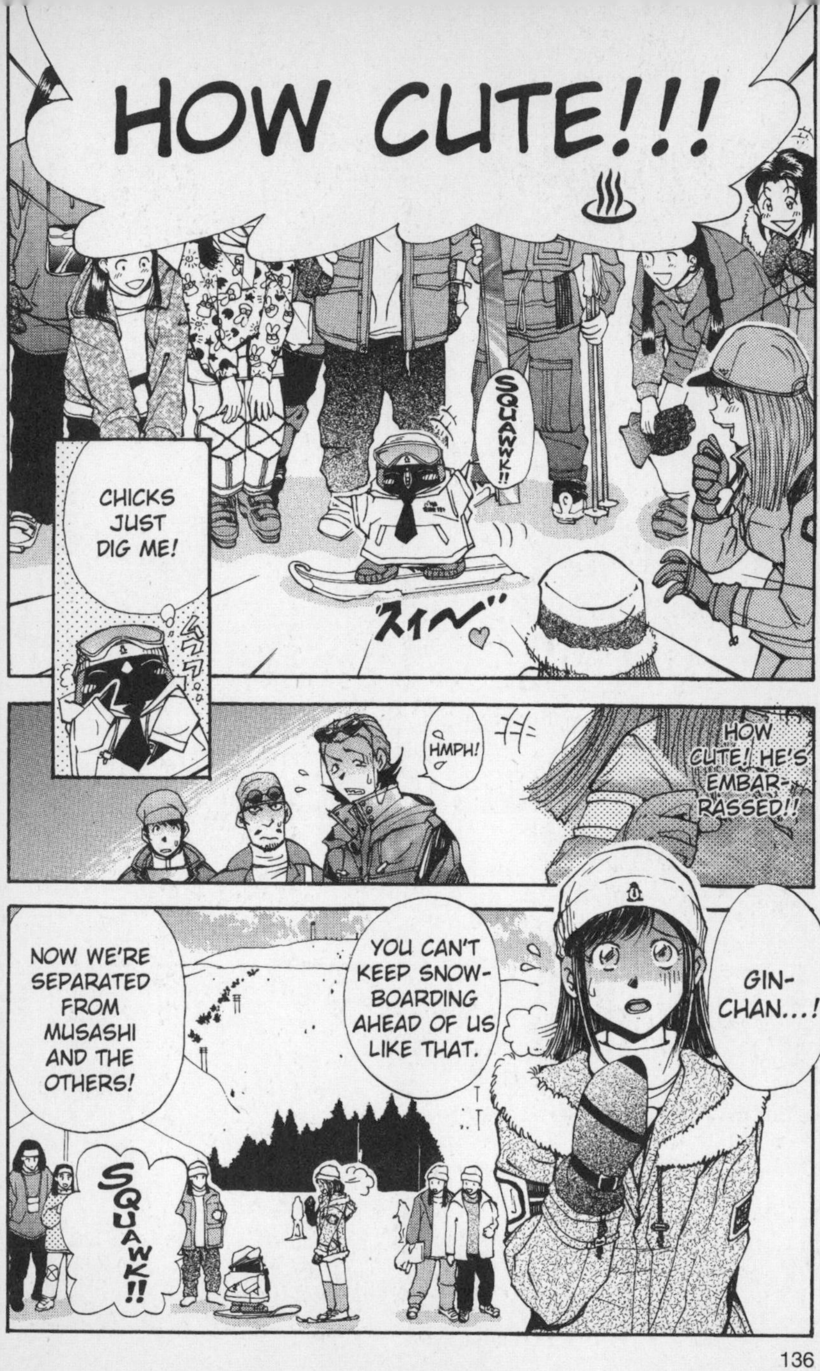
HOW CUTE!!!
SQUAWWK!!
スイ～
CHICKS JUST DIG ME!
HOW CUTE! HE'S EMBARRASSED!!
HMPH!
GIN-CHAN...!
YOU CAN'T KEEP SNOW-BOARDING AHEAD OF US LIKE THAT.
NOW WE'RE SEPARATED FROM MUSASHI AND THE OTHERS!
SQUAWK!!

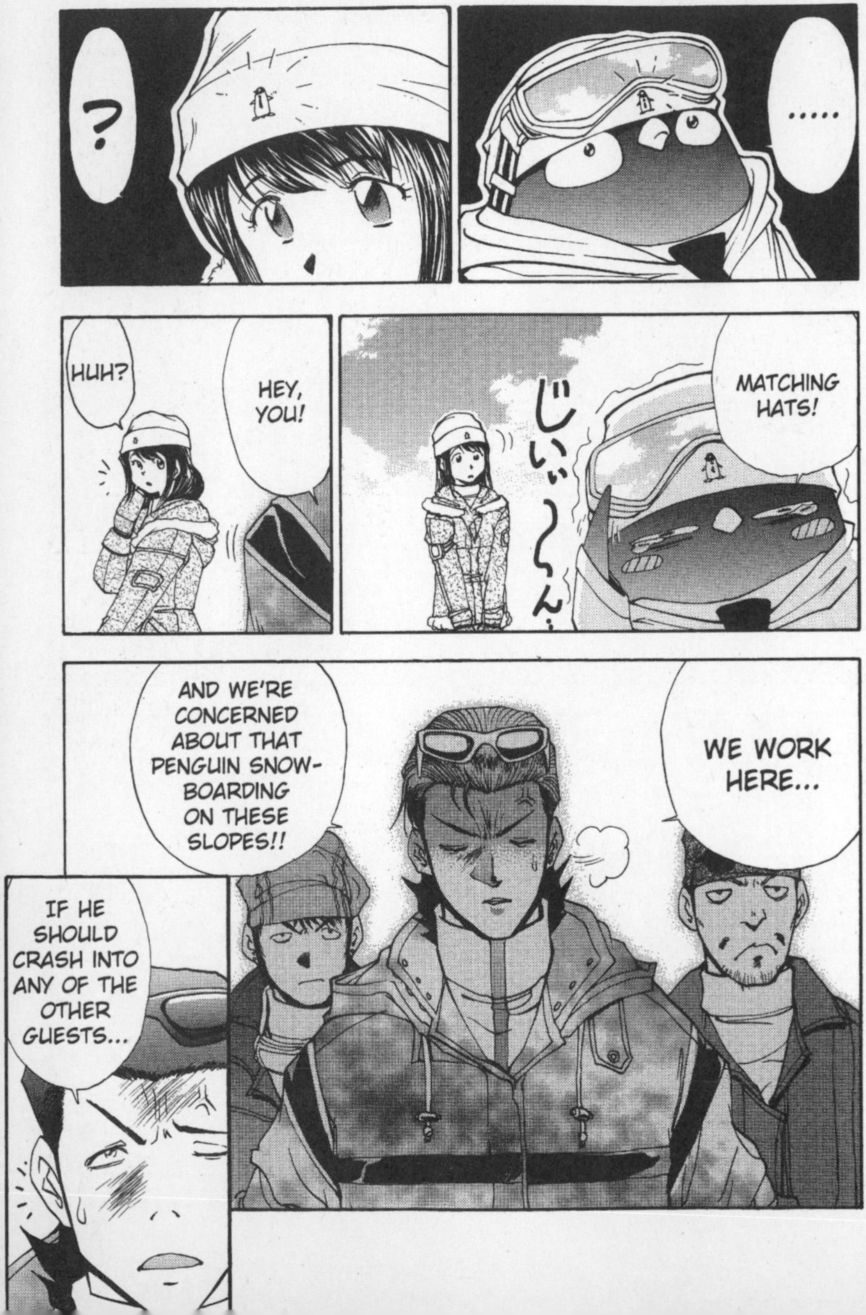
.....
?
MATCHING HATS!
じぃぃ～～ん
HEY, YOU!
HUH?
WE WORK HERE...
AND WE'RE CONCERNED ABOUT THAT PENGUIN SNOW-BOARDING ON THESE SLOPES!!
IF HE SHOULD CRASH INTO ANY OF THE OTHER GUESTS...

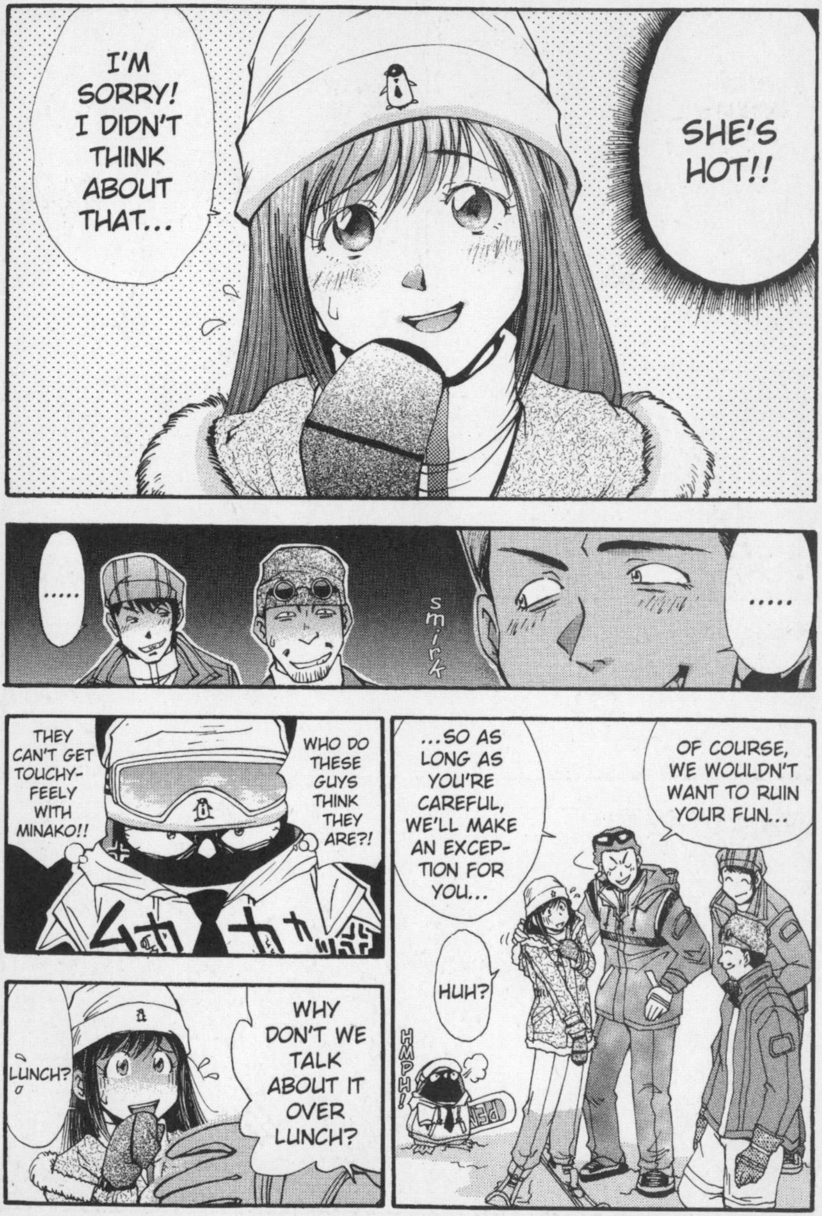

SHE'S HOT!!
I'M SORRY! I DIDN'T THINK ABOUT THAT...
.....
smirk
.....
OF COURSE, WE WOULDN'T WANT TO RUIN YOUR FUN...
...SO AS LONG AS YOU'RE CAREFUL, WE'LL MAKE AN EXCEPTION FOR YOU...
HUH?
HMPH!
WHO DO THESE GUYS THINK THEY ARE?!
THEY CAN'T GET TOUCHY-FEELY WITH MINAKO!!
WHY DON'T WE TALK ABOUT IT OVER LUNCH?
LUNCH?

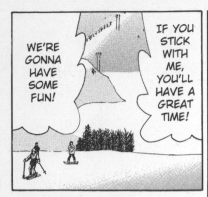

I'LL TAKE YOU TO A GREAT PLACE!
I KNOW THIS SKI RESORT LIKE THE BACK OF MY HAND!
IF YOU STICK WITH ME, YOU'LL HAVE A GREAT TIME!
WE'RE GONNA HAVE SOME FUN!
C'MON! LET'S GO!
UH... WAIT...
SHUNK
?!
SUPER MOVE! HIGH VOLTAGE UPPERCUT FROM HELL!!
GIN-CHAN...
ARE YOU OKAY?!
ARGH...

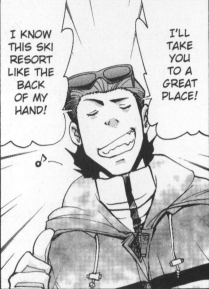

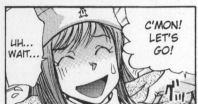

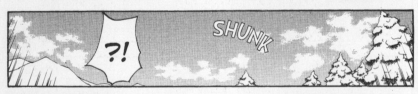

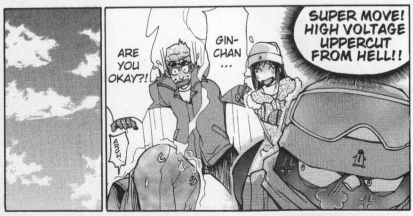

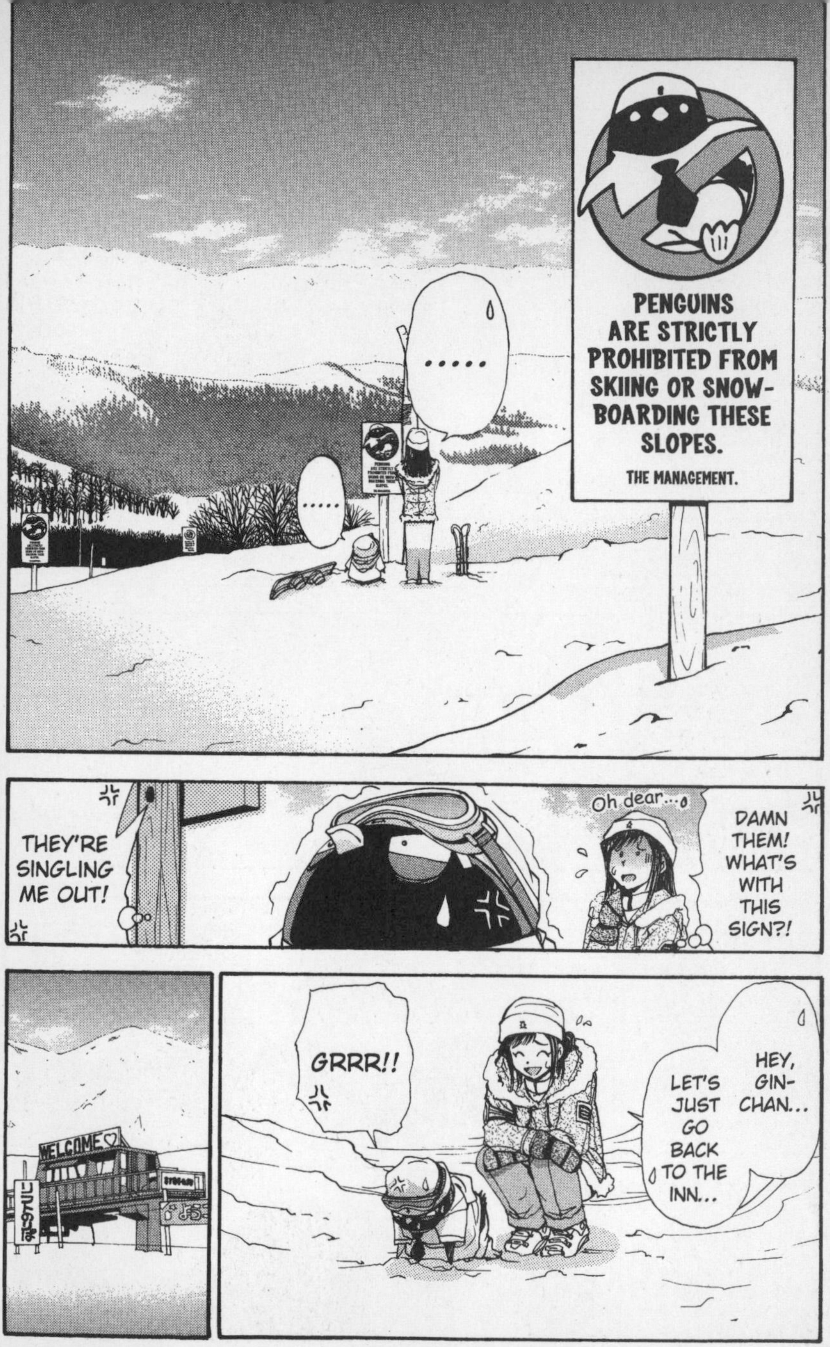
PENGUINS ARE STRICTLY PROHIBITED FROM SKIING OR SNOW-BOARDING THESE SLOPES.
THE MANAGEMENT.
.....
......
DAMN THEM! WHAT'S WITH THIS SIGN?!
Oh dear...
THEY'RE SINGLING ME OUT!
HEY, GIN-CHAN...
LET'S JUST GO BACK TO THE INN...
GRRR!!
WELCOME♡

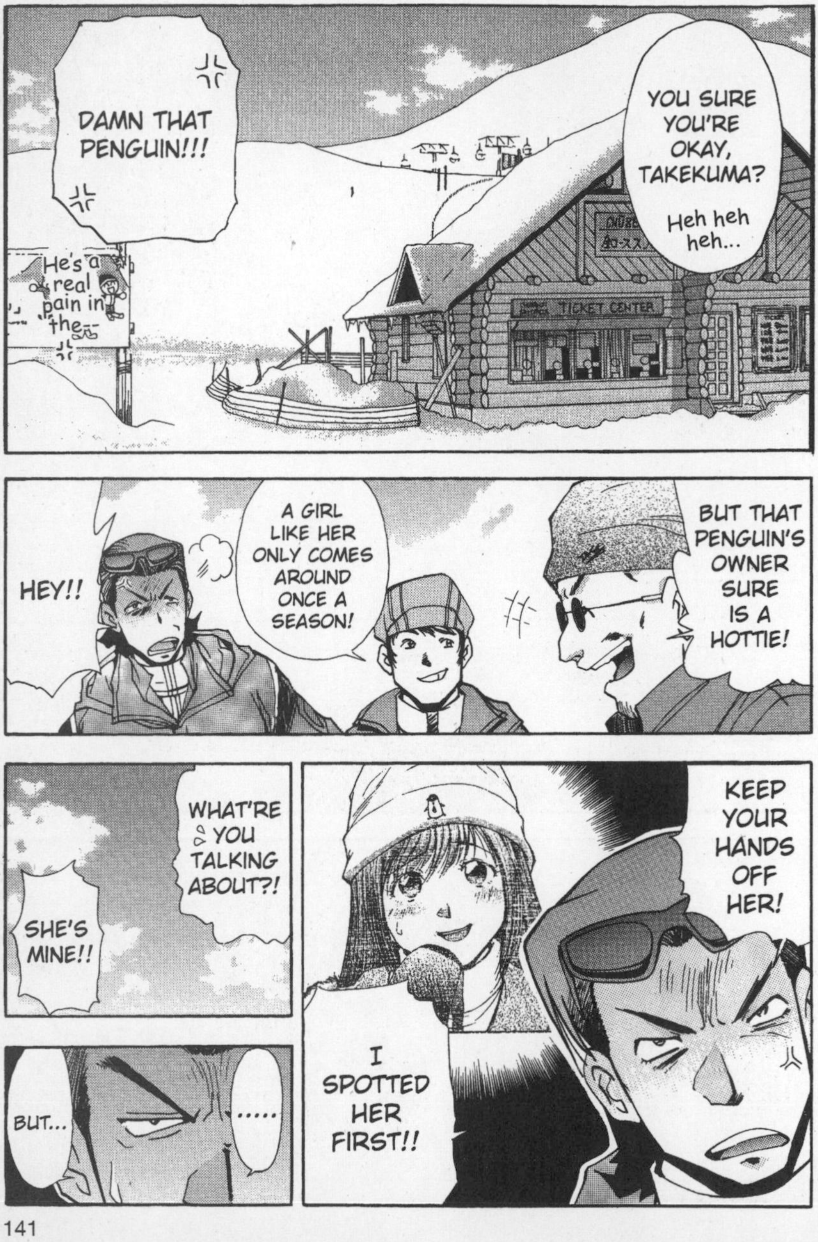
YOU SURE YOU'RE OKAY, TAKEKUMA?
Heh heh heh...
DAMN THAT PENGUIN!!!
He's a real pain in the--
TICKET CENTER
BUT THAT PENGUIN'S OWNER SURE IS A HOTTIE!
A GIRL LIKE HER ONLY COMES AROUND ONCE A SEASON!
HEY!!
KEEP YOUR HANDS OFF HER!
I SPOTTED HER FIRST!!
WHAT'RE YOU TALKING ABOUT?!
SHE'S MINE!!
......
BUT...

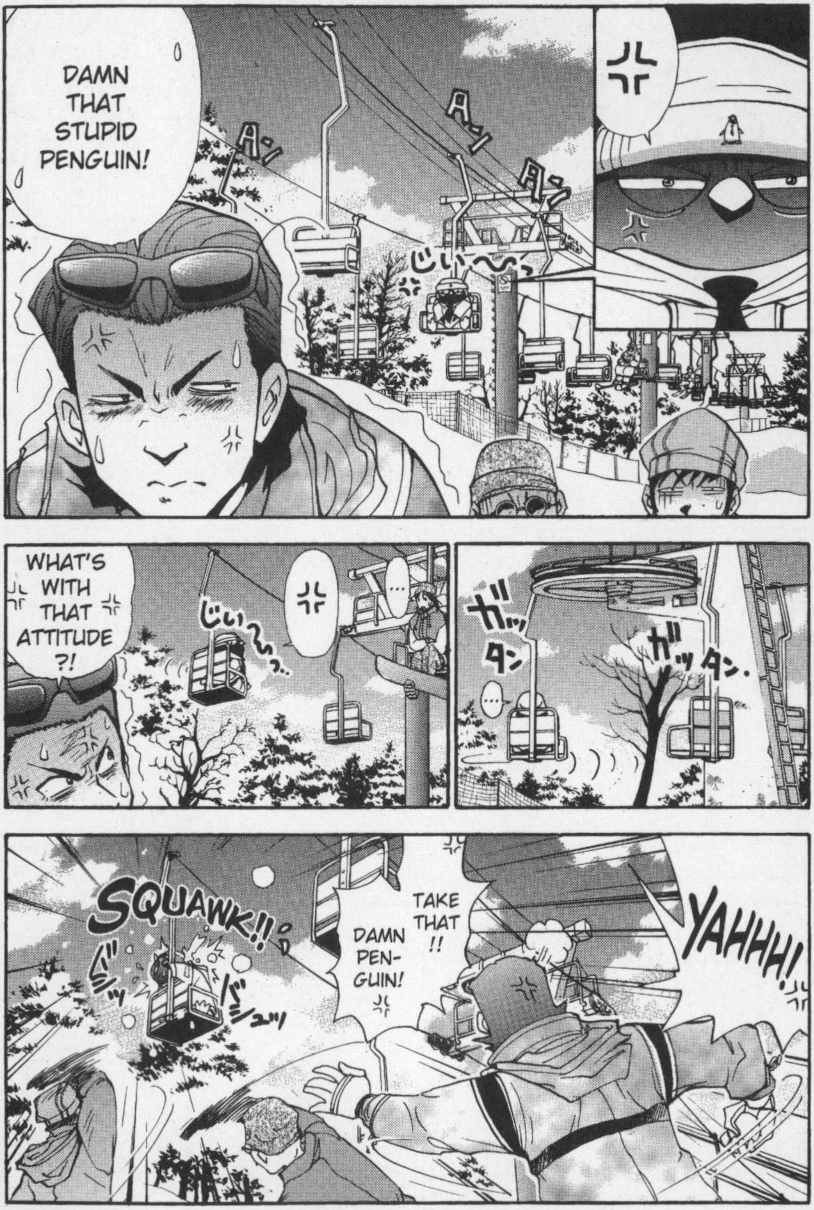
DAMN THAT STUPID PENGUIN!
じぃ〜っ
ガッタン
ガッタン.
...
...
じぃ〜っ
WHAT'S WITH THAT ATTITUDE ?!
YAHHH!!
TAKE THAT !!
DAMN PEN-GUIN!
SQUAWK!!

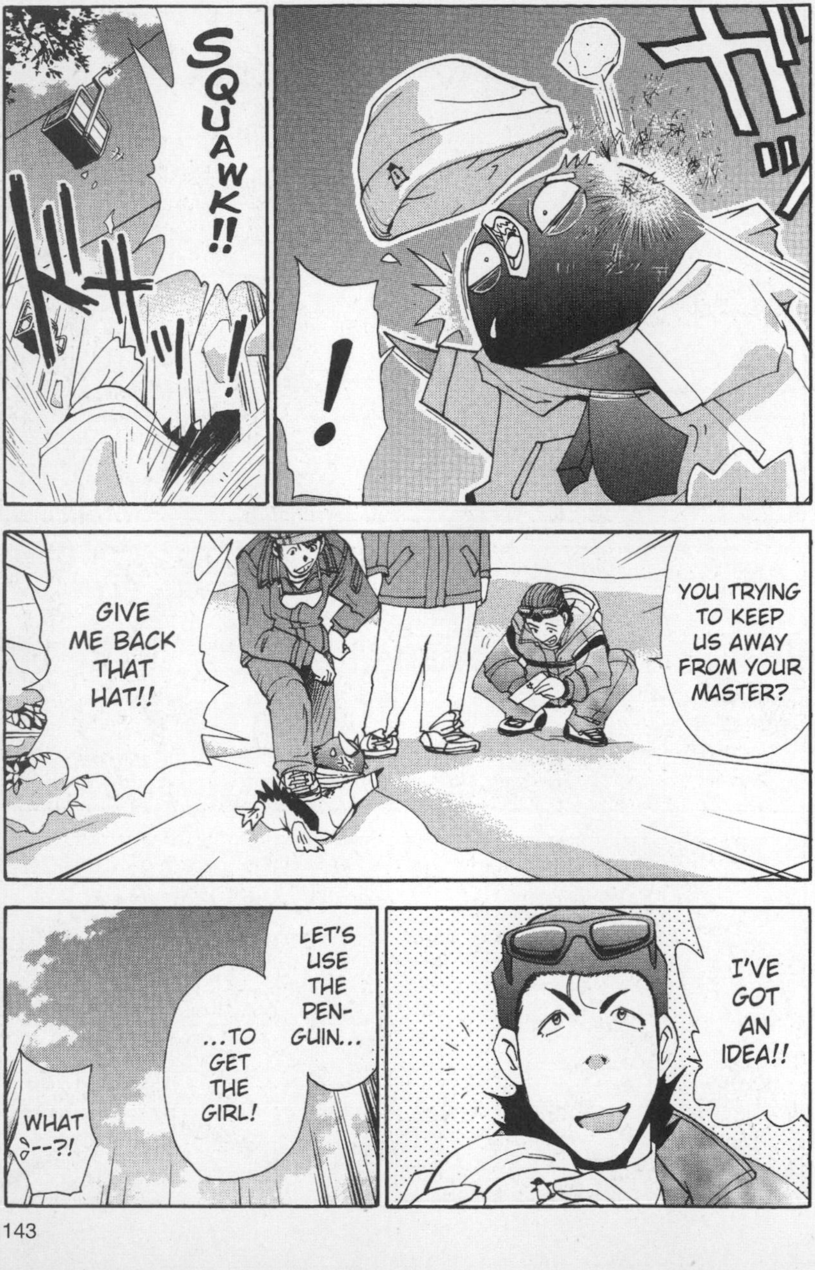
!
SQUAWK!!
YOU TRYING TO KEEP US AWAY FROM YOUR MASTER?
GIVE ME BACK THAT HAT!!
I'VE GOT AN IDEA!!
LET'S USE THE PEN-GUIN...
...TO GET THE GIRL!
WHAT --?!

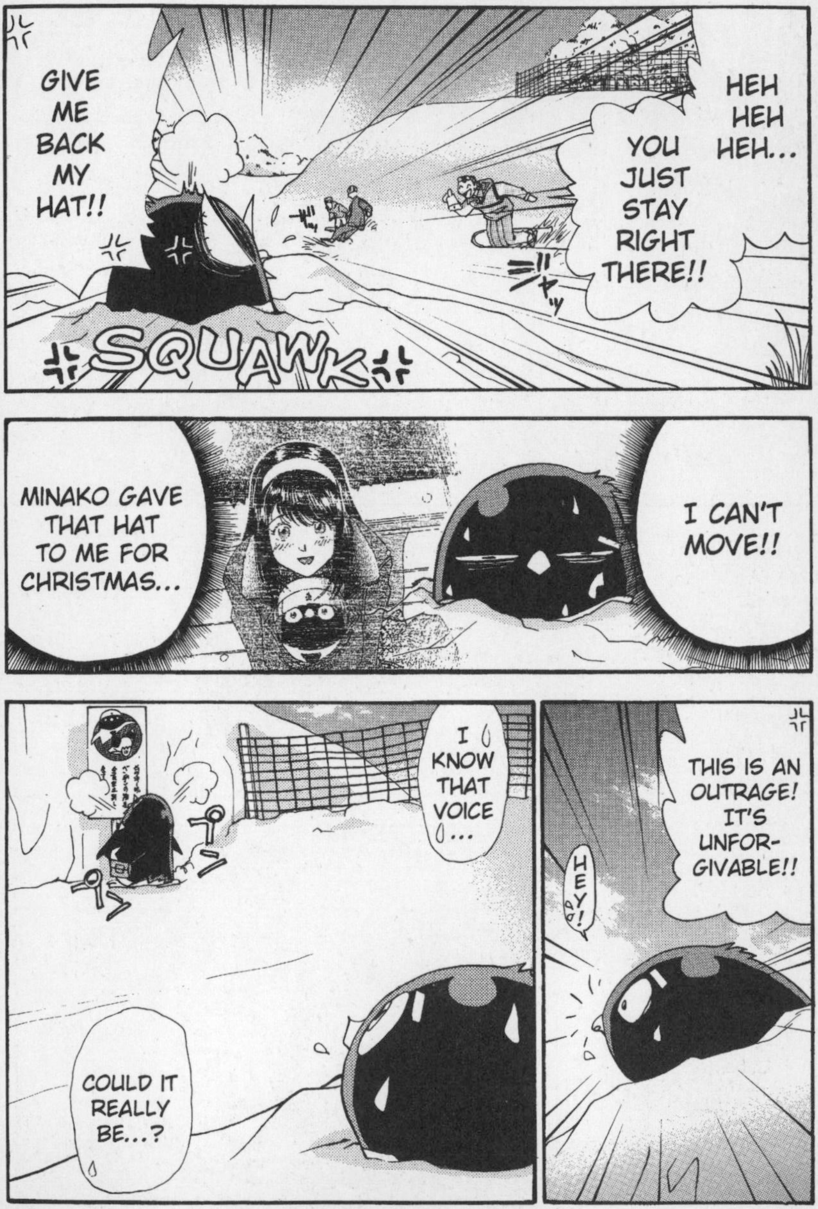
HEH HEH HEH...
YOU JUST STAY RIGHT THERE!!
GIVE ME BACK MY HAT!!
SQUAWK
I CAN'T MOVE!!
MINAKO GAVE THAT HAT TO ME FOR CHRISTMAS...
THIS IS AN OUTRAGE! IT'S UNFORGIVABLE!!
HEY!
I KNOW THAT VOICE...
COULD IT REALLY BE...?

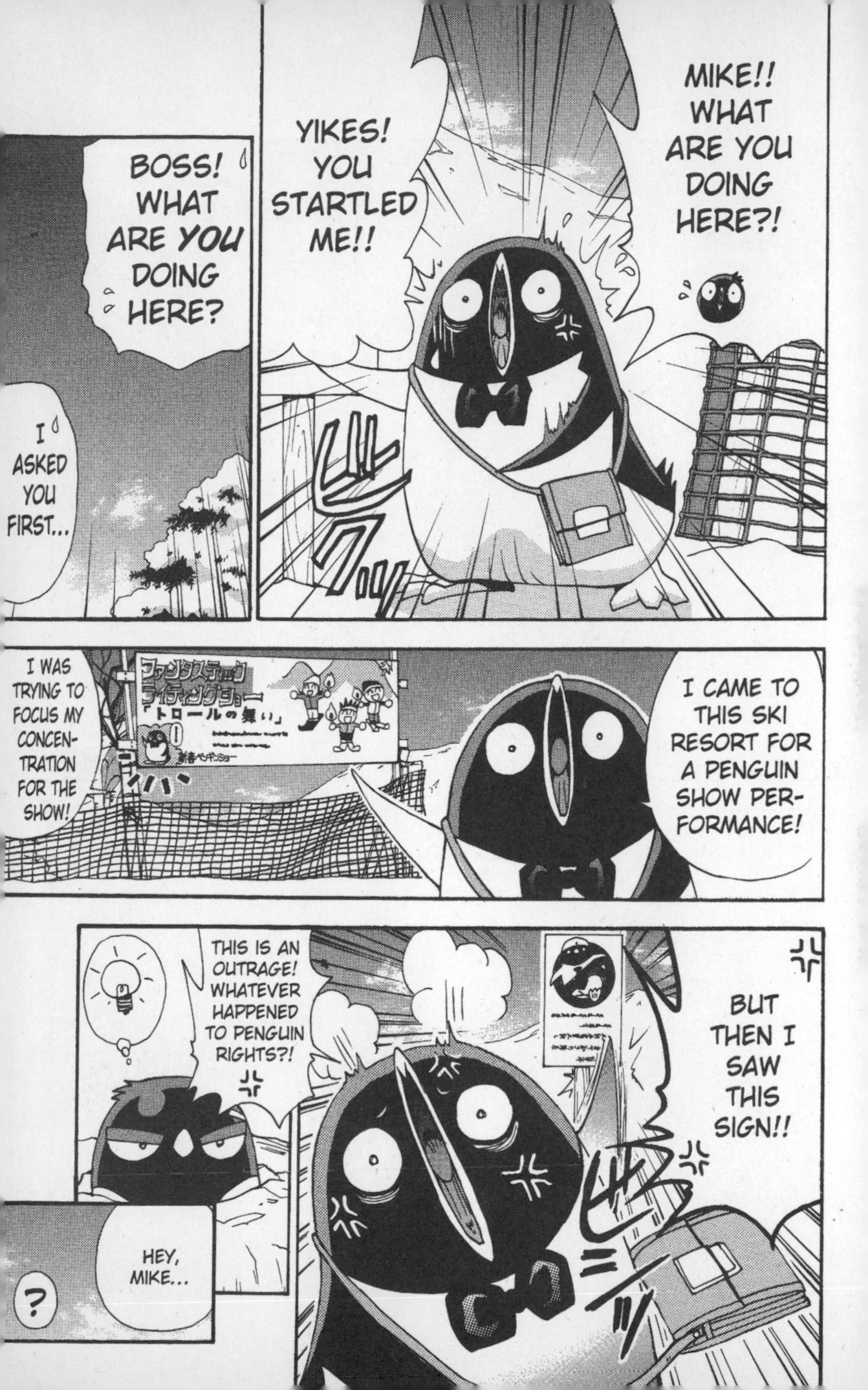
MIKE!! WHAT ARE YOU DOING HERE?!
YIKES! YOU STARTLED ME!!
BOSS! WHAT ARE YOU DOING HERE?
I ASKED YOU FIRST...
I CAME TO THIS SKI RESORT FOR A PENGUIN SHOW PERFORMANCE!
「トロールの舞い」
I WAS TRYING TO FOCUS MY CONCENTRATION FOR THE SHOW!
BUT THEN I SAW THIS SIGN!!
THIS IS AN OUTRAGE! WHATEVER HAPPENED TO PENGUIN RIGHTS?!
HEY, MIKE...
?

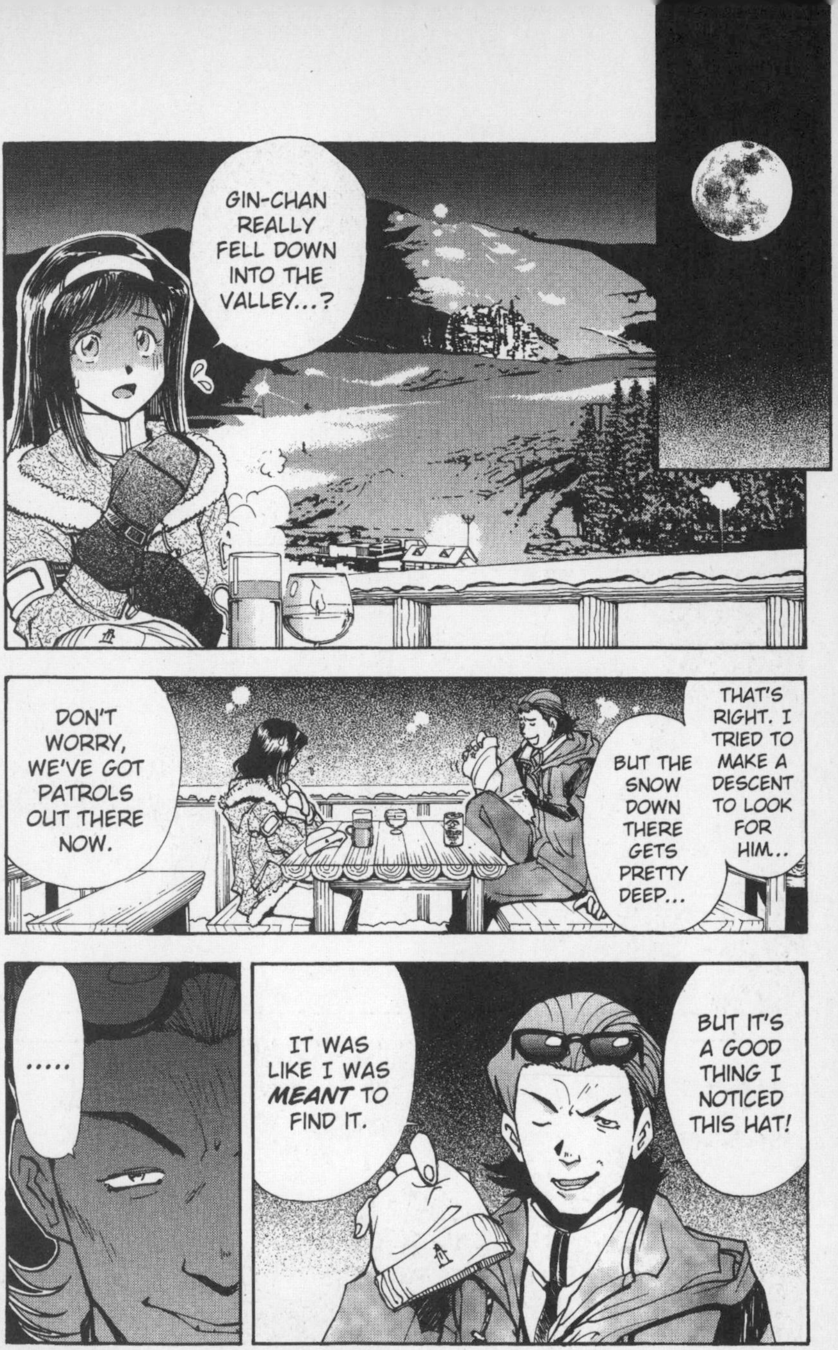
GIN-CHAN REALLY FELL DOWN INTO THE VALLEY...?
THAT'S RIGHT. I TRIED TO MAKE A DESCENT TO LOOK FOR HIM...
BUT THE SNOW DOWN THERE GETS PRETTY DEEP...
DON'T WORRY, WE'VE GOT PATROLS OUT THERE NOW.
BUT IT'S A GOOD THING I NOTICED THIS HAT!
IT WAS LIKE I WAS *MEANT* TO FIND IT.
.....

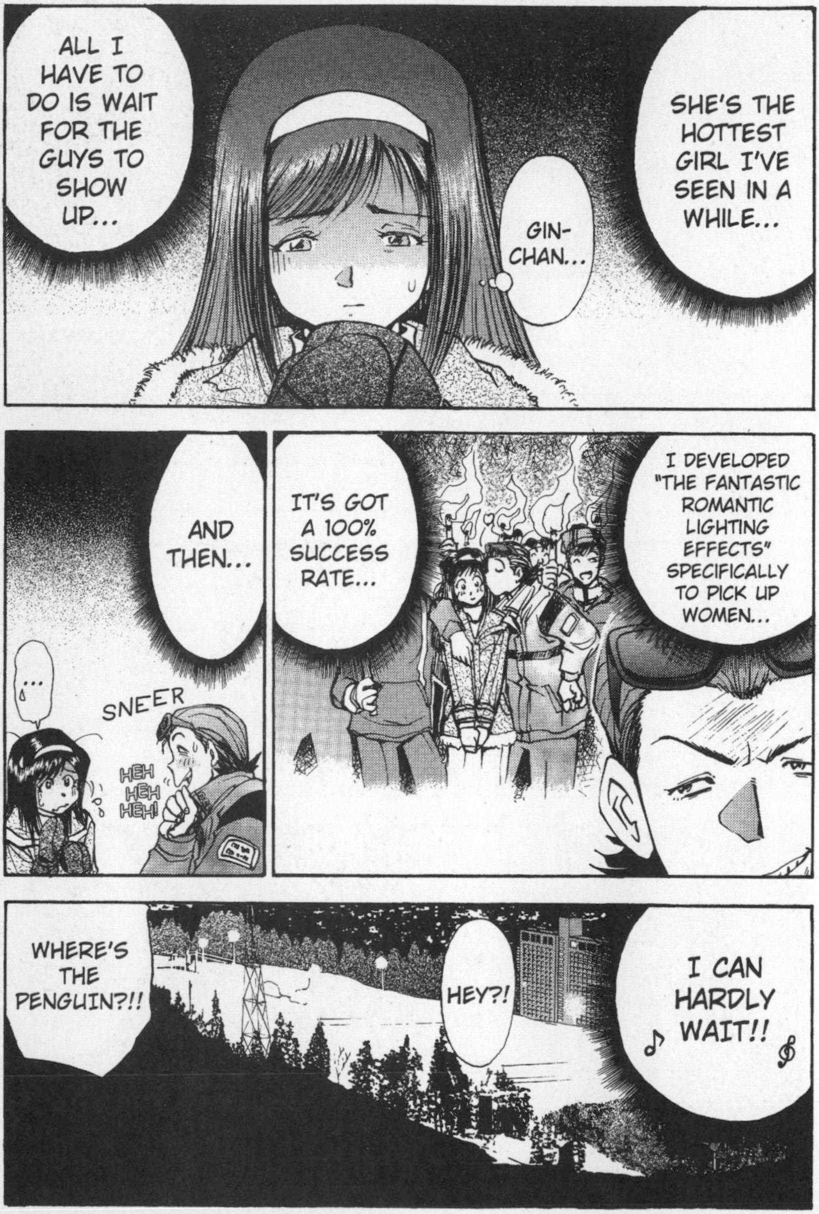
SHE'S THE HOTTEST GIRL I'VE SEEN IN A WHILE...
GIN-CHAN...
ALL I HAVE TO DO IS WAIT FOR THE GUYS TO SHOW UP...
I DEVELOPED "THE FANTASTIC ROMANTIC LIGHTING EFFECTS" SPECIFICALLY TO PICK UP WOMEN...
IT'S GOT A 100% SUCCESS RATE...
AND THEN...
SNEER
HEH HEH HEH!
...
I CAN HARDLY WAIT!!
HEY?!
WHERE'S THE PENGUIN?!!

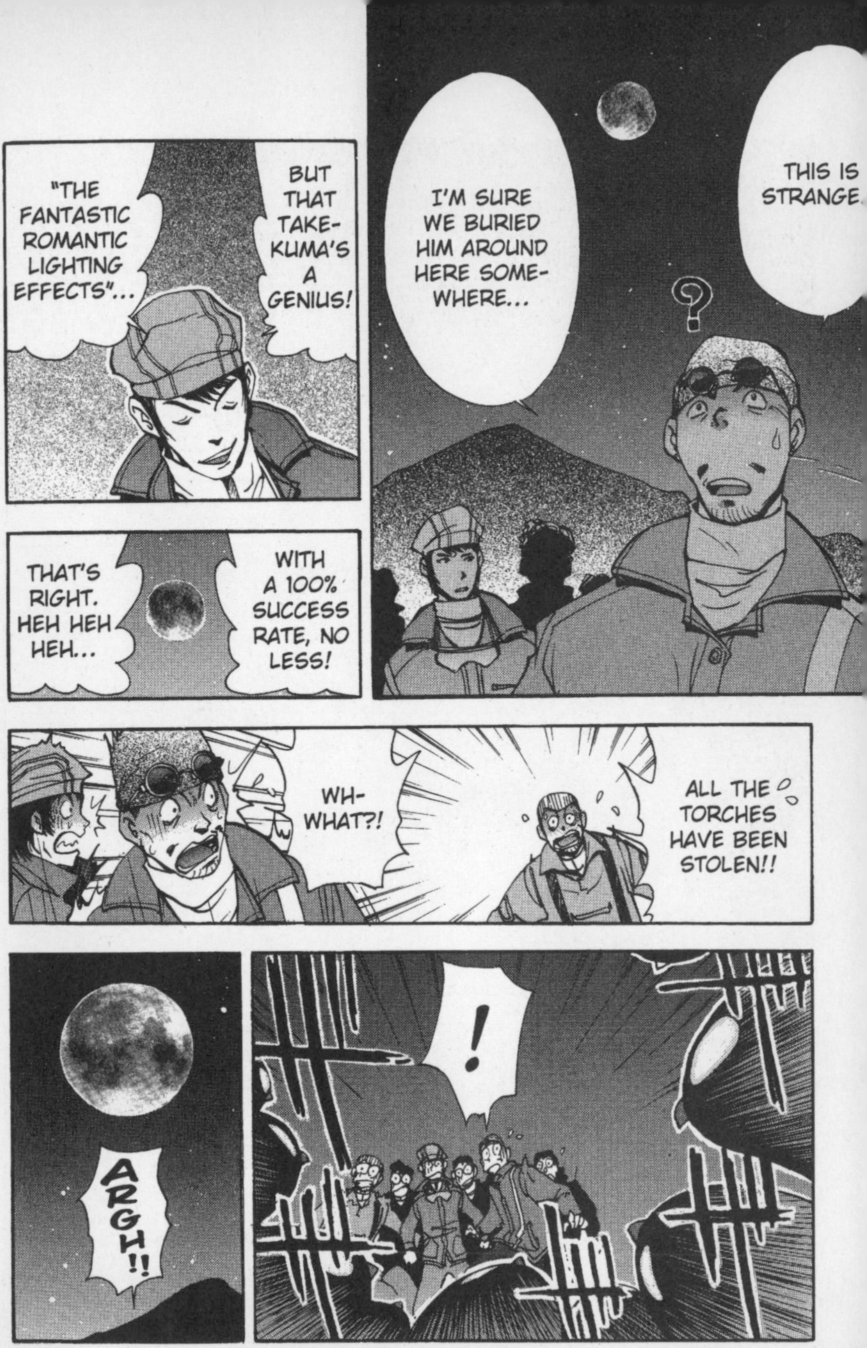
THIS IS STRANGE.
I'M SURE WE BURIED HIM AROUND HERE SOME-WHERE...
?
BUT THAT TAKE-KUMA'S A GENIUS!
"THE FANTASTIC ROMANTIC LIGHTING EFFECTS"...
WITH A 100% SUCCESS RATE, NO LESS!
THAT'S RIGHT. HEH HEH HEH...
ALL THE TORCHES HAVE BEEN STOLEN!!
WH-WHAT?!
!
ARGH!!

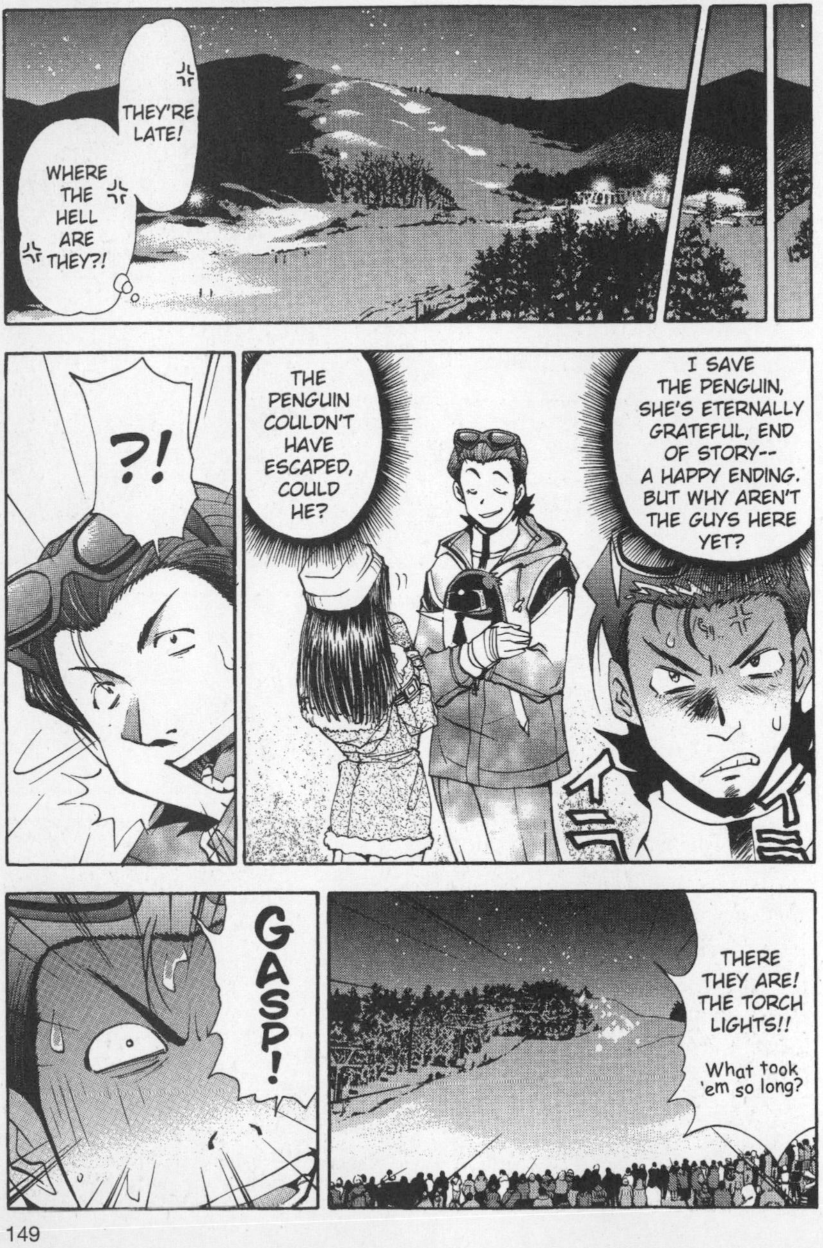
THEY'RE LATE!
WHERE THE HELL ARE THEY?!
I SAVE THE PENGUIN, SHE'S ETERNALLY GRATEFUL, END OF STORY-- A HAPPY ENDING. BUT WHY AREN'T THE GUYS HERE YET?
THE PENGUIN COULDN'T HAVE ESCAPED, COULD HE?
?!
THERE THEY ARE! THE TORCH LIGHTS!!
What took 'em so long?
GASP!

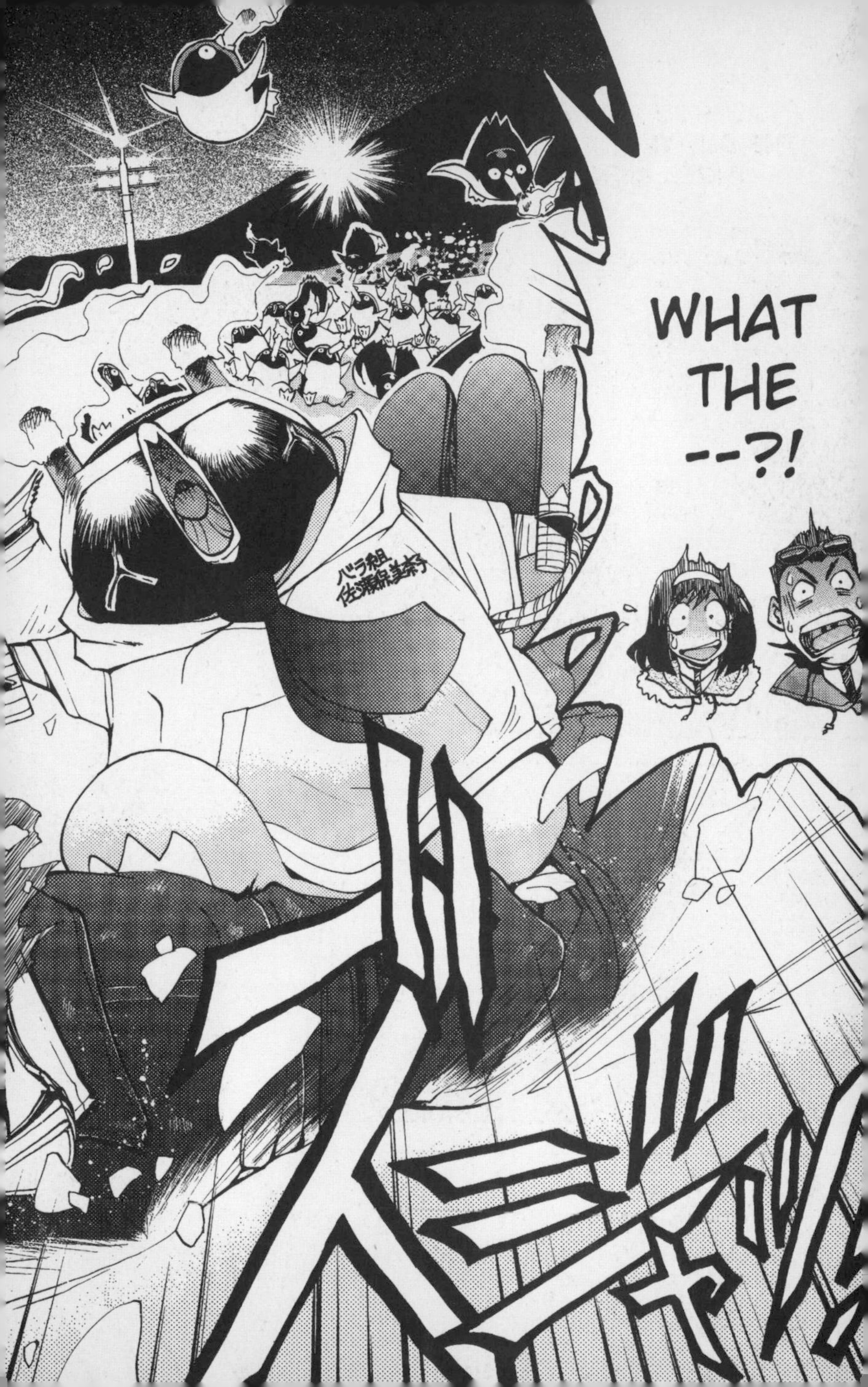
WHAT THE --?!
バラ組
佐須良美矛

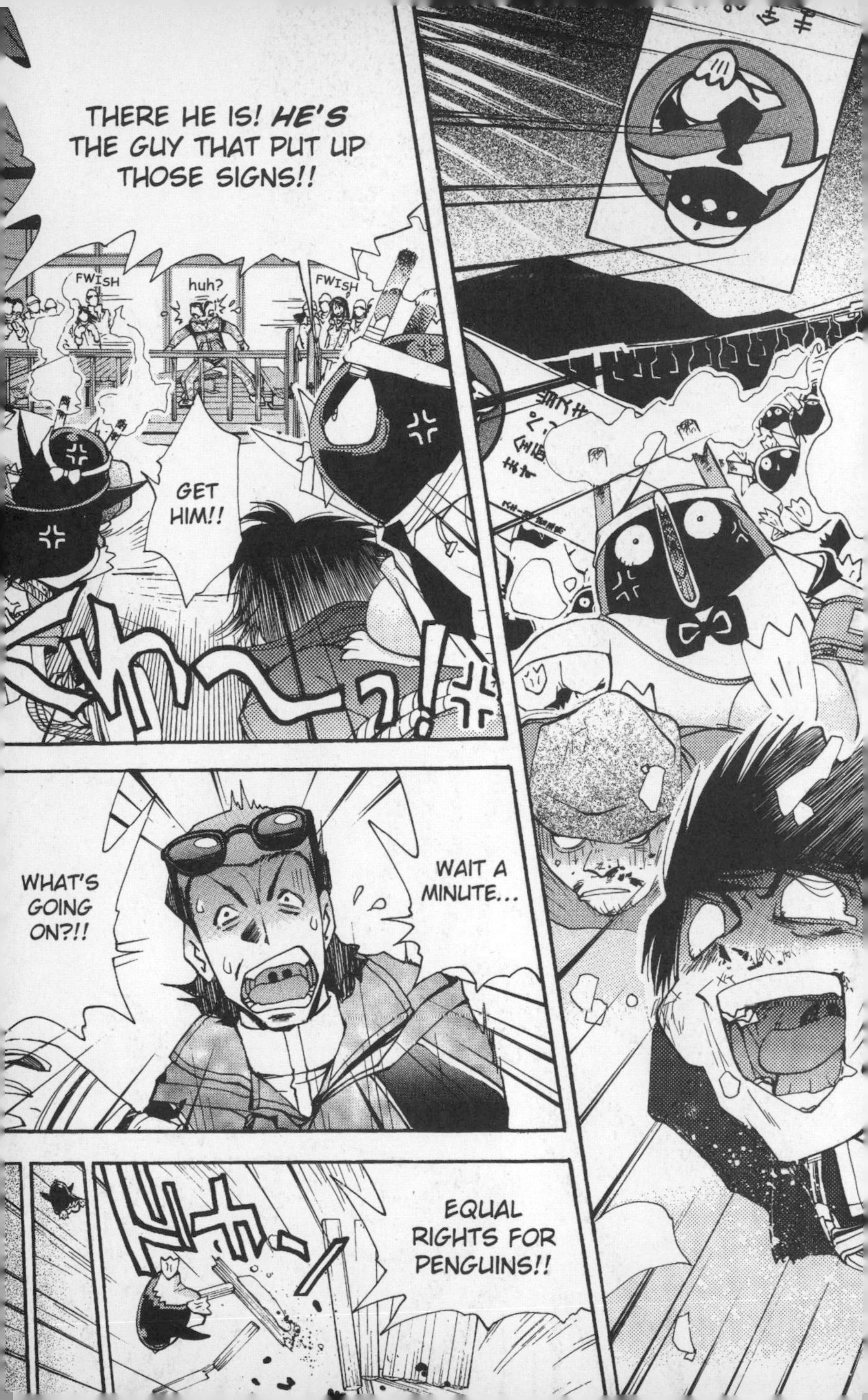

THERE HE IS! *HE'S* THE GUY THAT PUT UP THOSE SIGNS!!
FWISH
huh?
FWISH
GET HIM!!
WAIT A MINUTE...
WHAT'S GOING ON?!!
EQUAL RIGHTS FOR PENGUINS!!

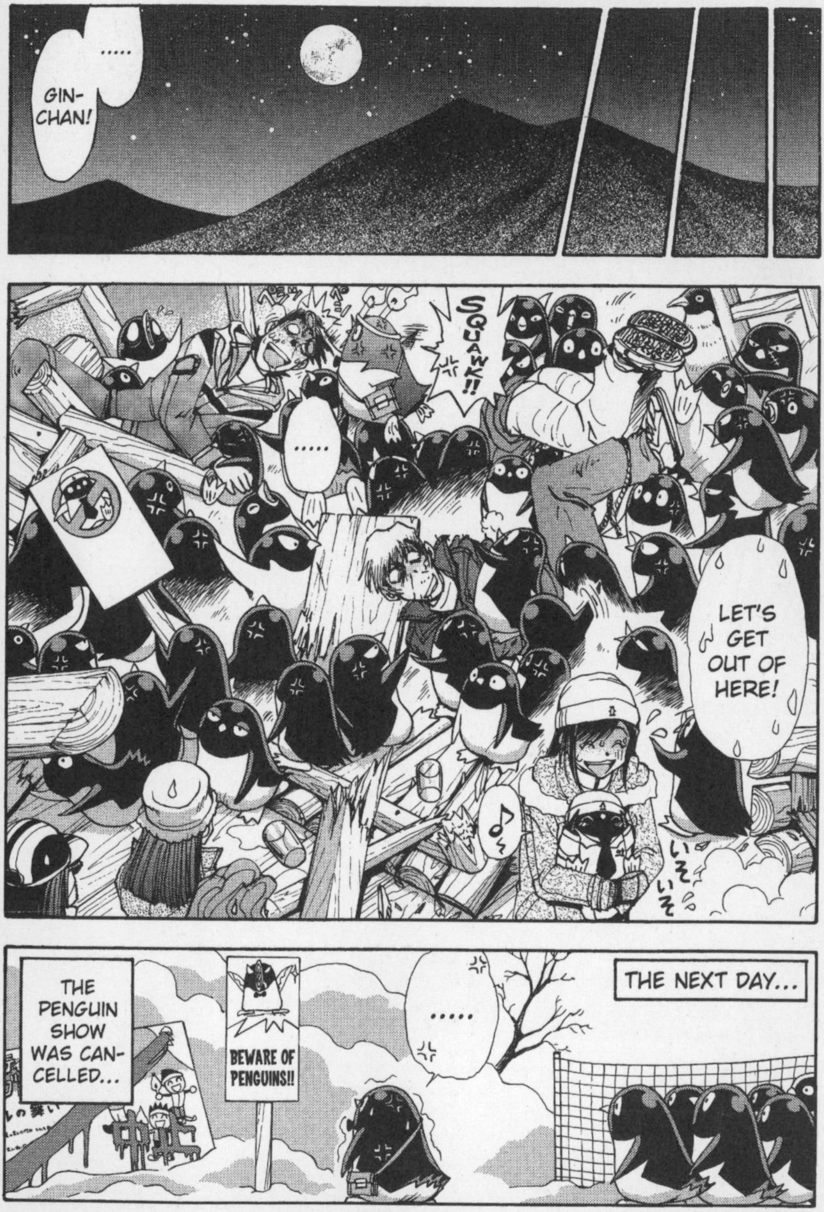
.....
GIN-CHAN!
SQUAWK!!
LET'S GET OUT OF HERE!
.....
いそいそ
THE NEXT DAY...
.....
BEWARE OF PENGUINS!!
THE PENGUIN SHOW WAS CANCELLED...

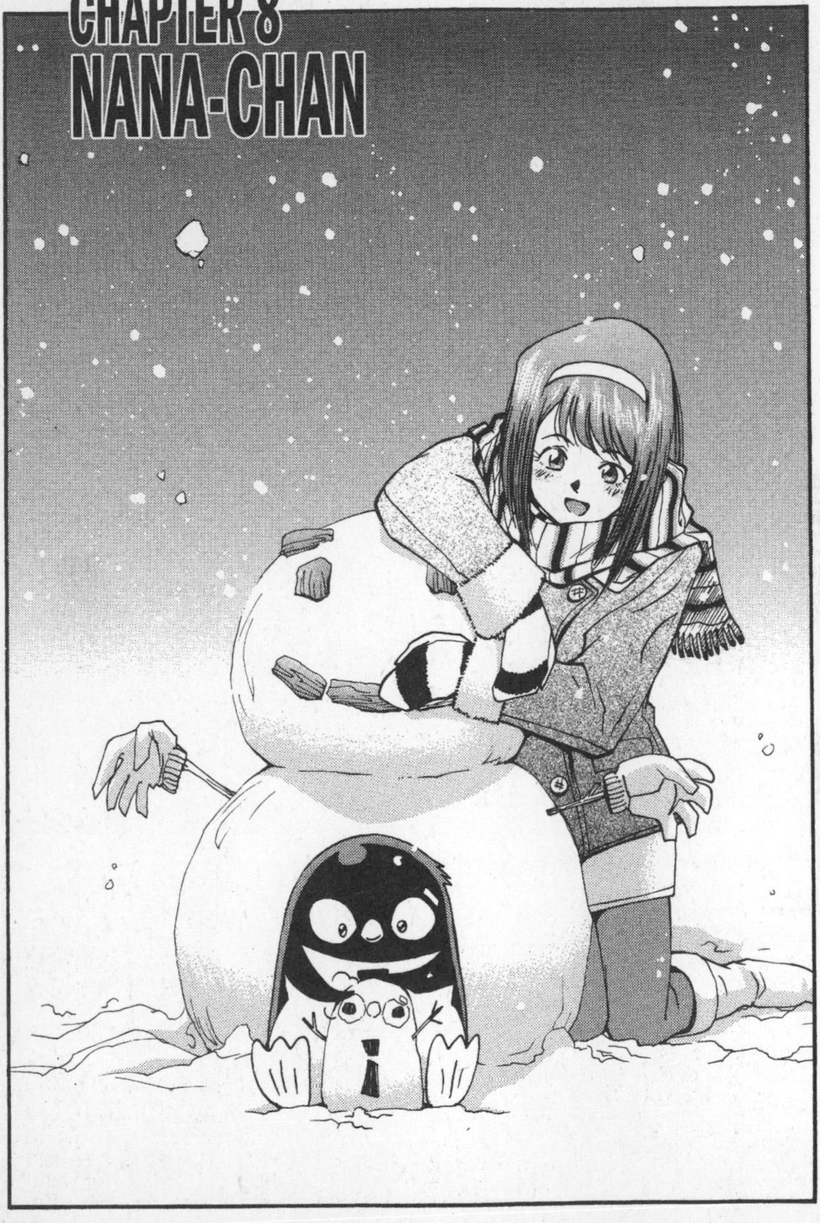
CHAPTER 8
NANA-CHAN

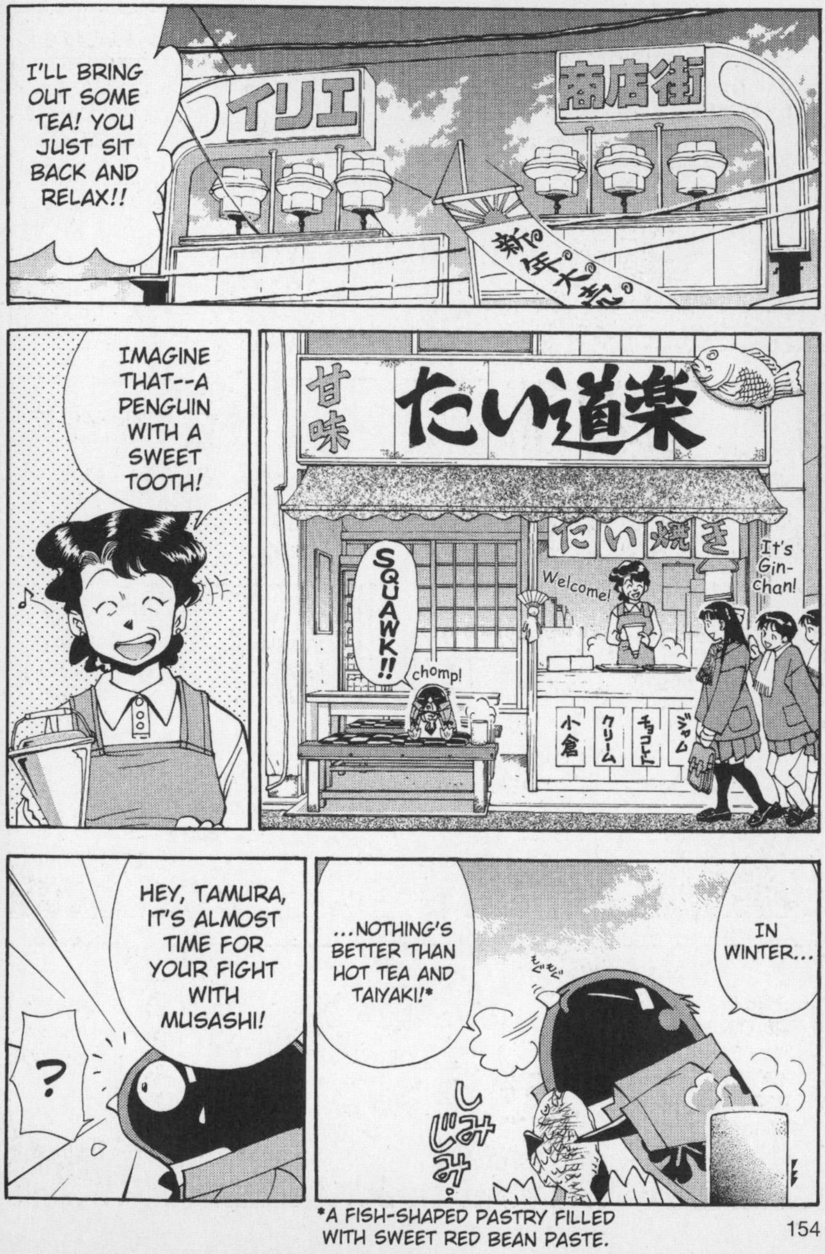

商店街
イリエ
I'LL BRING OUT SOME TEA! YOU JUST SIT BACK AND RELAX!!
甘味
たい道楽
たい焼き
It's Gin-chan!
Welcome!
SQUAWK!!
chomp!
ジャム
チョコレート
クリーム
小倉
IMAGINE THAT--A PENGUIN WITH A SWEET TOOTH!
IN WINTER...
...NOTHING'S BETTER THAN HOT TEA AND TAIYAKI!*
しみじみ
HEY, TAMURA, IT'S ALMOST TIME FOR YOUR FIGHT WITH MUSASHI!
?

*A FISH-SHAPED PASTRY FILLED WITH SWEET RED BEAN PASTE.

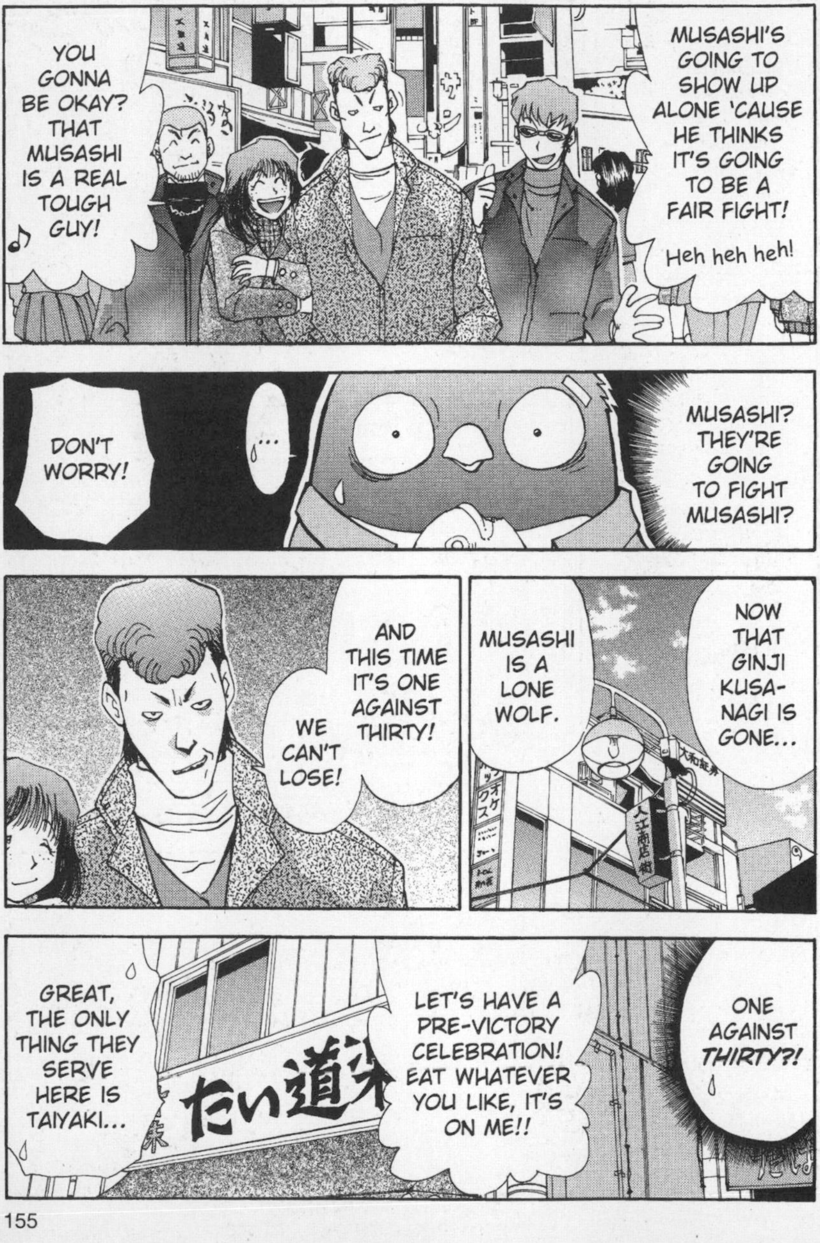
MUSASHI'S GOING TO SHOW UP ALONE 'CAUSE HE THINKS IT'S GOING TO BE A FAIR FIGHT!
Heh heh heh!
YOU GONNA BE OKAY? THAT MUSASHI IS A REAL TOUGH GUY! ♪
MUSASHI? THEY'RE GOING TO FIGHT MUSASHI?
...
DON'T WORRY!
NOW THAT GINJI KUSA-NAGI IS GONE...
MUSASHI IS A LONE WOLF.
AND THIS TIME IT'S ONE AGAINST THIRTY!
WE CAN'T LOSE!
ONE AGAINST *THIRTY?!*
LET'S HAVE A PRE-VICTORY CELEBRATION! EAT WHATEVER YOU LIKE, IT'S ON ME!!
GREAT, THE ONLY THING THEY SERVE HERE IS TAIYAKI...
たい道

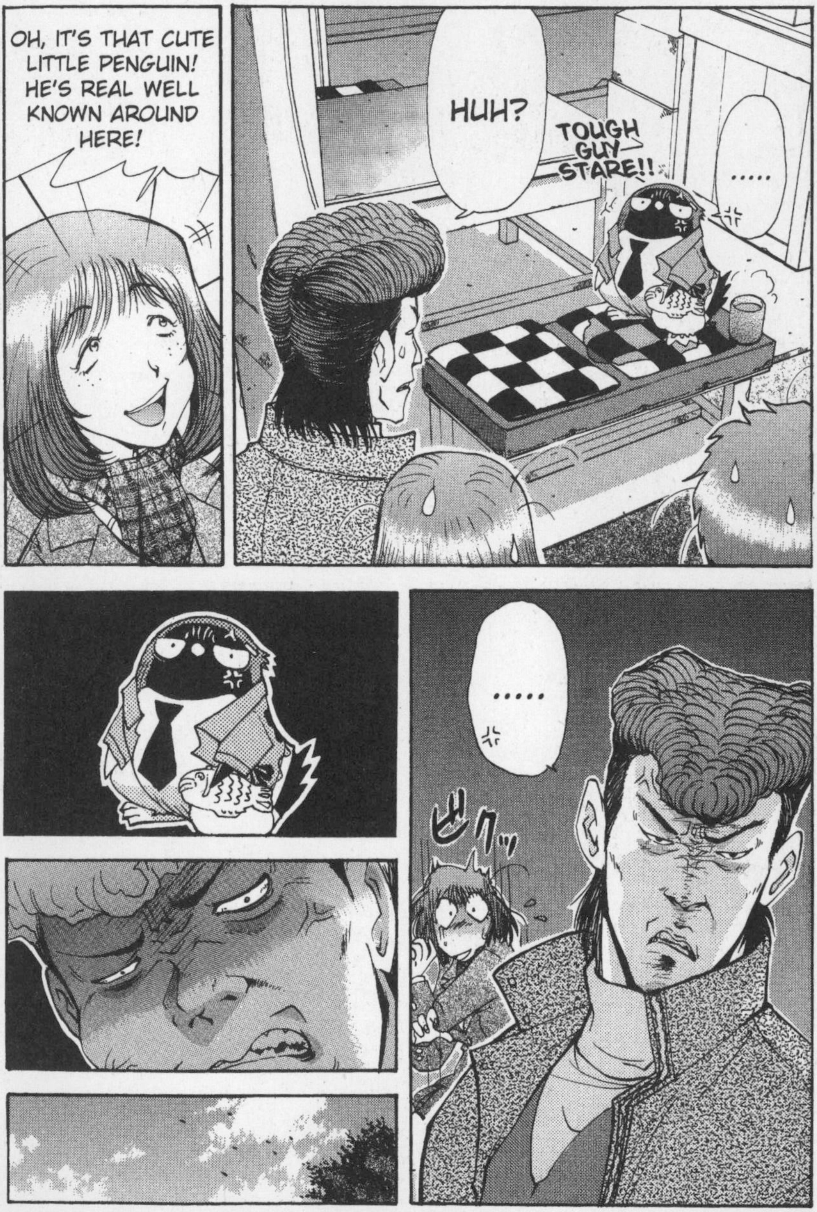
.....
TOUGH GUY STARE!!
HUH?
OH, IT'S THAT CUTE LITTLE PENGUIN! HE'S REAL WELL KNOWN AROUND HERE!
.....
ピクッ

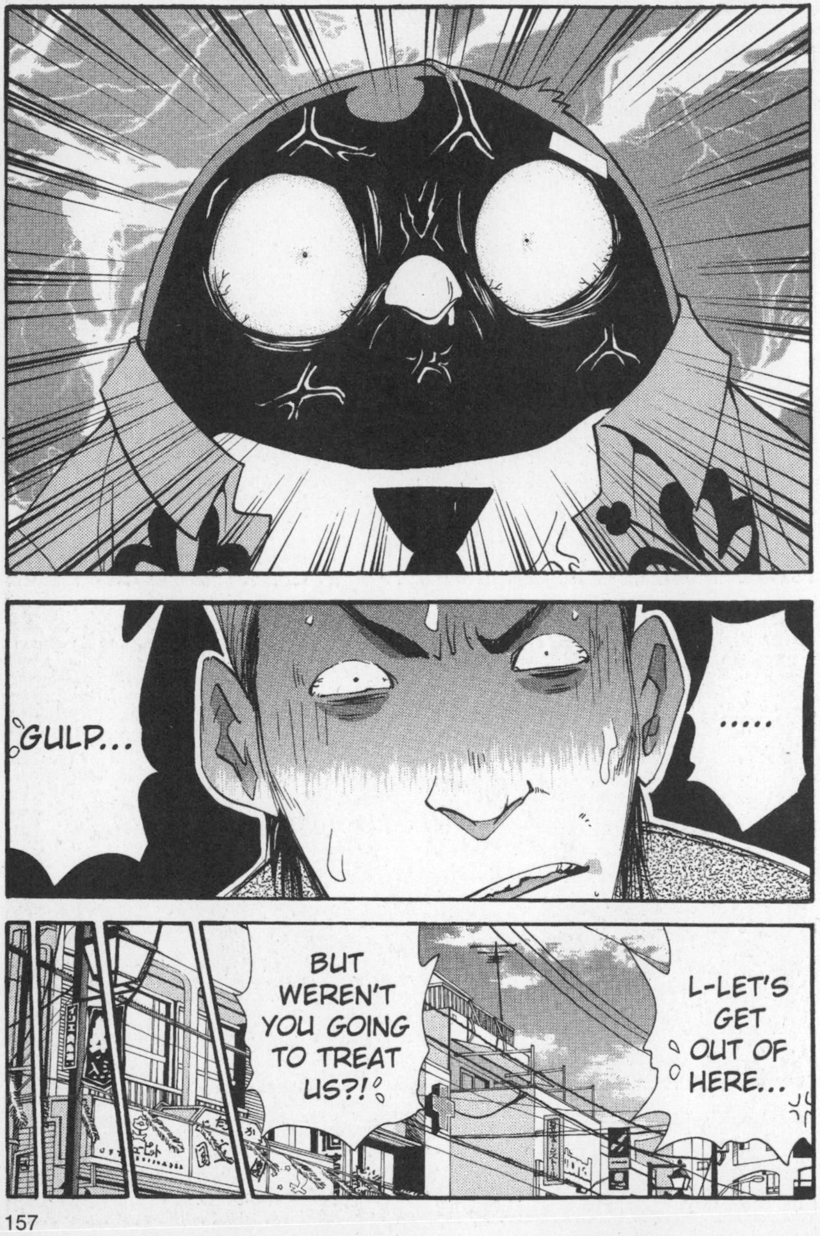
.....
GULP...
L-LET'S GET OUT OF HERE...
BUT WEREN'T YOU GOING TO TREAT US?!

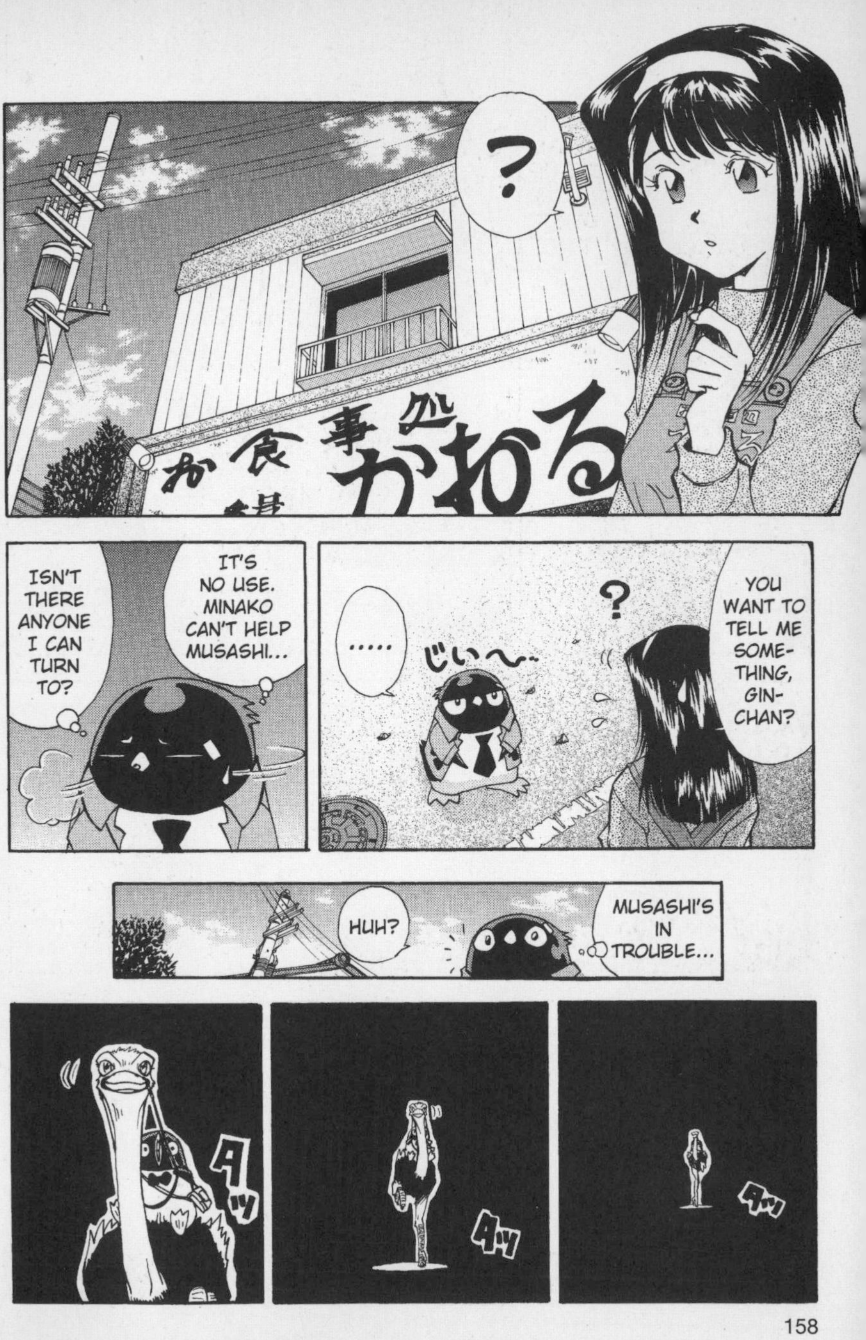
?
お食事処
かおる
YOU WANT TO TELL ME SOMETHING, GIN-CHAN?
?
......
じい～
IT'S NO USE. MINAKO CAN'T HELP MUSASHI...
ISN'T THERE ANYONE I CAN TURN TO?
MUSASHI'S IN TROUBLE...
HUH?
タッ
タッ
タッ

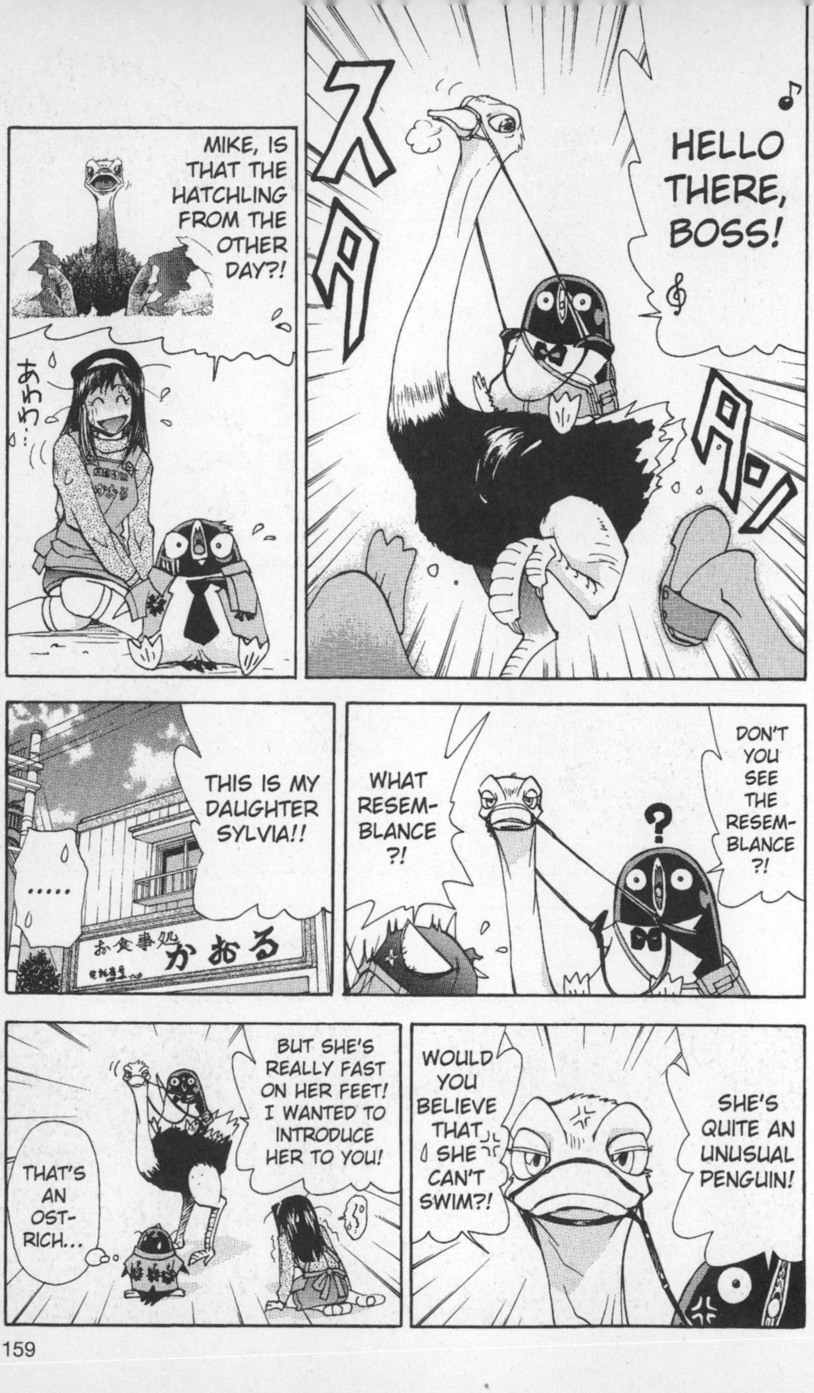
HELLO THERE, BOSS!
スタ
MIKE, IS THAT THE HATCHLING FROM THE OTHER DAY?!
あうう…
DON'T YOU SEE THE RESEMBLANCE?!
?
WHAT RESEMBLANCE?!
THIS IS MY DAUGHTER SYLVIA!!
......
お食事処 かおる
SHE'S QUITE AN UNUSUAL PENGUIN!
WOULD YOU BELIEVE THAT SHE CAN'T SWIM?!
BUT SHE'S REALLY FAST ON HER FEET! I WANTED TO INTRODUCE HER TO YOU!
THAT'S AN OSTRICH...

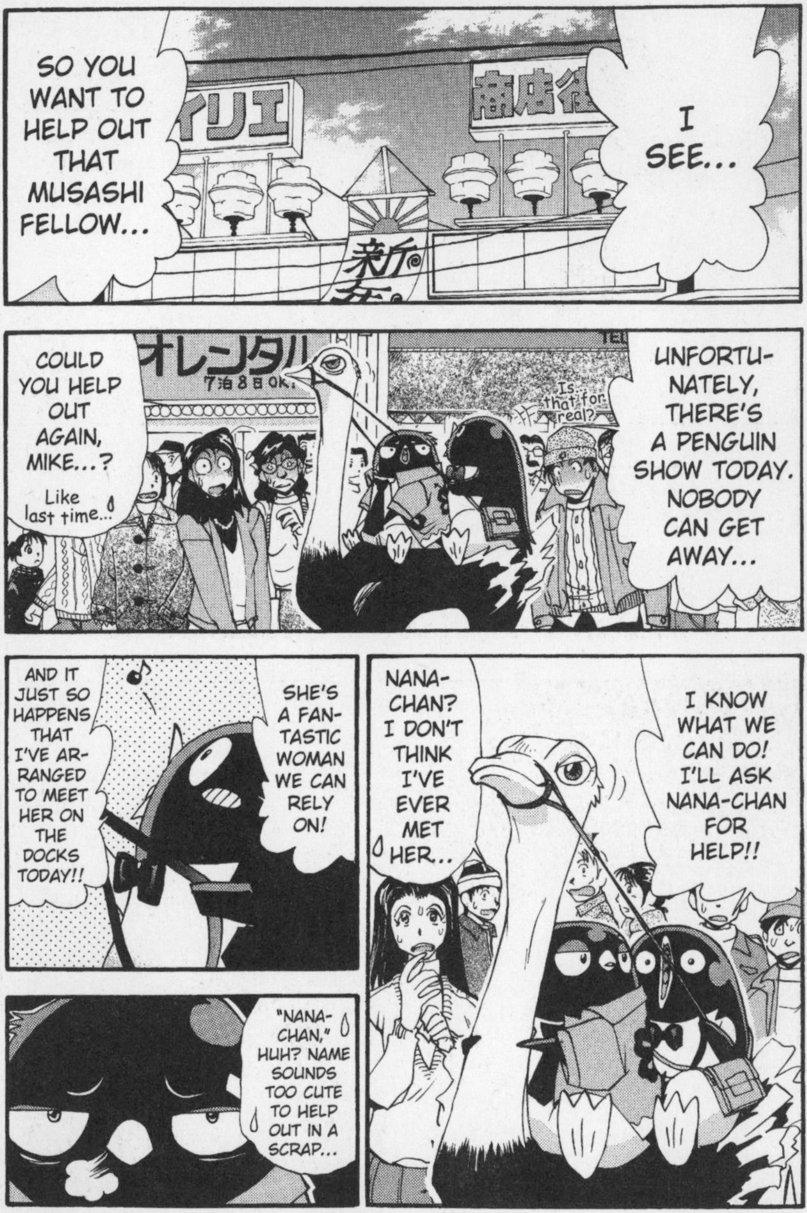
I SEE...
SO YOU WANT TO HELP OUT THAT MUSASHI FELLOW...
UNFORTUNATELY, THERE'S A PENGUIN SHOW TODAY. NOBODY CAN GET AWAY...
Is.. that for real?
COULD YOU HELP OUT AGAIN, MIKE...?
Like last time...
I KNOW WHAT WE CAN DO! I'LL ASK NANA-CHAN FOR HELP!!
NANA-CHAN? I DON'T THINK I'VE EVER MET HER...
SHE'S A FANTASTIC WOMAN WE CAN RELY ON!
AND IT JUST SO HAPPENS THAT I'VE ARRANGED TO MEET HER ON THE DOCKS TODAY!!
"NANA-CHAN," HUH? NAME SOUNDS TOO CUTE TO HELP OUT IN A SCRAP...

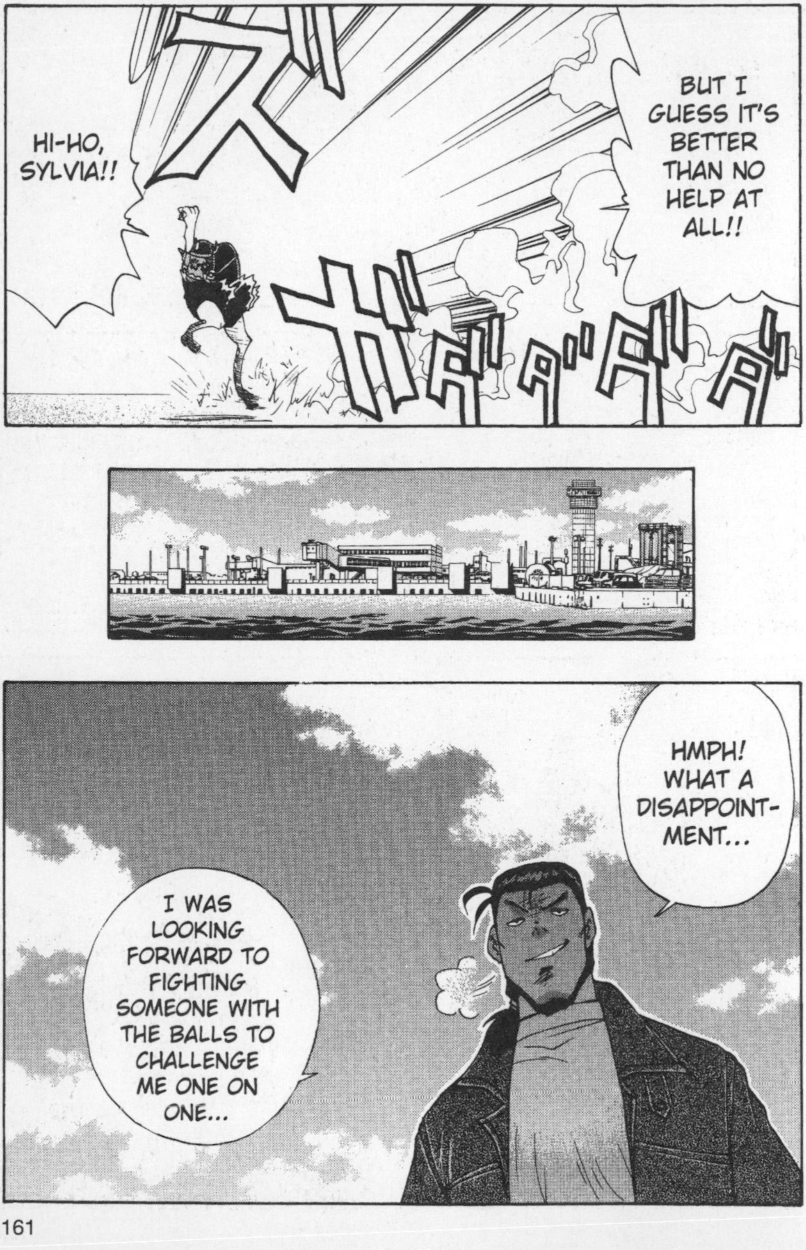
BUT I GUESS IT'S BETTER THAN NO HELP AT ALL!!
HI-HO, SYLVIA!!
HMPH! WHAT A DISAPPOINTMENT...
I WAS LOOKING FORWARD TO FIGHTING SOMEONE WITH THE BALLS TO CHALLENGE ME ONE ON ONE...

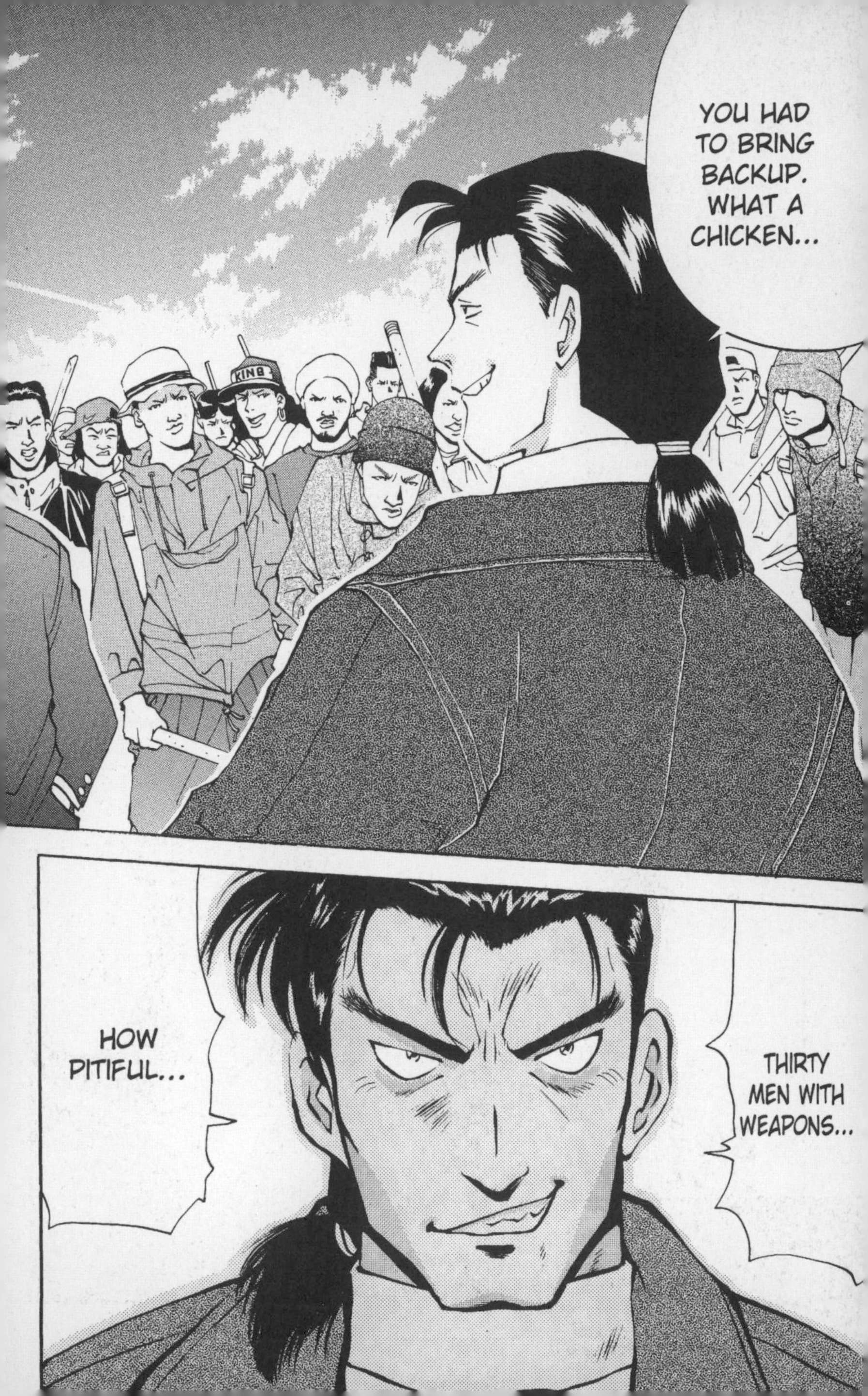
YOU HAD TO BRING BACKUP. WHAT A CHICKEN...
THIRTY MEN WITH WEAPONS...
HOW PITIFUL...

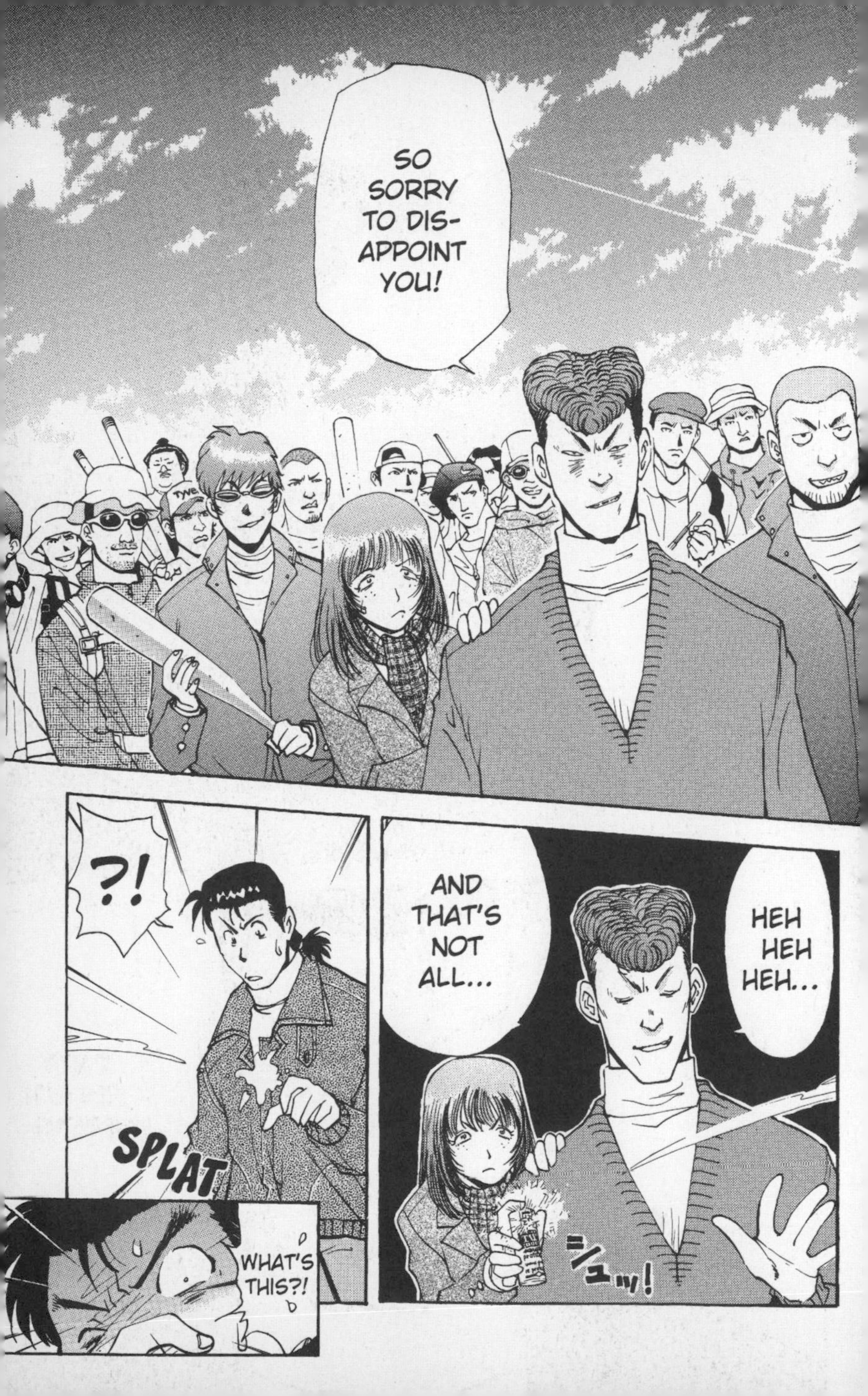
SO SORRY TO DIS-APPOINT YOU!
HEH HEH HEH...
AND THAT'S NOT ALL...
シュッ!
?!
SPLAT
WHAT'S THIS?!

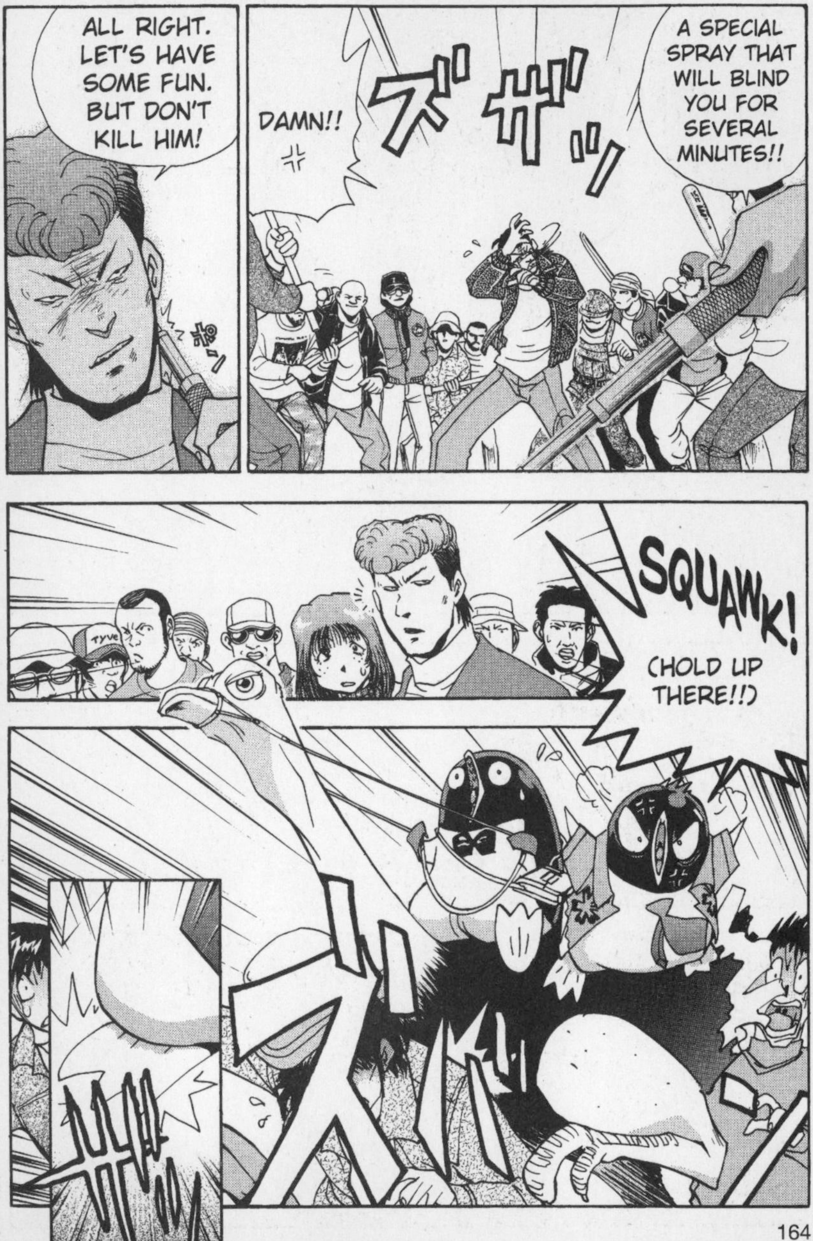
A SPECIAL SPRAY THAT WILL BLIND YOU FOR SEVERAL MINUTES!!
DAMN!!
ALL RIGHT. LET'S HAVE SOME FUN. BUT DON'T KILL HIM!
SQUAWK!
(HOLD UP THERE!!)

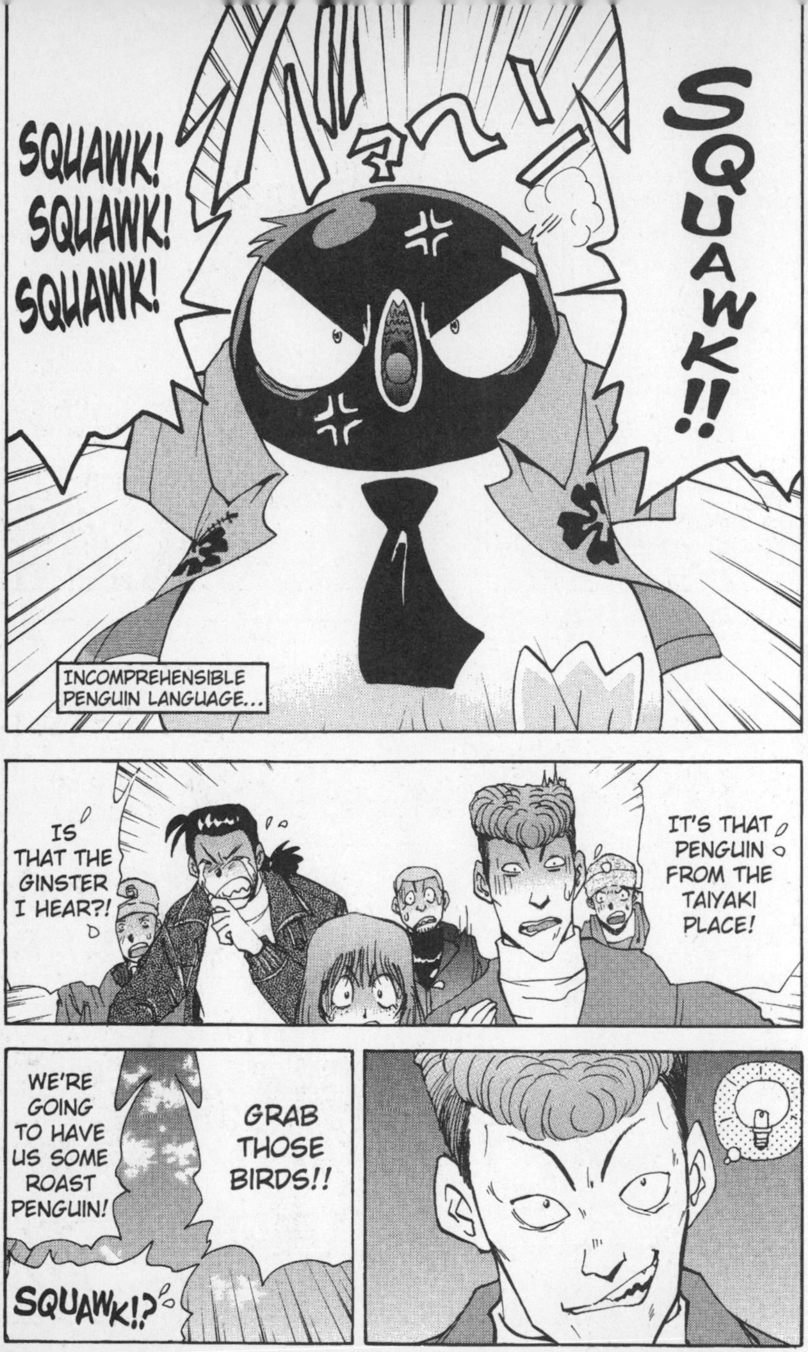
SQUAWK!!
SQUAWK! SQUAWK! SQUAWK!
INCOMPREHENSIBLE PENGUIN LANGUAGE...
IT'S THAT PENGUIN FROM THE TAIYAKI PLACE!
IS THAT THE GINSTER I HEAR?!
GRAB THOSE BIRDS!!
WE'RE GOING TO HAVE US SOME ROAST PENGUIN!
SQUAWK!?

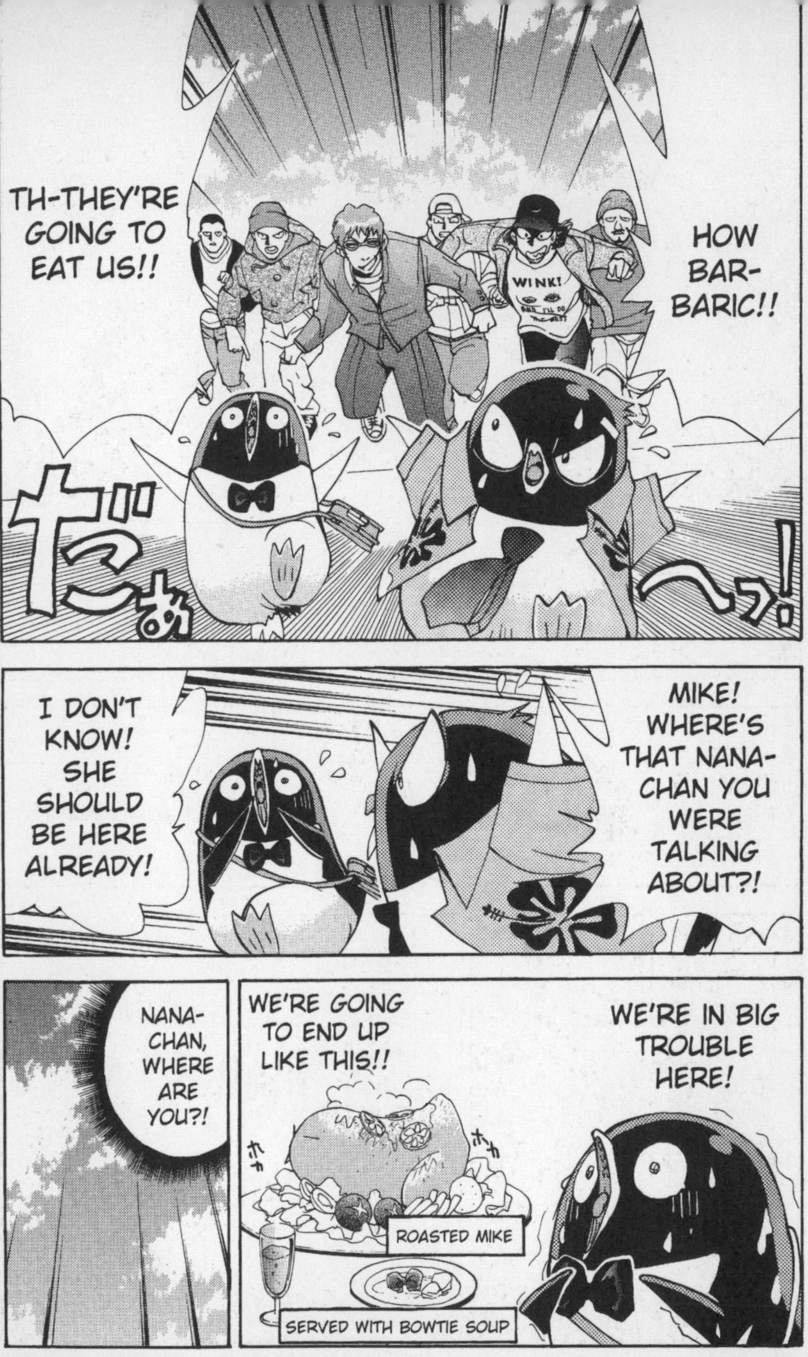
HOW BAR-BARIC!!
TH-THEY'RE GOING TO EAT US!!
MIKE! WHERE'S THAT NANA-CHAN YOU WERE TALKING ABOUT?!
I DON'T KNOW! SHE SHOULD BE HERE ALREADY!
WE'RE IN BIG TROUBLE HERE!
WE'RE GOING TO END UP LIKE THIS!!
ROASTED MIKE
SERVED WITH BOWTIE SOUP
NANA-CHAN, WHERE ARE YOU?!

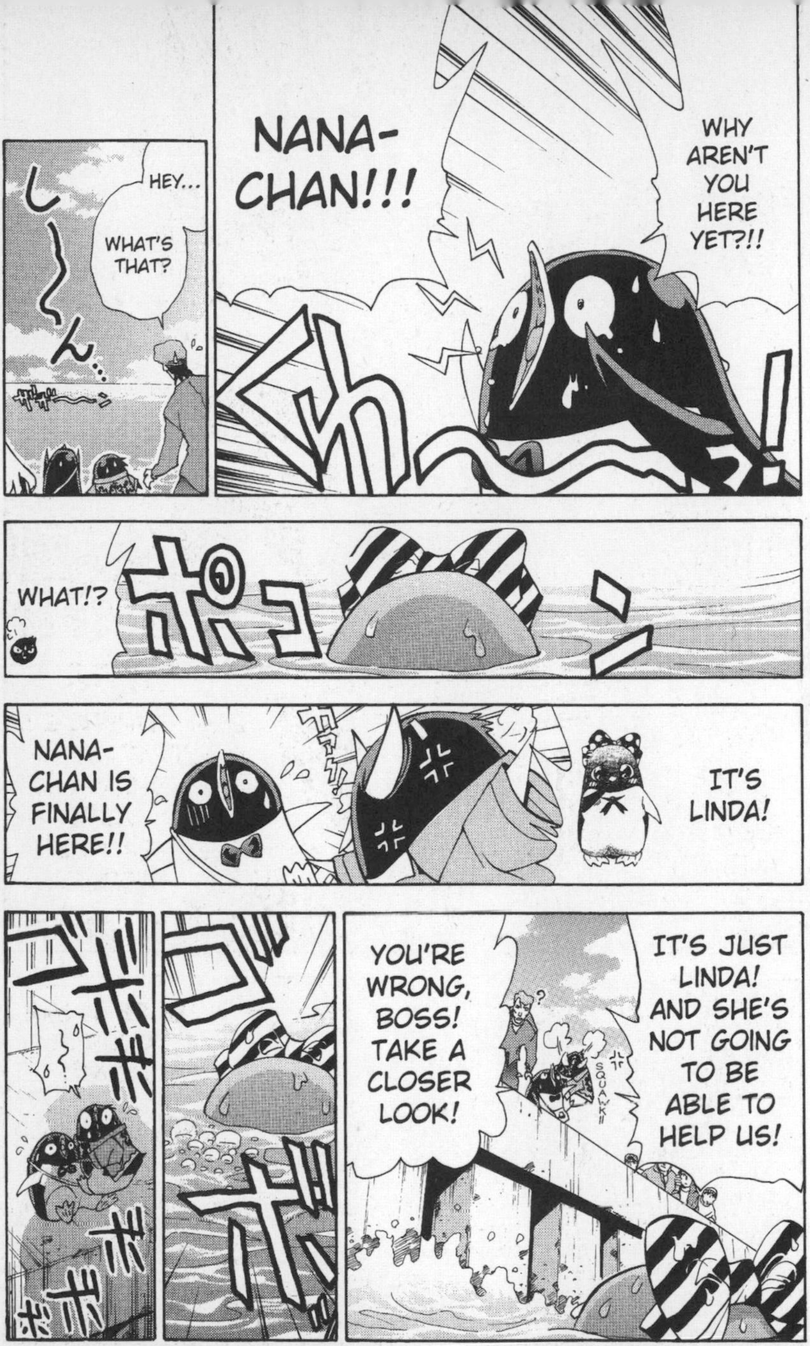
WHY AREN'T YOU HERE YET?!!
NANA-CHAN!!!
HEY...
WHAT'S THAT?
WHAT!?
IT'S LINDA!
NANA-CHAN IS FINALLY HERE!!
IT'S JUST LINDA! AND SHE'S NOT GOING TO BE ABLE TO HELP US!
SQUAWK!!
YOU'RE WRONG, BOSS! TAKE A CLOSER LOOK!

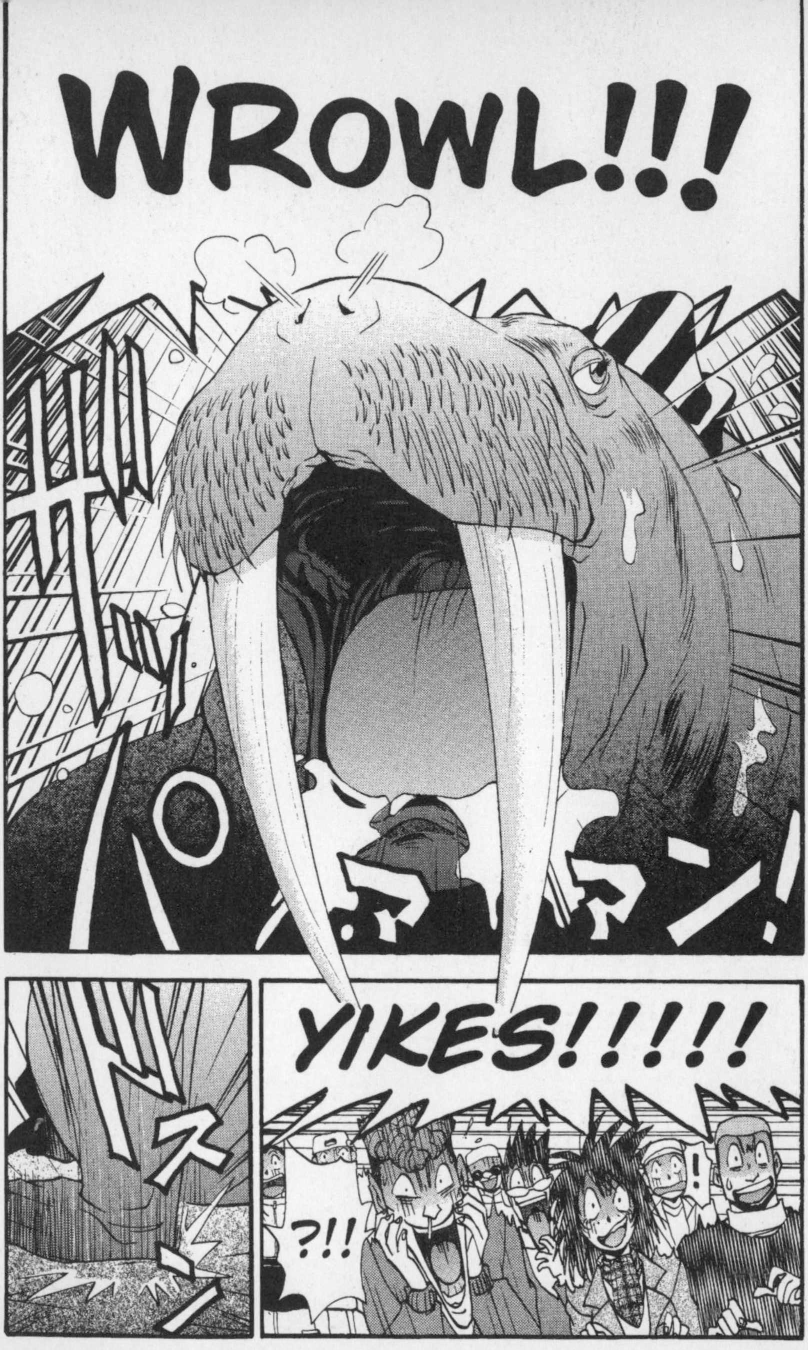
WROWL!!!
YIKES!!!!!
?!!

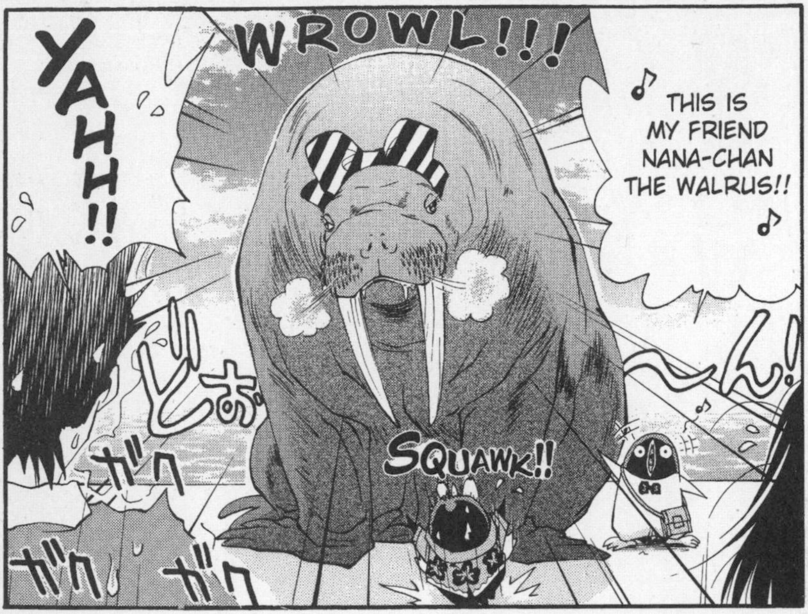
THIS IS MY FRIEND NANA-CHAN THE WALRUS!!
WROWL!!!
YAHH!!
SQUAWK!!

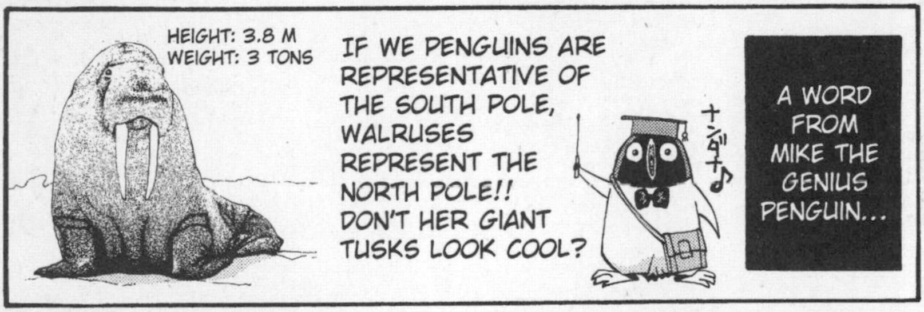
A WORD FROM MIKE THE GENIUS PENGUIN...
IF WE PENGUINS ARE REPRESENTATIVE OF THE SOUTH POLE, WALRUSES REPRESENT THE NORTH POLE!! DON'T HER GIANT TUSKS LOOK COOL?
HEIGHT: 3.8 M
WEIGHT: 3 TONS

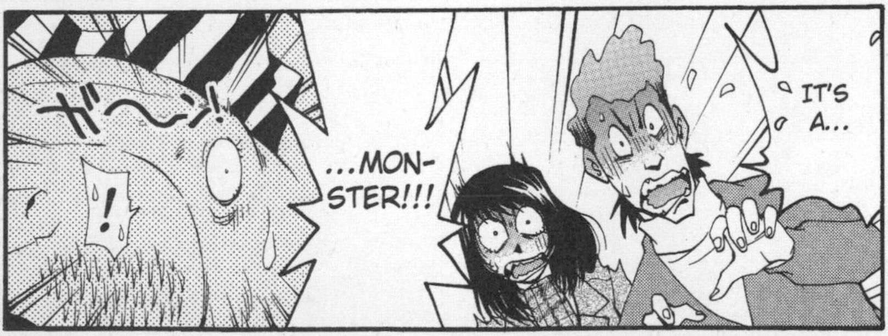
IT'S A...
...MON-STER!!!

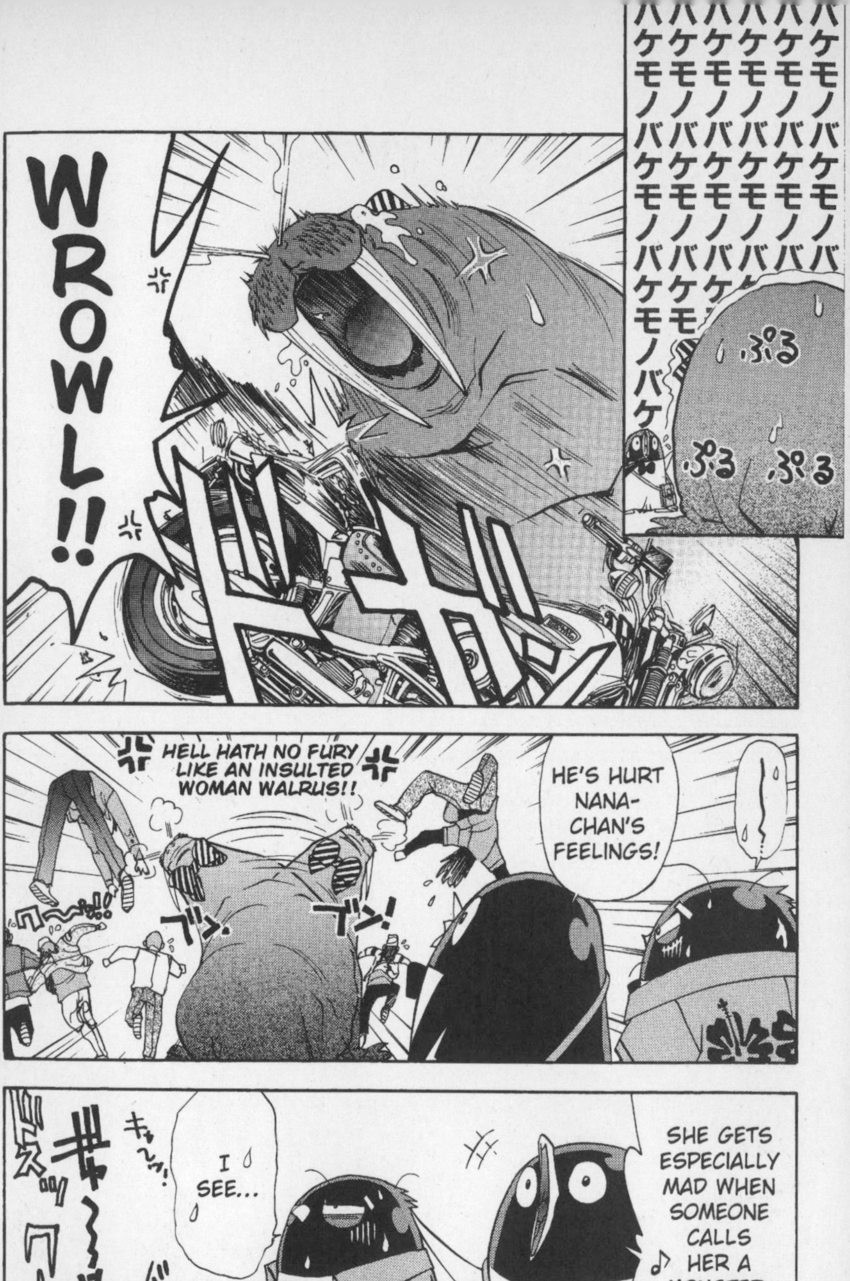

バケモノバケモノバケモノ
ぷる
ぷる
ぷる
WROWL!!
HE'S HURT NANA-CHAN'S FEELINGS!
HELL HATH NO FURY LIKE AN INSULTED WOMAN WALRUS!!
ブン!
ブン
SHE GETS ESPECIALLY MAD WHEN SOMEONE CALLS HER A MONSTER. ♪
I SEE...

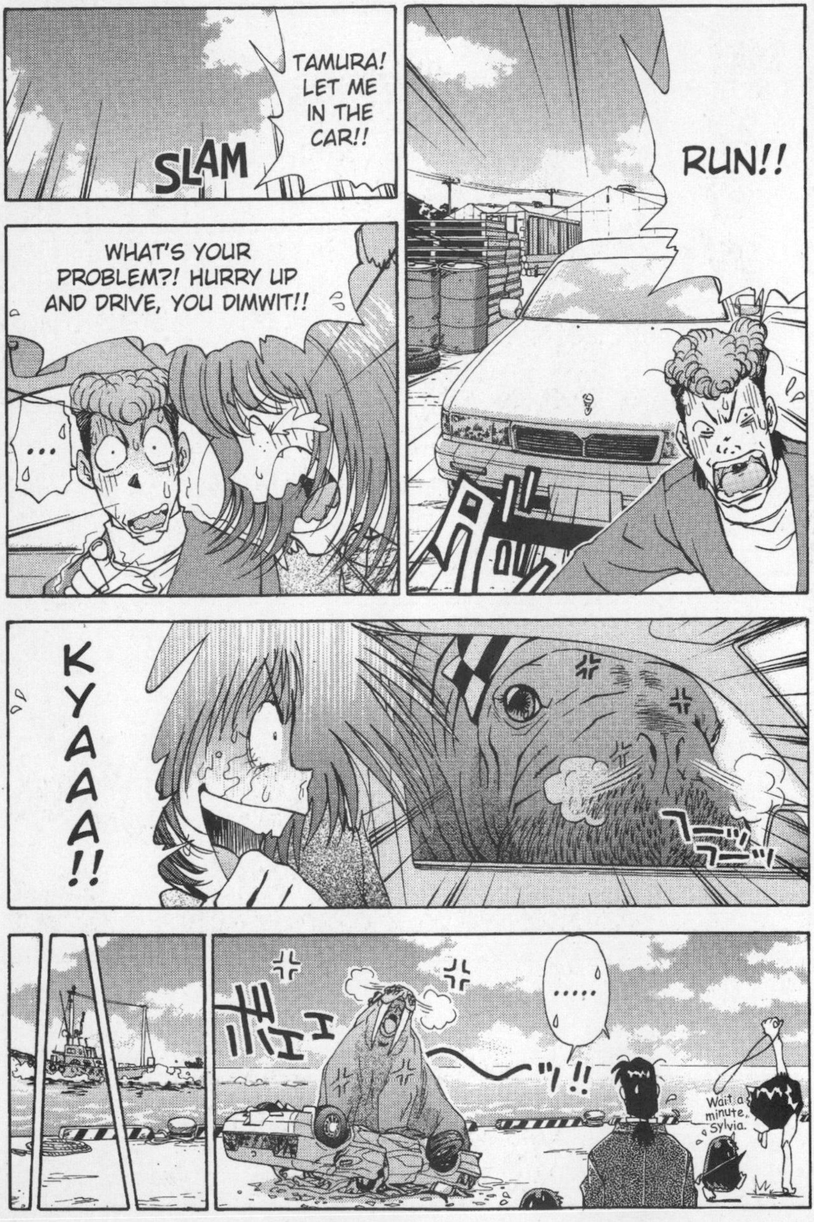
RUN!!
TAMURA! LET ME IN THE CAR!!
SLAM
WHAT'S YOUR PROBLEM?! HURRY UP AND DRIVE, YOU DIMWIT!!
...
フーッ
フーッ
KYAAAA!!
Wait a minute, Sylvia.
......
ボエエーッ!!

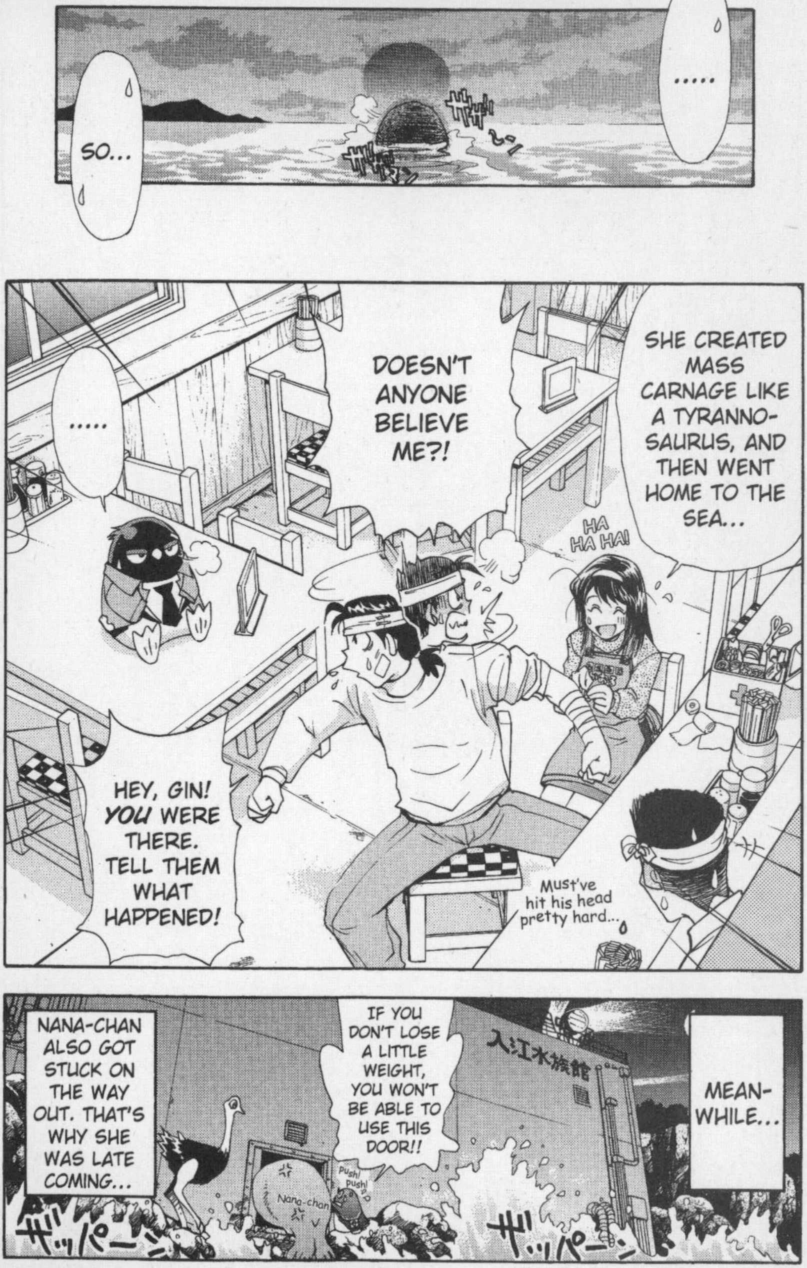
.....
SO...
SHE CREATED MASS CARNAGE LIKE A TYRANNO-SAURUS, AND THEN WENT HOME TO THE SEA...
HA HA HA!
DOESN'T ANYONE BELIEVE ME?!
.....
Must've hit his head pretty hard...
HEY, GIN! YOU WERE THERE. TELL THEM WHAT HAPPENED!
MEAN-WHILE...
入江水族館
IF YOU DON'T LOSE A LITTLE WEIGHT, YOU WON'T BE ABLE TO USE THIS DOOR!!
Push! push!
Nana-chan
NANA-CHAN ALSO GOT STUCK ON THE WAY OUT. THAT'S WHY SHE WAS LATE COMING...

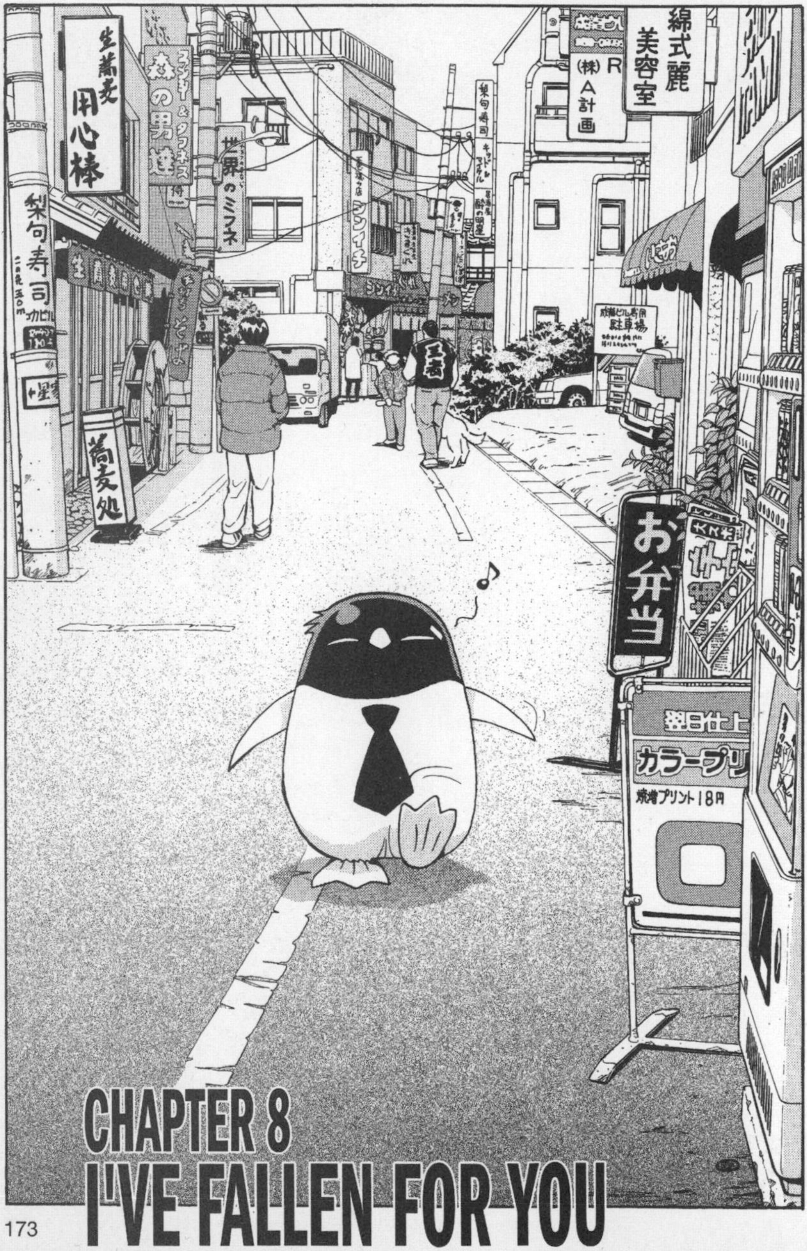
生蕎麦 用心棒
梨句寿司
森の男達
世界のミフネ
綿式麗 美容室
(株) R A計画
蕎麦処
お弁当
カラープリ
焼増プリント18円

CHAPTER 8
I'VE FALLEN FOR YOU

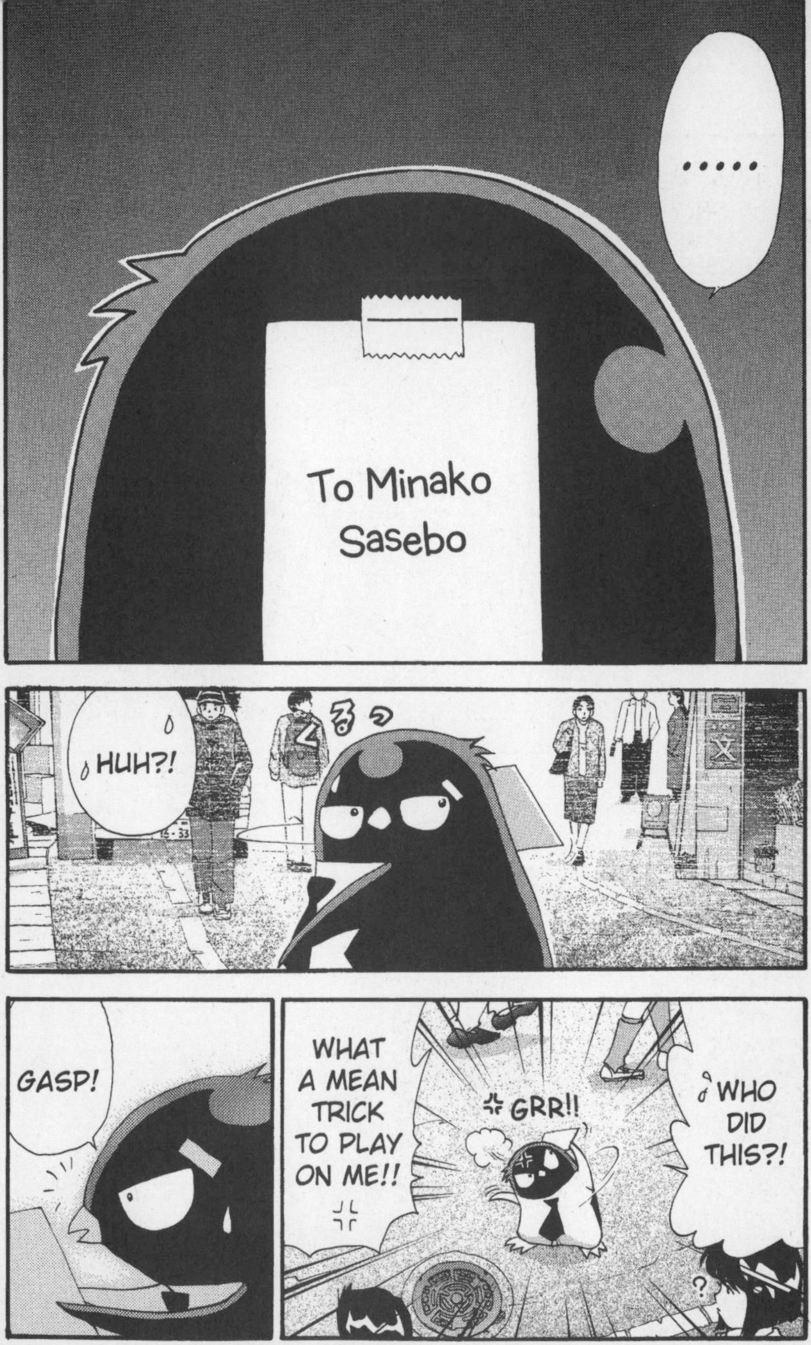
.....
To Minako Sasebo
HUH?!
WHO DID THIS?!
GRR!!
WHAT A MEAN TRICK TO PLAY ON ME!!
GASP!

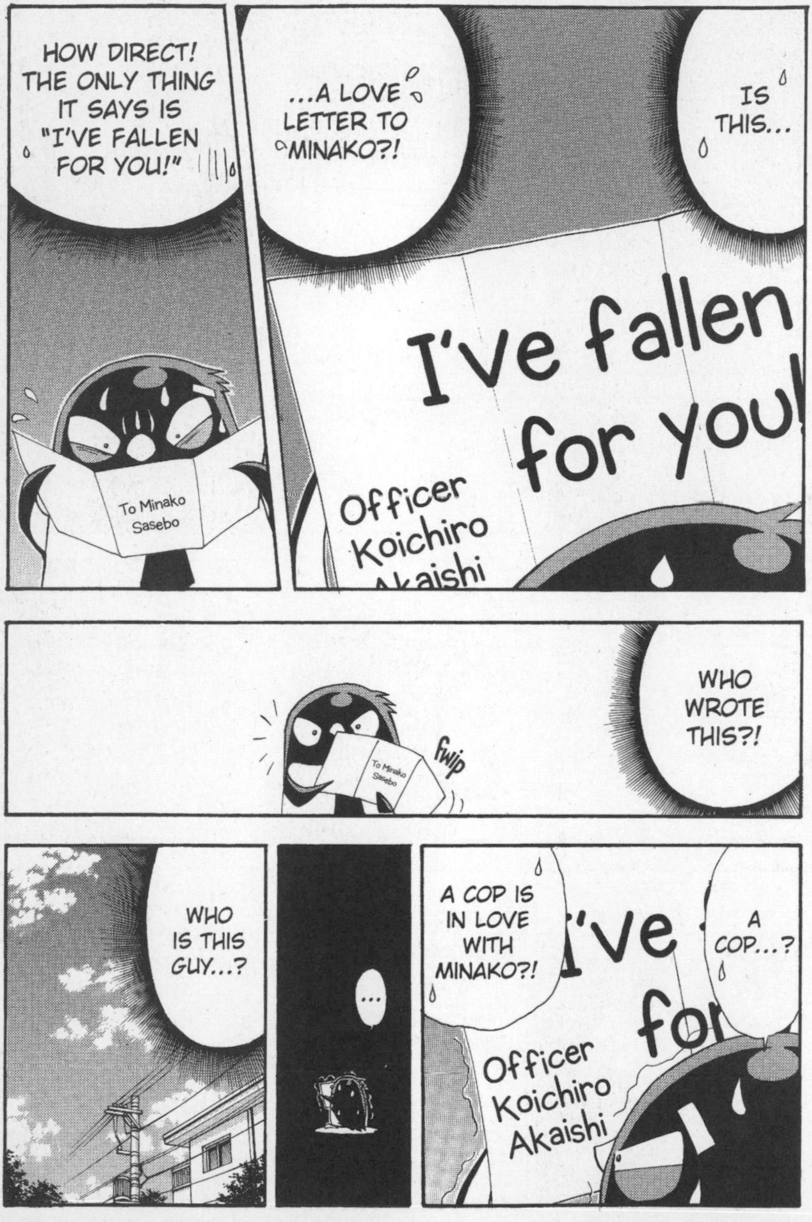
IS THIS...
...A LOVE LETTER TO MINAKO?!
I've fallen for you
Officer Koichiro
HOW DIRECT! THE ONLY THING IT SAYS IS "I'VE FALLEN FOR YOU!"
To Minako Sasebo
WHO WROTE THIS?!
fwip
To Minako Sasebo
A COP...?
A COP IS IN LOVE WITH MINAKO?!
Officer Koichiro Akaishi
...
WHO IS THIS GUY...?

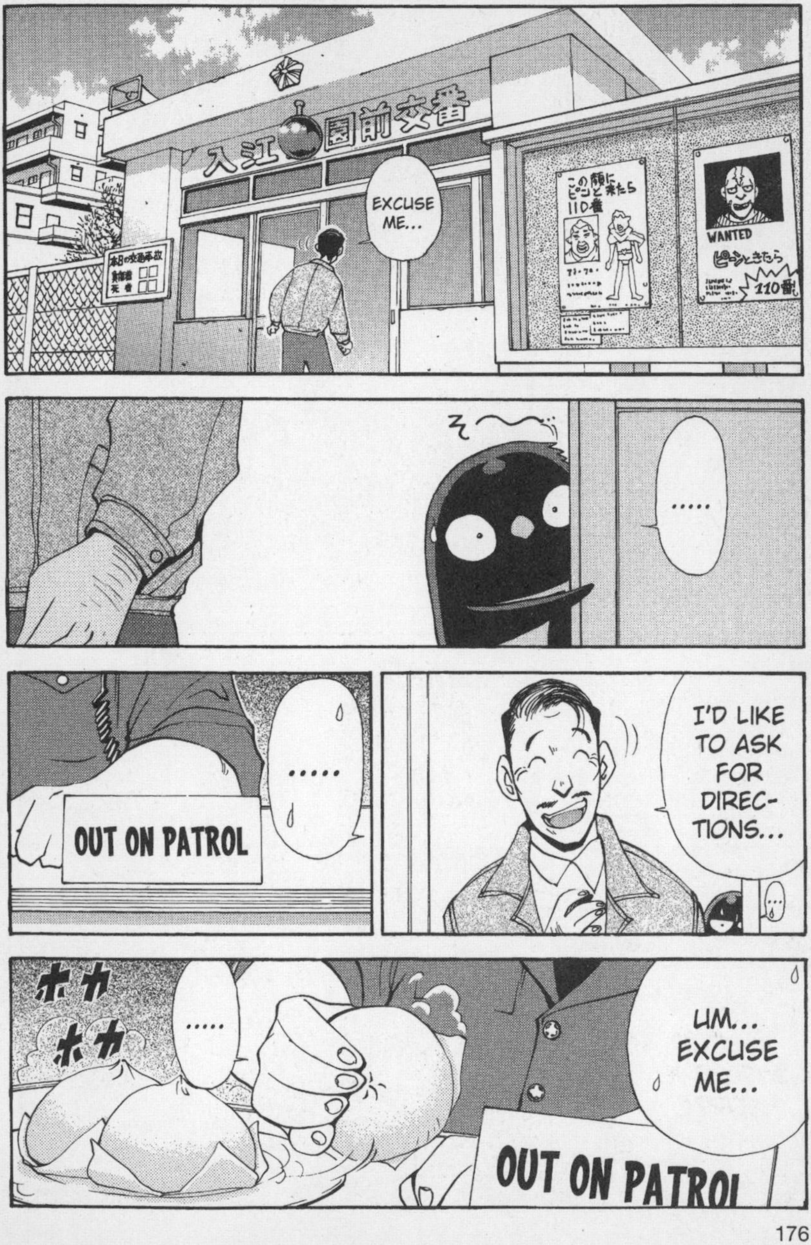
入江◯園前交番
この顔にピンと来たら110番
WANTED
ピンときたら 110番!
EXCUSE ME...
.....
I'D LIKE TO ASK FOR DIREC-TIONS...
...
.....
OUT ON PATROL
UM... EXCUSE ME...
OUT ON PATROL
.....
ホカ ホカ

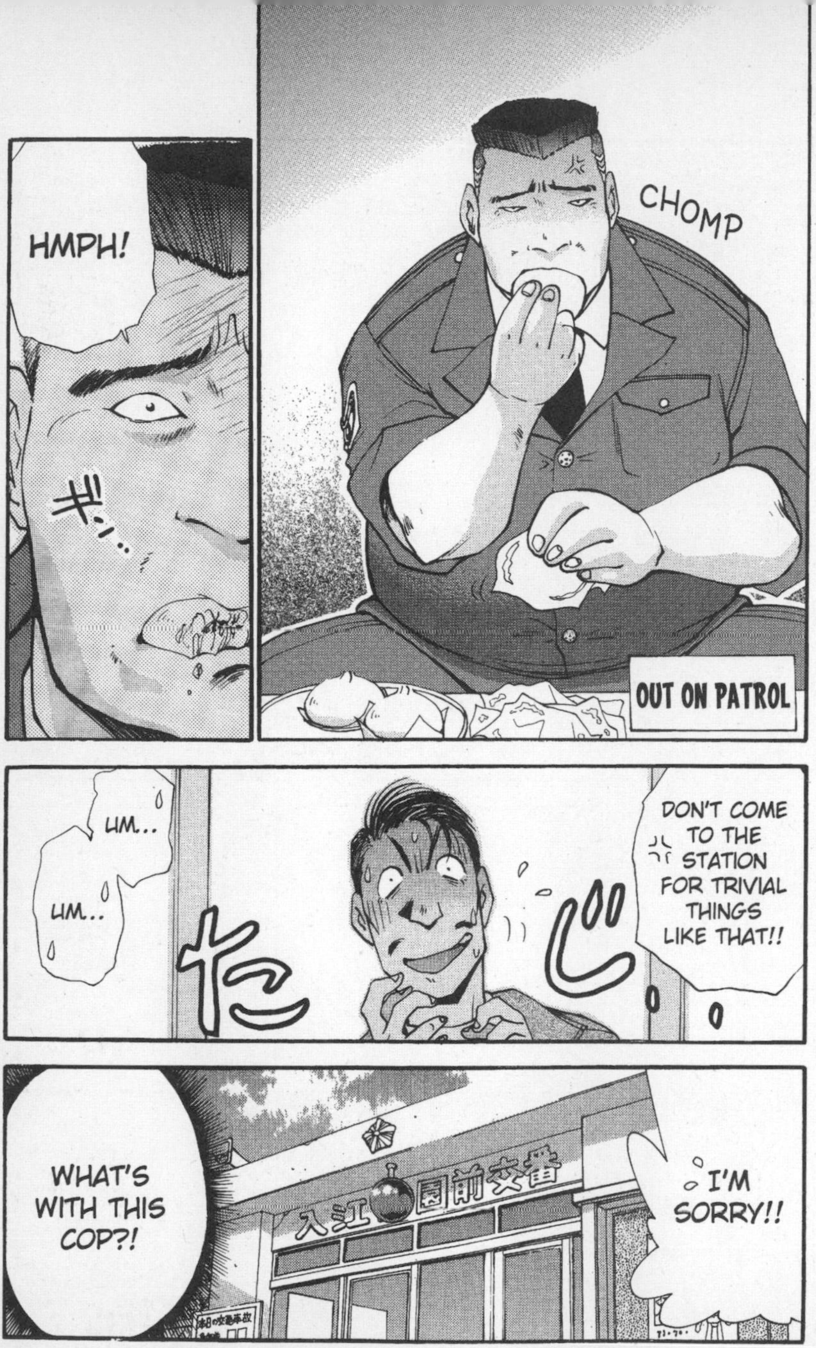
CHOMP
OUT ON PATROL
HMPH!
DON'T COME TO THE STATION FOR TRIVIAL THINGS LIKE THAT!!
たじ
UM...
UM...
I'M SORRY!!
WHAT'S WITH THIS COP?!

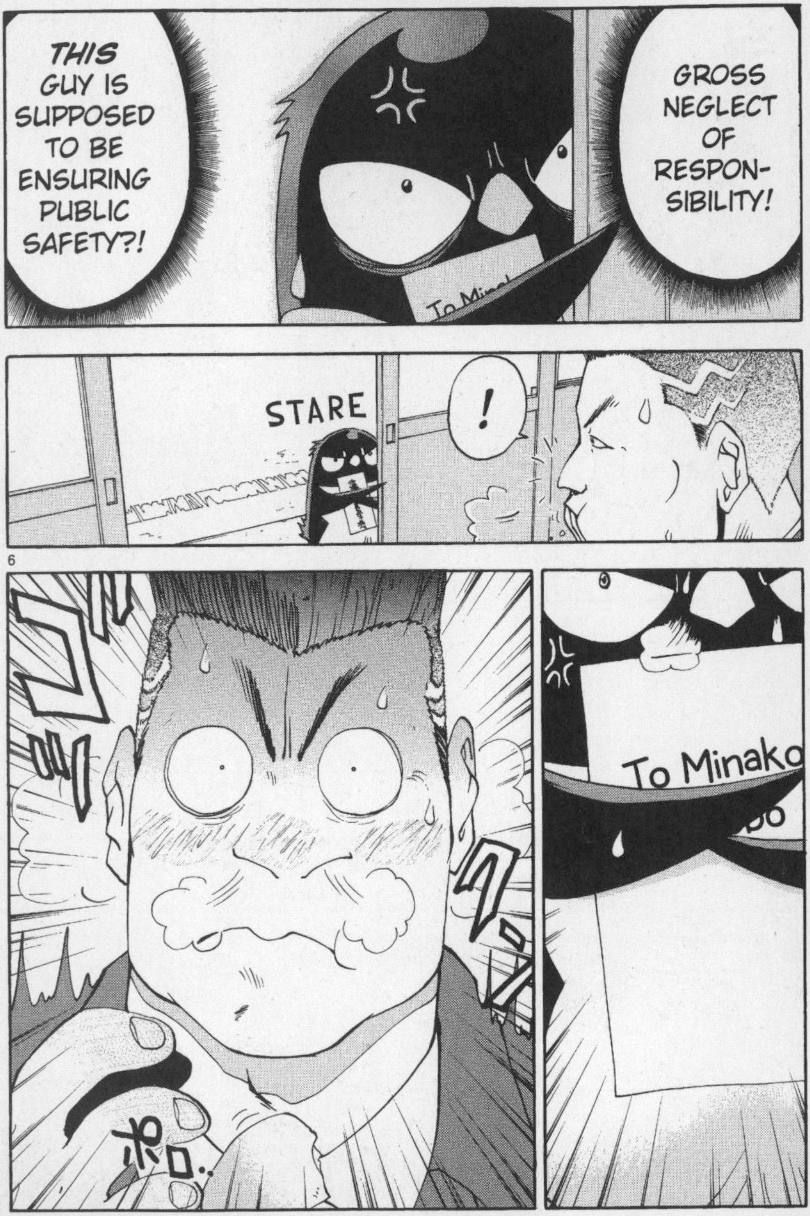
GROSS NEGLECT OF RESPON-SIBILITY!
THIS GUY IS SUPPOSED TO BE ENSURING PUBLIC SAFETY?!
!
STARE
To Minako
ポロ..

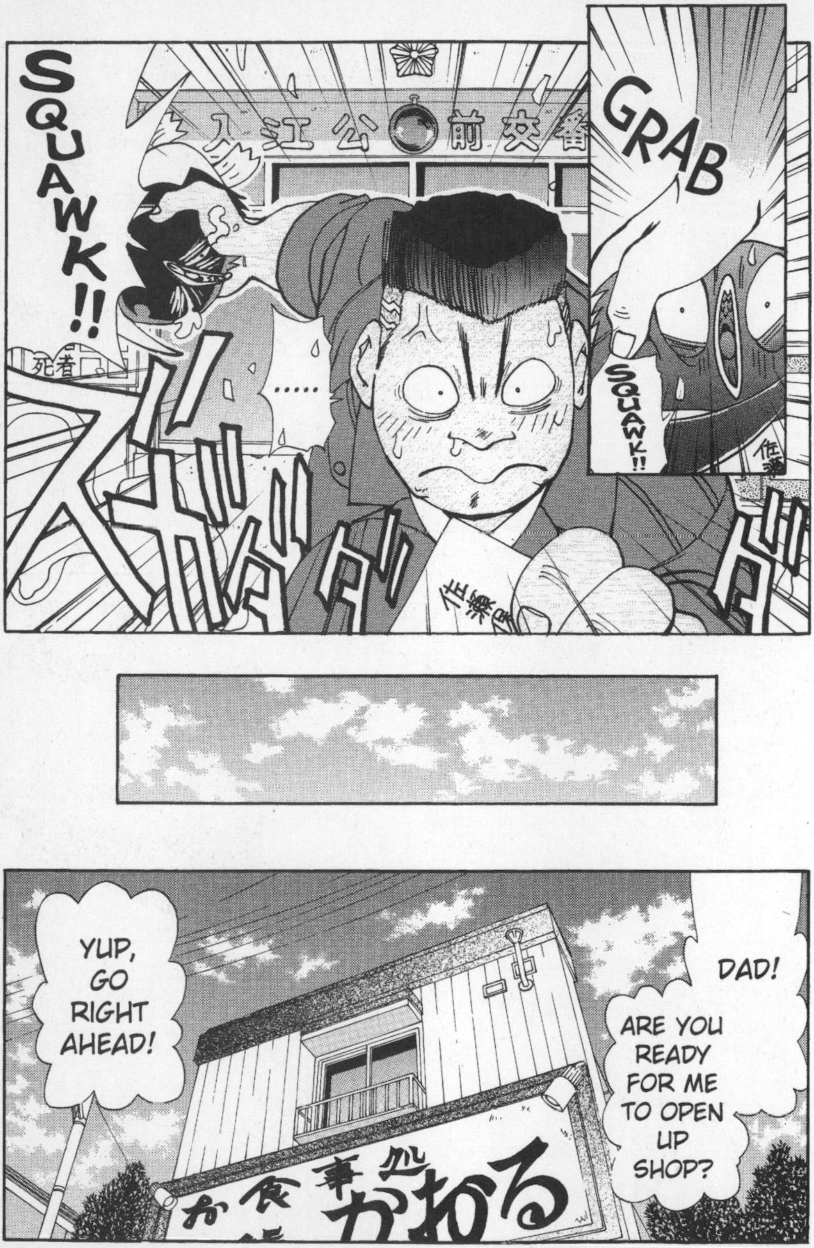
GRAB
SQUAWK!!
SQUAWK!!
......
DAD!
ARE YOU READY FOR ME TO OPEN UP SHOP?
YUP, GO RIGHT AHEAD!
お食事処 かおる

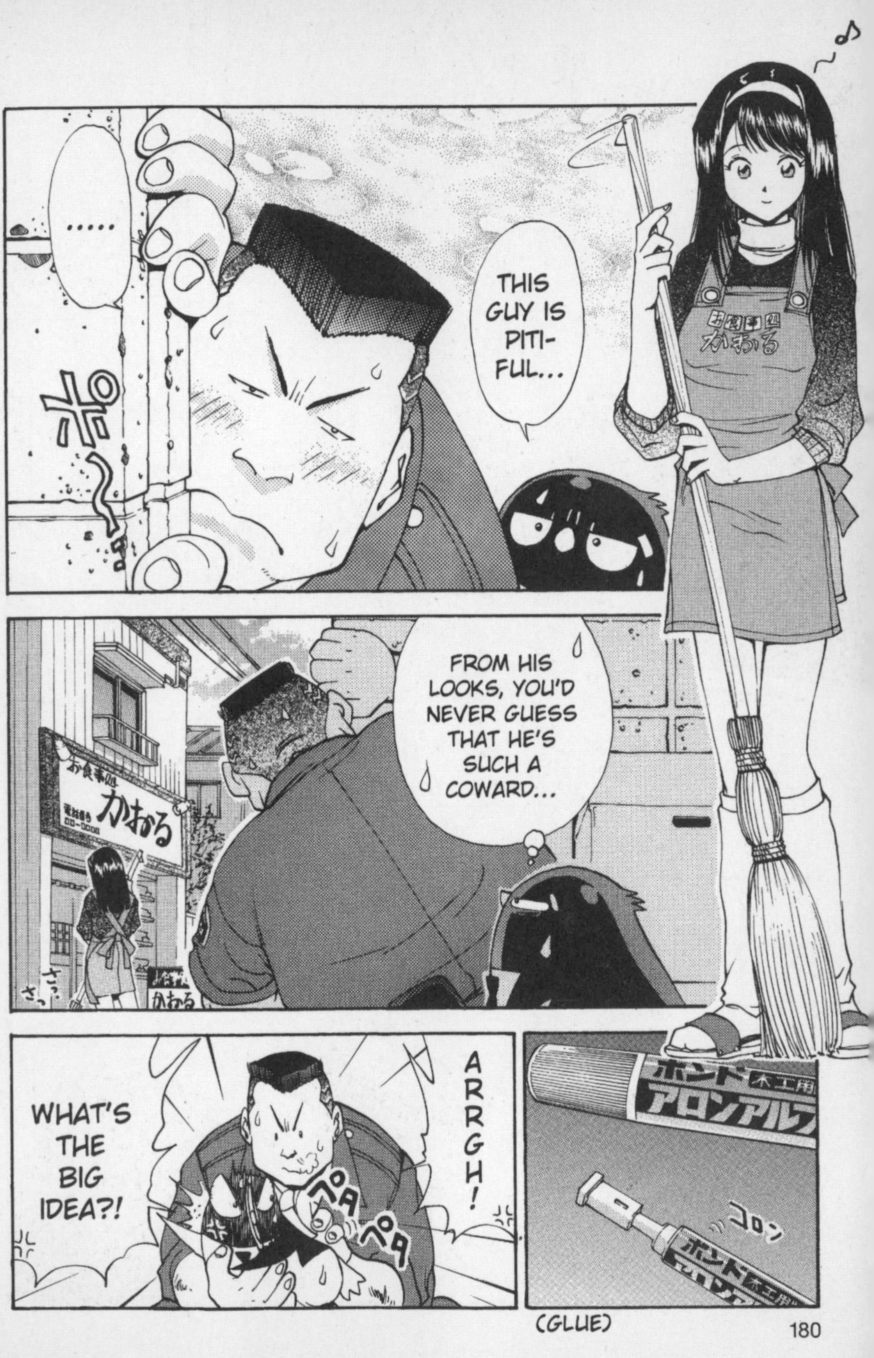
~♪
THIS GUY IS PITIFUL...
.....
ポ〜
FROM HIS LOOKS, YOU'D NEVER GUESS THAT HE'S SUCH A COWARD...
かおる
さっ さっ
かおる
コロン
ARRGH!
WHAT'S THE BIG IDEA?!
ペタ ペタ

(GLUE)

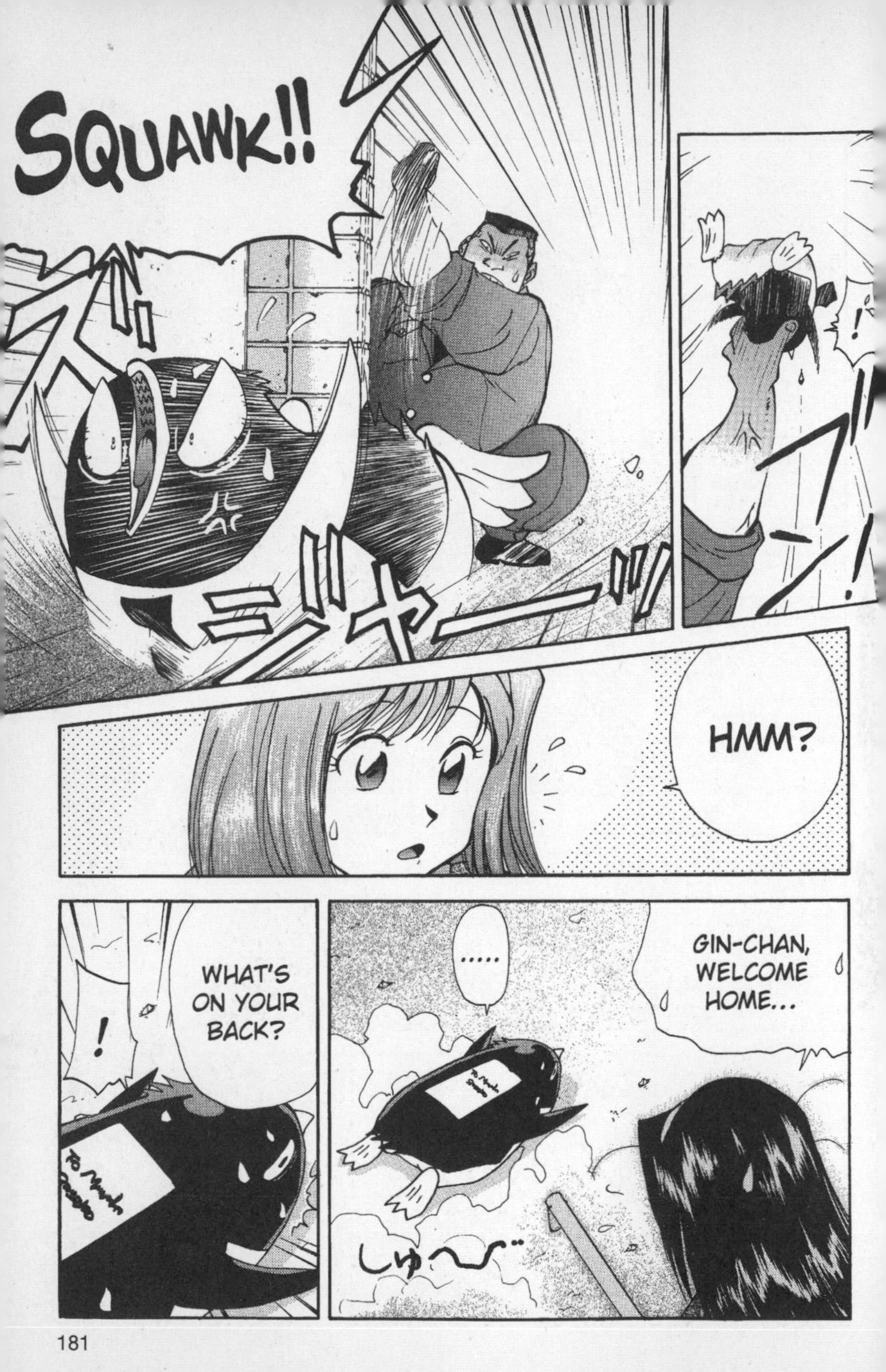
SQUAWK!!
HMM?
GIN-CHAN, WELCOME HOME...
......
!
WHAT'S ON YOUR BACK?

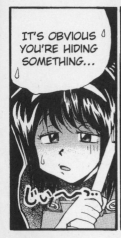

!!
To Minako Sasebo
ガバッ
IT'S OBVIOUS YOU'RE HIDING SOMETHING...
じぃ～っ…
FWOOSH
FWISH
SWOOSH
SWISH
To Minako Sasebo
HOP HOP HOP HOP
ぴゅん!
GIN-CHAN ACTS SO WEIRD SOME TIMES...

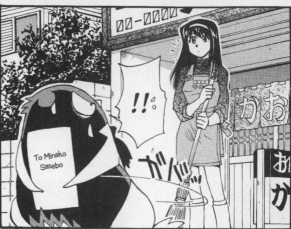

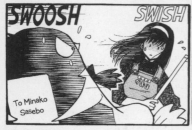

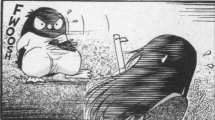

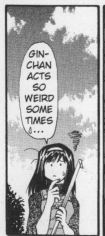

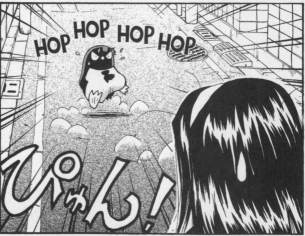

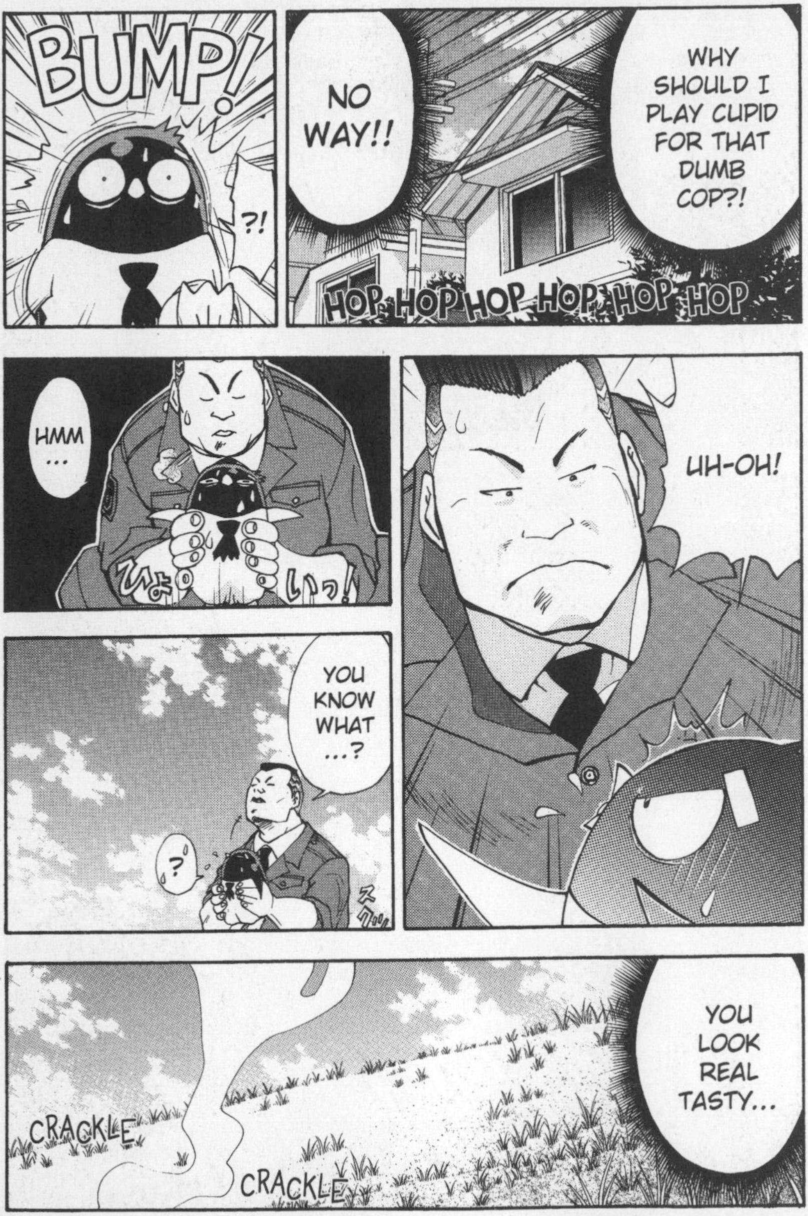
WHY SHOULD I PLAY CUPID FOR THAT DUMB COP?!
NO WAY!!
HOP HOP HOP HOP HOP HOP
BUMP!
?!
UH-OH!
HMM ...
ひょいっ!
YOU KNOW WHAT ...?
?
スクッ
YOU LOOK REAL TASTY...
CRACKLE
CRACKLE

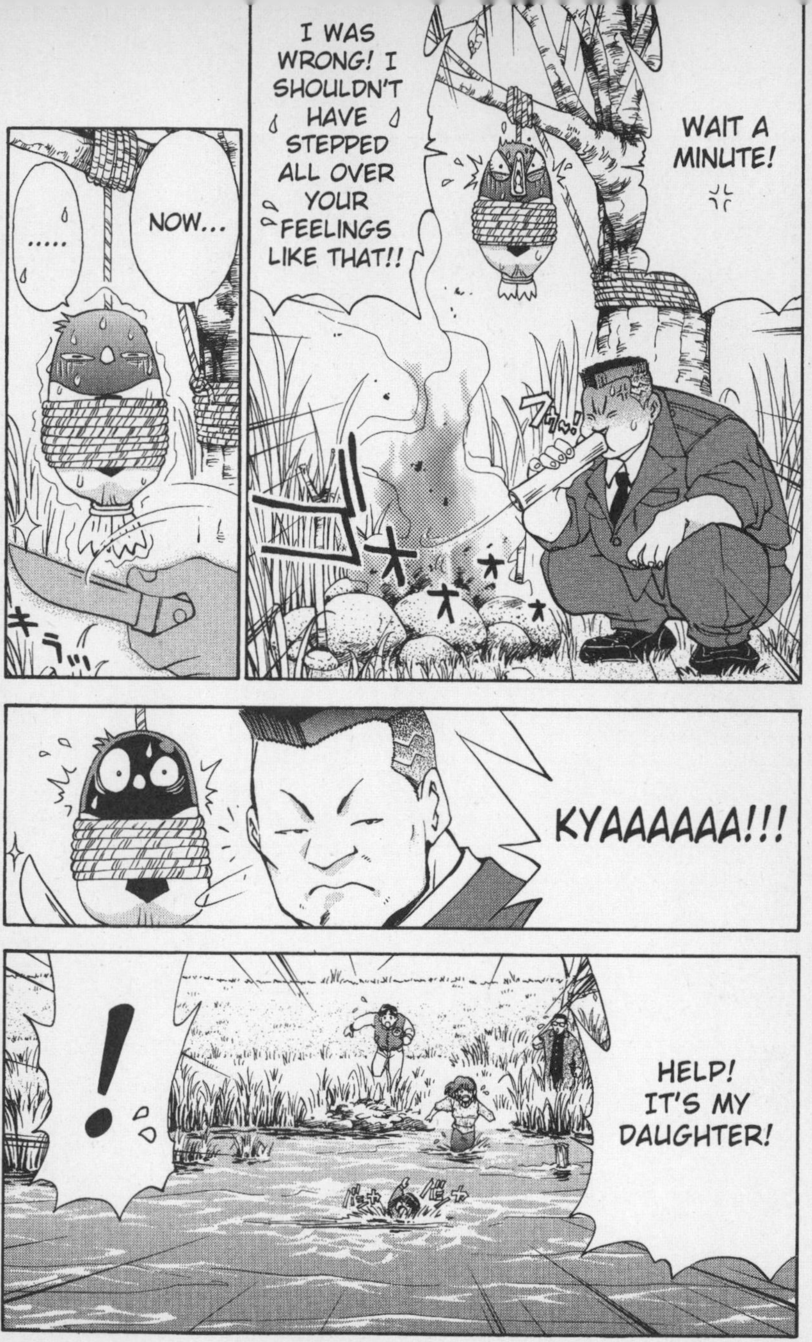
WAIT A MINUTE!
I WAS WRONG! I SHOULDN'T HAVE STEPPED ALL OVER YOUR FEELINGS LIKE THAT!!
NOW...
.....
キラッ
KYAAAAAAA!!!
HELP! IT'S MY DAUGHTER!
!

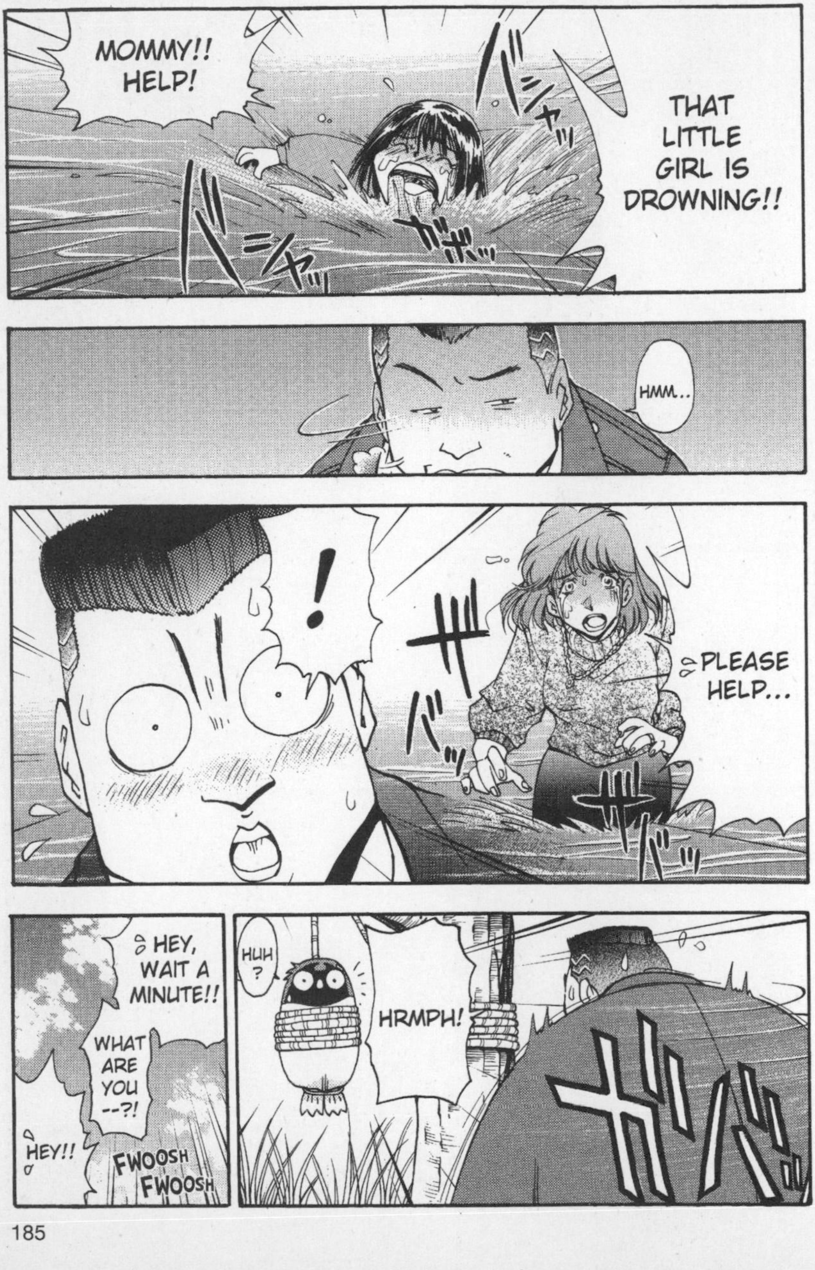

THAT LITTLE GIRL IS DROWNING!!
MOMMY!! HELP!
HMM..
PLEASE HELP...
!
HRMPH!
HUH?
HEY, WAIT A MINUTE!!
WHAT ARE YOU --?!
HEY!!
FWOOSH FWOOSH

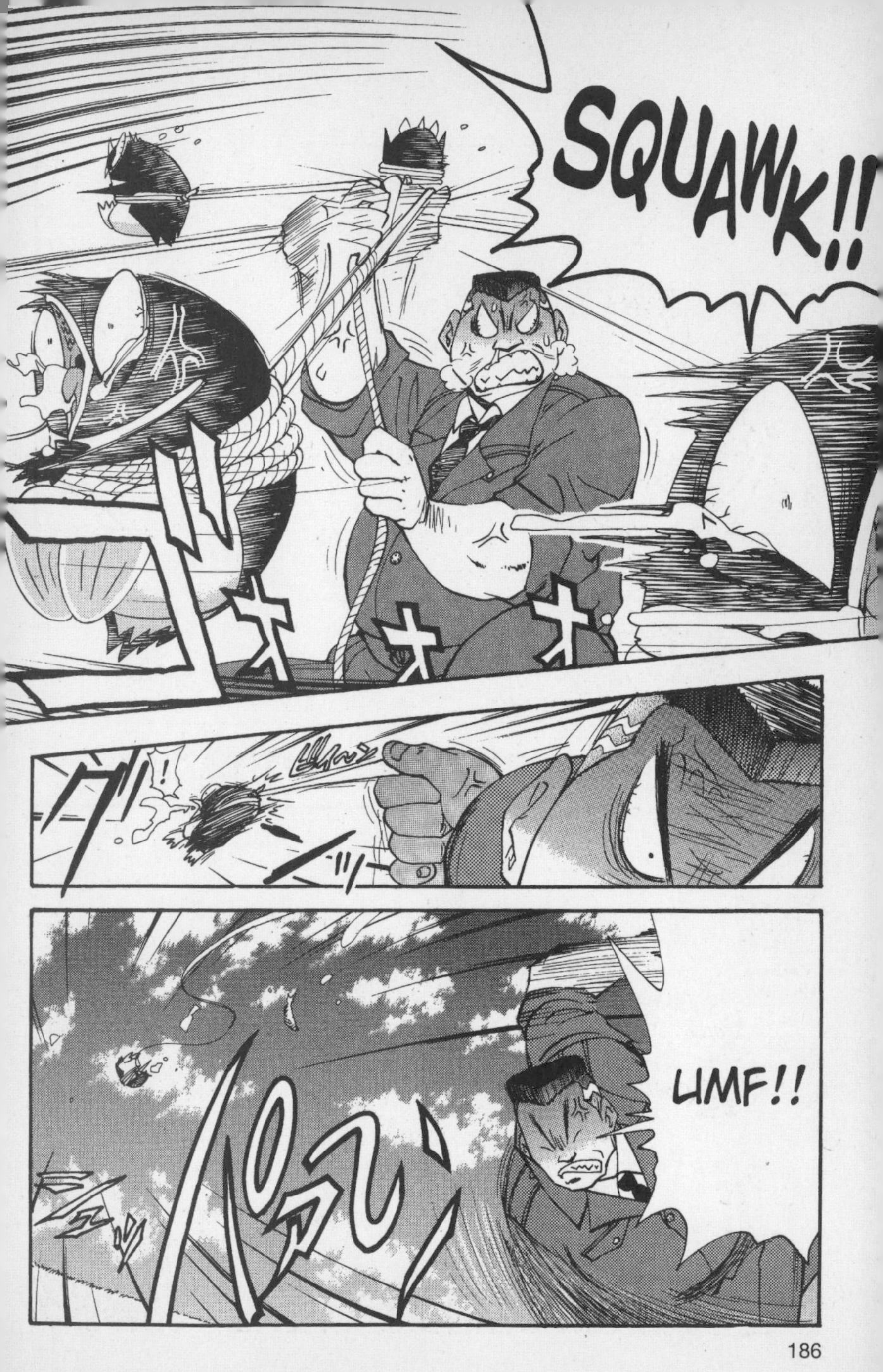
SQUAWK!!
UMF!!

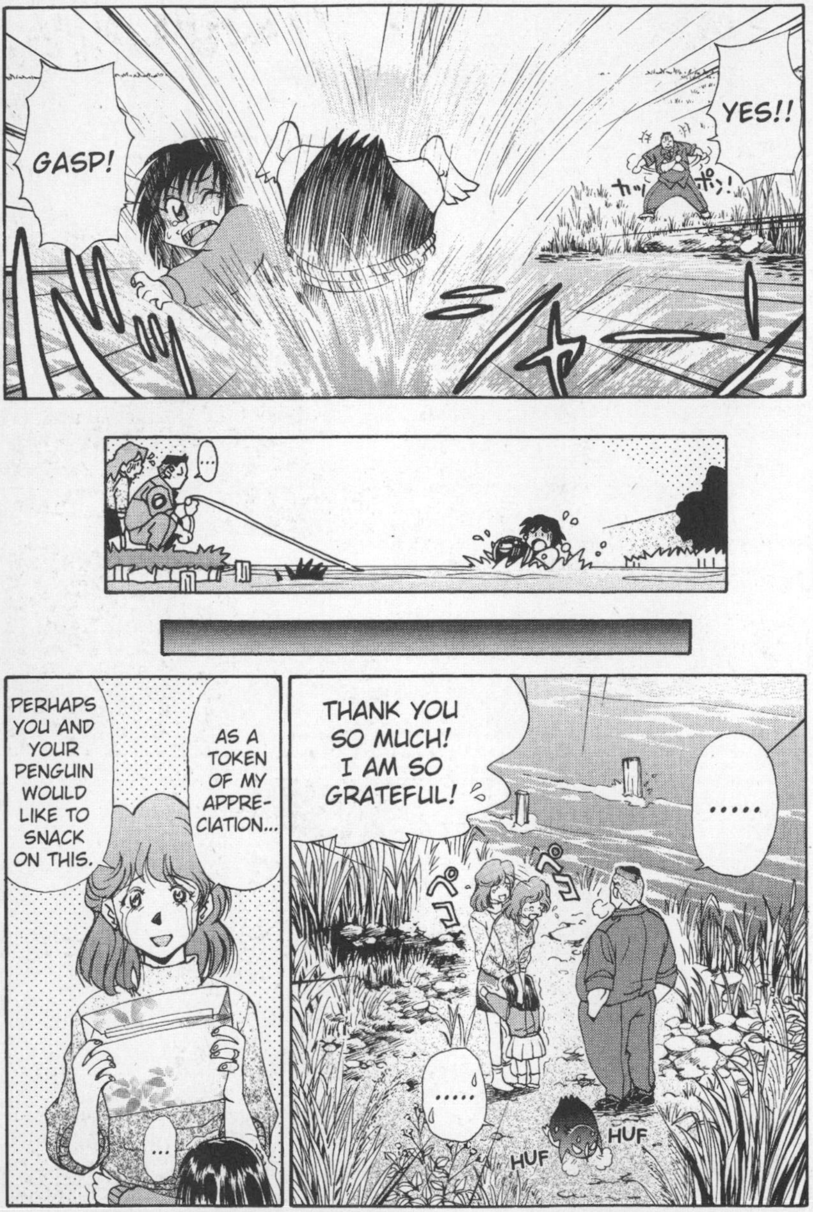
YES!!
カッ
ポン!
GASP!
...
THANK YOU SO MUCH! I AM SO GRATEFUL!
.....
ペコ
ペコ
.....
HUF
HUF
AS A TOKEN OF MY APPRECIATION...
PERHAPS YOU AND YOUR PENGUIN WOULD LIKE TO SNACK ON THIS.
...

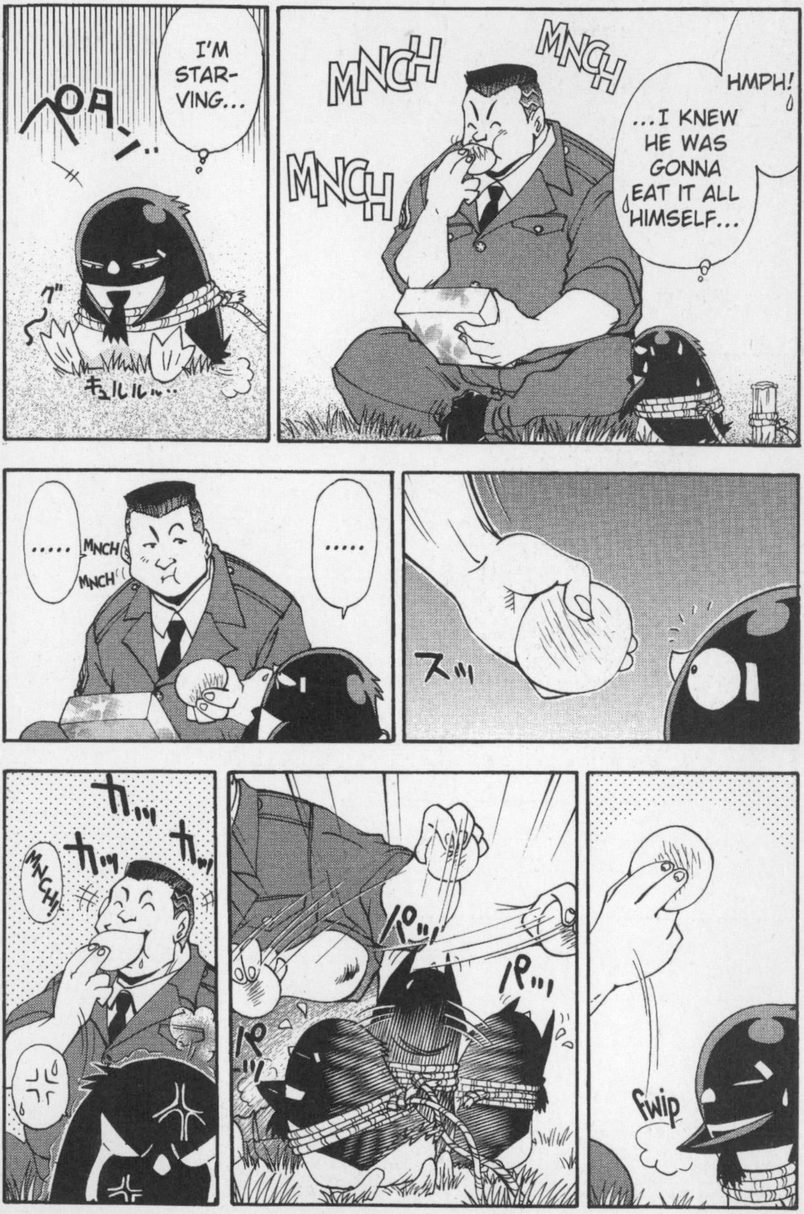
HMPH!
...I KNEW HE WAS GONNA EAT IT ALL HIMSELF...
MNCH
MNCH
MNCH
I'M STARVING...
ペタン‥
グ~
キュルル‥
スッ
.....
MNCH MNCH
.....
fwip
パッ
パッ
パッ
カッ
カッ
カッ
MNCH!

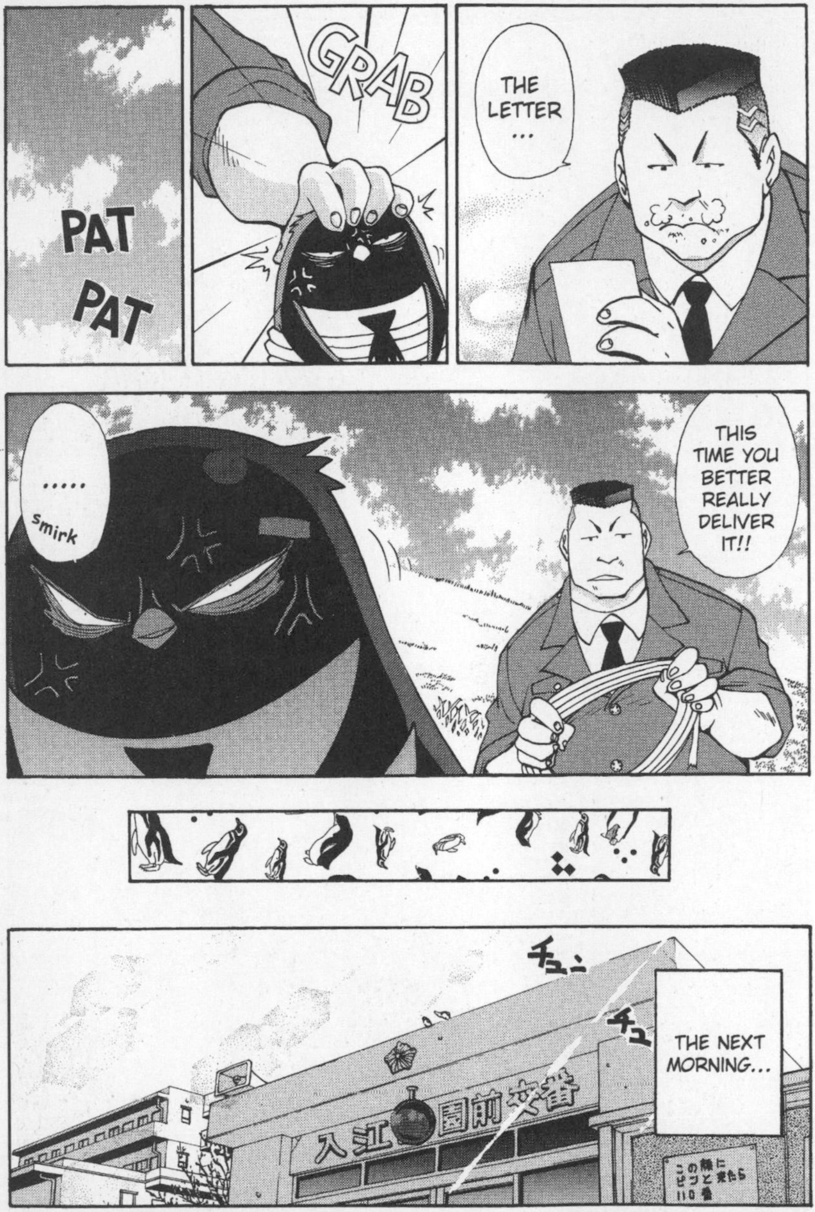
THE LETTER ...
GRAB
PAT
PAT
THIS TIME YOU BETTER REALLY DELIVER IT!!
.....
smirk
チュン
チュ
THE NEXT MORNING...

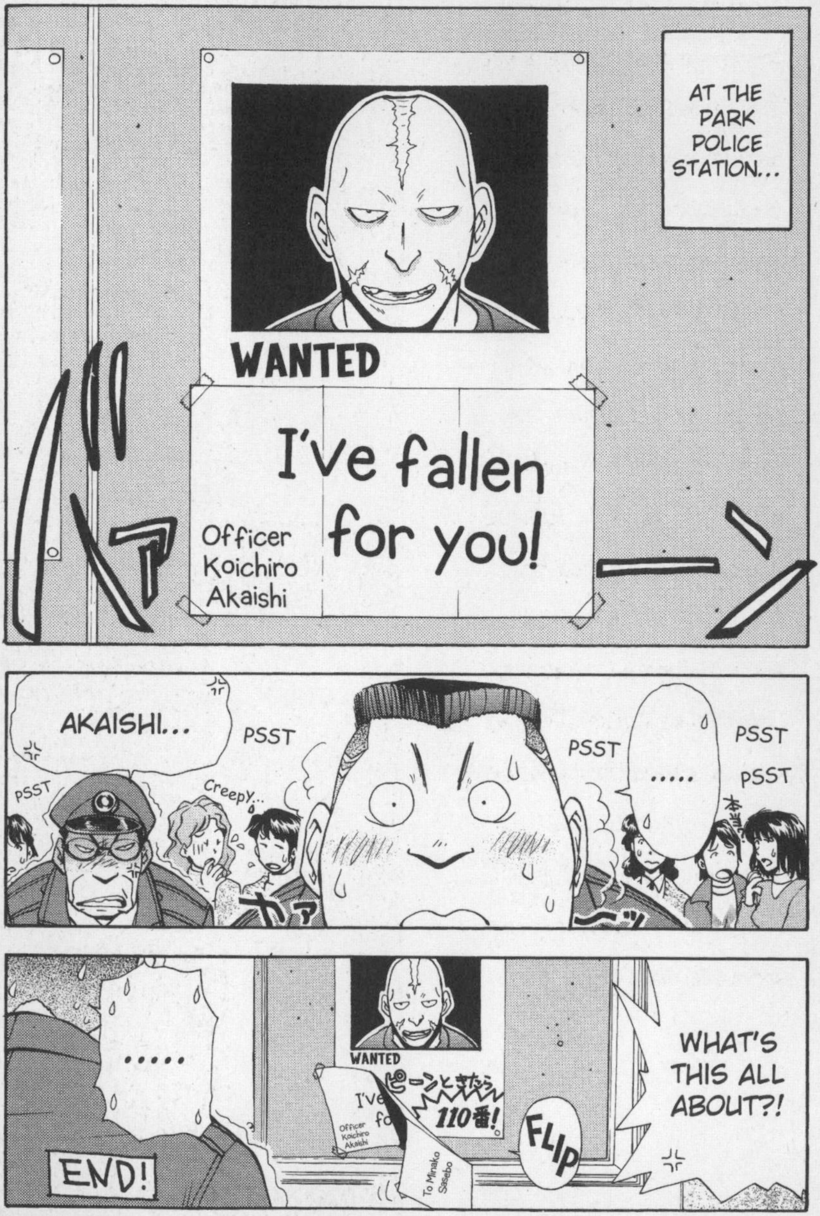
AT THE PARK POLICE STATION...
WANTED
I've fallen for you!
Officer Koichiro Akaishi
PSST
PSST
.....
PSST
Creepy...
AKAISHI...
PSST
WHAT'S THIS ALL ABOUT?!
FLIP
To Minako Sasebo
WANTED
ピーンときたら110番!
Officer Koichiro Akaishi
.....
END!

*O*shôgatsu or New Year's in Japan is a special time of year. Most people go back to their hometowns to spend time with family and to eat special New Year's food called *osechi*. Comprised of food that are a play on words, eating *osechi* brings on good fortune and health for the new year. For example, people eat *tai* (red sea bream) to have a *medatai* or prosperous new year. Another essential food for *Oshôgatsu* is *ozôni* – a savory soup served with *mochi* rice cakes. Eating is a very important part of Japanese culture as it is with many other cultures throughout the world. Food is great!

More Manga!
More Manga!

If you like TUXEDO GIN here are some other manga you might be interested in:

©1984 Rumiko
Takahashi/Shogakukan, Inc.

• Maison Ikkoku

A classic in the romantic love comedy genre, Rumiko Takahashi's MAISON IKKOKU is as heartwarming as it is hilariously wacky. Follow the exploits of chronically wishy-washy Yusaku Godai as he tries to win over his beautiful apartment manager, Kyoko Otanashi. All the while, the bizarre and nosey cast of characters that are the other residents of the building are there to chastise Godai as well as cheer him on.

©1988 Rumiko
Takahashi/Shogakukan, Inc.

• Ranma 1/2

Who could mention Rumiko Takahashi without mentioning RANMA 1/2 in the same breath? Ranma Saotome is an aspiring martial arts master who turns into a girl when doused with cold water and then turns back into a boy when showered with hot water. Ranma's odd physicality makes for hilariously comic situations and storylines. RANMA 1/2 has it all—a gender-bending romantic comedy with a healthy dose of martial arts.

©1989 Naoki
Yamamoto/Shogakukan, Inc.

• Dance Till Tomorrow

Romantic comedy for mature readers. Naoki Yamamoto presents a mixed-up wishy-washy main character, crazy relationships, and titillating sex. What more could a young man who's about to inherit a million dollars want?

Glossary of Sound Effects, Signs, and other Miscellaneous Notes

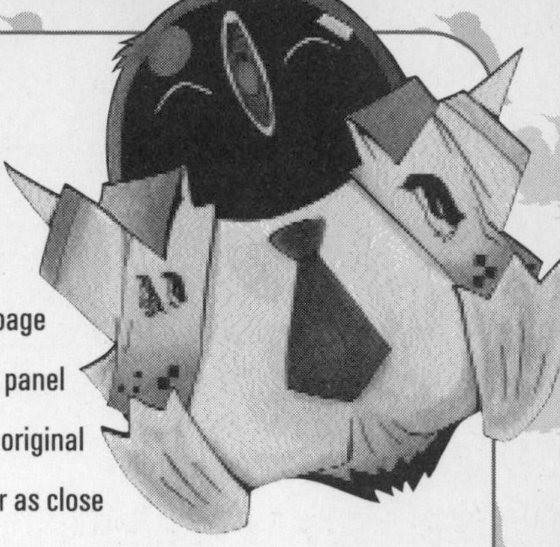

Each entry includes: the location, indicated by page number and panel number (so 3.1 means page 3, panel number 1); the phonetic romanization of the original Japanese; and our English "translation"–we offer as close an English equivalent as we can.

CHAPTER 1

6~7.1—FX: DOKI x 9 (heart pounding)
6~7.1—FX: HISHI! (hugs arm)
6~7.1—FX: KAAAA (Ginji turning red)
6~7.3—FX: JIIIIN (emotionally moved)
8.1—FX: WANA WANA WANA (trembling in anger)
8.1—FX: PURU PURU PURU (trembling in anger/sadness)
9.2—FX: DOGA (punch)
9.3—FX: PO... (turns red)
9.3—FX: PUN PUN (very mad)
15.1—FX: DAKI (hug)
16.2—FX: GURA... (shaking)
18.1—FX: GO (truck approaching)
20.2—FX: SU... (regains consciousness)
20.3—FX: PEKO... (bows)
22.2—FX: GU (squeezes)
23.2—FX: DOKI (heart jumps)
23.3—FX: BOOOO (dazed)
23.4—FX: BUROROROR... (truck moving)
24.2—FX: HISO HISO (whispering)
25.1—FX: TOKKO TOKKO (waddling)
25.3—FX: DON (bumps into)
26.1—FX: DO DO DO (bike engine)
26.2—FX: OOON (revving)
26.3—FX: VUOOOOON (bike engine)
26.4—FX: POTUUUN (alone)
27.1—FX: GARA GARA GARARA (crumbling)
27.3—FX: BIKU (startled)
28.2—FX: JIWA (tears coming out)

CHAPTER 2

31.4—FX: BIKU (startled)
33.4—FX: ZUI (pushes ice cream forward)
33.5—FX: MUKA MUKA MUKA (getting irritated)
34.4—FX: SAWA (nervous)
36.3—FX: DO DO DO (bike engine)
37.1—FX: VUKYAKYAKYA (skidding)
40.1—FX: DOUU (bike engine)
40.3—FX: KOOOOON (bike engine)
43.1—FX: BA (jumps out)
44.1—FX: DON (bump)

44.2—FX: ZUZAZA!! (skidding)

44.2—FX: DOTE (falls)

45.1—FX: ZUGYAGYAGYAGYA (skidding)

45.2—FX: ZA (standing firm)

46.1—FX: GUWA (truck approaching)

48.1—FX: ZUGYAGYA (skidding)

49.1—FX: DON (bam)

51.1—FX: ZUGYAGYA (skidding)

51.5—FX: GA (kick)

54.1—FX: VUOOOON (engine)

54.2—FX: HOWAWAWAWA (skidding)

54.3—FX: GOOOO (car running)

56.1—FX: GA (gets up)

57.2—FX: DA (runs over)

57.3—FX: PYON (jump)

57.3—FX: GAPO (takes off helmet)

58.2—FX: ZA... (falls to ground)

58.4—FX: KA (footstep)

60.1—FX: GA (punch)

68.5—FX: UIIIIN (auto door opens)

69.1—FX: BASHA (splash)

74.1—FX: GA (closes fist)

75.1—FX: HISO HISO HISO (whispering)

75.1—FX: NANDA NANDA (what? what?)

75.4—FX: KUI (points to himself)

76.2—FX: JIIIII (stare)

76.4—FX: KURU (turns)

76.4—FX: KUWA (penguin cry)

77.1—FX: GYUN (speeding in)

77.2—FX: DOKA DOKA DOKA (all bunching in)

77.2—FX: WAAAA! (kids cheering)

77.3—FX: MUGYUUU (squeeze)

77.4—FX: KYA KYA (kids laughing)

78.1—FX: WAI WAI (kids)

79.1—FX: JYUBO! (heat)

79.1—FX: KAN KAN (sound of furnace)

79.2—FX: GAN (hitting floor)

79.3—FX: PUSU PUSU (smoldering)

79.3—FX: DAAA (run)

79.4—FX: DOKA (slammed)

80.6—FX: SHIIIN (silence)

82.4—FX: TUKA TUKA TUKA (footsteps)

83.6—FX: GARA (opens door)

84.1—FX: DODON (drum)

84.2—FX: DON DODON x 6 (drum sound)

85.2—FX: AHAHA (laugh)

85.4—FX: GASA (rustle)

87.2—FX: DOKI (heart beat)

87.3—FX: DOKI DOKI DOKI (heart beating)

88.1—FX: KAPO (puts hat on)

88.2—FX: JIIIIN (moved)

89.4—FX: SU... (puts coat around)

CHAPTER 5

92.2—FX: WAI WAI GAYA GAYA (very loud crowd noise)

94.1—FX: GOKKUN (big gulp)

95.1—FX: GOOOON (temple bell)

96.1—FX: GOOOOON (temple bell)

96.4—FX: FU FU FU (heh heh heh)

97.2—FX: BATAN! (bam)

97.2—FX: GUSHA! (smushed)

97.3—FX: VUUUN (groaning)

97.6—FX: MUKU (gets up)

98.1—FX: BOOOOO (bright red)

98.2—FX: GAAAN (shocked)

98.4—FX: YURARI YURARI (swaying back and forth)

99.2—FX: GYUUUU (squeeze)

99.3—FX: PUAAAAN (car horn)

99.3—FX: KIKIKIKI (tires skidding)

100.3—FX: GOGOGO... (dragging concrete)

100.3—FX: SASASA... (clearing crowd)

100.3—FX: PA (stepping to side)

100.4—FX: KAAA! (yelling)

100.4—FX: BISHIII (points)

101.1—FX: RURARA (humming)

101.1—FX: GO (truck going by)

101.3—FX: DA (gets up)

101.4—FX: BA (gets up)

102.2—FX: GON (bell)

102.2—FX: NUFUFU... (laughing)

102.3—FX: BIKUN (startled)

103.1—FX: BI (raises hand)

103.4—FX: JIIII (stare)

103.5—FX: YURA YURA (off balance)

104.2—FX: DOTA BATA (struggle)

105.1—FX: GOOOOOON... (temple bell)

105.5—FX: DOKI (heart jumps)

106.4—FX: GOOOON (temple bell)

107.1—FX: CHARIIIN... RIIIN... (change going into box)

107.2—FX: GARA GARA (shaking the wishing bell)

107.3—FX: SU (puts out fins)

108~109.4 FX: GAKU (surprised)

110.2—FX: GOOOON (temple bell)

112~113.1 FX: KAPPOOOON (echoing in bath)

112~113.3 FX: SOWA SOWA (looking around)

114.1—FX: SHIIIIN (silence)

114.2—FX: DOSU... (sits down)

114.3—FX: CORON (rolls over)

114.4—FX: MOZO MOZO (wiggling)

114.5—FX: POTE... (drops)

115.2—FX: YANYA YANYA (enjoying)

115.2—FX: HIKKU (hiccup)

115.3—FX: GAKKUSHI (disappointed)

116.3—FX: KORO KORO KORO (turning umbrella)

117.2—FX: DA (runs)

117.3—FX: DOKA (hit)

117.4—FX: WAHAHA (laughing)

118.1—FX: KAPOOON (echoing)

119.4—FX: KAPOON (echoing)

119.4—FX: BYUO (strong wind)

120.2—FX: BACHA (splash)

120.3—FX: ZAA (gets out of water)

120.3—FX: BACHA (splash)

121.1—FX: KACHIIIIN (frozen)

122.1—FX: KAAAA (yell)

123.1—FX: POTE... (takes shape)

123.2—FX: YANYA YANYA! (enjoying crowd)

124.7—FX: DAN! (hits floor)

125.2—FX: ZUGADADADA (running with force)

125.3—FX: HAAA (monstrous breath)

126.5—FX: SUU (deep breath)

127.1—FX: DAN (kicks off)

127.2—FX: JYA (holds spear)

127.3—FX: BA (throws spear)

127.4—FX: PYON (jumps)

128.1—FX: BACHIN (fling)

128.1 —FX: BACHIN (slaps)

128.2—FX: KAPON (echoing)

129.1 —FX: DOSU (spear hits wood)

129.3—FX: BAIIN (spring-like sound)

129.4—FX: BIIIN (spring-like sound)

129.5—FX: GA (grabs)

130~131.1 FX: DOKA (crashing)

132.2—FX: KAPON (echoing)

132.2—FX: CHAPO (splash)

CHAPTER 7

135.1 —FX: ZABA (fwoosh)

135.3—FX: GA (snow)

135.3—FX: ZA (snow)

135.3—FX: SHUGO! (snow)

135.4—FX: ZUGA (braking)

135.5—FX: SU (flipping goggles up)

136.1 —FX: SUIII (sliding)

136.2—FX: MUFUFU... (heh heh)

137.3—FX: JIN (emotional)

138.4—FX: MUKAKAKA (getting angry)

139.3—FX: GU (pulling)

142.2—FX: TAN TAN (lift moving)

142.2—FX: JIIIII (stare)

142.3—FX: GATTAN GATTAN (clatter clatter)

142.4—FX: JII (stare)

142.5—FX: BASHU BASHU (snowballs hitting)

143.1 —FX: GA (hit)

143.2—FX: DOSA! (hits ground)

144.1 —FX: JYA (snowboarding)

144.1 —FX: ZA (snowboarding)

144.4—FX: PUN PUN (mad)

145.1 —FX: BIKU (startled)

145.4—FX: BISHI (points)

148.5—FX: ZAZAZAZAZA (something moving fast)

149.2—FX: IRA IRA (irritated)

150~151.1 FX: ZUJYA (snowboarding)

150~151.2 FX: KUWAAAA! (penguin cries)

150~151.4 FX: DOKAN (blow)

152.2—FX: ISO ISO (hurrying away)

CHAPTER 8

154.4—FX: MOGU MOGU (chewing)

154.4—FX: SHIMI JIMI (feeling happy)

156.3—FX: Biku (startled)

158.5—FX: TA (step)

158.6—FX: TA (step)

158.7—FX: TA (step)

159.1 —FX: SUTATAN (falls over)

159.2—FX: AWAWA... (out of words)

161.1 —FX: ZUGADADADADA (running)

162~163.3 FX: SHU (spray)

164.1 —FX: ZUZA (surrounds)

164.2—FX: PON (pats neck)

164.4—FX: ZUBAN (hit)

164.5—FX: ZA (lands)

165.1 —FX: BAAAN (bam!)

166.1 —FX: DAAAAA! (running)

166.3—FX: HOKA HOKA (steaming)

167.1 —FX: KUWAA (squawk!)

167.2 —FX: SHIIN (silence)

167.2 —FX: ZAZAAN (waves)

167.3 —FX: POKON (pops out)

167.6 —FX: GOBO (bubbling)

181.2—FX: ZUJYAA (skidding)

181.4—FX: SHU (dust settling)

182.1—FX: GABA (gets up)

182.2—FX: JIII… (stare)

182.5—FX: PYUN! (running off)

183.4—FX: PYOI (picks up)

184.1—FX: FU…! (blowing air)

184.1—FX: GO (flame)

184.2—FX: KIRA (shines)

184.4—FX: BASHA BASHA (splash splash)

185.1—FX: BASHA BASHA (splash splash)

185.1—FX: GABO (gulping water)

185.3—FX: ZABA ZABA (splashing)

185.4—FX: GABA (gets up)

185.5—FX: GYU GYU (squeezing)

186.1—FX: GO (swinging)

186.2—FX: BIIIN (tension on rope)

186.2—FX: GUN (tugging on rope)

186.3—FX: PAAAAN (throws)

186.3—FX: SHU (Ginji flies)

187.1—FX: KAPPON! (pose)

187.1—FX: BASSHAAN (splash)

187.3—FX: PEKO PEKO (bowing)

188.2—FX: PETAN (sits down)

188.2—FX: GU KYRURU (stomach sounds)

188.3—FX: SU (extends arm)

188.6—FX: PA PA PA (moves)

188.7—FX: KA KA KA (laughing)

189.6—FX: CHUN CHUN (morning birds)

190.1—FX: BAN (effect)

190.2—FX: KAA (blush)

167.7—FX: GOBOBOBOBOBO (bubbling)

168.1—FX: ZAPAN! (big splash)

168.3—FX: DOSUN (stomp)

169.1—FX: DON (heavy weight)

169.1—FX: GAKU GAKU GAKU (shaking)

169.4—FX: GAAAAN (shocked)

170.1—Background: The katakana for "Monster" fills the background

170.1—FX: PURU PURU PURU (trembling)

170.2—FX: DOGAN (hard hit)

170.3—FX: BUN BUN (swinging head)

170.3—FX: WAAA (people screaming)

171.1—FX: DA (runs)

171.4—FX: FUU FUU (breathing out of nose)

171.5—FX: BOE (Nana crying)

172.1—FX: ZAZAN ZAZAN (waves)

172.3—FX: ZAPPAN (waves)

172.3—FX: ZAPPAN (waves)

CHAPTER 9

174.2—FX: KURU (turns around)

176.2—FX: SOOOO (sneaking)

176.5—FX: HOKA HOKA (steaming)

177.2—FX: GIN (glare)

177.3—FX: TAJI (backing off)

178.4—FX: GOKKUN (big swallow)

178.4—FX: PORO… (falls out)

179.2—FX: ZUDADADA (running)

180.1—FX: POOOO (blushing)

180.3—FX: KORON (rolls out)

180.4—FX: PETA PETA (sticking)

181.1—FX: BUN (swings)

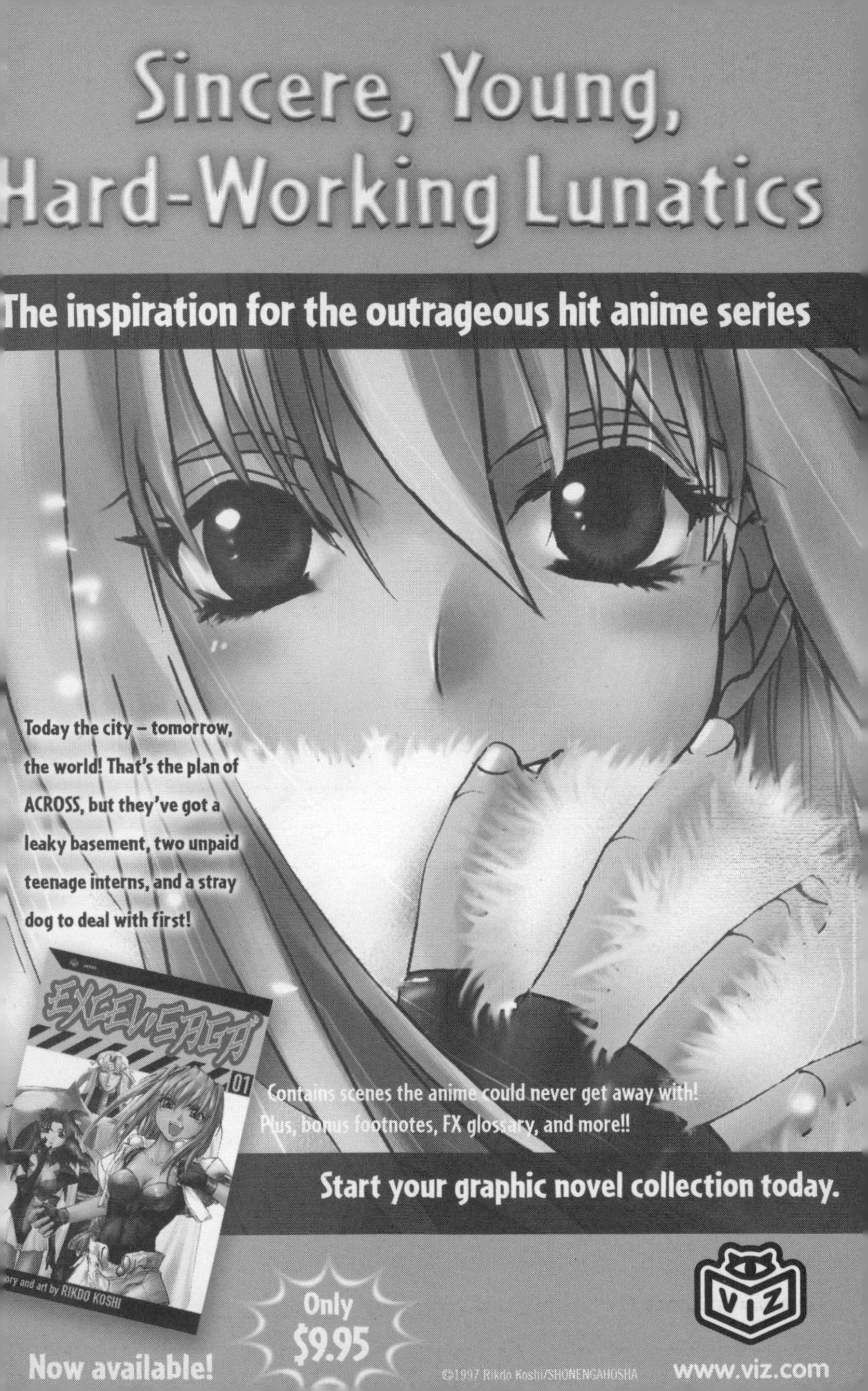

Sincere, Young,
Hard-Working Lunatics
The inspiration for the outrageous hit anime series
Today the city – tomorrow, the world! That's the plan of ACROSS, but they've got a leaky basement, two unpaid teenage interns, and a stray dog to deal with first!
EXCEL SAGA
01
ory and art by RIKDO KOSHI
Contains scenes the anime could never get away with!
Plus, bonus footnotes, FX glossary, and more!!
Start your graphic novel collection today.
Only
$9.95
Now available!
VIZ
©1997 Rikdo Koshi/SHONENGAHOSHA
www.viz.com

COMPLETE OUR SURVEY AND LET
US KNOW WHAT YOU THINK!

☐ Please check here if you DO NOT wish to receive information or future offers from VIZ

Name: _____

Address: _____

City: _____ State: _____ Zip: _____

E-mail: _____

☐ Male ☐ Female   Date of Birth (mm/dd/yyyy): ___/___/___   (Under 13? Parental consent required)

What race/ethnicity do you consider yourself? (please check one)

☐ Asian/Pacific Islander   ☐ Black/African American   ☐ Hispanic/Latino

☐ Native American/Alaskan Native ☐ White/Caucasian   ☐ Other: _____

What VIZ product did you purchase? (check all that apply and indicate title purchased)

☐ DVD/VHS _____

☐ Graphic Novel _____

☐ Magazines _____

☐ Merchandise _____

Reason for purchase: (check all that apply)

☐ Special offer   ☐ Favorite title   ☐ Gift

☐ Recommendation   ☐ Other _____

Where did you make your purchase? (please check one)

☐ Comic store   ☐ Bookstore   ☐ Mass/Grocery Store

☐ Newsstand   ☐ Video/Video Game Store ☐ Other: _____

☐ Online (site: _____)

What other VIZ properties have you purchased/own? _____

How many anime and/or manga titles have you purchased in the last year? How many were VIZ titles? (please check one from each column)

ANIME
- ☐ None
- ☐ 1-4
- ☐ 5-10
- ☐ 11+

MANGA
- ☐ None
- ☐ 1-4
- ☐ 5-10
- ☐ 11+

VIZ
- ☐ None
- ☐ 1-4
- ☐ 5-10
- ☐ 11+

I find the pricing of VIZ products to be: (please check one)

☐ Cheap   ☐ Reasonable   ☐ Expensive

What genre of manga and anime would you like to see from VIZ? (please check two)

☐ Adventure   ☐ Comic Strip   ☐ Science Fiction   ☐ Fighting

☐ Horror   ☐ Romance   ☐ Fantasy   ☐ Sports

What do you think of VIZ's new look?

☐ Love It   ☐ It's OK   ☐ Hate It   ☐ Didn't Notice   ☐ No Opinion

Which do you prefer? (please check one)

☐ Reading right-to-left

☐ Reading left-to-right

Which do you prefer? (please check one)

☐ Sound effects in English

☐ Sound effects in Japanese with English captions

☐ Sound effects in Japanese only with a glossary at the back

THANK YOU! Please send the completed form to:

NJW Research
42 Catharine St.
Poughkeepsie, NY 12601

All information provided will be used for internal purposes only. We promise not to sell or otherwise divulge your information.